AUSTRALIAN DIPLOMAT

AUSTRALIAN DIPLOMAT

DIPLOMAT

Memoirs of Sir Alan Watt

ANGUS AND ROBERTSON
in association with the
Australian Institute of International Affairs

Having as its object the scientific study of international questions, the Australian Institute of International Affairs, as such, does not express opinions or advocate policies. The views expressed in this book are therefore the author's own.

First published in 1972 by

ANGUS AND ROBERTSON (PUBLISHERS) PTY LTD

102 Glover Street, Cremorne, Sydney
2 Fisher Street, London
107 Elizabeth Street, Melbourne
167 Queen Street, Brisbane
89 Anson Road, Singapore

National Library of Australia
card number and ISBN 0 207 12354 3

Registered in Australia for transmission by post as a book.

PRINTED IN AUSTRALIA BY HALSTEAD PRESS, SYDNEY

A little time we gain from time
To set our seasons in some chime . . .
A little time that we may fill
Or with such good works or such ill
As loose the bonds or make them strong
Wherein all mankind suffers wrong.

Prelude, ALGERNON CHARLES SWINBURNE

PREFACE

MORE than half my life, to date, had expired when I joined the Department of External Affairs in April 1937 at the age of 36. Before I became a government official, I had spent three years at Sydney University studying English, Philosophy and History; three years at Oxford University, reading in the Honours School of Philosophy, Politics and Economics (PPE), with main emphasis on Economics; six months in Heidelberg, Germany, living with a German family; three years running an educational scheme for factory employees at the British-Australasian Tobacco Co., Kensington, Sydney; four years as Associate to a Supreme Court Judge in Sydney while I qualified as a Barrister; and five years at the New South Wales Bar.

With this background, it would scarcely be expected that I would fit into a public service job with the same ease as a young man who had just taken his first university degree and had little other experience of life. My interests and outlook were substantially already set, and these made me react strongly against rigidities and regulatory practices of the Commonwealth Public Service. However, the friendly advice of two senior public servants not in the Department of External Affairs, helped me to stay in the game until such time as attractive opportunities opened which made my frustrations seem unimportant by comparison.

For twenty-five years I was an Australian diplomat, posted at home and abroad. There were three interspersed periods of service in Canberra, while my overseas experience included five years in the United States, three years in the Soviet Union, two years in Southeast Asia, four years in Japan, two years in Germany, and participation in numerous international conferences under United Nations and other auspices. In July 1962 I retired, some four years before I would have been retired automatically on grounds of age. By that stage I had found the frustrations once again greater than the opportunities, and I preferred to pursue my international interests by other means outside the Public Service.

The pages which follow contain the story of those twenty-five years, with an introduction covering my earlier life without which my later career would scarcely be understood. It is a personal story, not an exposition in abstract terms of Australian foreign policy during that period; nor does it purport to be a confident and prophetic statement of what future Australian foreign policy should be. Those interested will find in Appendix I a list of books and articles published by me since retirement analysing and expounding Australian foreign policy since 1937, and expressing some personal views on its adequacy.

Here my main purpose has been to describe the life of an Australian diplomat from the inside during what can be called the 'developmental' stage of an Australian foreign office, as it passed from infancy to maturity. In 1937 the sole 'diplomatic' mission abroad was the Australian High Commission in London; by 1962 there were some forty-four diplomatic and consular offices in foreign and Commonwealth countries, and the number has since increased.

It is not easy for any country to find the appropriate staff, finance and expertise to create a substantial Service of this kind. In the process mistakes are made which need to be understood and recorded, even though by now many of them have been corrected. My generation of officials was in a very real sense a 'guinea-pig' generation, on which administrative experiments were carried out which were not always appreciated by the patients on the operating tables.

But although the story is personal, the environment is public and international. As a result, additional light is thrown on certain important aspects of Australian foreign policy, and upon the personalities, attitudes and activities of political leaders of various Parties who held responsible office between 1937 and 1962. Further, impressions of foreign countries recorded below are for the most part based upon substantial periods of residence, as distinct from fleeting visits. As such, they may help widen the reader's images of such countries.

The primary source of the chapters which follow is personal recollection, carefully checked as to dates and other facts from public records. Secondly, I was separated from my wife so often in the course of my official career that I sent her many letters, which she kept. These have provided valuable contemporary evidence of incidents and attitudes of mind and occasional quotations are made from their contents. Thirdly, over the years while abroad my wife kept a considerable diary, varying in detail with the time and energy at her disposal in different countries after family and official claims had been met. She has made these available to me and reading her records has reminded me of many things I might otherwise have forgotten, and has tested the accuracy of my recollection.

Finally, any writer of memoirs has to face two difficult problems. All memoirs tend unconsciously to be an exercise in self-justification or self-adulation. This, I think, is unavoidable. All one can do is to write what one thinks and believes, leaving it to others to point out mistakes, misinterpretations or attitudes based upon mere personal predilection, prejudice, or bias.

Again, an ex-official who writes of contacts with his political masters has to consider questions of propriety and good-taste. Judgments on what it is permissible to publish will vary, and there is ground for genuine difference of opinion. Some will feel that incidents should not be revealed prior to the death of the person concerned. Others, including myself, consider that the test should be whether or not such an individual is still exercising responsibility as a servant of the Crown.

An even more delicate question is whether reference should be made to the wives of political leaders who travel overseas with their husbands, and whose activities abroad do not always facilitate the tasks of Australian diplomats. On reflection I have decided to make no reference to wives in the text which follows, but feel bound to suggest here, in general terms, that wives would do well to realise that they are not themselves ministers of the Crown, and that interests and activities natural and permissible at home are not inevitably appropriate abroad.

A.W.

Canberra, August 1971

CONTENTS

Photographs between pages 204 and 205

INTRODUCTION

Early background, training and experience

MY ANCESTORS were simple folk, small farmers and carpenters. My father, George Watt, was born on 5 March, 1861 at Gight, Fyvie, Aberdeenshire, Scotland. At the age of nineteen, for reasons unknown, he migrated to Australia, arriving in Sydney in 1880 without capital assets. Within three years he married my mother, Susan Stewart Robb Gray, then aged nineteen. She was born on 8 October, 1863 at Cape Town, South Africa. Her parents had come from Scotland, and they continued their journey to Australia when Susan was eight months old. Grandfather Gray was a carpenter by trade, and I still have childhood recollections of splendid cedar cupboards and bookcases, made by him, with which his home was furnished.

In due course my father opened a general store at Gosford, then a small country town about fifty miles north of Sydney. His business prospered, he was made a Justice of the Peace, and eventually he became Mayor of Gosford, which still boasts an undistinguished 'Watt Street'. From Gosford he moved to Wollongong, a larger and growing coastal centre fifty miles south of Sydney where opportunities for running a general store seemed to offer better prospects. Here in the troubled 1890s disaster overtook him, as it overtook so many other Australians. An artificial boom built upon insecure foundations collapsed suddenly, and the general financial crisis was accentuated by the failure of numerous Australian banks and lending societies and by confrontations between employers and trade unions. An economic depression led to much unemployment and widespread personal hardship.

George Watt lost whatever equity he had in the Wollongong store and moved, with his growing family, to one of the poorer suburbs of Sydney. For many years he was employed as a commercial traveller for firms trying to expand their markets in the country. This work kept him away from home for five days a week. Thus the responsibility for bringing up the family fell mainly upon my mother, who had to use the slender and

I

uncertain family income to sustain, before I arrived, no fewer than seven sons and one daughter.

Eventually father moved to Croydon, a pleasanter suburb west of Sydney. There, at 7, The Avenue, I was born on 13 April, 1901. Ours was a two-storey house, set in adequate grounds, facing a longish avenue of tall pine trees. At the rear of the house was a pear tree with a crooked seat, the top of which became my place of refuge as a child. There I could escape from my teasing elder brothers, swing and sing as I wished, and talk with the tame galah whose wing had been clipped.

Like other large families, the children were a mixed brood, differing substantially in ability, interests and temperament. None other than myself had the opportunity for a university education, though one qualified as a chartered accountant, another as a civil engineer, a third as a pharmacist. Victor was a self taught artist whose water-colours of Australian land-scapes became widely known. Others engaged in business activities. Stanley and Leslie were of particular help to me when I was a moody, teenage adolescent. My only sister, Edna, left school early. She was a competent pianist, with some special gift as an accompanist. She was indirectly respon-sible for the development of my own keen interest in music.

At the Croydon and Burwood State Primary Schools I was at or near the top of my class and won a scholarship to Sydney Boys' High School. There my rating dropped rapidly, and my matriculation results in 1918 were quite undistinguished. There were, I think, a number of reasons for this. I had still not acquired the habit of orderly and sustained mental work. Five of my brothers volunteered for overseas service during the First World War, of the effects of which I was old enough to be conscious. Discipline and morale at Sydney High deteriorated markedly after retirement of an out-standing headmaster and his replacement by another who trusted no one.

There are few aspects of my time at secondary school worth recalling. My best subjects were English and History, my interest in which was stimu-lated by two excellent masters, one of whom discovered in me some gift for versification. Before leaving, I became editor of the school journal. During those years I was reading voraciously books chosen at random from the shelves of various brothers whose interests differed widely. At the same time I was reading the works of Henrik Ibsen, Oscar Wilde and Rudyard Kipling.

Secondly, I studied German instead of French. My choice was determined by the simple fact that on a wall of our living room there hung a print of Turner's painting of Heidelberg, showing the old bridge crossing the Neckar and the ruined castle on the hillside beyond.

Thirdly, I became a keen tennis player. I had no coaching, and learned to play against the wall of a house at Chatswood to which we had moved when father gave up commercial travelling and became a manufacturers' agent in Sydney. At tennis my grip was instinctive and wrong. As a result, although my forehand was excellent and and my capacity for low volleys on either hand good, my backhand was defensive and my serve and smash poor. However, keenness, a good eye, and a capacity to analyse the weak-nesses of an opponent took me into the school first team. In my last year I won the Schoolboys' Singles Championship of New South Wales.

At the matriculation examination held at the end of 1918 I qualified for courses in either Arts or Law or both, but the decision to attend the university was far from inevitable. I had no specific profession in mind, and my results were scarcely encouraging. A family conclave which included some of my returned soldier brothers decided that I should be given the opportunity. So my name was entered for first year Arts courses in English, History, Philosophy and Latin at Sydney University. My knowledge of Latin was minimal, but I had to take it to comply with University regulations insisting on a spread of subjects, knowing I could drop it after the first year.

My results at the University were much better than at secondary school. Taking Honours in Philosophy and in English, at the end of the first year I was awarded High Distinction in the former and Distinction in the latter. The Lithgow II Scholarship in Philosophy eased my financial situation and made it possible for me to increase my social contacts considerably. During the first year I played for the University Tennis Team against other Australian Universities, and was awarded a Blue.

After election to the Students' Representative Council in second year, and receipt of an invitation to join the Editorial Board of *Hermes*—the University Magazine—it was suggested to me that I should apply for a Rhodes Scholarship which would enable me to spend 3 years at Oxford University. So I applied, and in a very thin field was awarded the scholarship. By then my interests had become substantially literary, and my ambition was to write. My application stated that, if selected, I would read English Language and Literature at Oxford.

As the university year at Oxford began in October, it appeared at first that I could not graduate from Sydney at the end of 1921, as Pass Examinations were not held until November, while Honours Examinations did not take place until the succeeding March. Partly for this reason, and partly because problems of personal relationship were causing me some distress at the time, I decided not to sit for the second year examination at the end of 1920. Fortunately, I changed my mind at the last moment, and managed to scrape through the Pass Examinations. It was only then that I learned that an Honours Degree from Sydney was essential to entitle me to Senior Colonial Standing at Oxford, which would exempt me from preliminary examinations there prior to Final Schools. To comply with these regulations, I took Honours in English only in March 1921, and obtained permission from Oriel College, Oxford, to come up one term late. This enabled me to sit for the Pass Examinations and English Honours Examination at Sydney in November and December 1921, taking both at the same time under special dispensation of the Senate.

During my last year at Sydney University I won the University Tennis Singles from a better player who was thinking more of his Final Medical Examinations than of the match, and was included in a New South Wales Team to play New Zealand. In Auckland we won our main match and, as a shipping strike prevented us from returning to Australia, for three weeks we played informal matches throughout the North and South Islands.

Early in December 1921 I left for England aboard the steamship *Ceramic*, a one-class vessel carrying only sixty passengers and much cargo on a six week voyage around the Cape of Good Hope. My scholarship did not include costs of travel, but my family managed to find the capital for a single fare. During the voyage I became Sports Secretary for the first and last time in my life, and read Tolstoy's *War and Peace*. A short call at Durban for coaling introduced me to the South African colour problem. After further calls at Cape Town and Teneriffe, I disembarked at Southampton on 4 January, 1922, and took the boat-train to London.

For an Australian, first impressions of London in mid-winter are scarcely encouraging. It was dark and raining when we steamed into Victoria Station, but my forebodings soon disappeared in the company of my six foot Scottish cousin, Dr. James Watt, who had come up from Surrey to meet me. He piloted me to his home at Godalming, set in the grounds of the tuberculosis hospital of which he was the director. There I met Dorothy Watt and their two children. For some thirty subsequent years during visits to England I found a welcome from my cousins at Godalming. Their home was a place of perennial refuge, recuperation and stimulation.

Dorothy and James Watt were an improbable pair, differing in religion, temperament and outlook. James was the canny Scot, serious, hard working, realistic, highly qualified and responsible in words and action. Naturally, he had been brought up as a Presbyterian. Dorothy was English and Roman Catholic. Her interests were literary, and experience of the Continent of Europe had developed a capacity to operate fluently in several languages. Forthright in speech, she had a masterly command of invective, and was apt to say twice as much as she meant.

At the beginning of Second Term I took the train to Oxford and was assigned two rooms on the second floor of the Rhodes wing of Oriel, fronting the High, which in those days was mercifully less noisy than now. From my front window I looked out across the street to the porch of St Mary's Church, with its two fluted, winding columns topped by the statue of Mary holding the child Jesus in her arms. There was a small bedroom, the other room serving for all remaining purposes—work, entertainment and meals, except for dinner held in the College Hall. Undergraduates then spent the first two years in college and the rest of their time in approved diggings somewhere in the town.

It took me some time to settle in at Oriel. The freshers of my year had already had one term to adjust themselves to Oxford conventions. Had it not been for the presence of another Australian Rhodes Scholar at my college, I would have felt very isolated. Bill Merrylees had graduated in Philosophy at Melbourne University, and was pursuing a graduate degree. We had many common interests, though our physique and background were different. Bill was six feet tall, had been brought up on a farm, could handle machinery and mend anything. He had a keen analytical mind and was interested in meaning rather than form. We became life-long friends.

The Rev. Lancelot Phelps, Provost of Oriel, was a bachelor aged seventy, whose large beard contrasted with his bald head. He was known for his brusqueness of conversation and his mannerisms of speech, the most notable being the interpolation of a series of explosive Pchahs followed by a roar of laughter. He asked me about my proposed course of study, and obviously thought poorly of it. Discovering that my longer-term ambition was to write novels and verse, he told me that a course in English Language and Literature would not help me much, except perhaps to qualify me as a literary critic or linguistic expert. 'Do you want to spend your life arguing whether or not Bacon wrote Shakespeare, or discussing the meaning of obscure lines in Browning's *Ring and the Book*? Shakespeare knew small Latin and less Greek, but a great deal about life. What you need is something to stimulate your thinking on the problems of the modern world. I see from your record you have done some work in Philosophy and History. My advice is to put your name down for the new course of Philosophy, Politics and Economics, started only a year ago. It has not settled down yet, and covers too wide a field, but you can feel your way about it for a while and then decide which of the three main areas of study you want to emphasise.'

Though somewhat irritated by the Provost's manner and enormous self-assurance, I eventually decided, after discussion with Bill, that this advice made sense. So I entered my name for PPE, stressing philosophy for the time being, and was placed in the care of David Ross as Senior Tutor. Ross was a Fellow of Oriel and an expert in the Classics. In later years he edited the collected works of Aristotle, and became Provost. I owe a great deal to his training, unusual tolerance and human sympathy.

At the end of term I persuaded Merrylees to spend the vacation with me in Heidelberg. It was still winter when we arrived there. After a night spent at a hotel near the station, we ploughed our way on foot through the snow up to the castle. Nearby we found a pension with windows opening upon a glorious view across the Neckar to the Heiligenberg on the west bank. There we settled in for a month, found a German teacher, worked at the language, climbed through the pine forests to the top of Königstuhl, and took long walks through the hills.

Heidelberg made a deep and lasting impression upon me. Here was no dramatic landscape, no vast metropolis, but a university town large enough to be interesting and small enough to make a direct, personal appeal. Heidelberg seemed to contain in moderation everything one could want—pine-clad hills rising to about 2,000 feet; a broad and fast flowing stream spanned by a bridge of pinkish sandstone set on pillars supporting capacious arches; a battered castle which bespoke past authority and dignity; university buildings and churches; book shops and friendly restaurants.

But it was the change-over from Winter to Spring which took one's breath away. Any young Australian, coming from a country where many people have never seen snow and where the ubiquitous eucalyptus trees keep their leaves throughout the year, is likely to be stirred by the experience of his first European Spring. To be in Heidelberg, however, when the snow disappears from the gloomy pine forests and fruit blossom bursts out suddenly along the zig-zag ridges below the Philosophenweg on the western bank of the Neckar, is to be uplifted in spirit.

The vacation spent in Germany had a quite unexpected influence upon my studies at Oxford. Although my interests were still literary rather than political or economic, I could not but be aware of the effects of growing

B

inflation in Germany. In view of the swift depreciation in the value of the mark, Merrylees and I soon learned to keep our funds in sterling, to change sterling currency into marks to cover only our immediate needs, and to rush at once to pay our bills before the marks we had acquired depreciated further. The disastrous social effects of inflation upon those with fixed incomes was obvious. Though I did not realise it at the time, the way was being prepared for Hitler to take over.

At Oxford, Lipson's excellent lectures on economic history, and a reading of Engel's *Condition of the Working Class in England in 1844* stirred in me a sympathetic interest in the plight of those who had suffered greatly during the Industrial Revolution. I read Keynes' *Economic Consequences of the Peace Treaty* with enlivened understanding and began to study his views on currency and banking policy. Unconsciously, I found myself giving less attention to philosophy and more to economics, especially the effects of financial policy on unemployment and theories of the causes of trade cycles. Eventually I made the misguided decision to stress the economic aspects of my course and to take as my special topic Currency and Banking.

During the summer term of 1922 I played regular tennis matches for Oxford and was selected to play against Cambridge. At these universities much is forgiven those who achieve some success in sport. In my case the fact that I was a fresher and a colonial Australian became more or less irrelevant. My contemporaries at Oriel now accepted me, and I made more acquaintances at other colleges. I played for Oxford during three successive years, and captained the team in 1924.

Tennis also led me farther afield. In 1922 I was a member of an Oxford-Cambridge team which played against Belgian Universities at Spa. During the following summer a similar joint team spent five weeks in the United States, playing matches against various Clubs on the East Coast near to New York, culminating in a contest against Harvard-Yale at Newport. The American tour gave me my first experience of the United States. I learned how people in New York City can live on very different incomes; how an American can be very generous in his private activities and very tough in his official or business relationships; and how much of the law prescribing Prohibition was being evaded, leading to a considerable increase in crime.

Shorter university vacations were spent in Paris and Grenoble to improve my French, as the papers for Final Schools included unseen translation from two European languages. Merrylees and I also spent a month in the little fishing village of Mousehole, Cornwall, chosen because we thought it most unlikely that work would be interrupted there by any distractions. During one summer vacation I made a lone pilgrimage to Scotland, stopping off briefly at York, Durham and Edinburgh en route to Wartle, a village not far from Aberdeen. There I enjoyed a fortnight's stay with Scottish relatives who farmed a small property a few miles from the railway station.

In my third year Bill Merrylees and I moved out of college to diggings in the Banbury Road. We were old hands now, and enjoyed the comparative freedom of living away from college routine and discipline, except for occasional evening meals in hall. In one's final year one was expected to work hard, and life in diggings was less subject to interruption than life in college. In due course Bill submitted a thesis for a B.Litt. in Philosophy, qualified and returned to Melbourne to marry an Australian girl. His departure was something of a blow, but I was too busy to brood over it for long. I was working hard for Final Schools, while responsibilities with the Oxford Tennis Team took up much time and physical energy. An invitation to join Vincents Club, where University Blues and Half-Blues gathered, gave me yet another tie to wear.

But there were other interests besides academic work and sport. I had become a member of the Ralegh Club, which met periodically to discuss Commonwealth affairs. Well-known personalities, including occasional members of the British Cabinet, came to address its small, informal meetings and submitted themselves to fairly rugged questioning after the talk.

It was at a Ralegh Club Meeting held in 1924 that I first met Richard Gardiner Casey. On that occasion the address was given by Viscount Swinton in one of his earlier metamorphoses. When he finished he introduced Casey as the new Australian Political Liaison Officer in the Cabinet Offices, London, and invited him to tell us what he did.

Casey was then very much the young ex-Army officer who had won the D.S.O. and M.C. in the First World War. Tall, of good physique, with a clear, clipped voice, he explained that Prime Minister Bruce had sent him to London to improve consultation between London and Canberra at the formative stage of policy and before it had crystallised into British Cabinet decisions.

In the summer term of 1924 I was also elected President of the Colonial Club which, alas, subsequently died a natural death. In my time the Colonial Club had only one rule: that no serious business should be transacted at any of its meetings. It was a Club where colonials, who were generally expected by English undergraduates to be rough and rude, found satisfaction in living up to expectations.

My duties as President of the Club in Summer Term were light, but I was alarmed to discover that they included making a speech at the Annual Dinner for Rhodes Scholars given by the Rhodes Trustees, to be followed by a speech delivered by the President of the American Club. On the fatal evening I found myself seated at head-table between Lord Milner and Lord Grey of Falloden. The festive scholars listened impatiently to the former, and attentively to the latter. Then Rudyard Kipling proposed the toast of the Rhodes Scholars, to which we had to reply. I had made up my mind in advance that the only bearable speech by me in such surroundings must be flippant, ending on a more serious note of thanks. So I explained my brevity along the lines that I knew well that one misplaced word of mine would result in India being lost to the Empire, or Canada seeking incorporation in the United States.

Examinations for Final Schools came and went, with their customary tension and exhaustion. When they were over I thought I had done reasonably well, but I knew I was too close to the grind-stone to judge the probable results with any precision. The ordeal of the Oxford viva, held after written papers had been corrected, was still to come, but there was little point

7

in working for the viva, during which questions could be asked on the whole field of study. So I relaxed, and directed all my thoughts to the Wimbledon Tennis Tournament, for which my entry in Singles and Doubles had been accepted.

At Wimbledon I reached the last sixteen in the Singles, before being eliminated in four sets by Watson Washburn, a member of the American Davis Cup Team. For the Doubles my regular partner, Charles Kingsley, was not available. I played with Fisher, another Oxford man. We reached the last eight at Wimbledon, and were then eliminated in four sets by R. N. Williams and Watson Washburn, who eventually won the tournament. After Wimbledon I spent a few weeks in the north of England speaking about the League of Nations on behalf of the British League of Nations Association.

My viva at Oxford lasted twenty-five minutes, and I was questioned only by Professor MacGregor although four examiners, including David Ross, were present. MacGregor was Professor of Political Economy and he cross-examined me on classical economic texts and then on my special subject, Currency and Banking. My replies on the texts were scarcely illuminating, but I was able to defend my pro-Keynsian views on my special subject.

When the results were published some weeks later, I found my name in the Second Class. Ross told me that I had gained what would now be described as a good upper-second, that my best work had been on Politics, and that I had failed to convince MacGregor during my viva that I had earned a first, which he alone could grant in view of my selection of Economics for special emphasis.

I now had to face the future, and was at a loss what to do. Fortunately I was given some time for reflection, as F. R. Wylie, Rhodes Secretary at Oxford, told me I could return to Oriel for the term I had missed when I took up my scholarship. I applied for a graduate scholarship in Economics, available for two years, proposing to write a thesis on the effects of financial policy on unemployment, but the scholarship was awarded to someone with better academic claims.

At that time Queen's College awarded two Laming Travelling Fellowships, to be spent in foreign parts studying primarily languages and designed to lead either to diplomatic or academic work. An examination for these would be held about May 1925. The thought of spending a year in Germany attracted me. For reasons I no longer remember, I had also begun to acquire an interest in Japan. However, it would have been financially impossible for me to remain in England until the following May, especially at Oxford.

One day Ross summoned me and told me that Oriel College had decided to offer me its Bishop Frazer Graduate Scholarship of about £100-150, designed to assist some graduate to do further work at Oxford. I thanked him, but said that I would still lack the financial means of staying on in college until the end of the academic year, for the purpose of sitting for a Laming Fellowship. He then asked me what I would propose to do if I were not tied to Oxford. I answered immediately that I would spend the first half of 1925 in Heidelberg, living with a German family, improving my German and developing my understanding of international problems.

8

Two days later he sent for me again and told me that, although there was no precedent for the Frazer Scholarship being held away from Oxford, it had been agreed that I could take it out in Heidelberg. The College would want me to write from time to time to let them know how I was getting on. In my subsequent experience of universities, I have met no more imaginative example of tolerant encouragement. In my case the bread so cast upon the waters did not return for many years.

In December 1924 I proceeded to Heidelberg and arranged to live in Neuenheim with a retired architect, Herr Baurat Jablonowski, from whose wife Merrylees and I had taken German lessons in 1922. Then began six months of intensive work which had the strongest and most unexpected influence on my life. For about three months I was alone, but was then joined by Bill Merrylees and his wife Annie. Bill had decided to continue his philosophical studies in Heidelberg and to attend regular seminars at the University.

In 1922, with the German currency depreciating, our English funds had enabled us to live at a considerably higher standard than most Germans. But by 1925 the mark had been stabilised, living was expensive, and I had to ration my slender means most carefully.

Frau Jablonowski was stout, heavily corseted and severe in manner—in many ways a typical German Hausfrau. She was an intelligent woman, very religious and determined that her young charges should drink deeply from the wells of German culture as she understood it. She failed in an attempt to lure me into the study of German religious belief, but she was willing enough at my request to read through the Nibelungenlied with me in old and modern German, together with Goethe's Faust. I read a good deal of German poetry on my own, and travelled to Mannheim to hear Wagner's Ring series, whose librettos I read with some care. From these studies I began to form some views on the strengths and weaknesses of the German character.

But the deepest effect of Heidelberg upon me, strangely enough, related to Russian rather than German culture. I attended some public lectures given by Hans Ehrenberg, a professor of philosophy. His theme was 'Goethe, Shakespeare and Dostoevsky', whose respective outlooks on the world were compared. He interested me in Dostoevsky and insisted his major works must be read in a prescribed order if they were to be understood. Soon I was reading novel after novel, counting my slender capital each time to see whether I could afford to buy the next. I still have the six novels, bound in red, linen-backed covers. Reading the first volume took time, as the vocabulary was new. Later, I read with fair speed. No chapter in any book ever made as deep or lasting impression upon me as the chapter in the Brothers Karamasov entitled 'The Grand Inquisitor'.

I returned to Oxford in May 1925 to take the very informal Scholarship examination at Queen's. There were seven or eight applicants, and we were each handed a paper for unseen translation of extracts in Greek, Latin, German, French and Italian. I attempted the last three sections only, conscious that only my German was likely to measure up to requirements. We were also given a broad subject on which to write an essay. My mind was teeming with the ideas of Dostoevsky and of Professor Ehrenberg, which I poured out in all directions. I have often wondered since that time what the Examiners thought of my screed: I imagine that they regarded me as extremely odd, if not actually certifiable. Linguistically, the other candidates were well ahead of me and I was not awarded a Laming Travelling Scholarship.

By this time I had been away from Australia for three and a half years and isolated in a foreign country for the last six months. Suddenly the urge to return to Australia became irresistible. Heidelberg had attracted me as no other city abroad, but in my final summer month there I began to feel that I must break away from its romanticised atmosphere if I were ever to achieve anything.

There were also strong personal reasons for the growing urge to return home. I wanted to clarify relationships with an Australian girl with whom I had maintained a developing correspondence while overseas. So the decision was taken. My father had died in 1924 and the family home had broken up. As I had no capital, I sought and obtained free passage to Australia on the Government-owned *Jervis Bay*, in return for taking charge of a group of teenage migrants. These were delivered into other hands at Brisbane, and I returned to Sydney.

In Sydney I felt rather like a visitor from Mars, or at least like Ulysses returning from far wanderings. My family welcomed me but my friends of university days were now practising their professions, preoccupied with making their way in the world. Most of them had forgotten me and, in any event, had little interest in someone without concrete objectives and a settled job. The lady to whom I have referred discovered in a couple of months that she was more interested in someone else.

At this stage of my career, or rather lack thereof, my sister Edna came to the rescue. She invited me to stay with her and her medico husband at Ulmarra, a short distance from Grafton in northern New South Wales. There I found a comfortable home, with grounds leading down to the broad stretch of the Clarence River and with a view of cane fields on the farther side. Although hot in summer, this was a most attractive countryside. I settled down to get my bearings and to make plans.

Still hoping to write, I felt a strong urge to set down on paper my personal experiences overseas. For six months I worked hard on a first draft of a novel called Beginnings. It opened in Scotland with a picture of life on the farm I had visited not far from Aberdeen, then moved to Australia, Heidelberg, Oxford, and back to Australia again. Although it had some atmosphere and reflected ideas which I had drawn largely from Dostoevsky, it was immature and unpublishable. Yet writing it had a cathartic effect upon me. When I had finished it I began to look for a job which would at least make me independent of others.

Early in 1926 I was browsing through the Positions Vacant columns of the *Sydney Morning Herald* when I saw an advertisement for an Education Officer at the British-Australasian Tobacco Company, Kensington. I applied, was appointed and held the job for three years before deciding that it was a dead-end in which whatever talents I possessed were likely to be wasted. The management was at first rather dubious about my motives and kept an eye on me for awhile as a possible dangerous radical, but eventually I was left alone. Perhaps unconsciously, I was imitating the Russian Narodniks of the nineteenth century who went to the countryside to help the peasants and found their motives misunderstood by the peasants and suspected by the Czarist authorities.

My daily work was a great strain upon my energy but none at all upon my intelligence. Gradually I adapted myself to a non-university type of teaching. I was reasonably well paid and became financially independent. For a time I shared a flat in Darlinghurst with one of my brothers; later, my mother and I shared a house in Kensington with another family.

For a time I returned to Sydney University to enrol for a course in experimental psychology, which I had begun to feel might widen opportunities for handling staff problems in industrial establishments. I also joined a group, including a number of graduates, which studied and discussed social theories and problems. There I met my wife, who had graduated at Sydney University with the University Medal in Philosophy and was then teaching French at secondary school level.

Mildred Mary Wait was born at Wahroonga on the North Shore line in a pleasant house with large grounds including a grass tennis court and a garden which provided flowers, vegetables and fruit. In due course I proposed and, after a period of hesitation and consideration, was accepted. We were married on 19 December, 1927 in the Church of England, Wahroonga, and rented a house at Roseville with a splendid view towards the Blue Mountains very much like the view from my parents' old home at Chatswood. Despite normal difficulties of mutual adjustment, and special family strains and stresses resulting from frequent moves and changes at home and abroad, ours has been a happy marriage and any later achievements of mine have stemmed directly from it.

Sometime in 1928 the Sydney newspapers announced the appointment of Percival Halse Rogers, K.C. as a Judge of the Supreme Court of New South Wales. As such, I knew he would need an Associate, a position usually given to some recent graduate in Law to provide experience of the work of the Courts and to facilitate contact with solicitors, prior to starting practice on his own as a barrister.

The responsibilities of marriage had made me feel the need to plan for the future. I came to the conclusion that I must seek wider opportunities in a different job and that my withdrawal from the post of education officer would scarcely be noticed, either by the company or by my pupils. I therefore discussed with my wife the possibility of applying for the position of Judge's Associate, which would guarantee me a minimum income while I qualified as a barrister. I could not take a degree in law, as I would not be free to attend lectures, but I could take the bar examinations, for which I could work on my own. While I had no special attraction to the Law, I felt that a legal training would help settle my feet on the ground after years of wandering among the clouds. My wife agreed, I applied and I was given the job. So I went to work in Judges' Chambers, set in the old Supreme Court Building, King St, Sydney.

It was a major undertaking to seek a legal qualification under these circumstances. I was married, a first child arrived in 1930 and a second in 1932. While my responsibilities as Associate involved little tax upon my intelligence, the work in Chambers and in court took up all my time and much of my energy during the day. All my study had to be done at night and at week-ends. Moreover, I had no guidance from experienced teachers of law, which I would have gained through attendance at lectures.

Sometime in 1932 I qualified as a barrister. During the intervening years the burden of family responsibilities fell all too heavily upon my wife. We had moved from Roseville to Hunter's Hill, where I had bought a house, heavily mortgaged. It was an old stone building, with a stone fence in front and a side garden filled with oleanders, lassiandras, poinsettias and other shrubs. Here we found peace and quiet, undisturbed by the isolation of the suburb from the city. The trip to and from town by ferry was restful beyond compare.

Hunter's Hill had been a fashionable suburb in the nineteenth century and its established families were still somewhat exclusive in their associations despite a deterioration in its status. It also maintained a substantial legal tradition, residents including a branch of the Windeyer family and two barristers, Murray-Prior and Bowie-Wilson, who were Aldermen of the local Municipal Council. John Alvarez was a solicitor employed by the Maritime Services Board.

I came to know Alvarez and one of the Windeyers at the local tennis club, and the two barristers both as Associate and as fellow-travellers on the ferry. Through the influence of the latter I became an Alderman of Hunter's Hill Council and, after a time, Deputy Mayor.

Meanwhile, I had made plans to take the plunge into private practice at the Bar. After six months experience of the Equity Jurisdiction as Associate to Sir John Harvey, I decided to resign as Associate early in 1933. At that time Australia had still not recovered from the effects of the depression, and entering upon private practice as a Barrister was a hazardous undertaking. As I would have few or no briefs for some time, I looked around for other sources of income, and was fortunate enough to secure appointment as Temporary Lecturer in Philosophy at Sydney University for the year 1933. This again guaranteed me a minimum income for one year, which I hoped to supplement by marking papers in English for public secondary school examinations. But the diversion of energy needed to prepare lectures in early Greek philosophy interfered with the process of building up a legal practice, and the benefits of reading with a well-known junior Barrister, W. F. L., now Sir William, Owen—a Justice of the High Court of Australia.

When I look back, I realise how valuable were those four years' experience of Courts of Law while I was an Associate. My training at Sydney and Oxford Universities and my experience of Heidelberg had isolated me from the problems of life in the raw. Whereas most of my earlier interests had been bookish, my attention had now been forcibly directed to disputes between plaintiff and defendant, cross-examination of witnesses of every shade of reliability, charges of Crown Prosecutors and the evasive statements of prisoners in the dock.

Justice Rogers, whose expertise was mainly in Common Law and especially in commercial causes, nevertheless had to sit in Criminal and Divorce jurisdiction and travel on circuit to country districts of New South Wales. He tried cases of alleged murder, manslaughter, rape, and dozens of Divorce suits, defended and undefended. Before him appeared most of the leading barristers of New South Wales—'Dick' Windeyer, A. B. Shand, Maxwell, Curtis, Flannery, Jordan, Andrew Watt, H. V. Evatt, Spender, Cassidy and many others, men of diverse gifts and skills. Not only did I learn much about the seamier side of life and the mixed motives of human beings, I also gained valuable lessons which books cannot easily teach—how to clarify issues, to uncover relevant facts witnesses wished to hide, to select important aspects of a case and argue them, to treat a Judge with respect but without subservience, fighting a client's case to the end to ensure that his rights within the law were given due consideration.

I also saw from the inside how Supreme Courts worked, and gained a healthy respect for its judges, whatever their human frailties. No judge I knew would have hesitated for a moment in granting an application for issue of a writ of *habeas corpus*, providing a *prima facie* case was made out on sworn evidence, whatever the status of the person alleged to be holding someone wrongfully in custody. The speed with which such an application could be obtained in private Chambers impressed indelibly upon my mind how irrelevant written constitutional guarantees of individual liberty can be unless supplemented by adequate administrative machinery for putting them into effect and by a judiciary independent of Legislature and Executive.

Finally, I began to appreciate the very real camaraderie within the legal profession, particularly amongst barristers. The toughest arguments in court rarely militated against good-fellowship out of court, where the benefit of the wide experience of established seniors was not infrequently made available to new and struggling juniors.

In any profession there are, of course, a few scoundrels while some others sail close to the wind. The legal profession is no exception, and occasionally a solicitor or barrister is struck off the roll. But during the period when I was associated with the Law—from 1928 to 1937—I never met a lawyer suspected of sharp practice or unethical conduct who was not regarded by the overwhelming majority of his colleagues with watchful contempt.

As my lectureship at Sydney University ran out in 1933 and my briefs at the Bar were still few and far between, I sought other means of supplementing income. At that stage the Law Book Company of Australasia decided to engage upon a major publishing venture—a digest of the whole of Australian Case Law in many volumes. The editor was B. Sugerman, who had distinguished himself academically, was then practising at the Bar and was later elevated to the Supreme Court Bench where, as Sir Bernard, he now presides over the Court of Appeal. I applied for work on the Digest and was accepted, together with A. B. Kerrigan (now Q.C.), W. (now Judge) Dignam, and R. Hastings. The work was dull, with none of the excitement or drama or sufficient remuneration of Court work; but it had distinct advantages. It was legal work which could not fail to widen my experience. Moreover, it could be done in one's own time, thus making it unnecessary ever to forgo a brief. As the company's premises were in Phillip St, a message could always be sent to recall us to Chambers if we were wanted by a solicitor.

I worked on the Digest for a couple of years. While a few minor early titles were assigned to me, my main responsibility was the volume on Criminal Law and Procedure.

My income at the Bar between 1933 and 1937 never reached the point of sustaining my family or of enabling me to drop other supplementary work. So I did some legal journalism, lectured on Contracts at a business college, and in due course became an official reporter for *Weekly Notes*, published by the Law Book Company. For the rest, for a number of years I marked thousands of English papers for the Department of Education.

Since my return to Australia in 1925 my interest in international affairs had never flagged. I continued to read German and took further lessons in French with a view, at one stage, to possible employment with the League of Nations Secretariat. In 1925 the *West Australian* newspaper published several articles I had written on developments in Germany. My friends at the Bar used to tease me because of my preoccupation with international news.

While I expected that in due course I would make my way at the Bar, I had no sense that I was born to be a barrister. On the other hand, I was deeply interested in the cultures of other lands and disturbed at the possibility of another World War following Hitler's advent to power.

In 1935 the Department of External Affairs in Canberra, which for long had formed part of the Prime Minister's Department, was given independent status again under a separate head. Subsequently, applications were called for graduate staff, and overseas experience would clearly be regarded as an additional qualification. After much thought and discussion with my wife, I decided to apply for an advertised position. My main hesitation was doubt whether, after a free life at the Bar, I could stand the probable red tape of Canberra. But this doubt was weakened by the knowledge that much of my life would be spent overseas.

In due course the Commonwealth Public Service Inspector for New South Wales told me that I had been accepted, subject to medical examination. Shortly afterwards I presented myself to a very young Commonwealth Medical Officer who informed me, after the usual tests, that he would have to defer me for six months as I had high blood pressure.

I was puzzled and somewhat irritated by this verdict, and my first impulse was to withdraw my application. While I knew I had been working hard, I felt quite well and had been accepted for life insurance with a minor loading. On reflection, some innate Scottish obstinacy made me persist. I went to a specialist in Macquarie St who acted as Chief Medical Referee for the A.M.P. Society. He gave me a thorough overhaul, including an electrocardiogram, and pronounced me 'a first-class risk'. More bureaucratic red tape had to be cut, however, before my medical condition was accepted in Canberra as satisfactory. The Commonwealth Department of Health sent me to another specialist, chosen by it but paid for by me, who confirmed the verdict of his distinguished colleague. I was then told to report to Canberra to take up my new duties.

1

CANBERRA

One

I ARRIVED in Canberra in April 1937, at the ripe age of 36, to enter upon a new career. During the next twenty-five years life in the Australian Diplomatic Service brought many vicissitudes, both personal and official, but also many opportunities, much interest and a degree of satisfaction which I would not have found in any other profession open to me.

In those days, ten years after its founding, Canberra was a country town of 10,000 people, predominantly bureaucrats. The site had been chosen in accordance with the terms of S. 125 of the federal Constitution, which solemnly prescribed that the federal seat of government should be within the State of New South Wales, but 'not less than one hundred miles from Sydney'. This compromise, of course, stemmed from the jealousy between Sydney and Melbourne, each of which was determined to prevent the other from becoming the capital city of Australia.

Until 1927 Melbourne was the provisional capital, and the federal parliament met there after the Commonwealth was inaugurated in 1901. In 1937 there was still controversy as to whether the creation and development of Canberra was a wise decision. Many Australians, especially those who lived in Sydney and Melbourne, regarded it with something approaching contempt and resented the costs of its establishment. In later years, as Canberra grew, they tended to criticise its residents as pampered and privileged people. This attitude contrasted strangely with the strong disinclination and at times refusal of Commonwealth Public Servants in State capital cities to be transferred to Canberra. As one who was born and educated in Sydney, the first and largest of the State capitals, but who has lived in Canberra (when not overseas) since 1937, I have no doubt of the wisdom of the decision. Certainly I myself have found it much easier to think of Australia as a whole than would have been possible had I remained in Sydney.

On joining the Department of External Affairs I had left my family behind me in Hunter's Hill until such time as I could arrange accommodation for them in Canberra. I lived in a hotel for about a month and then, *mirabile*

15

dictu, was granted tenancy of a small, almost new, Government-built house in Bass Gardens, Griffith. Arrangements were then made for my wife and two sons, aged seven and five respectively, to travel from Sydney by the overnight train and to join me in the hotel until our furniture arrived.

One morning in mid May, 1937, about 5 a.m., my family stepped from the train onto the platform of the 'old' Canberra railway station, which had scarcely been designed to impress the visitor with the dignity of a national capital. The station was a couple of miles from the city, presenting to the bewildered traveller a vista consisting chiefly of fields, trees and hills. My eldest son, Alan, took one look around and exclaimed 'Where's Canberra?'

We soon found houses as we drove to our hotel, but the suburbs were separated from one another by so many open fields that they seemed to justify the current quip 'Canberra consists of six suburbs in search of a city'. Yet Walter Burleigh Griffin, the American whose design for Canberra had won an international competition, was no fool. An essential feature of his original plans was a series of artificial lakes, to be formed by damming the small Molongo River which passes through the centre of the city. These were intended to bind the areas north and south of the river by means of substantial sheets of water, crossed by two main bridges and providing a splendid foreground against which to view distant hills and mountains. Installation of the lakes scheme, however, was delayed until as recently as 1963 by inertia, procrastination and lack of funds. Meanwhile members of the local golf club, which included many of the bureaucratic establishment, acquired a vested interest in preventing action on the Griffin plan because their golf course had been laid out on the bed of one of the proposed lakes. It was due mainly to the persistence of Prime Minister R. G. Menzies who, unlike his Ministers, actually lived in Canberra and had a personal belief in its future, that funds were eventually provided for a modified lakes scheme. Viewed now from Red Hill, with the two well designed bridges pointing towards Mount Ainslie, one can appreciate at last the quality of Griffin's topographical imagination.

A second feature of Canberra's design is far more open to question. Griffin and his successors seem always to have preferred a pair of compasses to a ruler. It is almost impossible to drive straight from one point on the map to another for any appreciable period of time. One is constantly going round in circles, or semi-circles, or bends—all of which takes time, consumes petrol, increases the risks of motor car accidents and adds to the cost of inadequate bus services. Distances in Canberra are vast. Although there are sufficient buses to take one, slowly, to and from work at fixed times of the day, a housewife shopping wastes much time waiting, while cross-country travel involving change of buses is simply infuriating.

The newcomer to Canberra soon learns that ownership of a car is not a luxury but close to a necessity, whatever the cost. Nowadays, indeed, as suburbs have developed farther and farther from the centre, many families have two cars, one used by the husband to travel to work and for picnics and longer family trips, the other a small runabout used by the wife and older children for shopping and social purposes. As the number of cars grows, annual losses on the bus service tend to rise. The only compensation for the population as a whole is that, as roads are good, one can drive five miles in fifteen minutes save during peak traffic periods, although it is now a city of over 140,000.

In 1937 I could not afford a car, and we all had to operate by bus. Our house in Bass Gardens had only two bedrooms and a small alcove, and was blessed with a wood stove and chip bath heater. It had been built on bare sheep pasture; there were as yet no shrubs or flowers. Coming as we did from an attractive if old fashioned stone house at Hunter's Hill, with several wooden outhouses useful for storage and with a developed garden, our new home seemed small, restricted and bleak.

We had two weeks of autumn weather during which the vivid colours of the several million, European type trees which are a distinctive feature of the city helped us forget the absence of growth in our own garden. Then came the severe winter frosts. My wife had never before felt so cold. Like all Canberra 'pioneers', I soon learned how important the axe was as a household implement. Minimal comfort during the winter depended upon securing a supply of good wood—which was frequently impossible to obtain—and building up a reserve of cut wood and kindling for stove, fireplace and heater, near to and preferably inside the house. Otherwise one had to dash outside the house to the wood-heap before breakfast in a temperature often cold enough to freeze water in the outside pipes.

The winter climate of Canberra comes as a surprise to any newcomer who has merely looked up its latitude. The city is 2,000 feet above sea level, and is bounded by a semi-circle of mountains rising from about 5,000 feet towards the Snowy Mountains. Snow rarely falls in Canberra, but wind off the snow can chill to the bone. On the other hand, heavy frosts are usually followed by a clear sky, so that one can enjoy at one and the same time bright sunshine and an exhilarating nip in the air. Even during the three hot summer months it can be quite cool at night.

Perhaps as partial compensation for the discomforts of winter, during which residents who attended concerts in the only available building were apt to bring rugs and hot water bottles, Spring brought pleasant surprises. Indeed, there were three Springs. First there appeared the cheerful yellow and gold of numerous varieties of wattle trees; to be followed after a few weeks by different types of ornamental fruit-trees, especially prunus; last came the young green leaves of willow, poplar, Canadian pin-oak and dozens of other kinds of deciduous trees, which in their many thousands enliven the landscape without destroying the general Australian background of ubiquitous gum-trees.

The unkind critics, of whom there were a great many in 1937, would protest that man does not live by landscape alone. They missed the bright lights and variety of the big city, the range of entertainment to be found in Sydney or Melbourne, conversation with people who were not bureaucrats. For the young, especially those unmarried public servants who lived in uncomfortable hostels, Canberra was just plain dull. Whenever they could find time and sufficient money to pay for the trip, they fled to a State capital city seeking gaiety and means of escape from the ever-watchful eye of Big Brother government. They could scarcely be blamed for failing to foresee the extraordinary growth of Canberra during the late 1950s and the decade of the 1960s, which introduced variety, improved convenience, and made it in many ways a stimulating and attractive city in which to live.

With my family settled in, I was able to concentrate my own time and energy on my work in the Department of External Affairs. When I arrived in Canberra and presented myself to the Secretary, Lt Col. W. R. Hodgson, in the administrative buildings known as West Block, I was surprised to discover how few officers there were to carry out what seemed to me to be very important functions. The Political Division was headed by T. Mathew, who was assisted by P. R. Heydon and J. K. Waller. The International Co-operation Division was in charge of H. A. Peterson, whose assistants were D. F. Nicholson and J. S. Cumpston. At that stage Australia had no Diplomatic Missions in any foreign country, although we had had a High Commission in London since 1910, headed, with one exception, by an ex-member of the Cabinet, and a Political Liaison Officer in the British Cabinet Offices since 1924. In addition, a number of Trade Commissioners had been posted to selected foreign countries.

When first established, the High Commission in London was placed under the control of the Prime Minister's Department. This was natural enough at the time, but became more and more difficult to justify when External Affairs was once more separated out as a distinct Department under its own Head in 1935 and gradually grew under successive governments into a substantial Foreign Office represented in some fifty countries overseas. Nowadays the High Commission, London, is the only Australian diplomatic establishment abroad which is *not* under the control of the Minister for Foreign Affairs—the new title accorded in 1970 to the Minister for External Affairs.

The first Australian Political Liaison Officer in London was R. G. (later Lord) Casey. He was chosen by Prime Minister S. M. (later Viscount) Bruce and sent to London to improve consultation between the British and Australian Governments. Bruce hoped in this way to be able to express Australian views on impending British policy before being faced with a *fait accompli*. Casey remained in London from 1924 to 1931, with one short interruption when he returned to Australia. He then resigned to enter politics, and was succeeded by F. K. (later Sir Keith) Officer, who in 1937 was transferred to Washington as Australian Counsellor on the staff of the *British* Ambassador to the United States. He held that experimental post for three years. The precedent of attaching an Australian diplomat to a British Embassy was not repeated, because the Menzies government which came to power in 1939 decided to establish Australian Diplomatic Missions, the first of which opened in Washington in 1940, Officer being attached to its staff.

In 1937 A. T. Stirling, who in 1936 had become Head of the Political Division in Canberra, was transferred to London to succeed Officer as Political Liaison Officer, and Mathew was promoted to Stirling's Canberra post.

Such was the small staff of the Department of External Affairs, apart from records, typing and similar personnel, when I joined it in 1937, together with John Oldham, Noel Deschamps and Colin Moodie. My basic interest was in political affairs, but I found myself assigned to work under Peterson in the International Co-operation Division, which dealt mainly with trade, treaty and consular matters, apart from League of Nations and International Labour Office problems.

The tone of the Department was set by the Secretary, Colonel Hodgson, whose manner was blunt, gruff and insensitive. As a young man 'Hoddo', as he was invariably described in private by his irreverent juniors, had chosen the Army as a profession. He was trained as an officer at the Royal Military College, Duntroon, and graduated with the first group to complete the course after establishment of the College. He had been badly wounded at Gallipoli, and surgical operations left him with one leg shorter than the other, necessitating constant use of a walking stick.

A military career requiring normal physical fitness was closed to him. With much courage and pertinacity, he graduated in Law at the University of Melbourne, acquired accountancy qualifications and, after a period of work on military intelligence in the Pacific region, was appointed in 1934 Assistant-Secretary dealing with External Affairs problems in the Prime Minister's Department. He thus happened to be in position when External Affairs was re-established as a separate Department in 1935, and was appointed Secretary.

Hodgson, however, remained an Army man at heart and he never fully adapted himself to the world of diplomacy. He had plenty of courage, but little discretion and was temperamentally more inclined to offensive than to defensive operations. With his staff he was a bit of a martinet. I can never think of Hodgson without thinking also of the small, black, shaggy-haired dog which always accompanied him and which was privileged to sit in an old arm chair in his office. For recreation he played bowls, and not infrequently urgent telegrams, arriving out of office hours, had to be taken to him at the Bowling Club.

Peterson, the next senior officer, was a kindly but disappointed man. A clerical officer in the Third Division of the Commonwealth Public Service, he had graduated in Arts the hard way while in the Service and had hoped to be appointed Secretary. In the late afternoon Peterson would collect files from staff working under him, and take draft letters and telegrams to Hodgson for approval and signature. Hodgson treated these drafts rather roughly, regarding himself without justification as an expert on punctuation. Often the letters had to be re-typed before signature. About one year after my arrival in Canberra Peterson, somewhat irritated with Hodgson and seeing for himself no prospects of further advancement in the Department of External Affairs, transferred to the Department of Commerce. Before retirement he held several overseas Consular and Trade Commissioner posts.

Next in seniority after Peterson was 'Toby' Mathew, a man of considerable ability and complex personality. Though of obvious Irish ancestry, he had been born in England where his father was a well-known London barrister and author. Toby had been sent to Oxford, but he enlisted when very young for service in the First World War, which had left serious marks upon him. Apparently he found it difficult to settle down after the war, came to Australia and found employment in a library, eventually joining the Department of External Affairs. His written English was direct, simple and clear. Though his ability commanded respect, he was not an easy colleague, being irascible by temperament and apt to wound by too frequent use of his brilliant, mordant wit. Unfortunately, the strain of personal problems led to a breakdown around the time of the Munich crisis of 1938. Although he returned to the Department and was helped in various ways by two Ministers and some colleagues, eventually he had to be eased out of the Department and found work elsewhere, dying in middle age. His departure from Canberra was a great loss to Hodgson and the Department, and a tragedy for himself.

I did not find the transition easy from life at the New South Wales Bar to the Department of External Affairs. Privacy had always been an important concomitant in my work. I now found myself working in a large room with several other officers. On one occasion I could not avoid overhearing a colleague being interviewed by a Public Service Inspector in regard to an appeal lodged by the former against the promotion of another officer. The appellant described in detail all the reasons why, in his opinion, his own qualifications were superior. After ten minutes I could stand the conversation no longer, and went out into the corridor for a walk.

The files assigned to me by Peterson were on subjects which were not uninteresting but they were certainly not of any substantial political importance. Moreover, I rather resented the fact that they were collected by Peterson and taken to Hodgson for decision without my being present, unless Hodgson summoned me to discuss some point. Hodgson, I found, regarded me as a lawyer, simple if not pure: it did not cross his mind to discuss with me the kinds of political problems which alone had attracted me to the Department. I did not relish my official classification as Clerk, Third Division, although the name was only Public Service jargon. My annual salary of £510 was less than I had been earning before I came to Canberra. I sensed some antagonism amongst public servants who thought practical experience and seniority were far more important than tertiary education and who were disposed to resent the fact that I had been appointed under S. 47 of the Commonwealth Public Service Act to perform duties which, allegedly, could not be performed by others in the Service.

However, relations with most of my colleagues in the Department were friendly enough, and I developed some sense of being part of a team. Work of a legal or quasi-legal nature tended to come to me, and occasionally I had the feeling that my legal training and experience had some specific value. I think it was during the first year that I had one minor triumph, which was noted by Hodgson. Some question arose about ratification of treaties, and we discovered that the views of the British Foreign Office diverged from those of the British Dominions' Office. I pointed this out and gave an opinion as to the correct procedure, with supporting reasons. My paper was sent to Alfred Stirling in London, who passed it on to the Ministries concerned. After consultation and re-examination, they both agreed with the opinion I had expressed. What I wanted, however, was access to general telegrams and material on political problems, which normally were distributed only to the Political Division and to the Head of the

International Co-operation Division. Unless one knew the contents of these it was impossible to form any sound judgment on current matters of importance.

My earliest contacts with Cabinet Ministers had nothing to do with official business. Two of us played tennis occasionally with R. G. Casey (then Treasurer) and Dr. (later Sir Earle) Page. Although in later years Casey was apt to express considerable admiration for Page as a man of original ideas some of which had contributed substantially to Australian development, I was never able to forget that, on the tennis court, Page showed a strong tendency to call an opponent's ball out even when it was a foot inside the line. This seemed to me to reflect a curious meanness of spirit unlikely to be limited to sport.

Between April 1937 and September 1940, when I was posted overseas, there were no fewer than four Ministers for External Affairs—Senator George Pearce (November 1934-November 1937), W. M. Hughes (November 1937-April 1939), Sir Henry Gullett (April 1939-March 1940) and John McEwen (March 1940-October 1940). Even when I held a more senior position from 1938 to 1940, I saw them but rarely. Documents would normally be taken to them by Hodgson or, in his absence, by the Head of the Political Division. Each Minister, however, had a departmental reputation. Pearce was thought to be fair-minded and sensible. Hughes could be fiery; he was also capable of losing secret documents through carelessness and of leaving a late Cabinet meeting to drive off to Sydney—especially as the week-end approached—even though External Affairs items might remain untouched on the Cabinet agenda. Gullett was regarded as an able but somewhat vain and pernickety man. McEwen was competent and determined to be no mere rubber stamp.

I had been about a year in Canberra when Peterson suddenly decided to transfer to the Department of Commerce. This left a vacancy in the position of Head of the International Co-operation Division, to which Hodgson promoted me. At once my responsibilities increased and my interest was stimulated. As Head of a Division, the general range of inwards and outwards cables was circulated to me. It was my personal function to draft or supervise the drafting of instructions for Australian Delegations to League of Nations meetings and International Labour Organisation Conferences, which involved discussion of relevant agenda items with the Head of the Political Division, as well as with the Secretary. My new status entitled me to see important political and defence documents, such as British Foreign Office Blue Prints and defence appreciations by the British Committee of Imperial Defence (C.I.D.).

The most important document which came to my notice was a C.I.D. general strategic appreciation. From this it appeared clearly that British Naval, Air and Army resources were not such as to enable Britain to fight at one and the same time a war in the Atlantic, the Mediterranean and the Far East. British and French strength combined were thought sufficient to win a war fought in any two of these regions—against Germany and Italy, against Germany and Japan, or against Italy and Japan—but not against all three possible opponents together. The assumption, therefore, was that British foreign policy must be so adapted as to prevent a war in the three named regions at the same time.

When I read the paper, my naive reaction was to ask the question 'But suppose British foreign policy fails: what then?' The paper seemed to imply that it could not or must not fail. While I understood that there were limits to planning, imposed by available resources, and that probably no country could prepare in advance to meet every conceivable 'worst case', there seemed to me insufficient evidence to justify the basic assumption that a war in the three regions at once could be avoided. In that event, the consequences for Australia would be serious.

During the two and a half years when I was Head of the International Co-operation Division my views on political matters had little or no effect upon Hodgson. He looked to Mathew and later to John Hood for advice, although I became involved when League of Nations and I.L.O. matters came up for consideration. Any influence I had upon the Secretary or the Minister was indirect, through friendly relations with Mathew or Hood and occasional discussions with them.

Nor do I believe that the Department as a whole had substantial influence at the Ministerial level, except by providing basic information, mainly from British sources, together with comments which might include warnings as to the consequences of different courses of action. The Department of Defence seemed to me to have more influence upon the Government.

Yet it is clear from confidential documents made available to Australian historians of the Second World War that the Department of External Affairs was already making some serious effort to formulate a realistic foreign policy for ministerial consideration. Thus a memorandum prepared for the Australian Delegation to the Imperial Conference 1937 stressed that no situation should be allowed to arise 'in which Germany in the West, Japan in the Far East, and any power, such as Italy, on the main artery between the two, are simultaneously hostile'. No doubt this statement stemmed from the C.I.D. paper already referred to; but the memorandum also expressed the opinion that international relations were more 'strained' than in 1936, described the current situation as 'very tense' and prophesied, a year ahead of the event, a German 'move against Czechoslovakia'.[1]

Papers prepared for the same Conference by the Australian Department of Defence disclose concern at the 'unsatisfactory' situation in the Far East until 1942, by which time it was thought that completion of British defences, required if war should break out with Germany, would permit allocation of strengthened forces in the Far East to help restrain Japan. British opinion was sought on the possibility of Japan mounting an invasion of Australia. It was against this background that Prime Minister Joseph Lyons urged the United Kingdom to seek a general understanding with Japan and pursued without success, both inside the Conference and in unusual personal interviews with the Ambassadors in London of the Soviet Union, China, France, the Netherlands, the United States and Japan, suggestions for a pact of non-aggression in the Pacific.

[1] *The Government and the People, 1939-41*, by Paul Hasluck (Australian War Memorial, Canberra, 1952), pp. 56-58.

At the time of the Sudeten-German crisis in 1938, leading to the Munich settlement, I was suddenly and unexpectedly assigned responsibility for drafting a speech which Mr Lyons was to deliver in the House of Representatives. As mentioned earlier, Toby Mathew had a breakdown which made it impossible for him to do his ordinary work for about three weeks. I first learned of the situation when I received a telephone call from Percivale Liesching, then Official Secretary to the British High Commissioner in Canberra and one of a group which played tennis at his residence. Liesching asked me to see him and I discovered that, out of the kindness of his heart, he was looking after Mathew personally. As I felt that this should not be his responsibility, my wife and I agreed that Mathew should be transferred to our home.

By that time we had succeeded in securing a much pleasanter and more adequate house in Dominion Circuit, Forrest, with more bedrooms, sufficient grounds and an established garden—all within walking distance of the Department, across open country. After a week, however, we decided that the condition of my colleague was serious and beyond our capacity to handle. For another week, if my memory is correct, he stayed with John Oldham, who worked under him in the Political Division.

Meanwhile I was fully stretched in the Department. My instructions were to make the draft speech factual, leaving to the Prime Minister the vital last paragraph or two. I welcomed the opportunity, though not the attendant circumstances which had brought it to me. But as the date for delivery of the speech was postponed from time to time, the draft had to be modified on several occasions to keep it up to date. My own emotions were heavily involved,* as I disagreed strongly with the policy of Neville Chamberlain and was vain enough to think that my personal experience of Germany enabled me to form a more accurate judgment of Hitler than the British Prime Minister. However, I obeyed instructions, but interpreted them as allowing me to insert one sentence which I expected to be struck out as embarrassing to the Government.

The Lyons Government had informed Parliament and the Australian people that it supported the policy of the Chamberlain government on the Sudeten-German issue; it had not disclosed, however, that Australia had actually pressed Britain to press Czechoslovakia to make maximum concessions to Hitler. I felt that this non-disclosure was unjustified, and that the Australian Government was evading some of the consequences of its own policy. I therefore inserted in the draft the following words:

> The United Kingdom Government was also informed that the Commonwealth Government urged that the Government of Czechoslovakia should not delay in making a public announcement of the most liberal concessions which it could offer, and that representations should be made to the Czechoslovak Government with a view to securing an immediate public statement of such concessions.

Lyons had still not made up his mind when to deliver the speech before Mathew returned to the Department. He was far from well, but not obviously

* See Appendix II for 3 'political' poems written between 1938 and 1940.

disqualified from resuming his old duties. He took over my draft and added a second half as new circumstances developed. Eventually the Prime Minister decided to deliver it at 11 p.m. on September 28, 1938—a most unusual time for such a statement. The reason, unknown to his audience, but well known to us, was that Hitler had issued an ultimatum to the Czechs, expiring at midnight (Australian time) on September 28, which if rejected could have led to war. Presumably Lyons did not dare postpone his speech any longer without risking the charge that the Government had not disclosed to Parliament and people the extreme seriousness of the situation. As the Prime Minister did not indicate the reason for the timing, however, his speech struck members of Parliament as puzzling rather than illuminating, something of an anti-climax. They had feared the worst—an indication that we were on the verge of war—but had been told little more than that the international situation continued to be bad.

I have examined elsewhere in detail the question whether or not Chamberlain's policy was justified,[2] and have concluded that it was not. Here it is relevant to refer only to three more matters arising out of the speech and its preparation. First, the speech as read out in Parliament concluded as follows:

> If war is to come to the world it will not come by reason of anything that any British nation has done or failed to do. Our hands are clean. We have done our best to keep the peace. We have no selfish interest to serve. Even as the clouds gather about us, we still hope that peace may be preserved.

I can not conceive that any official drafted this ending, and have concluded that it was added by the Prime Minister himself: certainly it has an authentic Lyons ring. Secondly, the particular sentence I had deliberately inserted in the draft was not deleted. I suspect that its significance escaped notice. It stands upon the record, although no one inside or outside of Parliament drew attention to it at the time, so far as I am aware. Thirdly, this first personal participation in an international crisis reassured me about the correctness of my decision to leave the Bar and join the Department.

During the following two years of my first sojourn in Canberra I experienced, like others, many of the frustrations and disadvantages of government service, but my responsibilities were sufficiently wide and future prospects encouraging enough to make me feel that at long last I had found my metier. Relationships with Hodgson were not easy, but I was fortunate enough to make contact with two senior public servants, L. S. Jackson (Commissioner of Taxation) and H. F. E. Whitlam* (Commonwealth Crown Solicitor), whose friendly interest and sound advice filled a gap and taught me that, in the long term, what a public servant loses on the swings he may well pick up on the round-abouts.

My salary remained inadequate for growing family needs, especially after twins—a boy and a girl—were born in 1939. Early in that year, however, I

[2] The Evolution of Australian Foreign Policy (1938-65), by Alan Watt (Cambridge University Press, 1967), Chapter 1.
* Father of Mr. E. G. Whitlam, Leader of the Federal Parliamentary Labor Party.

obtained permission from Hodgson and the Public Service Board to apply for a Lectureship in Commercial Law at the Canberra University College, then under the wing of Melbourne University and designed mainly to enable public servants to do tertiary education work out of normal working hours. I was appointed, and the additional income enabled me to buy my first car. It was a single-seater Cadillac, vintage 1921, which a trusted friend sold me for £50. Although it was a monster which travelled only seven miles to the gallon, and one had to pump petrol and turn the windscreen wipers by hand, all members of my family developed a considerable affection for it. The material used to build it must have been magnificent. If the mudguard hit a tree, it was the tree rather than the mudguard which suffered. We could not use the car frequently, but when we did it added greatly to our comfort and range of activities.

When Hitler marched into Prague in 1939 the future looked grim indeed. Shortly afterwards I bought a radio set with short-wave facilities. So began a habit of listening to public news which, over the years, I have found of great value and which at times has driven my long-suffering wife almost to desperation. In an effort to reduce family wear and tear, I added ear-phones to the set.

Well before war broke out I had learned all the short-wave frequencies, and could turn to London, Washington or Berlin with accuracy and speed for news broadcasts at specific times. As the threat of war increased, I used to get up early to listen before breakfast to news items which the morning newspapers could not include because of their printing deadlines. At first I listened for my own edification only, but later thought some of the points important enough to jot down on paper. I showed these to Hodgson, but he showed little interest.

For a period of a few weeks after the actual declaration of war, however, short-wave news became of immediate practical importance. It reached Australia as much as twelve hours ahead of official telegrams from London if these were sent in code, and several hours ahead of telegrams sent in clear. Moreover, I could on occasion listen to Hitler's voice direct, and could form an impression of the effect upon his audience of what he was saying.

During this period I typed out a full summary of early morning news, which Hodgson transmitted to his Minister. One of these was taken into Cabinet which thereupon, to my great satisfaction, instructed Hodgson to instal a good short-wave set in the Department of External Affairs. This was found to be impracticable because of electrical interference by machines used in West Block for statistical purposes. Arrangements were then made for the machine to be installed in my home at Forrest, and for messages to be transmitted to the Department by land-line. I could thus telephone my wife at any time, ask her to tune in to a particular wave-length, and pick up news through earphones in my office.

This means of communication with the outside world became less import-ant after a few weeks from the outbreak of war, except at times of crisis. I remember, however, that our first news of the collapse of France in 1940 came over the land-line and I heard that Marshal Petain was forming a

government. The implications of this were obvious, and were passed on immediately to the Australian Cabinet.

The fall of France produced in me a mood of pessimism stronger than any other event in the war. I was no military strategist and, thinking in terms of the First World War, kept on expecting a French counter-attack to hold the Germans at some early point of time. It was only in later years that I learned that the Blitzkrieg had been foreseen by a comparatively junior French officer, Charles de Gaulle, whose views had been rejected or ignored by senior French generals but had been noted, understood and acted upon by the Germans. When I realised eventually that no effective French counter-attack was to be expected, I was plunged into greater gloom than when the fall of Singapore to the Japanese directly endangered Australia, because by then the United States was committed and I did not doubt ultimate victory.

Mathew left the Department of External Affairs in 1939 and John Hood was brought back from London to take his place as Head of the Political Division. Hood was a Tasmanian Rhodes Scholar who had taken a First at Oxford in Philosophy, Politics and Economics, and had then been appointed to the staff of *The Times* of London where he rose to sub-editorial rank. In many ways Hood was the opposite of Mathew, quiet in style and laconic in speech but with greater intellectual capacity as distinct from facility in expression. Our relations were friendly, and our common background at Oxford made it easy for us to work together. Hood seemed destined to go far in the Service and in later years he did in fact hold important overseas appointments. However, some family and personal problems hampered the complete fulfilment of his early promise and he retired in 1964.

Meanwhile my own contacts with senior officers in other Departments expanded, and I formed a high opinion of the capacity and sense of responsibility of most of them. As a departmental representative on an inter-departmental sub-committee which included Assistant-Secretaries from the Departments of Commerce and Customs I came to know E. (later Sir Edwin) McCarthy. I had already met him on the tennis court, and subsequent association led to a friendship which I came to value greatly. We both served in Washington during some of the war years. He became Secretary of the Department of Commerce, Deputy High Commissioner in London, Ambassador to the Netherlands and Belgium, and Ambassador to the European Economic Community. McCarthy was an expert on shipping and wheat, and as Chairman of the International Wheat Council and of the United Nations Committee dealing with international commodity arrangements won high international respect and trust.

On one occasion I was deputed to represent External Affairs on a selection committee for new appointees to the Department. In those days the system of selection was different from now, but the committee of three, including a Public Service Inspector, took their responsibilities seriously and decided to reject two applicants who, in different ways, seemed on paper to have significant qualifications. At a later stage when I was overseas these two were accepted into the Service and reached positions of some responsibility. Nevertheless, their official record confirms my belief that the decision to reject their applications was sound.

26

About July 1940 Hodgson found himself under sudden pressure from R. G. Casey, who earlier in that year had become first Australian Minister to the United States, to send to Washington a senior officer from Canberra to replace Keith Officer, who was to move to Tokyo to make arrangements for the opening of a Legation there. The only two who would have met Casey's requirements were Hood or myself, neither of whom Hodgson wished to lose. When he offered younger and less senior officers, Casey persisted. Eventually Hodgson decided that he could dispense with my services more easily than with Hood's, and he discussed with me a possible posting to Washington. I jumped at the opportunity, which I knew would give me direct political responsibilities in a country whose attitude towards the war was of outstanding importance to Australia. Moreover, I saw no opportunity of further advancement in Canberra, where Hodgson still regarded me as primarily a lawyer. In Washington, overseas allowances were likely to ease the domestic burdens which my wife was carrying, and bring her into a wider range of activities. So, after discussion with my wife, I readily assented to the proposal.

When Hodgson cabled Casey to say that he would send me, Casey agreed, but added a condition not previously mentioned. He said in his reply that, as the war would keep staff in Washington small for the amount of work involved, I should come without my family. When Hodgson showed me the cable, I objected to the condition, pointing out that Mrs Casey and the Casey children were in Washington and that, while the Minister's responsibilities would be far greater than mine as Head of Chancery, it was absurd to suggest that I would be less rather than more effective if my family accompanied me. I added that if I had been posted to a war area, including London, I would not have sought to take my family. Washington was not a war area, and I was being asked unnecessarily to go abroad for an indefinite period, leaving my wife to look after four children, including twins aged 10 months, on her own.

After some further exchange of cables, Casey withdrew the condition. It was not until many years later that I learned indirectly that Keith Officer, a bachelor, had intervened successfully on my behalf.[3] So began an overseas odyssey which kept me out of Australia, in various and widely different countries, for about seventeen years out of twenty-two, functioning as an Australian diplomat abroad.

[3] For an account of the personality and career of Keith Officer, see article by Peter Heydon in *Quadrant*, July-August, 1970, No. 66 (Vol. XIV, No. 4).

2

EASTWARD HO!

United States and United Kingdom

MINE was the first official, as distinct from ministerial, family to be moved overseas by the newly re-constituted Department of External Affairs. At that stage, sufficient thought had not been given to the rules and regulations which should apply in such a case.

Today, an officer posted abroad can in normal circumstances retain tenancy of a house in Canberra which he can sub-let, pending his return. He will be paid a basic salary, together with a cost-of-living allowance appropriate to the particular post, and an entertainment allowance varying with his status and responsibilities. In addition, he receives a substantial child allowance to help pay educational expenses at a boarding school if there are no suitable schools where he is sent, while the fares of children left in Australia are covered for one visit a year to parents abroad, up to the age of twenty-one if the child is at a university. None of these privileges was available when I was posted to Washington.

I was paid an arbitrary sum of $10,000 p.a. to cover all expenses in Washington; the tenancy of our house in Forrest had to be surrendered; as there were no educational allowances for children, the question of leaving any children behind, or sending any back to Australia, did not cross our minds. Each year I had to argue with the Australian Taxation Commissioner just how much of my emoluments could justly be regarded as salary.

My instructions were to report in Washington at the earliest possible moment. No air travel was available, so I was booked on the first ship, ahead of my family. This meant that my wife would have to cross the Pacific and the United States with four children, two of whom could not walk. In view of the dispensation we had been given enabling all of us to be together in Washington, we did not feel it right to make a fuss about this. There was a war raging, and members of thousands of families were being separated from one another. But as it was physically impossible for my wife to handle both twins and the two elder boys on her own, we had to engage a nurse to travel with her, pay the nurse's fare and undertake to return her to Australia provided she stayed with us for twelve months. To find the necessary capital for this, I had to sell the furniture in our house, and face the prospect of starting from scratch when we returned again to Australia.

I had no time to sell my old Cadillac in Canberra, and drove it to Sydney in the hope of disposing of it there. Busied with last-minute arrangements, I was unable to leave Canberra before dark and drove to Sydney, quite exhausted, through the night. I remember only two aspects of the journey: the dividing line on the road over which I drove most of the way, with occasional scampering rabbits darting across in front of me; and dawn light seen from the top of the Razorback Mountain near Picton, where I rested before facing heavier traffic.

No one in Sydney was interested in my car during the short time available, so I left it at a garage with instructions to sell. Nothing more was heard of it and no funds were received. I feel sure that the engine is still ticking over somewhere, perhaps on an outback farm where it might serve some purpose other than transportation.

My family had been booked to leave Sydney, about a fortnight after my departure, on the American steamship *Monterey*. The United States was not yet in the war, and it seemed sensible to put them on a vessel which would not be subject to interference by an odd German raider, though the risk was small. I travelled on a fairly modern British ship, the *Awatea*, which had been on the New Zealand run. Aboard were the first fifty Australians of the R.A.A.F., travelling to Canada for training under the Empire Air Training Scheme. They were an attractive bunch and their high spirits were infectious. We were blacked out during the voyage and at dusk and dawn airmen helped watch for raiders which—or so we were told—preferred such times for attack. If any raiders existed, none spotted us and the trip was quite uneventful.

My first port of call was Auckland. Finding that the ship would be staying there for a couple of days I decided, without instructions, to slip down to Wellington at my own expense and make contact with the New Zealand Department of External Affairs. My visit was welcomed by Alistair McIntosh, temporarily in charge of the Department because the Secretary, Carl Berendson, was out of town. Later I learned that Berendson was aboard a New Zealand warship visiting Tahiti to ensure it did not support the Vichy government. Australia had taken similar action regarding New Caledonia. McIntosh and I seemed to hit it off at first meeting. This was the beginning of a friendship and co-operation over a long period of years, during most of which McIntosh was himself Secretary of the Department. I came to respect his ability and judgment highly.

When the *Awatea* called at Fiji, I called upon the Governor, who was somewhat surprised but not displeased to see me. Somewhat intoxicated by these new contacts, I began to think it would be a good idea if I visited Ottawa en route to Washington from Vancouver, for talks with the Canadian Department of External Affairs. When I telegraphed Casey from Vancouver seeking his approval, I received a peremptory and entirely justified reply instructing me to proceed at once to Washington by the quickest route.

In Washington I booked in at the Wardman Park Hotel, which was within reasonable walking distance of the Australian Legation in Cleveland Av., N.W., and reported to Casey. With his assent I spent what time I could looking for a house for my family. Peter Heydon, who had been posted to Washington as Second Secretary, had already set some inquiries in train. Fortunately, as the United States was not yet at war, the extreme shortage of housing which developed after the Pearl Harbour attack was a nightmare of the future. I inspected numerous furnished houses, reduced the possibilities to six, and was able to take the risk of refusing to decide until my wife saw them. Two years later I would have snapped up the first house available.

In due course I met my family at the railway station. My wife told me that Alan and John, then aged ten and eight respectively, had expressed their point of view as the train steamed in to Washington by singing 'Advance, Australia Fair!' We all settled temporarily into an apartment and rooms I had taken for the family and nurse at the Wardman Park Hotel.

After inspecting the six houses I had lined up, my wife agreed with me that one on the corner of Cathedral Avenue and 29th St, N.W., was the most suitable. So we moved in, and stayed there for five years. The monthly rent of $200.00 consumed a larger proportion of my total income than I wished, but we never regretted the decision. The site was quiet and pleasant, with just enough lawn for the children to play when weather permitted, and sufficient trees and hedges to give some privacy. There were five bedrooms, three on the first floor and two on the second floor; living and dining room space on the ground floor were adequate; a basement was used as garage and an area for oil heating furnace, storage and laundry facilities.

Our landlord was a retired Marine Corps general and reasonable enough, but his wife ruled the roost and reacted strongly, on occasion, to the ravages of our boisterous children, who were constantly tripping over protruding portions of rocking-chairs, and struggling with one another over beds not designed for the purpose. When we left Washington, there were difficulties in agreeing upon reasonable compensation for minor damage.

Alan and John settled gradually into the American State primary school system. As foreigners, with a different accent and, at first, different clothes, there were some strains of adjustment, but they soon made a number of friends. In due course Alan went on to Junior High School, but educational standards were not high and he was unable to take courses in Chemistry and Physics until he returned to Canberra at the age of fifteen and found himself several years behind his contemporaries in these subjects. This complicated his work for matriculation and at the university. Following this experience, and the strong reaction of the two elder boys against leaving Australia again, my wife and I decided not to take any of the children overseas with us in future at the secondary school age, but to make arrangements for them to stay in Australia.

In Washington the twins were sent in due course to nursery school classes at Beauvoir, which was linked to the privately run Cathedral School. Beauvoir, unfortunately, had a habit of sending home any child thought to be ill, and our children's frequent colds resulted in their spending an undue amount of time away from classes. We thought the cost disproportionate to the benefits. By the time the twins were of nursery school age, the United States was at war, our nurse had returned to Australia, and coloured help in the house had become very difficult to obtain, as servants found they could get more attractive employment and better pay if they 'went government'. In later years at Washington our increasing social responsibilities, the large house and the normal demands of bringing up a family of four children threw a heavy burden upon my wife. After the experience of one humid summer in Washington without air-conditioning we decided that it was essential, despite the cost, for her and the children to spend the summer in a holiday resort to which I would commute on occasional week-ends. I discovered a pleasant house at Mountainhome in the Pocono Mountains, north-west from New York and 250 miles by road from Washington. There the family found fresh mountain air, and a group of houses provided with swimming pool, tennis court and restaurant facilities. After each summer they returned to Washington rejuvenated.

My wife and children had arrived in Washington during the autumn, when the city was looking its best. Around us were tree-lined streets bright with yellow and red leaves. Some of the trees in the spacious grounds of Secretary for War Henry Stimson nearby in Cathedral Avenue were magnificent; Rock Creek Park, only a few blocks away, was a riot of colour. This was the family's first experience of a non-Australian autumn, and simple pleasures such as wading through masses of fallen leaves helped the children settle in before the cold of winter kept them more indoors.

By comparison with Canberra, Washington seemed a large city, with far more impressive buildings and monuments and a much greater variety of shops, restaurants and places of entertainment. After three months I found it impossible to carry out my functions adequately without a car; so, despite a life-long aversion to hire-purchase, I made arrangements with a bank to buy a car on time-payment and bought a 1941 Dodge sedan for a mere $1,200—the best private car I had for the next twenty years. This not only enabled me to move with speed between the Legation and the State Department or to other diplomatic establishments, but also made it possible for the family as a whole to learn its way about Washington and the surrounding countryside. Soon the White House, the Capitol, the Supreme Court, the Lincoln and Jefferson Memorials and many buildings in Constitution Avenue were familiar objects, as also George Washington's old home at Mount Vernon with its magnificent site on the banks of the Potomac River. At week-ends we would sometimes take longer runs into the country, and learned to appreciate glimpses of the fertile Shenandoah valley, seen from the Blue Ridge Mountains, whence Southern forces were apt to emerge unexpectedly during the Civil War—to harry Union forces. On one occasion we drove along the 'Skyline Drive' to Charlottesville, to admire Jefferson's house and the University of Virginia. A visit to Williamsburg helped to create an image of the Southern past.

Yet, oddly enough, we found very real similarities between Washington and Canberra, despite the former's greater age and vaster scale. Both were

31

substantially artificial cities, infested with bureaucrats, the seat of federal government. I think it was one year before we met an American who had actually been born in Washington.

In a number of respects, Washington too was a planned city, although the results were at times the reverse of logical. It would seem to the new-comer simple to find a building at the corner of 10th and E. Streets—until he discovers that there are four of these, depending on whether the area is classified as North-West, South-East etc. Traffic, of course, moves on the right of the street—except, in my day, at Dupont Circle, where the street-cars came round the left half of the circle, allegedly because an important person who did not like noise had been able to arrange for a different rule of the road. Now that there is an underpass beneath Dupont Circle, perhaps the situation has changed.

Again, it seemed natural to my wife and to me that, living in 29th St N.W., and receiving an invitation to dinner in the same street and area, we should allow only five minutes to drive there. But we found, on the first such occasion, that our section of 29th St ran into Rock Creek Park. It took us 20 minutes to discover where the remainder of 29th St emerged from the other side of the Park.

One essential difference, of course, between Washington and Canberra was the high percentage of the American population which, in the local idiom, was 'coloured'. Some of the implications of the colour problem were brought home to us on a fine day in our first Spring, when bright sun-shine and burgeoning leaves tempted the family to take a long walk in Rock Creek Park. We speedily discovered that a large section of the coloured population had preceded us, including organised gangs of teenage youth very ready to show their superiority, resentment and power to any white children they might meet away from public places. We had to make the decision that our children could not be permitted to wander on their own through the parks of Washington, as the elder boys were accustomed to wander, on foot or bicycle, anywhere in Canberra.

Wherever I have been posted overseas, I have always tried to familiarise myself with the history and cultural background of the country where I was living, believing that a knowledge of the past is an essential element in forming judgments on current developments. So as opportunity occurred I began to read American history, and to visit places of historical interest within easy reach of Washington—especially Gettysburg, where the decisive battle of the civil war was fought. Two books in particular made a deep impression upon me: Stephen Vincent Benét(s) long poem *John Brown's Body*,[4] and Margaret Leech's *Reveille in Washington*.[5]

Many years before I had read Benét(s) short story 'The Last of the Legions' in which, through a tale showing the effects upon individuals of the with-drawal from Britain of the last of the Roman Legions, he foreshadowed weakening of the props supporting Western civilisation in Europe. So I

[4] *Selected Works of Stephen Vincent Benét* (Farrer & Rinehart, New York, 1942), Vol. 1.

[5] (Harper & Bros, New York, 1941).

was scarcely surprised to find that his long historical poem taught me more of the problems of the United States than twenty books of formal history.

The opening Prelude describes conditions below deck on a ship carrying slaves from Africa to the new world. If the captain had no doubts, because he was sure he got his 'sailing-orders from the Lord', not so the mate:

> The mate went up on deck. The breeze was fresh.
> There were the stars, steady. He shook himself
> Like a dog coming out of water and felt better.
> Six weeks, with luck, and they'd be back in port
> And he could draw his pay and see his girl.
> Meanwhile, it wasn't his watch, so he could sleep.
> The captain still below, reading that Bible . . .
> Forget it—and the noises, still half-heard—
> He'd have to go below to sleep, this time,
> But after, if the weather held like this,
> He'd have them sling a hammock up on deck.
> You couldn't smell the black so much on deck
> And so you didn't dream it when you slept.

And the mate's premonition of the distant future:

> Horses of anger trampling, horses of anger,
> Trampling behind the sky in ominous cadence,
> Beat of the heavy hooves like metal on metal,
> Trampling something down. . . .

Benét describes the Civil War, not as a partisan, but as someone who understands the courage of both sides. On several occasions I sat alone on Little Round Top at Gettysburg and brooded over the three-day battle with his eyes, wondering what I would have felt, had I been a Southerner, forced to realise that all hope of victory was vain:

> John Brown is dead, he will not come again. . . .

> Bury the South together with this man,
> Bury the bygone South.
> Bury the minstrel with the honey-mouth,
> Bury the broadsword virtues of the clan,
> Bury the unmachined, the planters' pride,
> The courtesy and the bitter arrogance,
> The pistol-hearted horsemen who could ride
> Like jolly centaurs under the hot stars.
> Bury the whip, bury the branding-bars,
> Bury the unjust thing,
> That some tamed into mercy, being wise,
> But could not starve the tiger from its eyes
> Or make it feed where beasts of mercy feed.
> Bury the fiddle-music and the dance,
> The sick magnolias of the false romance
> And all the chivalry that went to seed
> Before its ripening.

And with these things, bury the purple dream
Of the America we have not been,
The tropic empire, seeking the warm sea,
The last foray of aristocracy. . . .

Margaret Leech did not try to cover as wide a canvas as Benét. Hers is the story of Washington between the years 1860 and 1865. At first, she writes, it was no more than a Southern town, 'without the picturesqueness, but with the indolence, the disorder and the want of sanitation'. Malaria was prevalent, and parts of the city were malodorous. Shadows of the future can be read into her comment that 'It was a courageous man who ventured to walk alone by night in the ill-lighted streets of the capital of the United States. The inefficiency of the Washington police was as notorious as the prevalence of its footpads and hoodlums.' She thought that the grand scale of the city's design was responsible for many of its deficiencies. Adequate federal funds were not made available, and only the grounds around the Capitol and the White House suggested any desire by the national authorities to beautify Washington. Her description of the panic effect in Washington of the totally unexpected loss of the first battle of Bull Run (1861) is brilliant.

When R. G. Casey arrived in the capital in March 1940 he opened the Australian Legation at 3120 Cleveland Av., N.W. in a large, private house set in ample grounds studded with trees. The house was red-brick, somewhat old fashioned, but an adequate number of bedrooms and excellent reception rooms made it very suitable as a residence for a Head of Mission. Unfortunately, for many years the Chancery consisted of a series of attic rooms in the same building, neither dignified nor efficient and in too close contact with the Residence.

At first the property was rented from a rich American, who in due course wanted to sell it for $400,000. Casey was able to get him to hold his hand while pressure was brought to bear upon Canberra, and eventually managed to buy the property for $250,000. Although in Washington terms this was a bargain, it was not easy to secure Treasury approval to purchase. Now it is worth many times the purchase price.

After Pearl Harbour, it was necessary to rent additional premises in Washington to house Australian Service and technical staff dealing with war supplies procurement, shipping and other problems until eventually, after the war, the Chancery staff was removed altogether from the Ambassador's residence to a building at 1700, Massachusetts Av. In 1969 a new Chancery building costing approximately $A8 million was opened at 1601 Massachusetts Av. by Lord Casey, who by then had served as Minister for External Affairs for nine years, been made a Life Peer, become Governor-General of Australia and been dubbed a Knight of the Garter. The invitation to perform this ceremony was a fitting tribute to his long career of service to Australia and the Commonwealth of Nations.

Casey was a particularly good choice for the Washington post. Educated at the Universities of Melbourne and Cambridge, he had graduated as an engineer with honours in Mechanical Science, enlisted during the First World War, and subsequently interrupted a career in mining to become Australian Political Liaison Officer in London in 1924. He held this post for seven years, making valuable contacts in British official and political circles, before entering politics in Australia, where he held appointments as Commonwealth Treasurer, Minister for Supply and Development and Minister in charge of the Council for Scientific and Industrial Research. Casey had travelled widely, had visited the United States on several occasions, and admired American business and industrial entrepreneurs.

As an engineer, Casey enjoyed driving a Bentley car and flying a light aeroplane. There was an airstrip on his farming property at Berwick, and both he and his wife were qualified pilots. In Washington he soon became known as the 'flying diplomat'. Unfortunately the climate of the United States is not as suited to flying as Australia, and his staff was often uneasy about his safety when he flew during winter months. When I arrived in October 1940, I made it clear that I did not propose to fly with him. I had a wife and four young children, lacked the private means of the Minister, and was content to use ordinary air-lines.

Casey was fortunate to be able to call upon the services of Keith Officer during his first six months in the United States. Officer too developed wide British contacts when he succeeded Casey as Political Liaison Officer in London. More recently, he had served three years in Washington as Australian Counsellor within the British Embassy, and had come to know the Washington scene well.

Thus Casey was well settled in when I arrived. His relationships with two British Ambassadors—Lord Lothian and Lord Halifax—were close, as were also his contacts with Vice-President Henry Wallace, Secretary for War Stimson, Secretary for the Navy Knox, and Justice Frankfurter, a friend of President Roosevelt. Harry Hopkins, the President's most trusted adviser, and Assistant-Secretary of State Dean Acheson were always accessible. It has always been my view that Casey's work in Washington and the United States generally has been under-estimated in his own country. It was not easy, in advance of Pearl Harbour, to develop in isolationist America a favourable climate of opinion towards Australia. This the Australian Minister undoubtedly did.

No Head of Mission could have been more helpful to me personally when I took over my duties as Head of Chancery at Washington. Although I was more or less an unknown quantity to him, except on the tennis court, he made me feel at once that I was his chief political adviser and that he wanted to help me meet everyone relevant as soon as possible. Before my wife arrived he arranged a men's dinner at which a wide range of Commonwealth and foreign diplomats and American officials were present. Somewhat to my embarrassment, he took me with him when he next called upon Lord Lothian and Cordell Hull, Secretary of State. In the latter case at least, I felt it would have been better not to introduce me during an official visit arranged to discuss some specific problem; opportunity would soon come to be introduced informally at some function organised by the Minister.

Most important of all, from my point of view, was Casey's obvious receptiveness to new ideas or proposals, provided these were put forward as suggestions for his consideration and not advanced dogmatically as the only conceivable approaches to problems. Whereas in Canberra I had had practically no contact with Ministers for External Affairs, and Hodgson had rarely doubted the validity of his own judgment, in Washington I found an Australian of wide political and diplomatic experience and with substantial influence ready to listen to any sensible ideas which I or anyone else put forward.

As Head of Chancery, and the senior External Affairs adviser to Casey, I would become Chargé d'Affaires whenever he might be absent from the United States. But when he was in America, it was also my responsibility to co-ordinate the work of the Legation, and to ensure that messages to Canberra from any member of the staff did not run counter to general Legation policy as interpreted by the Minister. This meant that, on rare occasions, I might have to hold up some telegram from senior members of other Canberra Departments for further consideration. It was a delicate operation to do this in the case of J. B. Brigden, Casey's Financial Counsellor. Brigden, an economist, was older than I, and had held high State and federal positions. On the whole we got on well with one another and, with a little bit of give and take, managed to avoid rows.

In the early days, the other members of the staff from External Affairs were P. R. (now Sir Peter) Heydon who subsequently became Secretary, Department of Immigration,* and John McMillan. When Heydon was transferred to the Soviet Union by Dr. Evatt, his place was taken by L. R. (now Sir Laurence) McIntyre. The first Australian Naval Attache in Washington was Commander H. M. (now Sir Henry) Burrell, who became in due course Chief of the Naval Staff and a Vice-Admiral. He was succeeded by Commander Rosenthal, who was followed by Commander Harries. Harries, who later became a Rear-Admiral, was able but a difficult member of a team. Relations with all the rest were easy, while those with Heydon and McIntyre developed into personal friendships over the years.

During my time in Washington the only Commonwealth Missions were those of Britain, Canada, South Africa and New Zealand, although well before Indian independence Sir Girja Bajpai acted as Agent-General. The Australian Legation was in close touch with all of these, but relations with the British Embassy, which had seniority, adequate staff, experience and primary influence upon the United States Government during the war years, was of outstanding importance. The note from the British Ambassador to the Secretary of State requesting, on behalf of Australia, the opening of formal diplomatic relations with the United States had contained the sentence: 'This arrangement was not to denote any departure from the diplomatic unity of the Empire'. Casey's policy on arrival was to consult regularly with the British Ambassador, Lord Lothian and on occasion to go with him to see Cordell Hull. At that stage Britain and Australia were fighting a common war in Europe and the Middle East; both needed sympathetic American support. Casey believed he was serving Australian interests if Washington and London could be brought together in a common approach to a particular problem.

Yet even before Pearl Harbour, and the development of divergent British and Australian priorities in relation to the Pacific, Casey never forgot that he was representing Australia, not Britain or the Commonwealth of Nations

* Heydon died suddenly, at the early age of 58, in 1971.

as a whole. In his speeches in different parts of the United States and his regular contacts with journalists, the problems of the Pacific were uppermost in his mind. He had something of an obsession about 'public relations' and was inclined to take more seriously than his staff the recommendation of one alleged expert who advised the insertion in American newspapers of paid advertisements proclaiming the need for closer U.S.-Australia relations. The State Department was particularly sensitive to any such appeals to American public opinion over the heads of the American Administration, and made it clear that the latter would not be amused if such a publicity campaign were adopted by the Australian Legation. Casey's initiative in seeking an interview with the Japanese envoy Saburo Kurusu just before Pearl Harbour was a purely Australian initiative.

The unexpected death of Lord Lothian on 12 December, 1940 was an event of major consequence to the United Kingdom and, incidentally, provides evidence of the significant standing which Casey quickly won in Washington. Lothian had settled in well as British Ambassador, despite his earlier reputation as one who, before the rape of Prague by Hitler, favoured appeasement of Nazi Germany. His influence upon the American government and upon American opinion became of crucial importance to Britain. But Lothian was a Christian Scientist, and when he became ill towards the end of 1940 he refused to seek medical advice.

By a freak of mischance, the next senior member of the Embassy, Nevile Butler, was also a Christian Scientist. I do not know whether he reported the situation to London, but I do know that no medical aid was called in and that Casey became increasingly worried. Eventually Casey more or less forced his way into Lothian's bedroom to try to size up the situation for himself. Lothian died shortly afterwards and Casey was asked by the British Foreign Office to report upon the facts as he knew them.

Lothian's funeral was attended by all relevant diplomats in Washington. On many occasions since then I have pondered upon the responsibility of a second-in-command to report to headquarters if there is something amiss with his Head of Mission. Ordinarily, the responsibility must be carried by the latter, who is entitled to instruct his staff what to do and what not to do. But a nice question arises if the Head of Mission is so ill that his judgment is seriously affected. The situation is not dissimilar to that faced by the captain of a ship who, outside the harbour, hands over his vessel to the pilot. The pilot is in charge, but suppose he goes crazy and heads for the rocks: surely the captain must intervene and take the consequences if his intervention is subsequently judged to be unjustified.

The succession to Lothian raised delicate issues between the British and American governments. Reports reached President Roosevelt that the name of Lloyd George, then aged seventy-eight, was under serious consideration in London. When informal British soundings in Washington confirmed the reports the American reaction was one of consternation. Roosevelt felt that he could not convey direct to the United Kingdom his great reluctance to accept the nomination of an ex-Prime Minister of Britain, and Casey was called upon as a go-between.

A personal friend of Roosevelt and Cordell Hull asked Casey to see him

D

and explained the situation. Casey then sent telegrams to Menzies in Canberra, Bruce in London and the Australian High Commissioner in Ottawa. He also visited the South African Minister in Washington. After messages expressing doubt and concern about Press speculation regarding the nomination of Lloyd George had been sent to London by four Commonwealth Prime Ministers, the British Government took the decision to send Lord Halifax instead.

Halifax accepted the Washington appointment reluctantly, as a matter of public duty. As he himself has reported,[6] Churchill told him that 'The business we now have with the United States can only be handled by one who knows the whole policy of the Government and is in constant direct relation with us'. Churchill asked him to continue to sit as a Member of the War Cabinet during periodic visits to London.

The new British Ambassador was a man of much greater reserve than Lothian, and although Casey saw him frequently, their relations were not as close or as spontaneous. Throughout his time in Washington Halifax remained very much the aristocratic British Secretary of State for Foreign Affairs. There was little evidence that the British Commonwealth played any significant part in his thinking or affections, although he continued the regular meetings of representatives of Commonwealth Missions.

The arrival of Halifax in the United States was made by both Governments into a unique occasion. He was sent across the Atlantic in a new British battleship. When it steamed into Chesapeake Bay, Roosevelt broke protocol and went to meet him. By a quirk of chance, I had to represent Casey aboard the battleship.

Presidential inauguration ceremonies in the United States take place in January, in the middle of winter. It is a dangerous time for those who attend, especially if they go bare-headed, or fail to wear heavy overcoats. At the re-inauguration of President Roosevelt in January, 1941, Casey wore his Privy Councillor's uniform, stiff with gold braid. He did not take an overcoat, and caught a cold which developed into pneumonia. At first he resisted strongly his doctor's orders to lie in bed, relax and let the world go by until he recovered. Eventually he submitted, but even then left hospital and returned to work in the Chancery before he had fully recovered. It was obvious to us that he was taking an undue risk, and we helped persuade him to leave Washington for a week or two.

In Casey's absence I was invited in his place to meet the new British Ambassador, together with Commonwealth Heads of Mission. It was fortunate that Casey did not insist on attending personally, for it was a terrible day. There was heavy rain, and we all got drenched to the skin while climbing up the gangway of the battleship from a small boat which had taken us from the shore. At the top of the gangway we were met by the British Naval Attache, Captain Clark, looking like a drowned rat, and were shepherded into the Admiral's cabin to meet Halifax. He then left to meet Roosevelt on the President's yacht, after which both proceeded towards Washington, followed by dozens of reporters.

While we waited below until Roosevelt and Halifax were well clear of

[6] *Fullness of Days*, by Lord Halifax (Collins, London, 1957), p. 236.

Annapolis, we were introduced to a British team of high Service personnel, all of whom were in civilian dress. We now know that they had come to engage in confidential American-British staff talks designed to consider grand strategy for the war if the United States should become involved.[7] At the time I knew only that there would be informal discussions, and that the presence in Washington of the British Mission was highly confidential because any public leakage as to their presence and activities could seriously embarrass the President of the United States. The British team waited aboard until all the American reporters had departed from Annapolis, and then proceeded to Washington by car unnoticed. Subsequently a miracle resulted in the talks continuing in Washington until 29 March, 1941 without any information on this highly newsworthy subject appearing in the American press.

During the talks Casey received visits from time to time from members of the British team, but he was at no time informed, to my knowledge, of the basic result of the informal talks: that, in the event of the United States becoming involved in a war against both Germany and Japan, the war against Germany would be given precedence. The Australian Naval Attaché must also have been in touch with the British delegation, but I do not know whether he was given any more information than the Australian Minister.

Some American historians have criticised Roosevelt severely, since the war ended, for agreeing to the talks and entering into 'binding agreements' without the sanction of Congress. So far as I am aware, no binding agreement was made before Pearl Harbour; but, from the British point of view, it was of great importance to know in advance that the Americans accepted in principle the policy of 'beat-Hitler-first'.

When in May 1942 Dr. H. V. Evatt, as Minister for External Affairs in the Curtin Labor Party Government, visited London he learned of this policy for the first time and expressed 'great surprise'.[8] Yet it seems clear that the Australian Government had received telegrams from both London and Washington in February 1941 advising that Roosevelt had told Halifax the United States would have to fight a 'holding-war' in the Pacific if engaged against both Germany and Japan.[9] The reference to Washington puzzles me, unless a message was sent through separate naval channels. In any event, an Australian war historian has commented that 'there is considerable doubt whether Australian ministers had sufficient information about the [secret staff] discussions to be fully aware at that time of all the implications'.[10] One would also have assumed that all such messages would have been made available to members of the Advisory War Council in Canberra, which included senior members of the Labor Party Opposition; in that case, Evatt would have been aware of American policy early in 1941.

The reception of Halifax as British Ambassador by American public

[7] See *Roosevelt and Hopkins*, by Robert E. Sherwood (Harper, New York, 1948), pp. 272-74.
[8] *South-West Pacific Area—First Year*, by Dudley McCarthy, (Australian War Memorial, Canberra, 1959), p. 188.
[9] *The Japanese Thrust*, by Lionel Wigmore (Australian War Memorial, Canberra, 1957), p. 53, n. 4.
[10] Hasluck, *op. cit.*, p. 353.

opinion could scarcely be regarded as warm, as he was held responsible, after Neville Chamberlain, for the Munich Settlement. However, he did not allow minor Press irritations to disturb his habitual *sang-froid*, and won considerable applause by his nonchalant handling of a critical demonstration in the Mid-West. When some eggs and over-ripe tomatoes were thrown at him, he merely brushed the mess off his coat and commented thoughtfully 'What a lucky country to have eggs and tomatoes to throw around, when in England we only get one egg a month'. The contrast between rationed Britain and well-supplied America sank home.

Within the Embassy grounds he insisted when available in pushing personally the wheel-chair of a son, badly wounded in the War, treating the responsibility as a privilege in which he took pride. Despite his own physical disability in the left arm, he played occasional tennis on the Embassy court, holding one ball in his right hand together with the racquet, throwing the ball up to serve and adjusting his grip of the racquet to hit it as it dropped, and showing no self-consciousness whatever in the process.

These aspects of his character won our respect. Yet it is doubtful whether his experience in the United States during the Second World War led to any increased understanding of the new orientation of Australia and New Zealand, following upon diminution of British power in the Far East. To him, I suspect, political leaders from the old dominions should be dealt with as children who were sometimes wayward, and who might occasionally have to be humoured; they did not qualify even for junior partnership. His memoirs, *Fullness of Days*, contains in its index one reference to Australia, two to Canada, and no mention of Menzies, Evatt or Casey.

In the early part of 1941 Prime Minister Menzies visited London by way of the Middle East, and returned to Australia through the United States. He had been deeply moved by the patience and resilience of the British people under Nazi bombing, the results of which he saw in Plymouth. In Washington he spoke to the National Press Club, and made a strong impression upon that hard-bitten and unsentimental audience. After the speech, American friends telephoned the Australian Legation and asked how long Menzies 'would be around'. Told that he had to return to Australia quickly, they expressed regret, as Americans needed to know the situation in Britain better than they did, and Menzies was the person to tell them. 'He is number two', they said—by which cryptic phrase they meant that as a public speaker he was second only to Churchill.

To us this seemed a more vigorous Menzies, seized of the need to make the maximum effort towards winning the war. So we read with great interest news reports of his return to Australia. To our surprise, early favourable reactions were followed by rumours of dissention in the Government. On 29 August, 1941, Menzies returned his commission to the Governor-General and Mr. A. W. (later Sir Arthur) Fadden, Leader of the Country Party, became Prime Minister. The new Ministry remained in office only until 3 October, 1941 when, after the defeat of the Government in the House of Representatives with the aid of two Independents, Mr. John Curtin, Leader of the Labor Party, became Prime Minister. Curtin chose as Attorney-General and Minister for External Affairs Dr. H. V. Evatt, who in 1940 had resigned his position as a Justice of the High Court of Australia in order to enter federal politics.

My own contacts in Washington developed gradually. At the British Embassy I dealt mainly with Derek Hoyer Millar, who was Head of Chancery, and got to know Paul Gore-Booth well on the tennis court. I was also in close touch with Lester Pearson, Escott Reid and Ronald MacDonald (Canadian Embassy), Jordaan and Naude (South African Legation), and Cox (New Zealand Legation). Several of these held high office in later years, and association in Washington facilitated dealings with them in various parts of the world after the war.

At the State Department, my main contacts were Jack Hickerson, Ted Achilles and Robert Stewart. Stewart, who was Head of the British Commonwealth Desk, became my closest foreign friend. In due course he left the State Department to become Dean of the Fletcher School of Law and Diplomacy at Tufts College, Massachusetts. Although our paths diverged after I left the United States, we have kept in touch by correspondence, and I have twice stayed with him and his wife Charlotte. I still find it easier to speak frankly to him than to many Australians. This happy relationship greatly eased my official dealings with the State Department, as will be seen later.

Before Pearl Harbour the central objective of all members of the staff of the Australian Legation was to do everything possible to win sympathetic American interest in the problems of Australia. Casey sought constantly to induce the United States Administration to deter Japan from entering the war by issuing warnings or by sending warships to relevant areas such as Singapore or Australia. If our activities along these lines failed to have the desired effect, the aim was then, of course, to try to ensure that in a war with Japan the United States would be our fighting ally.

We all knew that President Roosevelt was sympathetic to the British cause when the British Commonwealth was fighting alone against Hitler and Mussolini, that he foresaw the most serious consequences for the United States if Britain were defeated, and that he would do all he could to prevent a Nazi and Fascist victory. But he had burned his fingers badly as early as 1937 when he made his 'quarantine' speech in Chicago, and had to be extremely cautious to limit practical assistance to the margins acceptable to isolationist sentiment in Congress and in the country at large.

When during the latter part of 1941 Cordell Hull and the special Japanese envoy, Saburo Kurusu, were engaged in the vital negotiations which preceded Pearl Harbour, Casey participated actively in the discussions which took place from time to time between the Secretary of State and representatives of the so-called ABCD powers (Australian, British, Chinese, Dutch) about the course of the negotiations. The new Labor Government which assumed office in Canberra in October 1941 was anxious that the talks between the United States and Japan should not break down, and encouraged Casey to take initiatives to this end.

On November 20 the Japanese envoys handed to Cordell Hull proposals for a temporary arrangement or *modus vivendi*, to the terms of which China took strong exception. In these circumstances Hull did not pursue the

Japanese proposals, but handed to the Japanese on 26 November a document detailing the fundamental principles upon which the United States believed a Pacific settlement must be based. He could not have expected that the Japanese Government would accept these principles. In short, the situation had become critical.

On 28 November Casey saw Hull and was given information regarding Japanese military activity in Indo-China and the possibility of further Japanese aggression within a few days. Next day he telephoned Evatt and suggested he should approach the Japanese envoy direct with an offer to act as an intermediary in order to get talks with the Americans started once again. Presumably, Evatt gave him authority to do this but Curtin, in view of the rapidly changing situation, sent Casey a message not to proceed with the proposal. This message was received too late, as he had already been to the Japanese Embassy.

My recollection of the circumstances surrounding the interview with Kurusu does not coincide exactly with the account given either by Casey[11] or by Hasluck.[12] The former discussed with me the desirability or otherwise of a talk with Kurusu. It seemed to me highly unlikely that any such last-minute intervention by an Australian could be successful, but I was more concerned about the possibility of serious misunderstanding it might lead to with our British ally and our American friends—to say nothing of the Chinese.

I pointed out that a meeting with Kurusu or the Japanese Ambassador, Admiral Nomura, could not be kept secret. China would be angry, the Americans might well feel that Australia was trying to take primary responsibility for the negotiations out of their hands, while the British might well react strongly and adversely because, at a time when the Americans seemed at long last to be ready to face up to the Japanese, Australia was taking a step behind the backs of the Americans which could easily be interpreted as an attempt to shore up the Japanese position.

I told the Minister that, in the state of near belligerence which existed between the United States and Japan, we had to assume that all telephone calls to and from the Japanese Embassy were being monitored by the Americans, and that all movements into and out of the Embassy would be known. If therefore he or the Australian Government decided to go ahead with the interview, it was essential that Cordell Hull and Halifax should be told in advance.

Casey accepted this latter advice, and saw the Secretary of State and the British Ambassador. Neither encouraged him to see the Japanese envoys, but they did not attempt to dissuade him, while making it clear that he would be acting solely on his own initiative, not theirs. It is my recollection that I thereupon telephoned the Japanese Embassy to say that Casey would like to call, if Kurusu thought it useful to see him. Later Kurusu telephoned Casey indicating assent, and the meeting took place. But there was no invitation from Kurusu; the initiative had been taken by Casey. He has since

[11] *Personal Experience* (1939-46), by R. G. Casey (Constable, London, 1962), pp. 57-58.
[12] Hasluck, *op. cit.*, p. 551.

written[13] that he told the Japanese envoy that he was not acting at the instance of either the Americans or the British, but would be glad to act as an intermediary if Kurusu had any proposal to make. The envoy had no power to make new proposals, so that the initiative bore no fruit. Casey, of course, reported the substance of the conversation to Hull and to Halifax.

December 7, 1941 (Washington time) was an unforgettable day. The news that the Japanese had bombed Pearl Harbour came like a thunder-clap. At first we did not know how severe the damage had been; nor could we understand how the American Navy could possibly have been caught napping. The Americans had broken the Japanese code. Although an attack on Pearl Harbour was not expected, other information indicating new Japanese aggressive intentions in the possession of the United States was communicated to Casey and transmitted to Canberra by our Legation. On December 5 Colonel Frank Knox, Secretary of the Navy, told the Australian Minister that the Japanese Embassy had received orders to burn their secret papers. In these circumstances despatch of warning telegrams to all American posts of the immediate danger of war would presumably have been automatic.

For myself, I could not understand at the time why Japan did not attack only British territory in the first instance, to test whether Roosevelt could have persuaded an isolationist Congress to declare war against Japan in such circumstances. No doubt the Japanese Government wanted to gain the benefits of surprise, which had been valuable to them in the war against Russia in 1905. Yet to force a largely isolationist America into war from which it might conceivably have abstained seemed to me a gambler's throw.

When we heard the news several of us went to the Legation to discuss the new situation. Our feelings were mixed—regret for American lives lost, chagrin that a surprise attack had been so successful, wonder as to what lay ahead for our own country. But the dominant emotion was one of tremendous relief that, whatever trials lay ahead, the resources of the United States would now definitely be thrown into the balance. However long it might take to make them fully effective, we did not doubt that the Axis powers would be defeated in the end. Hitler had attacked the Soviet Union; Japanese military leaders had attacked the United States—whom the gods wish to destroy they first make mad.

On 8 December, 1941, Roosevelt addressed Congress, declaring that 'hostilities exist'. I would have given much to be present, but the diplomatic gallery was barely large enough to house heads of missions, let alone smaller fry. So I drove around Washington in my car listening to the radio, smiling ironically to hear patriotic speeches by well-known isolationists. Then came a flurry of activity as America girded itself to fight. Mushroom departments were established, like the Board of Economic Warfare, hastily staffed with bureaucrats and outsiders, including 'dollar-a-year' men. When it was decided on the advice of General Marshall and his adviser Brigadier Eisenhower that Australia and the 'island-chain' linking it with the United States must be held,[14] the Australian Legation began to receive urgent requests for

[13] Casey, op. cit., p. 57.
[14] Crusade in Europe, by Dwight D. Eisenhower (Heinemann, London, 1948), pp. 21-2.

43

information which were sometimes duplicated by different branches of the same organisation.

After Singapore had fallen and Australia seemed in danger of invasion, I saw Casey and told him, following discussion with Heydon and McMillan, that we felt our services should be placed at the disposal of the Government for use anywhere and in any direction thought best. He replied that we should assume we must stay where we were unless and until we received instructions to the contrary.

It is my belief that, after Pearl Harbour, Casey felt that his main service to Australia as Minister in Washington was over. Although the Japanese had forced the United States into the war, he was entitled to think that his own contribution to the establishment of sympathetic and friendly relations between the United States and Australia had been substantial. This was a very considerable change from such relationships in the 1930s.

Moreover, Casey as a young man had played a direct part in the First World War. He was not the traditional diplomat, destined by temperament and experience to exercise influence behind the throne. As the danger to Australia increased, he had an urge to be closer to the firing line. Had Singapore not fallen so quickly after Pearl Harbour, I think he would have found most satisfaction in the position of British Minister of State in Singapore, co-ordinating both political and military functions.

Of course, the post of Minister in Washington continued to be one of outstanding importance for Australia. With the loss of the British battleship *Prince of Wales* and the battle-cruiser *Repulse*, followed by the fall of Singapore, effective military, naval and air support for the Pacific theatre could come only from American resources. While the war with Germany continued, there was sure to be the strongest British pressure upon the United States for concentration of effort and supplies upon the European and Mediterranean theatres. This could have involved the loss of Australia itself until the war with Germany and Italy was won—a policy which no Australian political party could conceivably have accepted. It was therefore essential that the most strenuous representations should continue to be made in Washington to ensure that sufficient forces and equipment were directed to the Pacific area to conduct at least a successful 'holding-war', even if Churchill and Roosevelt maintained that a policy of 'beat-Hitler-first' must have priority.

These considerations would have inclined Casey, who was an Australian first and foremost, to stay on in Washington, provided the Labor Party Government wanted him to do so. Yet in March 1942 he accepted an invitation from Churchill to become British Minister of State in the Middle East, with a seat in the War Cabinet. This decision led some Australians to criticise Casey, whose only public account of his reasons is his statement to Churchill, whom he met in the United States in January 1942, that his 'immediate future was . . . not very bright', as he represented an Australian Government of a different political colour to the one that had appointed him, and he thought he 'had only a limited tenure' in Washington.[15]

Casey, however, has not so far chosen to disclose that, with Dr Evatt as

[15] Casey, *op. cit.*, p. 94.

44

Minister for External Affairs, he had increasing grounds for believing that his own usefulness to his country in Washington was likely to be more and more restricted. Before Evatt reached the United States in March 1942 seeking Australian participation in decisions on war-time grand strategy and additional military supplies for the Pacific area, there was considerable evidence that the Minister for External Affairs would either bypass the Australian Minister to the United States or ignore his existence.

First, there was the telegram from Evatt familiarly known in our Legation as the 'Lynchburg telegram'. Peter Heydon telephoned me from the Legation in the middle of the night. A 'Most Immediate' telegram had been received from Australia, and decyphering had commenced. The introductory words were 'To be decyphered by McMillan only'. John McMillan was a Third Secretary, the most junior member of the diplomatic staff, and he was away from Washington at Lynchburg on short leave. I told Heydon that the accidental absence of McMillan was no ground for refraining from decyphering a 'Most Immediate' telegram in war-time; he himself should proceed with the decyphering. I then tried unsuccessfully to return to sleep, but the circumstances were so unusual that I soon decided I had better go to the Legation myself to see what the message was about.

The telegram proved to be a message from Evatt to Justice Felix Frankfurter, whose personal relations with Roosevelt were well-known. It dealt with official, not personal matters. The opening words of the telegram, together with instructions to McMillan to deliver the message to Frankfurter, implied that Casey, the representative of Australia in the United States, was not to be made aware of its contents.

I had to make an awkward decision. I was a member of the staff of the Australian Minister in Washington, subject to his instructions. Circumstances had brought to my knowledge information of which he would be unaware unless I brought it to his attention. Yet he was the representative of Australia, not I. If I told Casey, on the other hand, I would be running counter to the implied instructions of the Minister for External Affairs.

Next morning I went to Casey and said: 'Sir, last night we received a "Most Immediate" telegram, the first words of which contained an instruction that it was to be decyphered by McMillan. As he is out of Washington, I authorised its decypher. It is a message from Dr. Evatt, on official matters, for Frankfurter and McMillan is to deliver the message. What are your instructions?'

Casey looked at me for awhile and then, without further comment, said: 'Bring McMillan back and let him deliver the message'. We telephoned McMillan and told him to return to Washington immediately. He delivered the message to Frankfurter, who brought it at once to Casey. Until then, Casey had not seen the telegram.

This experience alone must have given Casey considerable food for thought. It was clear evidence of Evatt's suspicious nature, and of his reluctance or inability to trust a senior member of a different political party. This attitude was not limited to Casey. In 1965 it was revealed that Evatt later sent a similar telegram to London containing a message to Sir Stafford Cripps which Alfred Stirling was to decypher and to deliver to Cripps. 'Stirling carried out his orders, and Cripps promptly told him to show the message to Bruce!'[16]

Secondly, difficulties arose in Casey's relations with L. R. MacGregor, Australian Trade Commissioner in New York. While MacGregor was an official of the Department of Commerce and Agriculture, with the right to approach relevant American Departments directly, he was, of course, subject to the general authority of Casey, whom it was his duty to keep informed of important developments.

After the change of Government in Canberra in October 1941, however, it became increasingly clear that MacGregor saw himself as a competitor of Casey, rather than as a subordinate. He was in direct touch with Evatt through his own communications channels in New York, and succeeded in making Evatt think that he had personal relations with the White House which could result in Australia getting greater war supplies. Casey could scarcely view with equanimity the prospect of Evatt using MacGregor as a second channel of communication dealing with matters of which the Australian Minister in Washington was unlikely to be made aware. MacGregor, who was transferred to Washington in due course in charge of Australian War Supplies Procurement, was appointed by Evatt after the war Australian Minister to Brazil—a post for which he had few obvious qualifications.

Thirdly, it is Casey's published recollection, based upon diary entries made at the time, that when he met Evatt in San Francisco on the latter's arrival in mid-March, 1941, the Minister for External Affairs made no attempt to dissuade Casey from transferring to Cairo. According to Casey,[17] Evatt took the view that, with General MacArthur about to assume command in Australia in April, the latter's voice would be much louder in Washington than any Australian voice. It was Curtin, not Evatt, who opposed the move, although the final decision was left to Casey.

We do not have Evatt's account of this discussion, and it has been suggested that Evatt was taken aback at the news that Casey might transfer to Cairo.[18] We do know, however, that when Evatt arrived in Washington with his own special advisers, namely, W. S. Robinson and A. S. V. Smith, his conduct of negotiations with the Americans was such that members of the Australian Legation were left with the strong impression that their advice and assistance were not required.

Against this background, it is scarcely surprising that Casey concluded that his position in Washington, in relation to his own government, was not likely to be such that it would tip the balance against acceptance of Churchill's invitation to become British Minister of State in Cairo, especially when Frankfurter, Harry Hopkins and President Roosevelt himself advised in favour.

The impending visit to the United States of Dr. H. V. Evatt was a matter of great importance to Australia. Accompanied by his wife, he arrived

[16] *Bruce of Melbourne*, by Cecil Edwards (Heinemann, London, 1965), p. 338.

[17] Casey, *op. cit.*, pp. 95-96. See also, *The Government and the People, 1942-45*, by Paul Hasluck (Australian War Memorial, Canberra, 1970), p. 160.

[18] *Evatt, Justice and Politics*, by Kylie Tennant (Angus and Robertson, Sydney, 1970), p. 140.

in San Francisco on 17 March, 1942, after the fall of Singapore and before the battle of the Coral Sea. On 19 February the Japanese had bombed Darwin. The Australian Government and the Australian people feared an actual invasion of metropolitan Australia.

It was my responsibility to ensure that suitable air bookings were arranged for the Minister for External Affairs and his party. These were made by the most direct route from San Francisco to save time, and the State Department informed us that the Under-Secretary of State, Mr Sumner Welles, would meet Evatt on arrival at the Washington airport. I flew to San Francisco to meet the Minister, explain the arrangements and be at hand to transmit any messages or instructions to Washington.

I had not met Evatt previously, although I had seen him in action in Court when I was Associate to Mr Justice Halse Rogers. Further, when I was practising at the Bar of New South Wales from 1932-7, I was aware of the views of his professional colleagues regarding his standing as a Barrister.

In those days Evatt was regarded as an ambitious man of unusual academic ability, more effective in a Court of Appeal than in a jury case. He was not a naturally gifted speaker. On the other hand his learning, his analytical mind and his persistence were such that he was a formidable opponent, particularly in matters of constitutional law. His appointment by a Labor Party Government as a Judge of the High Court of Australia at the unprecedented early age of 36 was viewed, in the light of his former political activities in the parliament of New South Wales, with some disfavour; but few would have disputed his qualifications in regard to that Court's most important function, namely, the interpretation of the Commonwealth Constitution.

But although I had views regarding Evatt as a legal practitioner, I knew little about his policies as Minister for External Affairs. I flew to San Francisco anxious to do my best to be of assistance, despite a degree of uneasiness as to his methods of operation following the incident of the Lynchburg telegram.

When I was introduced to Evatt, our first conversation ran somewhat as follows:

E. How have you got me booked to Washington?
W. Straight across country by the most direct route. Arrangements have been made for the Under-Secretary of State to meet you at the airport, and reporters have been notified of time and date.
E. Cancel the arrangements.
W. I beg your pardon?
E. I said cancel the arrangements. Book us to Washington via Los Angeles.

I was taken aback. The situation in the Pacific and the justified concern in Australia seemed to call for earliest contact with the American Administration. To risk antagonising the State Department needlessly by changing existing arrangements and delaying arrival was to me simply incomprehensible. I made an attempt to put these views in permissible English, but was told curtly to do as I was told. So I telephoned Washington, cancelled the old bookings and took out tickets via Los Angeles and El Paso, on the Mexican border. It was only much later that I learned the reason for Evatt's decision. Air travel disturbed him greatly, and W. S. Robinson had told him that the route via Los Angeles would be less bumpy.

I accompanied the Evatts to Washington. At that time we had to travel by D.C.3s which, though very safe aeroplanes, were slow, unpressurised and had to come down about every four hours of a flight which took at least eighteen hours to cross the United States. As we started to lose height approaching Los Angeles, we struck some turbulence. Mrs Evatt was sitting near a window alongside her husband; then came the corridor and I was sitting in the single seat on the other side of the plane. When the bumps came, Evatt jogged me with his arm across the corridor:

E. It's bumpy.
W. (As this seemed to me a simple statement of fact, I replied) Yes, Sir.
    (Silence for a few minutes, after which came some more bumps, and another jolt with the arm)
E. And I don't like it.

I wondered whether it was appropriate to say 'No, Sir', but as this seemed somewhat ambiguous, I decided to say nothing.

We landed safely, and Evatt instructed me to see the weather people at every landing-place en route to make sure that the weather ahead was all right. So I solemnly made inquiry at each stop, putting my question rather in the form 'Surely the weather between here and Washington is wonderful, isn't it?', feeling that I simply had to deliver the body at the newly designated time. Sometimes the answer I got was 'Well, for the next 500 miles it's all right, but then . . .' In such cases I did not wait for the full reply, but returned to Evatt and reported favourably. During the remainder of the trip we had poor weather occasionally and then Evatt glared at me suspiciously. Eventually, to my great relief, we arrived in Washington, the door opened and there was Sumner Welles to greet the Australian Minister for External Affairs, with attendant publicity.

Evatt's negotiations with the United States Administration were kept entirely in his own hands. Although Casey accompanied him once to see President Roosevelt and the Legation made formal arrangements for some of his interviews, the only advice he wanted was from 'W.S.' and 'Smithy', not from the Australian Minister in Washington or his staff. Evatt's suspicions were not limited to political opponents like Casey. When I took him around the Legation to meet individual members of the staff, we entered Peter Heydon's room. I introduced Heydon, and Evatt advanced his right arm to shake hands. Before the two hands met, however, the Minister's roving eye caught a photograph of Menzies on the wall. This was a personal momento of the time when Heydon had acted as private secretary to Menzies. As soon as he saw the photograph Evatt withdrew his hand, turned away and walked out of the room. Outside, he instructed me not to allow Heydon to see confidential telegrams to and from Canberra. My attempts to explain the absurdity and unfairness of such a procedure were ignored, and it took me a couple of weeks to obtain permission for Heydon to resume his normal responsibilities. Even then, before the end of 1942 Evatt transferred Heydon to our Legation in the Soviet Union. At that time the Soviet Government was operating from Kuibyshev and living conditions were very difficult. When later Mrs. Heydon joined her husband, she had to travel with her baby via Siberia.

On March 31, 1942 Mr and Mrs Casey left Washington for New York en route to London and Cairo, leaving their two children temporarily in the care of Dean Acheson and his wife who had offered to look after them. Before Casey left, Evatt instructed him to write to Cordell Hull stating, in vague terms, that after Casey's departure Australian interests in the United States would be in the hands of Dr Evatt. A telegram was also sent to Curtin in terms similarly vague.

It is difficult to reproduce the effect upon Australians posted in the United States of Evatt's first overseas Mission as Minister for External Affairs. Lest it be thought that my memory has played me false, I reproduce here an extract from a letter of mine sent to an official colleague in Australia on April 16, 1942:

> . . . This last month here has been far the worst of my public service life. While Mr. Casey and the Mission were both here, there was complete confusion. I had two masters, no discretion, and Legation work suffered. After Mr. Casey left things eased somewhat, but only somewhat. I managed to secure some decisions on principles to be adopted in the future, but many things requiring discussion and decision remain undiscussed and undecided.
>
> I have done my best to hang on to the coat-tails of every senior Australian here to prevent him resigning or otherwise going in off the deep end. I have seen everyone from Sir William Glasgow Australian High Commissioner in Ottawa, to Geoff. Bridgland and all senior Australians in Washington (including myself) trodden on, discarded, not used. There was room for a Mission to Washington and for firm handling of the supply organisation, but other things have occurred which I can scarcely put on paper. . . .

When Casey left the United States, I informed Evatt that the State Department expected urgent advice that a member of the staff of the Australian Legation had been appointed Chargé d'Affaires *ad interim*. Normal protocol required that, in the absence of a Head of Mission, there must be some identifiable Acting Head of Mission to take responsibility for the activities of the Mission and members of its staff. To my astonishment, he instructed me to see Sumner Welles, Under-Secretary of State, to arrange for Evatt himself to be included in the State Department List as Australian Envoy Extraordinary and Minister Plenipotentiary. I said that I knew of no precedent for this, and that in any event it seemed quite unnecessary as he, of course, as Minister for External Affairs, could instruct any Australian Head of Mission or Acting Head what policy he was to pursue. I added that listing as technical Head of Mission could not give Evatt any greater authority to deal with the American Administration than he already had as Minister for External Affairs. My comments were ignored, and the instruction was repeated.

I knew that the Americans would view this request with considerable displeasure. It was therefore with the greatest reluctance that I sought an interview with Sumner Welles. The Under-Secretary expressed surprise at the request, and asked whether Dr Evatt proposed to present credentials as Head of Mission signed by the King. I replied that I had no information on that point. After some hesitation Welles said that the State Department would not be 'stuffy' about protocol. It would accept the requested entry of Evatt's name in the Diplomatic List as Attorney-General and Minister of State for External Affairs, Envoy Extraordinary and Minister Plenipotentiary provided the letters 'apptd' were included after the letters 'E.E.M.P.' In accordance with American protocol the abbreviation 'apptd' stands for 'appointed', and implies that the person concerned, though designated Head of Mission, has not yet presented credentials.

For two successive months Evatt's name was so included in the Diplomatic List. I was instructed not to inform Canberra of what had been done, and no Letters of Credence were sought or presented. As Evatt was Attorney-General of the Commonwealth, I thought it would be impertinent for me to question whether there was any constitutional impropriety in an Australian Minister of the Crown being listed as Australian Minister in Washington. Of course, he received no financial remuneration for the new office. When I took a copy of the List to him to see, he smiled and said 'Well, it's only their document'. I sought no further explanation.

The State Department was not amused by this interlude, and Bob Stewart made it quite clear to me that Evatt would have to nominate a Chargé d'Affaires when he himself left the country. Before he flew to London in May 1942 he agreed to nominate me.

During the visit of the Minister for External Affairs to Washington, the Pacific War Council was established and he represented Australia at its first meetings. The Australian Government had felt it was essential to have direct contact with the United States regarding overall strategic problems, and had never been content with the similar body established by Churchill in London and on which there was no American representative. Although the Washington Council was advisory only, and grand strategy continued to be decided by Roosevelt and Churchill, together with their Combined Chiefs of Staff, the Council provided Australian and other national representatives with regular access to President Roosevelt and with some continuing evidence of what was passing through his mind.[19]

Creation of the Council was a matter of great satisfaction to Evatt. It should not be assumed, however, that Evatt's personal intervention in Washington was primarily responsible for the decision. While Australian pressure and Evatt's own initiatives before he left Australia were no doubt an important element in overcoming Churchill's reluctance, the historical record shows that Roosevelt proposed to Churchill as early as 9 March the establishment of an advisory Council in Washington, and that Churchill agreed in substance in a telegram dated 17 March, the day when

[19] For comments by Sir Owen Dixon and Sir Paul Hasluck on the significance of the Council, see *The Government and the People 1942-45, op. cit.*, pp. 228, 475, n9. In my opinion both unduly minimise the value to Australia of membership of the Council.

Evatt arrived on the West Coast of the United States.[20] The influence of Harry Hopkins on the creation of the Council also deserves recognition.[21] Evatt's arguments in Washington no doubt reinforced Roosevelt's conclusion that the Council should be set up, and probably affected the timing of the published decision.

During the month of April 1942 a telegram was received from Australia instructing the Legation to secure the agrément for the nomination of Sir Owen Dixon as Australian Minister to the United States, in succession to Casey. I took the telegram to Evatt, who read it without comment but with every physical sign of surprise. The clear inference to me was that Prime Minister Curtin had taken the decision without reference to Evatt.

At that time Dixon was a Justice of the High Court of Australia. Although I had never met him, I knew the great respect in which he was held by the legal profession in New South Wales and was delighted that someone of his standing had been chosen. Hastily I telephoned Bob Stewart and asked him if he would clear the agrément quickly with the White House, as leak-ages of such appointments were always likely to occur. Stewart promised to do what he could, on condition that I solemnly assured him in advance that Dixon, when presenting his credentials, would also present in accordance with custom Dr Evatt's Letters of Recall. I knew that Stewart was teasing me and that he was well aware that, as Dr Evatt's Letters of Credence were unlikely ever to be presented, no Letters of Recall could be issued. Shortly afterwards the State Department informed us verbally that Dixon would be welcome. The message was relayed to Canberra and the appoint-ment was announced there on 19 April, 1942.

Apart from the establishment of the Pacific War Council, we in the Legation had no means of measuring the success of Evatt's visit. We were not told whether specific additional forces or supplies had been obtained for the Pacific area, while responsibility for any follow-through regarding supplies was assigned to MacGregor, who was transferred from New York to Washington as head of Australian War Supplies Procurement.

When Evatt reported to Parliament on 3 September, 1942, he stated that '. . . one result of our work was a very substantial flow to Australia and other Pacific areas of aircraft, tanks and other vital equipment and supplies'. Later in his speech he added 'Again, I cannot give figures, but comparing April 1st. last with the latest available data there has been a very great improvement in the Australian stock position in respect of such vital materials as tinplate, aviation spirit, motor spirit, power kerosene, illuminating kero-sene, lubricating oils, diesel oil, cotton, raw rubber and aluminium'. He also referred to 'an important increase' in materials received from the United States for the manufacture of munitions in Australia, including machine tools.

In Washington we did not doubt that Evatt and his team had made the maximum effort to put the Australian case to every relevant American from the President down. We were uneasy, however, at Evatt's methods of opera-tion. We resented his suspicion of the loyalty of members of the Australian Legation, while here and there we heard echoes of strong reactions in

20 See Ph.D. thesis on American Diplomatic Relations with Australia, 1941-5, by J. J. Reed (Univ. of Southern California, 1969), p. 231.   21 Sherwood, op. cit., p. 515.

American circles to his abrasive style. The most notable of these stemmed from an interview with General Marshall, during which Evatt's criticism of British 'selfishness' in pressing demands for the European theatre led Marshall at one stage to rise from his chair to tell the Australian Minister in measured terms that he did not propose to continue a conversation in which Evatt denigrated the motives of 'our most important ally'. Marshall subsequently conveyed this information direct to a distinguished Australian, who repeated it to me.

When Sir Owen Dixon left Australia to take up his new post in Washington I flew to the West Coast to meet him. He had assented to the appointment with great reluctance and under the strongest pressure from Curtin as a war-time duty. A special Act of Parliament had to be passed to enable him to return to the High Court of Australia in due course.

By training, career and temperament Dixon was neither a politician nor a diplomat, but a lawyer. Ten years' experience of Dr Evatt as a colleague on the High Court had left him with no illusions that difficulties could be avoided in a post in which he would be subject to the directions of the Minister for External Affairs. Curtin, however, had assured Dixon that he would have the Prime Minister's support.

Dixon, whose attitude towards bureaucrats was almost as sceptical as his attitude towards politicians, had insisted on bringing with him at least one person of ability on whom he could rely, namely, his associate, Keith Aickin, now a Queen's Counsel in Victoria. Keith had been made a Third Secretary and shared some of his chief's doubts as to the efficiency of government officials. I am afraid I was not amused when, during an early conversation with Aickin, he told me that Dixon's standards were high and that he would expect certain things to be done. My reaction was to tell him that, as Head of Chancery, I was quite capable of judging what was and what was not proper or necessary, and that he (Aickin) was subject to my directions. When we got to know one another better we got on quite well.

I found that Dixon had had an unpleasant trip across the Pacific, but was far more interested in other people's troubles than his own. He agreed without question to the arrangements we had made for continuation of the journey to Washington, and cross-examined me effectively regarding the functions and problems of the Legation. It was obvious that he was a person of outstanding intelligence, whose interests ranged from the Classics and Archeology through History and Law to current affairs. He combined in one and the same person acute analytical capacity, clear apprehension of general principles, thorough attention to detail and ability to express himself in clear, logical terms.

Yet if his approach to life's problems was analytical, factual, concrete, ironic and pessimistic, he had attractive human qualities which at times seemed to contradict his general outlook. Something of a Puritan regarding personal conduct and a teetotaller himself, yet he enjoyed lively conversation with people of diverse interests, and provided liquor for their entertainment. His ready laugh—almost a cackle—was infectious. He had the trained barrister's gift of speaking to his brief. When he received a cable instructing him to make certain representations to the Secretary of State—

instructions with which he sometimes disagreed—he could analyse all the weaknesses in the argument and yet make the best case in carrying out the instructions. He and Lady Dixon, who joined him later, were invariably considerate in relation to Legation staff and their families, and my wife and I were the recipients of many kindnesses from both. In short, Dixon quickly won the respect of his staff and was always ready to consider advice, without feeling at all bound to accept it if he concluded that arguments in a different direction were stronger.

Dixon's tasks in Washington were very different from those of Casey, who had had to publicise Australia and to attract American attention towards Australia at a time when the United States was substantially isolationist. With the United States now in the war and Australia's main source of support, the objective of the Australian Legation was to further Australian interests while maintaining friendly relations with the Americans and, when decisions had been taken, to try to ensure the most efficient technical co-operation between allies.

The new Minister took some time to settle in to his Washington responsibilities. As Barrister and Judge he had been accustomed to doing his own work, with help from Junior Counsel or an Associate. Capable of intense concentration over long hours, he was inclined to assume too many responsibilities himself and to rely too little upon his staff. Unlike Casey, he had a positive aversion to publicity, saw the Press when he could not avoid them, and left Washington when compelled by circumstance.

He came to Washington only because he felt it his duty to try to contribute to winning the war, and this task absorbed his interest and energy. I suspect he also hoped that by accepting the Washington post during a difficult period he might be able to do something to save Australia for the British Commonwealth and minimise American influence on its future.

The Americans with whom he had closest relations at first were mostly 'technical' people—General Marshall, Admiral King and others who did not speculate much and were not politicians but who assembled facts, i.e., guns, ammunition etc., and planned the war on the basis of what had been assembled. They in return showed respect and trust for Dixon.

In the early days we of the Chancery staff found we had far less discretion to handle things ourselves than before. Dixon's passion for perfection made him tend to read everything himself before anyone else—an impossible aim for a busy Head of Mission, and to insist on approving every telegram which left the Legation, no matter how unimportant the subject.

Further, he arrived from Australia with strongly critical views of American efficiency, and for some months almost seemed to have convinced himself that he could not understand Americans nor they him. His interest in post-war questions was slight and he seemed to think that despatches to Canberra on current political developments in the United States were a waste of time. Like Carlyle, he wanted facts, facts, facts—but facts of only one kind, namely, those which could be held in the hand. Propaganda, mental attitudes, the likes and dislikes of individuals seemed to him unimportant and ephemeral. Events determine policy. If Great Britain won battles and regained strength and power, the world in general and the United States in

E

particular would respect her again. If she did not regain strength, any action we could take to make her better understood was doomed to failure.

Yet Dixon's attitude did change in a number of important respects during his tenure of the Washington post, and we gradually found ourselves working more easily with him and to better effect, especially after a visit to Australia which he made in the first half of 1943. His reading of British 'Blue Prints' containing British Foreign Office despatches and reports had the odd effect of making him somewhat more critical of British diplomacy. I think he also acquired more respect for his staff of bureaucrats, whose knowledge of the local scene he found valuable. Moreover, a close relationship developed between him and Assistant-Secretary of State Dean Acheson, a man of ability with a very different outlook from that of the American 'technicians'.

Acheson was a lawyer and well aware of Dixon's reputation in the field of law. As Acheson came to know Dixon, he developed a profound respect for the latter's capacity and at times, as during the UNRRA Conference at Atlantic City in November-December 1943, found Dixon's support and advice very valuable to him as Chairman of the Conference. When Dixon retired from the Washington post in late 1944, Acheson gave him a farewell dinner during which he described the departing Australian Minister as a person who, though a foreigner, would 'adorn' the Bench of the Supreme Court of the United States if it were possible to appoint him to it. He added that Dixon would be greatly missed in Washington, where he had made himself 'beloved'.

Dixon's relations with the British and Commonwealth Embassies and Legations were also good. He saw much of Sir Girja Bajpai, then Agent-General for India and later Secretary-General of the Indian Department of External Affairs. The two men used to walk back together from Commonwealth meetings at the British Embassy and, though of very different height and temperament, developed a strong regard for one another. I have sometimes wondered whether Indian assent to Dixon's appointment in 1950 as United Nations mediator on the Kashmir issue was facilitated by Bajpai's opinion of him, formed during the days when they were colleagues in Washington.

As soon as my new Chief had settled in, I thought it my duty to warn him that Dr Evatt would probably send personal telegrams through the Legation, some of which would relate to official matters. I urged him strongly to make an issue of any such telegrams when the first appeared or, failing that, to allow me to report to Evatt that the Head of Mission in Washington saw all telegrams. For reasons which I have never understood, Dixon decided not to raise this issue himself, and told me not to do so.

I believe his judgment was seriously at fault in this respect. In any event, his decision had important effects upon my subsequent career. It was all the more surprising, because Dixon had serious reservations about Evatt's personality and character, and his instinctive approach to difficulties with Evatt was to attack. I assume that Dixon took it for granted that, as a member of his staff, my responsibilities were to him and not to the Minister for External Affairs. I doubt whether it crossed his mind that anyone could conceivably adopt any different point of view. Moreover, the circumstances of Dixon's appointment were such that he regarded himself as Curtin's representative rather than Evatt's and, in the early stages at least, he was over-optimistic about Curtin's ability to keep a brake upon Evatt.

Within a year of Dixon's arrival in Washington he had begun to doubt the wisdom of his acceptance of the appointment and the usefulness of his continued tenure of the post. Differences regarding Evatt's methods of operation were discussed with the latter during a subsequent visit to Washington by the Minister for External Affairs, and the conversation included criticism by Dixon of personal telegrams sent by Evatt through the Australian Legation. For the first time Evatt became aware that Dixon had seen all such messages, and he was furious with me. Evatt insisted that my duty was to him and not to Dixon, and he asked whether, if he had sent a message to Roosevelt in a sealed envelope through the Legation bag, I would tear open the envelope and show it to Dixon. When I said 'No', he asked 'Why not?' I replied that no member of the Legation staff would know what was in a sealed letter, so that there could be no question of any member of his staff being in possession of any official information which was denied to the Head of Mission. Evatt brushed this explanation aside. I did not feel free to inform him that I had advised Dixon to take up the issue with Evatt at the earliest stage, or to allow me to do so, and that my instructions had been in effect to let sleeping dogs lie.

Evatt never forgave me this 'betrayal'. It is my belief that my posting to Moscow in 1947 was substantially due to his conclusion that in seeking a Secretary for the Department of External Affairs in that year he must look elsewhere for someone whom he thought he could rely upon to accept his methods of operation without hesitation or question.

During the first half of 1943 Dixon returned to Australia to discuss the Washington situation with Curtin. He found the Prime Minister sympathetic and helpful and ready to promise necessary support in Dixon's dealings with Evatt, but on the return to Washington there was little noticeable change. Eventually Dixon decided to resign and pressed for a replacement. When there was delay at the Australian end, he himself set a term to his own stay. This forced the issue, and on 18 September, 1944 Curtin announced Dixon's retirement.

My own work while Dixon was still Australian Minister to the United States was extensive but, for the most part, unexciting and frustrating. As the war progressed, Australian Service representation in Washington increased substantially and MacGregor's staff at War Supplies Procurement grew by leaps and bounds, including a 'personal assistant' for Evatt when in America. Our diplomatic staff, however, remained small, Australian civilian manpower being in short supply. 'Jim' McIntyre and I were kept extremely busy, and at times began to wonder whether our work was degenerating into that of a tourist agency. Every new specialist member of the Legation staff involved increasing demands upon typing and cables facilities, problems with housing, transportation and office accommodation. As Head of Chancery I had general responsibility for seeing that the machine as a whole continued to function.

Moreover, every Australian who came to the United States passed through Washington, and expected special attention. Hotel accommodation became more and more difficult to obtain, and we were blamed if what was regarded as suitable accommodation was not found. W. S. Robinson, for instance, high in Ministerial favour, would telephone me from San Francisco, perhaps when I was just sitting down to dinner after a long day. The conversation would run like this:

> Is that you, Alan? W.S. speaking. Just arrived in San Francisco. I shall be over in Washington for 3 or 4 days in 2 days time. I'd like you to get me a suite at the Shoreham. You know, old chap, not one looking out over the street, but over Rock Creek Park. See you soon.

I would groan to myself, and next day we would do our best to achieve the impossible.

Australian journalists passing through, with one notable exception, were very demanding. Most carried letters from the Minister for External Affairs requesting that they be given every consideration. They seemed to expect that we could arrange for them to continue to London via Lisbon in comfortable aircraft, instead of flying out in bombers being delivered from Montreal. When we explained patiently that all we could do was to ask the British Embassy, which controlled priorities for the Lisbon route, for seats, and warned them in advance that applications were likely to be rejected for anyone under the age of sixty who did not have heart disease or some other severe complaint, they assumed that we were apathetic, disinterested and inefficient.

Even senior Australian public servants tended to think we treated them badly. One Head of Department whose request for a seat via Lisbon had been rejected when submitted by us told us contemptuously that he had met Lord Halifax, who had said he would look into the matter. The Australian was not pleased when the Second Secretary at the British Embassy whose responsibility it was to award seats again rejected the request. As our visitor had no inclination to travel by bomber, we got a booking for him on the Queen Mary with some 14,999 other passengers; but when he found he would have to share a cabin with a Colonel and make his own bed, he instructed us to take his name off the list. After we had done this, he went to New York, where he saw the Queen Mary lying at a wharf. He rather liked the look of the ship, and telephoned us to get him put on the list again. The necessary arrangements were made, though our popularity was not increased in the process.

The same person saw Mr Bruce in London, told him how inefficient the staff of the Australian Legation in London was, and asked for a return flight to the United States via Lisbon. Somehow or other he was given this privilege. To our considerable satisfaction everything which could go wrong with the flight did go wrong: the journey took him much longer and was far more tiring than if he had returned by sea.

Dealings with Stewart in the State Department were a diplomat's delight. He had written his doctoral thesis on the British Commonwealth of Nations and was the only American I met in the State Department during the war years who really understood how the Commonwealth worked or failed to work. We served different governments and, of course, acted on instructions; but as confidence developed between us we were soon able to speak to one another with a degree of frankness unusual in diplomatic relations. As a result, information in both directions could be conveyed informally, without the Secretary of State or my Minister becoming involved in formal exchanges.

When the Pacific War Council was established in Washington in April 1942, for instance, the State Department had no representative at its meetings. President Roosevelt was attended by Harry Hopkins and looked to him to supply information he did not have at his own fingertips. Also present were the Heads of Diplomatic Missions of Britain, Canada, Australia, New Zealand, China and the Netherlands. After a meeting concluded, Dixon would send a telegram to Canberra to inform the Australian Government what had taken place. With Dixon's permission, I would then call upon Stewart, tease him by referring to the extraordinarily interesting statements his President had made at the last meeting of the Council, and then show him a copy of our telegram.

In diplomacy one does not acquire much information unless occasionally one has some to give. Knowledge of what we were sending to Canberra encouraged Stewart to reciprocate with other information, when he judged this to be practicable and consistent with the interests of the United States.

While Dixon was absent in Australia for consultations, Winston Churchill visited Washington in May, 1943. President Roosevelt arranged a 'Band Party' on the lawns of the White House intended primarily to facilitate contacts with Churchill by various representatives of the British Commonwealth including MacKenzie King, Dr Evatt and Heads of Commonwealth Missions in Washington. I was invited to attend as Australian Chargé d'Affaires, an appointment to which Dr Evatt had again agreed reluctantly only after heavy pressure from the State Department.

The Band played a few marches and Southern ditties while Churchill walked around to meet people, but when rain started there was a general move back towards the shelter of the White House. There, by pre-arrangement, Commonwealth guests separated from Americans and were escorted into the State Dining Room where Churchill proposed to give a general review of the war. Around the table were grouped, *inter alia*, Churchill, Halifax, Field Marshal Wavell, Sir John Dill and Malcolm McDonald (U.K.), MacKenzie King, Ralston, Norman Robertson and Chiefs of Staff (Canada); Evatt and myself (Australia); Close (South Africa); Cox (New Zealand Chargé d'Affaires); and Bajpai (India).

Before the meeting opened, I could not help thinking of the occasion, so long ago, when British troops had burned the White House. How strange the changes which had led to a British Prime Minister being a welcome and honoured guest in the same place. Now an American State room had been placed at the disposal of Britishers for a British Commonwealth Meeting, designed to strengthen Commonwealth ties—and no one even seemed to think this was a matter for surprise. I was quite prepared to believe that the room was lined with concealed microphones, but the two Allies had little to conceal from one another.

Churchill lit a long cigar and plunged straight into a review of the war, dealing with each arm of the service in turn. He spoke for about an hour without notes, turning for confirmation now and then to one of his Chiefs of Staff, or putting a question to some other adviser. He was in his best form, fluent, confident and effective. Never at a loss for a word, at the appropriate times he was amusing, or earnest, or dramatic, or adroit. An occasional friendly remark about the United States seemed to be addressed to the possible microphones; for the rest, he said practically nothing which could not have been justifiably overheard by American Cabinet Ministers or American Chiefs of Staff.

I was in no position to judge the accuracy of the account of the war which Churchill gave. For all I knew, half of his facts or inferences might have been wrong. I was also prepared to believe that his insatiable curiosity, his susceptibility to bright ideas, his irrepressible enthusiasms might carry him away into deep waters unless strong hands were near to help control the tiller. But of one thing I had no doubt—that he was the most outstanding political personality I had met. As a leader, a person who could rouse others in time of war to do things which were difficult, he seemed to me on that day to stand head and shoulders above everyone, and considerably higher than President Roosevelt.

Adroit references to Dominions and to individuals like Wavell were notable features of Churchill's review. At the right moments he referred to the eagerness of the Canadian army in England to come to grips with the enemy; to the pressure of the Japanese upon 'our beloved Australia and New Zealand'; to the splendid work of the Australian Ninth Division, which had subsequently been returned to Australia from the Middle East 'to defend its homeland'; to the New Zealanders and South Africans, the work of the Navy and Air Force, and the rehabilitation of the Army in Africa. I could not help feeling that if Churchill's public acts and utterances had always been as suited to the occasion as his remarks in private conclave in the White House, a number of Empire and Commonwealth wheels would have run more smoothly.

Sir Owen Dixon left Washington in September 1944 and was succeeded in October by Sir Frederic Eggleston. During the interval I again became Chargé d'Affaires. One morning I received a telegram from Lord Gowrie, who had recently completed a most successful term as Governor-General of the Commonwealth of Australia, intimating that he and Lady Gowrie were on a ship in the Panama Canal; that the vessel would be travelling in convoy, which was expected to reach New York in a stated number of days; and that they would be staying at the White House while the ship was in port, before proceeding to England.

I was taken by surprise, as I had received no word from Australia that they were coming to the United States, still less that they had been invited to stay at the White House. Hastily I telephoned Bob Stewart, explained the facts and asked him to check with one of the President's entourage. Before he had time to obtain an answer to his inquiry a second telegram from Lord Gowrie informed me that his ship would be breaking convoy and would arrive in New York several days earlier than anticipated. When I passed this news on to Stewart, he told me he had just heard from the White House, which was not aware of any invitation having been issued to the Gowries. The most probable explanation, we decided, was that Mrs Roosevelt, who had visited Canberra in 1943 and been received by the Governor-General, had said on leaving 'If you ever come to Washington you must of course stay with us'.

President Roosevelt was out of Washington at the time and would not return until after the Gowries had passed through New York. This complicated the visit still further. Time passed while further checks were being made and eventually I had to say to Stewart in desperation that a decision one way or the other was essential, as I had to leave for New York to meet the Gowries and must know whether there was an invitation to the White House, or whether I should make arrangements for them to stay at the residence of the Australian Minister. I added that they were the last people to impose themselves upon anyone. They had won many friends in Australia, and I hoped something could be done even if there were some misunderstanding about the visit.

Stewart was extremely helpful, and Mrs Roosevelt proved to be both generous and gracious. On the afternoon before the ship was due I found myself in the train for New York with a charming letter of invitation from Mrs Roosevelt in my pocket, explaining that her husband was unfortunately out of Washington, but that she was expecting them to stay with her for three days. This resolved all my difficulties and made it unnecessary for me to explain to the Gowries what had really happened. I met them aboard ship, handed over the letter, accompanied them by train to Washington and delivered them at the White House. Then I excused myself and returned home, feeling that my responsibilities were over.

While my wife and I were having a late lunch, however, a telephone message from the White House informed us that Mrs Roosevelt invited us to afternoon tea that afternoon, and that the British Ambassador and Lady Halifax would be present. It was typical of Mrs Roosevelt's courtesy that she should not only arrange for her guests to meet others in Washington, but that she should include an unknown Australian Chargé d'Affaires in the list. I have often contrasted her whole attitude towards this visit with the typical European cartoonist image of Americans as inevitably rude, vulgar and insensitive.

In October 1944 I flew to San Francisco to meet my new Minister. In the Legation we viewed his arrival with a degree of uneasiness. The Government had found it difficult to find the right man for the job, and we had the impression that Eggleston was being sent to Washington rather as a stopgap. When Casey opened the Legation he was fifty; Dixon was fifty-six on arrival; Eggleston was sixty-nine and was known to suffer from arthritis. A solicitor by profession, with experience of Ministerial office in the Victorian Legislative Assembly, he had been Chairman of the Commonwealth Grants Commission, a strong supporter of the Australian Institute of International Affairs, a participant in several unofficial British Commonwealth and Institute of Pacific Relations Conferences and, from 1941 to 1944, first Australian Minister to China. His interest in international and political affairs was undoubted, as his published books and articles proved. In short, his record seemed to establish many important qualifications for his new post. But his age, some physical disability, and the absence of a wife or family to help him run the large Legation residence made us wonder whether he could successfully meet the strains and stresses of busy, wartime Washington.

In the event, these doubts proved justified. His staff did not find in Eggleston the endearing qualities described so sympathetically by Tristan de Buesst in the introductory biographical sketch written for Eggleston's last book *Reflections on Australian Foreign Policy*, published after his death. Perhaps we came to know him too late in life; perhaps we erred in comparing unfavourably his qualities as Australian Minister in Washington with those of Casey and Dixon, different as these two were from one another; yet, fundamentally, I think we were judging less the human being than his suitability for a particular post at a particular time. In any event, I must describe him as we found him, leaving it to others to fill out the picture of the man they knew in other surroundings.

It is my understanding that Eggleston had done well as Australian Minister in Chungking. There, however, age tended to be revered. There was little routine Chancery work, so that he had ample leisure to read, to reflect and to converse. Even his physical disability, which made it difficult for him to move around, could be overcome when necessary by use of a sedan chair. But Washington in 1944 was a madhouse, requiring energy, mobility, initiative, a wide range of contacts, permitting no leisure at all and little time for quiet thought.

Moreover, Eggleston's earlier experiences were in some respects a disadvantage in Washington. The United States which he knew was academic, liberal, interested in general ideas; the American Administration which we knew in the war years, whatever its high-falutin' phrases, was tough, self-centred, realistic, practical and pragmatic. It took Eggleston perhaps a year before he was ready to admit that the friends he had met in Conferences organised by the Institute of Pacific Relations were not in control of the foreign policy of the United States. Further, he seemed unable to realise how busy American Cabinet members and officials were, and how many demands were made upon their time. In the early days after presentation of his Letters of Credence, he would tell us to arrange a dinner and give us a list of senior Americans and others to invite. He would not listen to the advice of McIntyre or myself that a Secretary of State, for instance, would not accept an invitation to a function at less than three weeks notice, if at all. The invitations would go out, the refusals come in and Eggleston would be dejected without cause.

In the large Ministerial residence he was alone, save for servants. He tended to expect his staff to drop in after dinner for casual talk, when they were either dropping off to sleep or thinking about the files they had planned to deal with at night and which must now be added to those appearing on the desk next morning.

Whereas Dixon had tended to over-centralise and try to do too much himself, the amount of work he could get through was enormous. He was dour and ascetic by temperament, possessed of outstanding intelligence and iron will. He had been suspicious of all generalisations and statements of principle. Eggleston's approach to problems was more theoretical, and he gave less attention to detail.

Whereas Casey had hundreds of acquaintances in various parts of America and would dash off to see them at the drop of a hat, Eggleston's mobility was limited and he seemed to expect people to come to see him. I soon began to realise that a number of functions which Casey and Dixon had carried out themselves, including outside contacts, would inevitably devolve upon me, although I did not have the standing and authority of a Head of Mission, or the necessary freedom from routine work.

In short, although Eggleston's period of service in Washington was not in broad terms unsatisfactory from the Australian point of view, we were conscious of a gradual decline in the status and influence which the Australian Legation had acquired under its first two Ministers.

There was one aspect of the Washington scene, however, in which Eggleston was interested and which was of great importance for six or seven months after his arrival, namely, the problem of post-war organisation. During the First World War he had enlisted as a private and, as he was too old for combat service, had been placed in the legal corps. This led to appointment to the staff of the Australian Delegation to the peace conference in Paris. With this background, and his general interest in problems of world order, it was natural that he should wish to participate in the United Nations Charter Conference held in San Francisco from 25 April to 25 June, 1945. He studied carefully the draft Charter drawn up by representatives of the United States, United Kingdom and Soviet Union at Dumbarton Oaks and assented to, with minor modifications, by China, and gave much thought to the adequacy or otherwise of the principles enunciated in the draft. His inclusion in the Australian Delegation to the Conference was taken for granted, and he looked forward with keenness and pleasure to playing a substantial part at San Francisco.

I too was deeply interested in the problems of post-war organisation, but saw no chance at all, in view of Evatt's attitude towards me, of participation in the Conference. Moreover, with Eggleston absent from Washington, our staff position would be even worse than it had been over the years since Pearl Harbour. To my surprise and delight, I found my name included in the list of the Australian Delegation. I knew well that my nomination did not reflect any measure of Ministerial favour or recognition of competence. But as the oldest Australian staff member in Washington, it was thought I might be useful as a 'contact' man with the numerous members of staffs of Diplomatic Missions, the State Department and other American institutions who were proceeding to San Francisco from their Washington base.

However, the reasons for my inclusion did not worry me. After four and a half years in Washington I was stale, frustrated and weighed down by routine. Here was an opportunity at last to participate in a conference of world importance, to use any intelligence I still had left, and to make some personal contribution to the establishment of the new organisation designed to maintain international peace and promote general welfare. I regret to say that, on this occasion, I sternly repressed pangs of conscience at the additional load in Washington which would have to be borne by my patient, long-suffering and uncomplaining colleague, 'Jim' McIntyre.

THE SAN FRANCISCO CONFERENCE 1945 AND ITS AFTERMATH IN LONDON

The part played by Australia in the formation of the United Nations has been described elsewhere more fully than most other aspects of Australian foreign policy.[22] Here it is sufficient to give some personal impressions of the Australian Delegation and of the Conference.

To Evatt's chagrin, Prime Minister Curtin insisted on including in the Delegation Mr Francis M. Forde, Minister for the Army, who took with him two senior advisers, Dr R. (later Sir Roland) Wilson and Mr P. E. Coleman, an Assistant-Secretary, Department of Defence.

As Deputy Prime Minister, Forde outranked Evatt, and was presumably intended to be named Leader of the Delegation and to act as some kind of a brake upon Evatt. Forde was a pleasant, friendly soul inexperienced in foreign affairs and innocent of constitutional knowledge. None of us had any doubt that the *de facto* leader would and must be Dr Evatt. In the result, both Forde and Evatt were listed together without one or the other being given clear priority. Forde made the opening speech for Australia, but it was drafted under Evatt's supervision. Thereafter, Evatt simply ran the show. It was he who represented Australia on the Steering Committee, composed of the Heads of Delegations, and, more important, on the Executive Committee of fourteen, of which Australia was elected a member.

The Australian Delegation was housed in the Sir Francis Drake Hotel, Forde and his advisers being accommodated on the tenth floor and Evatt and his advisers on the seventeenth floor. Although there were occasional meetings of the delegation as a whole, these tended to be rather formal. Any communication between the two groups of advisers was discouraged by Evatt, and as his team had most of the documents it was not easy for Forde's team to know just what was going on. Nevertheless, the two groups of advisers did in fact keep in touch with one another as much as practicable.

In these circumstances it would be natural to expect that the work of the Australian Delegation would be chaotic, and the results ineffective. On the contrary, it may be doubted whether any previous Australian Delegation to an international conference was better briefed and prepared, at least so far as the Evatt team was concerned.

There were a number of reasons for this. The Post-Hostilities Division of the Department of External Affairs had for a year previously produced a series of planning papers. Discussions in Canberra with New Zealand representatives during negotiations for the Australia-New Zealand Agree-

22 See 'Australia and the Formation of the United Nations', by P. Hasluck, Royal Australian Historical Society, *Journal and Proceedings*, Vol. XL, (1954), Part III, pp. 133-78; *Australia and the United Nations*, by N. Harper and D. Sissons (Manhattan Publishing Co., New York, 1959), pp. 47-78; Watt, *op. cit.*, pp. 78-93.

ment of January 1944 were followed by similar discussion in Wellington (N.Z.) in November of that year. By the latter month the Dumbarton Oaks Draft of the United Nations Charter had been circulated, and the two Dominion governments were able to agree upon twelve points of principle which were approved by the Australian cabinet. These formed the basis of subsequent Australian amendments to the Dumbarton Oaks text.

The Conference in San Francisco was preceded by British Commonwealth discussions in London where, according to Hasluck who was present as an officer of the Department of External Affairs, Evatt for the first time addressed his mind fully to the problems of the Charter and made a strong impression through his mastery of the issues involved.

Finally, the text of the Australian amendments was hammered out during a three day trip from Washington to San Francisco in a conference train specially provided for members of delegations. For three days and three nights we were locked up with our Minister for External Affairs in adjacent compartments, liable to be called upon at any hour to discuss problems or work on drafts. As a result the Australian amendments were in excellent shape by the time the journey came to an end, though at a cost of considerable delegation blood, sweat and tears.

Including clerical and typing staff and junior military aides, the Australian Delegation comprised no less than forty people. These included, apart from Forde and Evatt, four members of different political parties, separate representatives of employers' organizations, the Returned Soldiers League and women's organizations, a newspaper editor, the Federal President of the Australian Labor Party, senior advisers on defence matters, three journalists, and a limited number of External Affairs officers. It is no derogation of the interest shown by most of these or of their readiness to do what was practicable to help to say that the main burden of work fell upon officers of the Department of External Affairs, together with Professor K. H. Bailey (then consultant to the Attorney-General's Department) and Dr Roland Wilson, Secretary of the Department of Labour and National Service.

Hasluck in particular was stretched to the limit. As Head of the Post-Hostilities Division of the Department of External Affairs he was Dr Evatt's chief adviser on matters relating to the United Nations Charter. In addition, he had to attend meetings of the vital Executive Committee and Co-Ordination Committee, in addition to carrying out responsibilities on a main Conference Committee to which he had been assigned. He has commented that '. . . we were doing something close to an eighty-hour week for ten weeks, and taking a large proportion of our meals from "room service" while we wrote, or read, or dictated or telephoned. We were all slightly mad at the end of it. . . .'[23]

Forde and Evatt were named as Australian Delegates to all main Committees, and alternates acted in their place unless and until some crucial issue or difficulty arose, when Dr Evatt would enter the room and take over responsibility for expounding the Australian case. This constant insistence on personal intervention did not amuse the representatives of some other countries, particularly the Great Powers. Many years later a member of

23 Hasluck, 'Formation of the United Nations', *loc. cit.*, p. 171.

the British Delegation, Sir Dingle Foot, wrote that, at San Francisco

> The leader of the rebels was Dr Evatt, from Australia. He became the principal spokesman of the small countries. He was a distinguished jurist, an able politician and a man of abounding energy. But he lacked the capacity to delegate. It was always necessary, it seemed, that the most important speech on any committee debate should be delivered by Dr Evatt and that we must if necessary await his arrival.[24]

I was assigned to work on Security Council matters, acting as alternate to the Ministers in normal charge of the handling of issues dealt with by Committee I of Commission 3 (Structure and Procedures) and also on Committee IV of Commission 3, dealing with Regional Arrangements. I was also listed as an adviser on Committee II (Peaceful Settlement) and Committee III (Enforcement Measures). My main responsibilities were in relation to the problem of the 'veto' rights of Permanent Members of the Security Council, and the Charter provisions for regional arrangements.

It is my considered opinion that Evatt reached the peak of his international influence during the San Francisco Conference, despite the fact that he later held important U.N. offices, including the Presidency of the General Assembly in 1948. If he drove his own staff to the point of utter exhaustion, he himself worked harder than any other Head of Delegation. To quote Hasluck again, 'It was an amazing display of physical energy and sustained combativeness on a dozen different fronts'.[25] He had mastered the Dumbarton Oaks draft of the Charter and all relevant amendments thereto which had been tabled, and he fought tooth and nail for his own points of view, irrespective of Great Power reactions or the susceptibility of other delegates. He also used the press to maximum advantage, both to publicise Australian policies and to sow seeds of criticism of policies he was opposing. During the Conference the New York *Times* published a small edition in San Francisco dealing especially with Conference matters, and Evatt found this a valuable basis for pressure.

This, of course, was not a peace conference which had to concern itself with the carving up of territories or the payment of reparations: it was a constitutional convention where Evatt was on familiar ground. He was far better qualified to analyse, clarify, advocate and contest than others without his background of legal training and experience. He chose to speak for the Middle and Small Powers, most of whose representatives felt less free to criticise Great Power policies in public than he. This was a popular stance, except amongst representatives of the Great Powers. Whether or not Evatt's policies were wise, from the point of view of securing international harmony and co-operation and protecting Australian long-term interests, his influence upon the Charter was greater than Australia's current influence in the world at large.

Evatt's most extraordinary achievement at the Conference was his influence upon the 'domestic jurisdiction' provisions of the Charter. Art. 2 (7) now reads as follows:

[24] Article in *Canberra Times*, 11 July, 1970.
[25] Hasluck, 'Formation of the United Nations', *loc. cit.*, p. 170.

Nothing contained in the present Charter shall authorise the United Nations to intervene in matters which are essentially within the domestic jurisdiction of any state or shall require the Members to submit such matters to settlement under the present Charter; but this principle shall not prejudice the application of enforcement measures under Chapter VII.

To obtain approval of this clause, the Australian Delegation had to upset a Dumbarton Oaks draft, as amended by the sponsoring Powers at San Francisco, limited in its operation to the section dealing with the Pacific Settlement of Disputes. This draft, even as amended, appeared to Evatt to permit the Security Council to impose a settlement in a matter of domestic jurisdiction, provided there was an actual threat to the peace, and thus to encourage an aggressor to threaten the use of force, in the hope of extorting concessions as the price of Security Council support for the country threatened.

For instance, suppose Japan or China demanded that Australia should accept one million migrants within a year, and threaten Australia if she refused. On appeal to the Security Council, the Council might agree to deal with the threat, *provided* Australia accepted 500,000, or 200,000 or less. The Australian amendment was designed to limit the powers of the Security Council, in such a case, to preventing aggression or defending the victim of aggression.

Although I had no personal responsibility for the handling of this issue, I was present when the crucial vote was taken in Committee. A roll-call vote had been demanded by those opposing the Australian attitude, and before it was taken none of us was certain of the outcome. In the result, the present paragraph was approved by thirty-one votes to three, with five abstentions. At the time I was convinced that a number of those present voted in favour, not because they had been completely convinced by Evatt's arguments, but because they knew he regarded the outcome as important and were prepared to help him because of his advocacy of middle and small power points of view during the Conference as a whole.

Over the succeeding years, of course, new majorities in the General Assembly have re-interpreted the paragraph and reduced its original significance to a minimum, while Evatt himself, in his handling of the Indonesian, Spanish, and religious trials issues, did not maintain a consistent attitude towards Art. 2 (7).[26]

I have summarised elsewhere Evatt's influence on those Articles of the Charter dealing with Trusteeship, Non-Self-Governing Territories, the Powers of the General Assembly, and the status of the Economic and Social Council.[27] Here it seems relevant to comment further only on Australian policy towards the 'veto', and towards Regional Arrangements, with the discussion of both of which I was closely involved.

Evatt was opposed in principle to any Great Power veto which would give to Permanent Members of the Security Council a privileged status denied to other members; but he was realistic enough to limit his formal

[26] See Harper and Sissons, *op. cit.*, pp. 164-66.
[27] Watt, *op. cit.*, pp. 91-93.

opposition to any right of veto upon matters arising under Chapter VI (Peaceful Settlement of Disputes). He argued that if the Security Council had to use force to maintain international peace and security, this must come predominantly from the Great Powers. In these circumstances he was reluctantly prepared to accept a right of veto by each of the Permanent Members. Why, however, should any Permanent Member have the right to prevent such action as establishment of a Committee to investigate facts, report and make recommendations to the Council?

Evatt made a very strong case in support of his point of view, and gained much sympathy from the representatives of many Small Powers. Here, however, the Sponsoring Powers dug in their heels and, in effect, flatly refused to sign a Charter so limiting their rights. The only concession made to the smaller powers, after much debate, was agreement that the veto could not be used to prevent an item being placed on or removed from the Agenda, or to prevent an inscribed item being discussed. Middle and Small Powers had to be satisfied with this, together with a statement by the Sponsoring Powers protesting at the implication that Permanent Members of the Council would misuse or abuse their right of veto.

I was able to persuade Evatt to include, in a speech he made commenting on the final result, a section I had drafted in an attempt to make the most of this promise of future responsible behaviour. It ran as follows:

> I can only hope . . . that during the next few years the Great Powers will demonstrate to the world by their actions in the Council that they will not in practice exercise to the full the veto rights which they possess under the Charter. If it can be agreed that all peaceful means of settling disputes must be adopted and exhausted and that in practice the veto will not be used to block such procedures, I am convinced that we will make a great step forward. This would remove many of the doubts which middle and smaller countries have felt regarding acceptance of the present text . . . The Great Powers can perform a great service to the world if they demonstrate in practice that the powers given to them under the Charter will be used with restraint and in the interests of the United Nations as a whole.[28]

Subsequent experience, alas, proved that this hope was unjustified, the Soviet Union in particular having used the veto over one hundred times.

At San Francisco, therefore, the Smaller Powers were compelled to accept the view of the Sponsoring Powers that world peace depended upon securing unanimity amongst the Permanent Members of the Council and that, if such unanimity did not exist, the Security Council would be unable to act. In these circumstances it seemed to Evatt and many others essential to ensure that there should be no Great Power veto upon amendment of the Charter. If after a trial period of, say, ten years, it were found that the veto had in fact stultified action in the Security Council to the serious detriment of international peace, then the issue should be re-considered and the Charter amended. Here again the Sponsoring Powers were rigid and obstinate and insisted upon the right of each Permanent Member of the Security Council to veto any proposed amendment. In other words, it became more difficult to

[28] Quoted in Watt, *op. cit.*, p. 87.

amend the Charter than to create it: at San Francisco a two-thirds majority could approve the text of the Charter; thereafter, any amendment required a two-thirds majority which must include the affirmative votes of every Permanent Member of the Security Council. An Australian proposal that amendments should require a two-thirds majority including only the affirmative votes of three of the five Permanent Members was rejected. The inevitable result of such rigidity was to encourage revision of the Charter by way of re-interpretation, whether or not the new interpretation was legally justified.

In view of the possibility that action by the Security Council could be prevented by use of the veto, the Australian Delegation was concerned to ensure that there was specific recognition in the Charter of the inherent right of self-defence, individual and collective, if an armed attack occurred against a Member State. We argued that the over-all jurisdiction of the Security Council should not preclude the existence of regional arrangements or agencies designed to deal, at least in the first instance and in appropriate cases, with problems of international peace and security. Articles 50, 51 and 52 of the Charter substantially met Australian wishes, and when the text was approved Senator Vandenberg of the United States paid tribute to the contribution made by Dr Evatt.

Sir Frederic Eggleston found himself in a difficult position in San Francisco. In theory he should have been Dr Evatt's chief adviser; in practice he was largely ignored by the Minister for External Affairs, who primarily wanted help in giving effect to policy upon which he had already decided. Eggleston's immobility made it impossible for him to be used as a 'runner' to try to obtain high-level support from other Delegations, while his age made it impracticable for him to be available late at night as well as throughout the day. Nor could he be given a substantial degree of discretion in Conference Committees, because Evatt insisted on taking charge in every Committee when crucial problems arose.

I felt that Eggleston would have done well if he had told Evatt he proposed to return to Washington to carry out there his important duties as Head of Mission. It seemed to me undignified for him to stay. However, he may have concluded that personal reactions to Evatt's methods of operation were less important than possible opportunities to contribute his own views.

In general, I found the experience of the San Francisco Conference invaluable. There I learned many lessons which I used later at other conferences, met a very wide range of people with some of whom I would be working again elsewhere, and formed impressions of individuals and national attitudes which I could have gained by no other means.

Thus, it was at San Francisco that I first saw high representatives of the Soviet Union in action, and had the opportunity to study their attitudes and methods closely. The first quality which all of them showed, from Molotov down, was pertinacity and determination to continue to fight for their policies even in the face of great opposition. They were serious-minded men not given to levity, and they addressed themselves to their respective tasks after full preparation prepared to play the game right to the bitter end even when everyone else had become tired of it. On several occasions when issues had been decided against them or when they could not command majority support, they refused to give up trying and at times were ultimately successful in securing a compromise substantially favourable to their points of view.

At San Francisco I saw no signs amongst the Soviet Delegation of revolutionary enthusiasm or of impulses towards idealism. On the contrary, they showed at times that they could be tough, pragmatic bargainers, ready to make concessions only at the very last minute after all other methods had failed, including an occasional threat to walk out of the Conference. One of the inferences I drew was that when we take up a matter with the Soviet Government we should not regard too seriously their preliminary reactions or an actual refusal to agree to a proposal. Instead, we should hold our ground, keep on trying, convince them we are determined to continue to press for something we regard as important and justifiable, and demonstrate that we have no more concern for their susceptibilities than they have for ours. Further, if we have something which they want, we should not make it available to them without taking very good care to get from them as much as we can of what we want. If we throw in our hand too early, we will get no thanks and little respect.

Molotov himself made a considerable impression upon me. In the early days of the conference I was sitting about six feet away from him and I was able to watch him closely. He was not an amiable individual at all, and his delegation seemed to regard him with some fear; but he was a notable personality, more than able to hold his own in the company of Foreign Ministers and not at all disturbed by wide-spread opposition to any of his views. He knew the techniques of conferences and missed no point to which he was entitled, including questions of procedure. He left an impression of dourness and toughness. While he was still in San Francisco he seemed to have power to take most decisions on his own; after he left Gromyko had to refer many things to Moscow and this led to considerable delays.

While it is a common Soviet technique to admit to minimal knowledge of foreign languages and to insist on speaking in Russian—partly, like the French, to make others aware of the existence and importance of their own language—at that time few members of the Soviet Delegation seemed even reasonably at home in English or French. Two exceptions were Gromyko, whose English was more than adequate, and Manuilsky of the Ukraine, whose French was excellent. Communication with most of the others was often difficult, as if some psychological obstacle had to be overcome.

I found that whenever I had views to express in a committee to which the Russians were likely to be opposed, I was always asking myself the question 'Does the Soviet Delegate really understand the precise point I am making?' At San Francisco simultaneous translation of all five official languages had not yet been introduced, and the translation which was made into English and French was sometimes shortened by the interpreters. This increased the difficulty of communication between East and West. It is only gradually that one learns, as experience of foreign countries increases, that it is often wise to express oneself in English more slowly than usual, avoiding unusual words and slang, particularly when one is transacting official business.

Finally, I came to the conclusion that one of the strongest arguments for creating a World Organisation, however imperfect, was the need for regular contact and consultation between representatives of countries which have been mutually suspicious of one another and isolated from one another's influence. Thus I found it impossible to believe that even the Russian guards brought over to the United States to live for nine weeks in San Francisco could remain unaffected by the atmosphere of that prosperous, cheerful and attractive city. Contrast with their own conditions of life must make some impression. The effect upon more sophisticated Russians would be stronger.

After some five years in the United States, I learned at San Francisco little about Americans that I did not already know, but I formed definite impressions of particular representatives at the Conference, and of their capacity or otherwise to work as a team.

Not unnaturally, there was much less unity of purpose and of common action amongst the Americans than amongst the Russians. This was due in part to the variety of American representation, as the Delegation included Democratic and Republican leaders from Congress, officials and Dean Virginia Gildersleeve (head of Barnard College). Still more, however, did it result from lack of effective leadership by the Secretary of State, Edward R. Stettinius Jr.

When the Conference completed its work everyone praised Stettinius, but most must have done so with tongue in cheek. I had met him when he was Lend-Lease Administrator. At that stage he seemed to be an earnest man doing a pretty good job. At San Francisco, on the other hand, he proved a hopeless Chairman and never seemed on top of the problems with which he had to deal. Perhaps he deserved praise because he exuded confidence and never gave up hope of reaching agreement, but his only real interest appeared to be in the field of 'public relations'.

Stettinius never missed an opportunity to ensure that the flood lights were sufficiently strong to facilitate dozens of photographs being taken, and he showed great anxiety for the comfort of the one or two thousand press and radio men who riddled the Conference and took up a disconcerting amount of space. But whenever he struck a real problem as Chairman he had to have a special adviser seated close behind him to explain the answer to a question. At times he did not seem to know the difference between a motion and an amendment, and when several motions were before the meeting was capable of saying with a smile 'Now I think we are all agreed'. Almost without exception his speeches were read textually from a little black book, and he spoke without conviction. In short, he showed no signs of intellectual capacity and was ever ready to pour oil on wheels the working of which he did not fully understand.

This was a tremendous disadvantage to the United States, whose luminaries amongst the Delegates were Vandenberg and Stassen, both Republicans. Senator Connally, a Democrat, was attached to the Committee which dealt with the veto, and I heard many of his declamatory speeches. Whenever he

F

rose to defend this Great Power privilege we were always cheered, because his arguments were likely to be so inadequate that they would probably help us rather than the American Delegation. Connally undoubtedly had a personality and his style, though somewhat florid—he had a tendency to wave a finger and turn in a circle while speaking—could be picturesque on occasion, but his understanding of the Charter was limited. If given time to assimilate a problem or have it fully explained to him, he could speak with effect, but in the quick to and fro of debate he was not sufficiently agile to be able to choose the most telling arguments.

I saw little of Stassen, because I had nothing to do with the Committee dealing with trusteeship problems, but once he was introduced to speak on the veto. Although somewhat school-masterish in style, his manner and self-control were good and he left the impression that he knew what he was talking about.

Senator Vandenberg spoke frequently and to very good effect in the Committee in which regional arrangements were discussed. An experienced politician, he was undoubtedly more intelligent than Connally. On several occasions he made very adroit speeches as new situations arose, and I felt he would be a valuable member of any Republican Administration.

John Foster Dulles played an important part as an Adviser. On one occasion I was at a lunch with him and Dr Evatt alone. He struck me as an able experienced man, well versed in law and international affairs and accustomed to taking into account the particular idiosyncracies of people with whom he was dealing. In somewhat difficult conversation he knew exactly where he wanted to go, at what pace to proceed, and the pitfalls to avoid. He was a forceful speaker, able to think on his feet without notes and to marshall arguments in good order. Some of the Australian Delegation were critical of him because he fought our views on the 'full employment' pledge. They objected to the fact that after we had had a clear win in Committee Dulles came along and managed to brow-beat members into reversing the position temporarily. But if Evatt had done the same thing the same critics would probably have praised his capacity. Dulles was really trying to recover ground which Dean Gildersleeve had lost.[29]

In due course the San Francisco Conference came to an end and exhausted delegates and advisers returned to their own countries or overseas posts. In Washington, the battles of San Francisco long continued to be fought again by those who had been there. As if drawn to one another by the sight of an old-school tie, they tended to congregate together at cocktail parties, and their continuing reminiscences greatly bored colleagues who had not shared the experience.

The war with Germany had ended while the Conference was in session. When on 2 September, 1945 the Japanese surrender ceremony took place aboard the U.S.S. *Missouri* in Tokyo Bay, I decided that the time had come for me to fight my way out of Washington. In wartime one carries out the job assigned, but by the latter half of 1945 I had served five years in the United States and had become saturated with the American scene. I had

29 For a detailed account, see 'The Australian Full Employment Pledge at San Francisco', by L. F. Crisp, *Australian Outlook*, Vol. XIX, No. 1 (1965), pp. 5-19.

served under three Heads of Missions and for a longer period than any other member of the diplomatic staff, and the myth had grown up that I was the 'American expert', to be taken over by succeeding Heads of Mission with all the other fixtures at the Legation. There were educational problems for our eldest son; our daughter's American accent was indistinguishable from that of her American friends at nursery-school; my own future advancement in the Service required movement and other experience.

Oddly enough, it was my participation in the San Francisco Conference which led to my transfer from Washington. Evatt wished to maintain Australian influence on United Nations activities and wanted staff to participate in the work of the U.N. Preparatory Commission which was to meet in London and prepare the way for the first meetings of the Security Council and of the General Assembly. Apparently he had found my work at San Francisco of some value as he made specific mention of the work of 'Bailey, Burton, Forsyth, Hasluck and Watt' in the formal report of the Australian Delegation presented to Parliament. Out of the blue he sent a telegram to Eggleston asking the latter to release me for work in London.

Eggleston called me to his office to discuss the matter, and showed me a reply which he proposed to send stating that my continued presence in Washington was essential. I decided that the time had come to make a stand. I pointed out that five years was an unusually long period at one post for members of the Australian Diplomatic Service, that all other members of the staff had changed, that understaffing, strain and saturation with the American scene had reduced my effectiveness substantially, that if I were not transferred now there was no obvious reason why I should ever be transferred, that I was forty-four years of age and that continued presence in Washington could only result in failure to attain higher status and responsibility elsewhere. In conclusion I said that while it was of course a matter for him to decide what reply should be sent to Evatt, I felt I should make it clear that if I were kept on in Washington beyond December 1945 I proposed to retire from the Service.

Eggleston was rather hurt by what I had said, but he held his reply until the following morning. The telegram he then sent stressed the need to keep me in Washington but added that, if the Minister felt he must transfer me to London, two conditions regarding staff would have to be met which Eggleston thought it unlikely to be fulfilled. To his surprise, the Minister for External Affairs agreed in principle to the conditions, and a booking was made for me to leave by flying boat from Baltimore to Southampton via Ireland.

In October 1945 I found myself skimming along the water off Baltimore, and as the seaplane rose slowly into the clouds I began really to believe that my Washington days had ended. The transfer, however, involved family difficulties and a heavy burden fell upon my wife.

The war was scarcely over, and it seemed to make no sense to take with me a wife and four children, two of them aged only six, straight into a London winter, with schooling, food and accommodation problems—at least until I had arrived, settled in and found a suitable house. We therefore decided, and the Department of External Affairs agreed, that my wife and family would stay on in Washington for the time being, then return to Australia for summer holidays and join me in England early in 1946.

It was 20 years since I had been in England. London looked shabby and dejected, as if it had not had a coat of paint for a decade. Here and there—particularly around St. Paul's Cathedral—gaps between buildings on which rubble still lay reminded one of what Londoners had been through during German bombing raids. Food was still heavily rationed, and English people seemed to have acquired the habit of forming queues even in order to buy a newspaper.

I found my cousins, Dorothy and James Watt, in very good heart. Once again they made me welcome at their home in Surrey whenever I was able to slip down there. Dorothy was having trouble with her coal merchant, who would promise but fail to deliver. I suggested that, now the war was over, she should tick him off and threaten to make other arrangements. She had grown so used to war-time restrictions, to be accepted as a patriotic duty, that the idea had not seemed to cross her mind. She went straight to the telephone, exercised her undoubted verbal gifts telling the coal merchant what she thought of him, and returned to the living-room uplifted in spirit. What was more to the point, the merchant delivered next day.

Technically, I had been appointed Senior External Affairs Officer, London, charged with the responsibility, with the aid of a tiny staff, of keeping in touch with the British Foreign Office and the Commonwealth Relations Office on a very wide range of matters. I was also adviser to the Australian High Commissioner on foreign policy issues, and had to pass on to Australia relevant information from British sources, including much original material from British Missions abroad.

At that time we still had a room in the British Cabinet Offices, conveniently situated near Whitehall, though our main office-space was at Australia House. But soon I became so busy with United Nations meetings that it was impossible for me to carry out effectively the functions of External Affairs Officer. For that reason, I have never regarded myself as having occupied that post which, even technically, I held for six months only.

Colonel Hodgson led the team of Australian officials attending the U.N. Meetings, where Rules of Procedure for the Security Council and the General Assembly were slowly hammered out by national representatives, many of whom had been at the San Francisco Conference. Australia urged that the President of the Security Council should be elected for a period of one year, and that the best available person should be chosen. This view was rejected by the majority, on the ground that every member of the Council should be given the opportunity to act as President. The approved rules therefore laid down that the Presidency should be held for one month only in the year, after which it should rotate to each member in turn. As a result Australia, which had alphabetical priority amongst those elected to the first Security Council, supplied the President for its first meeting, which opened in London on January 17, 1946.

By the irony of circumstance, Evatt did not come to London to carry out this important function. It is inconceivable to me that he did not wish to do so, and I have always assumed that Prime Minister Curtin refused to let him leave Australia again so soon after long absence abroad during 1945. Whatever the reason, the leader of the Australian Delegation at meetings of the Council, and its first President, was Mr Norman Makin, whose friendly goodwill towards the members of his team scarcely compensated for the fact that his understanding of the United Nations Charter was slight.

Before the Council opened, Bailey and I strongly urged Makin not to give a quick ruling if a point of order were raised, but to throw the matter open for general discussion, during which the arguments for and against would emerge and there would be time to think. We wanted at all costs to avoid the use of the veto by one of the Permanent Members of the Council. I still have a photograph of the Council meeting, with Makin in the Chair, and Bailey and myself sitting close behind him in the next row, looking distinctly edgy.

During my stay in London I looked around for accommodation for my family as opportunity occurred, and eventually managed to arrange to take over a house which had been occupied by John Oldham, who had replaced me in Washington. It was not particularly attractive, but conveniently located in Chelsea, only a short ride to Whitehall. If desired, one could continue in the same bus to Trafalgar Square and up the Strand to Australia House.

The Chelsea House was unfurnished, so I drew a rough plan of it to send to my wife who, I hoped, might be able to buy in Washington some suitable furniture to replace what we had had to sell before leaving Canberra. My wife did in fact buy some important items of furniture for the house which we were destined never to occupy, although I rented it for three months in order to retain control. In the Diplomatic Service officials propose and Governments dispose. Suddenly, in February 1946, I was transferred back to Canberra on a few days' notice.

At the end of 1945 my wife left for Australia with the children. Before departing from Washington she had had to wrestle with our landlady, who maintained firmly that some damage to her 'antique' furniture could not be classed as 'fair wear and tear' and demanded compensation, which was paid. Priorities for travel were still very difficult to obtain, and the length of stay in hotels in cities like San Francisco was heavily restricted, because American soldiers were returning from the war and being demobilised in their tens of thousands.

'Jim' McIntyre, though overwhelmed with Legation work, had given her noble assistance, and eventually she found herself with seats on a train to San Francisco and with bookings on a Swedish ship, the *Paracoola*. On the way across America there were long queues in the train for a limited number of meals, and it was a constant battle to ensure that the children were fed. In Chicago, where she had to change trains, she lost the two elder boys temporarily in Marshall Field's store, and was lucky to find them again in time to catch the train. At the station, in accordance with American procedure, passengers are not allowed to pass through entrance gates to the platform until ten or fifteen minutes before the train is due to start. At Chicago a large crowd collected outside the gates, and when they were opened swept down stairs in a crush which carried the members of my family along with it, precariously holding hands to avoid separation. On this occasion the family only succeeded in boarding the train just before it moved out.

Bookings for a San Francisco hotel had been made for three days, but departure of the ship was delayed and it was with great difficulty that my wife obtained permission to stay on in the hotel for a further seven days. During the voyage the twins developed measles, one after the other. We had lost our tenancy of a house in Canberra, and it was necessary for the family, on arrival in Australia, to rent a house at Woodford in the Blue Mountains, one mile from shops and schools.

In those days there was no provision for home leave for officers serving overseas, and I am still puzzled at the Department's readiness to facilitate the return of my family to Australia, knowing that all or most of its members were to rejoin me in London early in 1946. Though the return was reasonable enough, I have wondered whether the Secretary had plans, not yet communicated to me, to recall me from London to Canberra.

In 1945 Colonel Hodgson had been posted overseas, and W. E. (later Sir William) Dunk had been appointed Secretary in his place. This was an unexpected appointment because Dunk, though an experienced and able Commonwealth public servant, had previously occupied posts connected with accountancy and auditing, until during the war years he had been put in charge of Australian Reciprocal Lend Lease. This responsibility brought him into close touch with American problems and took him on occasion to Washington.

Dunk was frank and somewhat blunt in conversation, and Evatt must have been impressed by his administrative capacity. Yet while Dunk had an interest in broad economic problems, his knowledge of international political affairs was inevitably limited. At some stage he must have come to the conclusion that he needed alongside him a senior External Affairs officer with overseas experience and expertise on the political side. He therefore persuaded the Public Service Board to agree to the creation of a new post in the Department entitled Assistant-Secretary (Political). At that time there were no other Assistant-Secretaries on the establishment.

In February 1946, just as the sessions of the Security Council were ending, Dunk sent me a telegram indicating that he proposed to appoint me to the new post and wanted me to return to Australia immediately. This, of course, involved a complete change in our family plans, including abandonment of the lease of the Chelsea House. Discussion with my wife was impracticable, as telegrams would be useless and letters would take too long.

I knew that she would prefer the children to be in Australia, for educational and other reasons. For myself, the proposed appointment had a number of attractions. After five and a half years overseas, I was plain homesick. More important, however, was the fact that I would have clear status in the Department as the second senior officer, with assigned responsibility for political matters. This was a key position which must bring me into regular touch with the Minister for External Affairs, and which would be an excellent jumping-off post for appointment either at home or abroad.

On the other hand, I knew that relations with Dr Evatt were sure to be difficult; yet I had grounds for hoping that my work in connection with the formation of the United Nations had changed his attitude towards me somewhat for the better.

All things considered, I concluded that this was an opportunity to influence policy which could not be rejected. I telegraphed my acceptance to Dunk, and flew back to Australia with Mr Makin and four other officials in a converted Lancastrian bomber which carried only six passengers, sitting with their backs to one side of the plane. We completed the journey in three days—the same length of time it had taken from Baltimore to London. So far as I can remember, we landed for fuel only in Israel, at Cocos Island and at Perth, before reaching Sydney. It was a most tiring journey, but a pleasantly swift transition from Europe to Australia.

At the airport I was met by John Quinn, whose appearance shocked me. I remembered him before the war as a tall, keen, extremely intelligent young External Affairs officer whose French was first-class. He had been posted to Singapore and on the fall of that city had been taken into custody by the Japanese, together with V. G. Bowden, Australian Government Representative. What happened thereafter I never discovered, but suffering was written plainly on Quinn's face. The alert mind seemed dulled, speech had become somewhat mechanical, the spark of life had been dimmed.

Over the years, Quinn recovered, and even agreed to being posted as Australian Minister to Saigon, although that was an area likely to awaken old memories. Later, while Australian Ambassador to Cairo, he was killed in an accident to a French aircraft.* Whom the gods love die young.

---

* A monograph on John Paul Quinn, containing recollections of the man by some of his colleagues, was published privately in 1968. A copy is in the National Library, Canberra.

3

CANBERRA

Two

M<small>Y SECOND</small> official sojourn in Canberra lasted only 13 months, from February 1946 to March 1947. Although all the members of my family were glad to be back in Australia, I found great difficulty in making any suitable household arrangements. The children also had some problems of adjustment to the local educational curriculum.

The house my family had taken at Woodford was isolated and inadequate, and my first responsibility was to find better housing for them on the Blue Mountains while I searched for accommodation in Canberra. Fortunately, I was able to secure a much pleasanter place at Wentworth Falls, although it was a considerable distance from the train which the two elder boys had to catch to take them to the nearest high school at Katoomba. The twins attended primary school at Wentworth Falls, but found it rough and tough and remained there only a few weeks.

In Canberra it proved impossible to rent a Government house in my own right. I had lost my place in the Canberra queue, and service overseas was regarded, in my case, as supremely irrelevant. During my absence in Washington the regulations had been changed, so that other External Affairs officers posted abroad temporarily could now retain control of houses they had inhabited in Canberra. But the house I had had to surrender was occupied, and no exception was made for my special circumstances by the Department of the Interior.

Eventually I had to settle for the only house I could find. It was at Wells Gardens, Griffith, furnished and under the control of another External Affairs officer of comparatively junior rank posted in New Zealand. There were only two bedrooms, and a small dining room which, in view of our family of six, we had to convert into a bedroom. All meals were taken in the kitchen, one of the children having to crawl under the table to get to the far side.

I took the house only because it was essential to bring the family together again, and in Canberra. I had been absent from them for about seven months;

my wife was carrying far too heavy a burden; schooling at Wentworth Falls was unsatisfactory; my work as Assistant-Secretary (Political) consumed all my energy, and I simply could not find the time to try to find better accommodation, or afford to pay more for the only kind of furnished house which was likely to be available. Most of the furniture we had acquired in America for the house in London had to be stored.

The family moved to Canberra after Easter, 1946. Alan and John rode their bicycles to the Canberra High School, where the former had to fit into two years work on Physics and Chemistry normally spread over four years. The twins settled somewhat uneasily into Telopea Park Primary School, both discarding their American clothes during the first week in the face of ribald remarks by their school-mates. They travelled by bus. On the first day Mary got lost returning from school, because she could not explain to the bus-driver where she lived. My wife shopped at Manuka, a considerable walking-distance from Wells Gardens.

I myself acquired a bicycle which I used to get to and from the office at night or over week-ends when facilities for travel by bus were minimal. As soon as practicable, I bought a second-hand car for £250. It was a Nash sedan, of uncertain vintage and monstrous proportions, with a petrol consumption of seven miles to the gallon. It had to be started with a hand-crank requiring the strength of an elephant. As there was no garage at Wells Gardens the car had to be left out in the open each night. In winter the frosts were so severe that I felt obliged to drain the water from the radiator every evening, fill it again every morning and start the engine with expenditure of more muscular energy than I had to spare. I found I could afford to run it only to and from work once a day, with an occasional week-end jaunt for the family.

After spending about six months at Wells Gardens, I managed to transfer to a much more suitable house in Barkly Crescent, Forrest, rented from the Government by Dr Anstey Wynes, another External Affairs officer then posted in Ottawa. This was near the house in Dominion Circuit in which we had lived before moving to Washington. Forrest is a pleasant suburb, and Barkly Crescent is lined with magnificent Canadian pin-oaks which in autumn are a riot of colour. The area was much closer to schools and to work, and I could walk across the fields to West Block without losing too much time.

During this period of thirteen months in Canberra I was over-worked and under-paid. The former I did not mind, because it was the kind of responsibility I had joined the Department to assume. As to the latter, Dunk as Secretary did his best to secure approval from the Public Service Board and Treasury of an adequate salary, but the best he could obtain was £1200 a year. As a result, my second sojourn in Canberra cost me an additional £500 from capital saved while overseas.

At the Department of External Affairs, my relations with the Secretary were frank and friendly. Dunk was a somewhat rough diamond, but he was a man of independent mind with the courage to express his own opinions to his Minister even when they were not welcomed.

My functions as 'Assistant-Secretary, Political' were not defined very

77

precisely, but in practice they worked out as follows. The Secretary kept personal control of administrative matters, interesting himself especially in reforms involving the creation of new positions, recruitment of staff, appointments, salaries and other conditions of service and the like. Senior overseas appointments he discussed with me in advance where my experience or knowledge of personnel seemed relevant. He dealt with international problems in the economic field himself, although I always had ready access to him to put forward any point of view. He saw the Minister personally whenever he thought it necessary, and kept me informed of Ministerial attitudes and decisions.

For the rest, I had unrestricted access to all telegrams and other material coming into the Department, while no limitations were placed upon my access to Dr Evatt. I kept my eye on the distribution of all political material coming into the Department, especially telegrams, and called upon relevant officers of the Department of External Affairs for preparation of draft ministerial submissions or speeches, adapting them in accordance with my own judgment after discussion with Dunk when this seemed necessary. He would always know what I proposed to recommend to the Minister and could, of course, override my views. I kept him closely informed of actual ministerial decisions, although urgent draft telegrams altered by the Minister often had to be despatched before the Secretary could be told of the changes. Dunk and I never had any violent differences of opinion. Looking back in the light of further years of experience, I think he allowed me a lot of latitude, and showed me considerable tolerance.

My relations with Dr Evatt, on the other hand, were never easy. Indeed, they were usually difficult, tense and frustrating. Time was often lost waiting upon the Minister's pleasure, sitting in the office of his private secretary while members of parliament, journalists and others went into or came out of his room without restriction. When eventually admitted to the Minister's sanctum, Evatt would take a long draft telegram, go through it meticulously and make numerous alterations in scarcely legible handwriting, inserting words or phrases which were written all over the front or back of the document, with lines and arrows indicating their position. Sometimes he would ask for the relevant file, which he would flick through with uncanny skill, as he had some sort of sixth sense with documents. If one relevant document happened to be missing from the file, he would be likely to discover the fact.

After leaving the Minister, it would take me at times half an hour or even an hour to decypher his alterations of the original draft. On several occasions he accused me of sending off telegrams in a form which he had not approved. To counter such charges, I eventually decided to keep a separate file in my own room containing all original drafts with the Minister's alterations in his own handwriting. One Saturday morning he made a very unusual call upon me in my office. I left the room to get something for which he had asked, and returned to find him standing by my filing cabinets, one drawer of which was open. In his hand was the file in which I kept the draft telegrams he had altered.

He had pulled open the cabinet in a fit of idle curiosity, and his sixth

78

sense led him to this particular file. He glared at me and demanded to know why I kept these drafts, which he rightly judged were intended to provide first-hand evidence of what his actual instructions had been. The only reply I could give was that he had charged me on occasion with despatching telegrams which he had not authorised, and that I felt the best way to justify my actions was to keep the originals. Evatt thrust the drawer of the cabinet inwards with a bang, and stalked out of the room.

My problems as Assistant-Secretary, however, were far less important than those of the Secretary. He, not I, had been appointed by the Cabinet and charged with the responsibility of running the Department as a whole. It was his authority which was undermined, if the Minister chose to ignore him and to work through others. The delicate situation in Indonesia provides an illustration of the kind of unexpected difficulties which Dunk was apt to meet.

Australian policy towards the Netherlands East Indies in the early days after the Japanese surrender was somewhat ambivalent. As explained in the House of Representatives by Dr Evatt on 13 March, 1946, Australia had a vital interest in the preservation of the war-time friendship with the Dutch in relation to the Netherlands East Indies. At the same time, it was important to do everything possible to establish good relations with the Indonesian and other dependent peoples of the world who were advancing towards a far greater degree of self-government.[30] In the same speech the Minister for External Affairs said that Australia had had special representation in the Netherlands East Indies since V-J Day, including Mr MacMahon Ball and then Mr Keith Officer. Both representatives had kept in close consultation with the British Military Command.

Ball spent most of the month of November 1945 in Indonesia, whither he had been sent 'in order to find out how far the Republic was a genuine nationalist movement and to assess the calibre of the Republican leaders'.[31] On his return to Australia, Mr A. D. Brookes was sent to Indonesia as Australian Political Representative, and carried out his functions there from December 1945 to June 1946, although in April 1946 Officer was appointed Australian Political Representative in South East Asia, with the rank of Minister. When Brookes became ill and returned to Australia, Judge (now Justice Sir Richard) Kirby, who was in Indonesia for other purposes, acted as Political Representative in June, July and August 1946 until Mr B. C. Ballard became Political Representative on 10 August, 1946.[32]

Ball, though not a career official, was a man of wide experience in the study of international problems. Officer was the senior overseas officer of the Department of External Affairs, while Ballard was a lawyer of linguistic capacity who had been recruited into the Department during the Second World War, partly in view of his specialist knowledge of the New Hebrides. On the other hand, Brookes was a young man without governmental training

[30] Current Notes (Department of External Affairs, Canberra), Vol. XVII (1946), p. 148.

[31] See *Australia in World Affairs (1956-60)*, Greenwood and Harper (Eds) (F. W. Cheshire, Melbourne, 1963), Chapter by J. A. C. Mackie, p. 275.

[32] Australia and Indonesian Independence (1942-49), by Margaret L. George, (B.A. Hons Thesis, A.N.U., Canberra), especially pp. 53-58, 80-81, 153.

or international expertise, suddenly launched with Dr Evatt's approval into an extremely delicate international situation of special importance to Australia. I have been unable to trace any public announcement of his appointment.

On 17 April, 1946 Dr Evatt and his Private Secretary, Dr John Burton, left Australia for London, arriving there on 19 April. During their absence overseas a telegram was received in Canberra from Brookes. It was despatched from Batavia, addressed to Burton and 'repeated' to the Secretary, Department of External Affairs. The telegram dealt with matters of high policy in which Brookes was involving himself with Indonesian Republican leaders.

Dunk was annoyed that Brookes seemed to regard a junior officer, Burton, as the person to whom he had primary responsibility for reporting. But even if the message had been intended for Dr Evatt, Dunk was deeply concerned that a person of such limited experience was involving himself in difficult and delicate political problems without effective departmental control, and without his reports being submitted to the Minister together with departmental comments. When Brookes returned to Australia he brought with him a formal letter from Prime Minister Sjahrir requesting that the Australian government raise the Indonesian question before the United Nations on certain terms.

Dunk gave me to understand at the time that he had taken up directly with Evatt the question of Brookes' activities in Indonesia and control over them by the Department of External Affairs. In reply Evatt, while not specifically endorsing what Brookes had been doing, minimised their significance and ascribed them to excess of zeal. In fact, the Australian Government did not agree to the Sjahrir proposal, and did not raise the issue in the United Nations until about a year later, in very different circumstances. The appointment of Ballard in August 1946 strongly suggests that Dunk's objections to the Minister had some effect. I have no doubt, however, that the Brookes experience contributed to Dunk's eventual conclusion that he could not work with Evatt and that it would be best to seek another position.

Meetings of Commonwealth Prime Ministers in London lasted from 23 April to 23 May, 1946. The Australian Prime Minister, Mr J. B. Chifley, left London on 6 May, and thereafter Dr Evatt represented Australia. Evatt then proceeded to New York, where he acted as Australian Representative on the U.N. Security Council and attended meetings of the Far Eastern Commission in Washington. Then he flew to Paris, where the Paris Peace Conference opened on 19 July, 1946 to consider the draft Treaties of Peace with Italy, Rumania, Hungary, Bulgaria and Finland. Evatt returned to Australia from Paris on 29 August, handing over the leadership of the Australian Delegation to Mr J. A. Beasley, Australian Resident Minister in London. During 1946, therefore, Dr Evatt was away from Australia for approximately four and a half months. His return from Paris was made necessary by impending federal elections in Australia, scheduled for 28 September, 1946.

As I only returned to Australia towards the end of February, and left

Canberra in October to attend the Second Part of the First Session of the U.N. General Assembly, which met in New York from 23 October to 16 December, I was in Australia with Dr Evatt for only four or five weeks in the early part of the year and for about six weeks in the second half of the year. On the other hand, Dunk took three weeks leave soon after I returned from London, during which I was Acting Secretary in practice though not in name. Dunk also attended the Paris Peace Conference, and in his absence from Australia for a period of two and a half to three months I was Acting Secretary.

While Dunk was on leave I was fully stretched. On 13 March Evatt gave a general review of the international situation in the House of Representatives, while there was much to do administering a rapidly growing Department, at home and overseas. But when Dunk returned, and the Minister left for London, the strain eased greatly.

At this stage of his career Evatt more or less dominated decisions on Australian foreign policy. By then he had become the acknowledged expert on international affairs in the Cabinet. He was frequently abroad and while there for the most part took his policy, so to speak, with him, using External Affairs officers posted overseas or travelling with him for drafts, and reporting to Canberra in somewhat general terms or after the event. No Acting Minister was likely to do more than make occasional suggestions to the Minister, while carrying on in Canberra with necessary routine decisions. The Prime Minister received copies of all important cables despatched by and received by the Department of External Affairs, and was capable of intervening, for instance, on some issue affecting relations with the United Kingdom. But Mr J. B. Chifley, who had become Leader of the Labor Party and Prime Minister on the death of Mr Curtin in 1945, gave Evatt a lot of rope. On the few occasions when I had to seek some decision from him as Acting Minister for External Affairs, I found him approachable, tolerant, shrewd in posing questions and blessed with a fundamental common sense which enabled him to deal with issues with which he was not specially familiar.

After his experience in London as President of the U.N. Security Council, Mr N. J. O. Makin became at times Acting Minister when Evatt was abroad, and in September 1946 was appointed Australian Ambassador in Washington, where the Legation had been converted into an Embassy. There could be no greater contrast than the respective personalities of Evatt and Makin. Evatt's characteristics have been described already. Makin was a kindly man who had left primary school at an early age and who had had to make his career in the world the hard way. His intellectual capacity was limited, but he had considerable experience of political life both within the Labor Party, as Speaker of the House of Representatives, and as Minister of the Crown. He won friends by his very simplicity and lack of pretentiousness.

If I rang his Private Secretary to secure an appointment, the Minister as likely as not would inquire what time would suit me best. On arrival, I would be shown into his office at Parliament House immediately unless there was another caller in the room already. When presented to the

Minister, he would shake me warmly by the hand, and if the time was relevant, suggest we should have a cup of tea before dealing with the files I had brought over. Recommendations would be accepted rather too readily, and he was prepared to sign most documents without alteration. There were occasions when I returned to my office somewhat uneasy at the fact that the Minister had signed them all, and determined to give some further consideration to one or two in order to protect him from the consequences of ill-judged or too hasty advice.

At the Paris Peace Conference Dr Evatt overplayed his hand. Dizzy with success as a result of the influence he had exerted at the U.N. Charter Conference at San Francisco, he tabled on behalf of the Australian Delegation no fewer than seventy amendments to the five draft treaties presented to the Conference by the Council of Foreign Ministers, failing to realise that the two Conferences were entirely different in nature. The U.N. Conference had been a constitutional convention; but the most important issues at Paris related to such matters as disposal of territory or payment of reparations. These were European and Mediterranean problems affecting Australian interests far less than countries closer to hand. Nor could Australia justifiably claim any special expertise entitling its representatives to play a special part in the Conference.

In the event, the activities of the Australian Delegation were strongly attacked by representatives of the Soviet Union. Referring to Evatt's objections to decisions being taken by a two-third rather than a simple majority, the Soviet Foreign Minister, Mr Molotov, spoke on 8 August, 1946, as follows:

> What is most important to him [Dr. Evatt] is to secure the most convenient method for the conference to adopt such recommendations as will not be acceptable to the Soviet Union. It is for this reason that he is so busy in his activities in this conference. . . . The Soviet Union believes it is not the purpose of the Peace Conference that one power or *bloc* of powers should obtain the upper hand over the Soviet Union or any other State. If anyone attempts to play this part he is sure to fail in his schemes and to cause political damage—first to his own State and then to the authority of this conference.[33]

The Soviet Union, Molotov added, took pride in the fact that it had saved European civilisation from Fascist barbarity.

On 27 August there was a 'stormy dispute between Australian and Soviet Delegates during meetings dealing with the peace treaty with Italy'.[34] For Australia, Colonel Hodgson moved for a fact-finding committee to examine documents regarding Italian frontier questions, including those which had been considered by the Council of Foreign Ministers. Mr Vyshinsky commented that the Australian Delegation wanted to ignore the work done by the Council, and added:

> Why have we wasted so much time? Why does the Australian Delegation put forward amendments in limitless numbers? We find that 35%

[33] *Keesing's Contemporary Archives*, p. 8125.
[34] *Ibid.*, p. 8136.

of all the amendments put forward are submitted by Australia, yet Australia is farthest removed from Europe. These are delaying tactics. The aim is to destroy the work of the Foreign Ministers' Council.[35]

By this date Dr Evatt may have left Paris, for he arrived in Australia on 29 August. Mr Beasley, presumably as Acting Leader of the Australian Delegation, entered the fray and is alleged to have shaken his fist at Vyshinsky. ' "We may be 15,000 miles away," he shouted, "but we have fought in two European wars and lost some of our best men in them . . . I refuse to be bounced or bullied by anybody".'[35]

On the same day Dr Walker (Australia) moved an amendment designed to set up a commission to fix reparations. In reply, Molotov declared that the Soviet Union had borne heavier sacrifices in the War than Australia, and contributed more to victory. He continued as follows:

> The Australian delegation have almost drowned us in a pile of amendments. This suggests there is someone who helps them. It is obvious that no delegation alone would be able to prepare so many amendments. The proposals made by Australia on the reparations question are directed against the Soviet Union and are not made for the sake of the countries which have to pay reparations.[35]

On the following day Dr Walker's proposal was rejected, receiving the affirmative votes only of Australia and New Zealand, although Canada, South Africa and the Netherlands registered abstentions.

Press reports of these altercations were cabled from Paris to Australia, together with hints that there was disagreement on policy within the Australian Delegation. On his return to Sydney Evatt strongly denied to journalists that there had been any such disagreement. In a subsequent cartoon by David Low, Evatt was depicted standing in front of three mirrors, each of which reflected an image of himself from a different angle. Below the drawings were the words 'Gentlemen, are we not all agreed?'

When Dunk was leaving for Paris and I was about to become Acting Secretary, I asked for his general instructions and received my answer in one sentence: 'Hold the fort until I return'. I interpreted this to mean that I should not try to initiate significant administrative changes, that I should avoid as far as possible disputes with the Minister on administrative matters, but that I was free to suggest lines of policy for ministerial consideration, subject to known views of the Secretary, as I would have done had Dunk been in Canberra.

But to hold the fort was easier said than done. An 'acting' position at any stage of a diplomatic career is not attractive, except for the purpose of gaining wider experience and strengthening claims to promotion. But the position of Acting Secretary is particularly frustrating. The Secretary of the Department of External Affairs is appointed by Cabinet, whose specific choice gives him very considerable authority. Whatever difficulties he may experience with his particular Minister, he is a 'Permanent Head' who cannot be removed from office without public questioning by the mass media and probably in Parliament. Under the Commonwealth Public Service

[35] *Ibid.*, p. 8136.

Act he has wide powers, including the power to promote, subject to appeal. An Acting Secretary, on the other hand, has no Cabinet backing, and whatever his technical powers under the Public Service Act he would not in fact exercise them so far as important administrative decisions are concerned, at least without prior consultation with the Secretary. In short, an Acting Secretary has far more responsibilities than powers.

I found the period between Evatt's return to Australia and my departure for New York distinctly unpleasant. There was no longer an Acting Minister, and I had to obtain decisions from the Minister or make them myself. His Paris experiences and the reporting of the Paris Conference in the Australian Press had soured him somewhat, but his interest and energies were soon devoted almost exclusively to the federal election campaign, as part of which he travelled widely throughout the Continent on behalf of his Party. Until 28 September, 1946, the date of the elections, I was frequently out of contact with him and when in contact I received no encouragement whatever to discuss any but urgent and vital problems. In these circumstances I had to take more upon myself at times than I would have wished, quite conscious of the fact that, in due course, he might disagree with my actions and blame me for not consulting him.

One administrative problem which led to difficulties was the adequacy of the staff of Mr W. McMahon Ball, who took up duty in Tokyo on 3 April, 1946 as British Commonwealth Member of the Allied Council for Japan, representing the governments of the United Kingdom, India and New Zealand, as well as Australia. He was a lecturer at Melbourne University, and became well-known as a radio commentator on international affairs before his war-time appointment as Controller of Overseas Broadcasting during the years 1940-44.

In 1945 Ball edited a book of Evatt's speeches and wrote an introduction analysing and explaining the main points of the Minister's foreign policy from November 1941 to September 1944. He was an adviser to the Australian Delegation at the U.N. Charter Conference held in San Francisco in 1945. Subsequently, after acting briefly as Australian Political Representative attached to the Commander, Allied Forces Netherlands East Indies, he had been sent to Japan in the capacity mentioned above. He held this post from 3 April, 1946 until 17 August, 1947; led an Australian goodwill mission to ten countries in Asia in 1948; and from 1949 to 1968 held the Chair of Political Science in the University of Melbourne. His published works include two books, *Japan—Enemy or Ally* (1949), and *Nationalism and Communism in East Asia* (1956).

My first contact with Ball was at the San Francisco Conference in 1945. There he was generally regarded by officials in the Australian Delegation as a man with a deep interest in international affairs, sympathetic towards the policies of Dr Evatt but with independent ideas of his own. However, we did not find him an easy colleague. He was sensitive on questions of status, and resented the incursions of Dr Evatt at moments of crisis or special importance into the Committee where Ball had primary responsibilities, despite the fact that Evatt took the same course with every other member of the Australian Delegation, however senior.

It is a common experience of career officers of the Department of External Affairs that when someone from outside the Department is appointed to a high position within it or a temporary representative position abroad, he expects consideration and privileges far beyond those accorded to his colleagues, who have been processed rather roughly over the years through the government machine.

Ball's appointment to Tokyo must have been decided before I returned to Australia from London. His staff as announced at the time when he assumed duty was substantial, including Lt Col E. Longfield Lloyd (Counsellor), B. C. Ballard (First Secretary and Australian Adviser), E. Ward (Second Secretary and Economic Adviser), D. McNicol (Second Secretary) and H. Plumridge (Press Attache).

Before Evatt returned to Australia from Paris, Ball began to press me strongly regarding his administrative problems. In particular, he sought the appointment of an administrative officer, and the recruitment from outside the public service of a designated woman as his secretary in Tokyo. As to the former, all External Affairs officers were supposed to perform administrative work, and McNicol as Second Secretary would be expected to perform much of this in Tokyo. Recruitment from outside the service was difficult to arrange and came within the jurisdiction of the Public Service Board, which twice turned down Ball's request when submitted by the Department. I offered him a 'competent' departmental secretary within a fortnight, but he expressed grave doubts of public service 'competence' and demanded his own nominee.

Late in August 1946 he telegraphed complaining of the 'scandalous' treatment he had received on staff questions. I replied rejecting any imputation that the Department had not done its best to help him, within the framework of the Public Service Act and Regulations. I added that Evatt was returning to Australia shortly and that I would discuss Tokyo problems with him.

Early in September I met Evatt in Sydney, discussed Ball's requests with him, and received instructions to help solve Tokyo administrative problems. Ball was informed of this, but I refrained from adding that Evatt's mind was concentrated upon the federal elections. In fact, the Minister began to campaign throughout Australia, was often inaccessible to me by telephone, and impatient if I raised with him any but the most important questions of policy.

After one more week, with Evatt still in Western Australia, Ball sent me a telegram containing a blistering series of complaints against the Department, and threatening to resign 'within the week' if his various requests were not granted. I knew that he had real problems, and was prepared to forget the imperious tone of someone under strain in the field; but I regarded the threat to resign just before elections as impermissible in any officer, temporary or permanent. Resignation at such a stage would be highly embarrassing to any government in power. The telegram required a ministerial reaction.

I was unable to raise the matter with Evatt for four more days. I flew to Sydney to meet him on his return there. He continued to Canberra by car, and told me to accompany him so that outstanding matters could be discussed en route. Just before we reached Liverpool I showed him the exchange of telegrams with Ball. He reacted violently, and criticised me for not having informed him in Western Australia by telephone. He dictated a telegram to Ball, ejected me from the car, told me to take the train to Sydney and to telephone the message through to Canberra. It expressed distress at Ball's complaints, which were 'new' to him, undertook to do everything possible to ease the great burdens Ball was bearing, asked for fullest details of staff alterations wanted, and proposed Ball should visit Australia to discuss matters 'in about a fortnight's time'. By the end of that period, of course, the elections would be over.

I had several policy matters to discuss with the Minister, but these he regarded as of secondary importance. Returning to Sydney, I carried out instructions and flew back to Canberra.

The tone of Ball's reply to the Minister's message was entirely different from that in the telegram to me. He explained his difficulties and 'frustrations' in Tokyo, gave reasons why it would not be wise for him to leave Tokyo at that time to report personally in Australia, and sought, *inter alia*, Ministerial help to secure the secretary he wanted.

MacMahon Ball did not resign until the following year and over much more important issues. As Commonwealth Representative on the Allied Council he had an impossible task. Australian policy was to press for a tough peace treaty with Japan, including limitations upon the maintenance of armed forces and upon economic development, to be supervised by an Allied Occupation Army. This was not the policy of India, nor, eventually, of Britain.

Secondly, American policy towards Japan in the early post-war period was dominant. On the Far Eastern Commission in Washington the four Great Powers had rights of veto. This enabled the United States, if it so wished, to prevent a majority recommendation being put into effect—in which case the United States could issue an interim directive to General MacArthur. The United States increasingly favoured a much 'softer' peace treaty with Japan than Australia or New Zealand approved.

Thirdly, the Supreme Allied Commander resented the establishment of the Allied Council, and 'from first to last his senior officers treated it contemptuously . . . on balance, the Allied Council was a fiasco.'[36] According to William Sebald, who himself served for some time on the Council as United States member, 'MacArthur made no secret of his dislike for the Allied Council, which he regarded as an unwanted intrusion into the Occupation and an undesirable vehicle for Soviet propaganda'.[37]

Despite these difficulties, which no Australian representative in Tokyo could have overcome, Ball and his Australian associates did have considerable influence in helping to ensure substantial rural land reform in Japan, which enabled some three-quarters of all farmers to acquire the land on which they worked.

When, in 1947, Dr Evatt visited Japan and apparently patched up differ-

[36] See Greenwood and Harper (Eds), *op. cit.*, p. 248.
[37] *With MacArthur in Japan*, by William Sebald (Norton & Co., New York, 1965), p. 62.

ences with General MacArthur regarding Australian policy, Ball must have felt that the ground had been cut away from under his feet. He has himself commented that reports of meetings between the Supreme Commander and the Australian Minister 'exuded an atmosphere of cordiality and mutual confidence. From that point Australian official policy became remarkably resilient.'[38] Ball's resignation from the Council took effect on the same day that Dr Evatt, reporting in Australia on his visit to Japan, stressed the 'cordiality and friendship' of his reception by General MacArthur and claimed that no country had 'exercised as much influence on American policy towards Japan as Australia'.[39]

The Labor Party won the elections and Evatt retained his portfolios as Attorney-General and Minister for External Affairs. As soon as the election results were clear and Prime Minister Chifley had announced his new Cabinet, I flew to Sydney with a sheaf of outstanding files requiring Ministerial attention. Evatt's Sydney office was in the group of Commonwealth Offices on the higher floors of the Commonwealth Bank Building on the corner of Martin Place and Pitt St. Thither I repaired, but was kept waiting for a considerable time before the Minister would see me. When eventually I was ushered into his room, his manner was such that I came to the conclusion that he had decided to impress me with the fact of his continuing power.

Having disposed of the files after a long interview, he began to question me about the organisation of the Department and to comment about individual officers. He said that a foreign minister was entitled to ensure that particular officials who sympathised with his policy were given the opportunity of putting it into effect. He mentioned two officers by name, and expressed the opinion that they should be promoted. Alan Dalziel, his Private Secretary dealing with electorate matters, was called into the room and asked to support the principle enunciated by the Minister—which he readily did. Evatt seemed to enjoy my additional discomfiture at such a conversation in the presence of a junior official who had nothing to do with External Affairs policy matters.

I found the situation extremely embarrassing. I had no doubt that Evatt was pressing me to promote particular officers, while avoiding an explicit instruction to do so as he knew as well as I that such promotions were the clear responsibility of the Secretary and not of the Minister. As Acting Secretary, I would not have promoted any officers without the Secretary's specific approval. Nevertheless, I felt it unwise to start a further dispute with Evatt by challenging his right to make such suggestions. I therefore listened to what he had to say, and suggested that he would no doubt wish to discuss the matter with Dunk on the latter's return. When the Minister persisted, I remained silent, promising nothing and subsequently doing nothing whatever to give effect to the Minister's wishes.

On 11 September, 1946 Mr Norman Makin, who had been appointed Australian Ambassador to the United States in succession to Sir Frederic Eggleston, presented his credentials. Soon afterwards he was nominated as

[38] Greenwood and Harper, *op. cit.*, p. 253.
[39] Current Notes, Vol. XVIII (1947), pp. 469-70.

Leader of the Australian Delegation to the Second Part of the First Session of the U.N. General Assembly, which was to open in New York on 23 October. The other Australian delegates were Professor D. B. Copland, Professor K. H. Bailey, Paul Hasluck and myself. At that time Hasluck was Counsellor-in-Charge of the Australian Mission to the United Nations, New York.

I need hardly say that I shed no tears at the thought of handing over to Dunk the administrative responsibility for the Department. My main concern was to let him know just what had happened during his absence, and this could not be done by telegram or personal letter. The Secretary was due to return to Canberra some two days after I left Sydney. By great good fortune Dunk's plane from San Francisco and mine from Sydney spent half-an-hour together on the airfield at Nadi, Fiji. I told him what had happened, and as he walked out to his aircraft I thought he looked pretty grim.

The flight from Fiji to Canton Island, which I visited for the first time, was rough and unpleasant. We then flew to New York via Honolulu and Vancouver. As the General Assembly did not begin for a few days, I took the opportunity of slipping down to Washington by train to discuss Assembly problems with Makin and to see how the Embassy was getting along since I left it twelve months earlier. 'Jim' McIntyre put me up, and we gossiped to our hearts' content.

Over the week-end I made contact with other members of the staff. John Oldham had succeeded me as Head of Chancery, and I found that the atmosphere had changed. We now had an Ambassador—not a mere Minister, like Casey, Dixon and Eggleston—who must not be disturbed until ready. The British Embassy practice of referring to the Ambassador as 'H.E.' (His Excellency) had been taken over. Black coats and striped pants seemed more in order. I am afraid I didn't show sufficient reverence for the new dispensation.

Oldham stressed the tremendous changes which had taken place since I left—more work, more staff, a different political situation. When he began, with customary assurance, to express opinions about certain General Assembly items about which he was not well informed, I excused myself. I was happy to return to New York after a friendly conversation with Makin.

In New York the sheer physical complications in carrying out our Delegation work were very substantial. The Australians were accommodated at the Vanderbilt Hotel; our offices were on the forty-fifth floor of the Empire State Building; plenary sessions of the Assembly at that time were held at Flushing Meadows, one-half to one hour by car, depending upon traffic and the driver's experience; Committee Meetings were held at Lake Success, twenty to thirty minutes further away from New York City. In short, we spent anything from one to three hours a day travelling.

As the senior External Affairs officer it was my responsibility to co-ordinate work for Makin's opening speech in plenary, get various people to contribute, throw it together and clear it with Canberra. Eventually it was finished and sent into the Secretariat for translation. Then the Soviet Foreign Minister, Mr Molotov, managed to get his name inserted in the list of speakers ahead of Makin's, and made a provocative speech. This meant a hectic night re-writing certain sections of the completed Australian speech in order to reply to Molotov. Only after Makin's speech was delivered could I concentrate upon my own work in Committee, although I still had to co-ordinate cabled reports by the Delegation to Canberra.

My own special interest and experience in United Nations affairs had been in the security field, which were dealt with in Committee I. But Hasluck was Head of our Permanent Mission in New York, and was acting as Australia's representative on the Security Council. For him to serve on another Committee would have interrupted the continuity of his work and diminished his prestige. I therefore offered to serve on Committee III (Social, Economic and Cultural). Despite the help of Colin Moodie, Alf Body and Mrs Moore, it took me some time to familiarise myself with the new problems, particularly the question of refugees, which was of sufficient interest to the Soviet Delegation to induce Molotov to send Vyshinsky into the Third Committee to do battle. However, things settled down in due course, and I enjoyed the Conference work. Makin was a friendly and tolerant leader who genuinely appreciated the efforts of his team. Although our instructions from Canberra were often difficult and usually critical, the physical absence of Dr Evatt reduced tension within the delegation.

The problem of most immediate importance for Australia during the Assembly sessions was the question of approval of a trusteeship agreement in respect of Australian New Guinea. Responsibility for handling this issue fell upon Bailey, whose expertise in this field was far greater than that of any other member of the delegation. He had been Professor of Public Law at Melbourne University before becoming a special Consultant to the Commonwealth Attorney-General's Department in the later war years; subsequently he became Solicitor-General. At the first election of Members of the International Court of Justice, his name was sixteenth on the list. Had he been one place higher, he would have become a member of the court. Few Australians could have presented our case to the Trusteeship Committee more effectively.

In the result, the trusteeship agreement approved by the United Nations was one with which Australia could be well satisfied. Had the agreement come before the Assembly some fifteen years later—by which time Afro-Asian membership and influence had greatly increased—it is highly unlikely that an agreement as favourable to the Australian point of view would have been approved. Bailey worked day and night, trying to give effect to difficult and sometimes impossible instructions from Australia, and receiving little thanks from Canberra for the results he achieved.

It is the custom at Sessions of the General Assembly for each Committee to report formally to a Plenary Session of the Assembly on the work done. Only when resolutions are approved in Plenary Session do they become Resolutions of the Assembly. These final plenary meetings are normally routine, in that the work of the Committees, on which all Members of the United Nations have the right to be represented, are summarised, explained and endorsed. The proper person to handle them was the Leader of the Delegation, or the individual in charge of the Committee from which the

Report came. No such difficulties were foreseeable in respect of matters dealt with in my Committee.

During 1945 and 1946 I had been absent from my family on official business for some eight months. I was therefore particularly anxious to be home for Christmas. Transportation across the Pacific was infrequent and difficult to arrange. I therefore sought permission by cable to Canberra to leave New York when my work in Committee was finished. In reply, Dr Evatt sent instructions that no member of the Delegation was to leave New York until the last Plenary Meeting of the Assembly ended. As a result, I was unable to join my family for Christmas.

It was not long after my return from New York that I realised that Dunk had decided he could not continue to work under Evatt. When the position of Chairman, Commonwealth Public Service Board became vacant, Dunk applied for the post and Evatt made no attempt to persuade him to stay. On 5 February, 1947 Cabinet approved Dunk's new appointment, which was gazetted on 3 March, to take effect as from 27 March.

This development placed me in the direct running for promotion to the position of Secretary, Department of External Affairs. Of the three officers senior to me, Hodgson had held the post for many years and was unlikely to be returned to it from overseas; Officer and Stirling were at their best in overseas diplomatic activities, which they preferred. While I had few illusions about myself as an administrator, I believed that the responsibilities I had carried out, at home and abroad, gave me the strongest claims to appointment.

Yet I knew perfectly well that Evatt would be unlikely to select me for this most important post in the Department, save on terms, express or implied, which I would not accept. I decided, therefore, to take no positive steps to seek the position, but not to refuse it if it were offered, despite the inevitable and continuing difficulties in relations with the Minister.

At that time the Moscow post was vacant. Evatt had offered it to an Australian whose very distinguished war record and subsequent business activities had made him a well-known public figure. The person invited gave serious consideration to the proposal, but eventually turned it down.

Eventually the Minister told me he was thinking of sending me to Moscow as Australian Minister and of appointing John Burton as Secretary, Department of External Affairs. He asked whether I had any objection to the Moscow assignment. I told him I regarded the Moscow post as important and interesting, but it would involve certain family complications which I would prefer to discuss with my wife before giving an answer.

My wife would have preferred the whole family to stay in Australia, where we could hope to acquire a house of our own and the children could be educated in the company of their friends. But we had taken the major decision to join the Department of External Affairs, which inevitably involved overseas service, and she was ready to accompany me wherever my career led, provided satisfactory arrangements could be made for the children. Neither of us thought that a diplomat should refuse a foreign assignment, except on health grounds. We both agreed that we would seek no favours from Dr Evatt.

After a long night's discussion we decided that I should intimate my readiness to go to Moscow. The twins, then aged seven, would obviously have to come with us. As there was no 'international' school there for foreign children, their education would be a problem. We would make arrangements to receive Australian material from the New South Wales Department of Education, which had a well-developed Correspondence School for children who lived in 'outback' Australia. If necessary and practicable, my wife would act as their teacher; otherwise, a governess would be sought, if we found we could afford one. The two elder children wanted to stay in Australia and some arrangements must be made for them in Canberra until matriculation, after which they would go to a university college.

In deciding to send me to the Soviet Union Evatt, of course, had not the slightest idea of my long-standing interest in nineteenth century Russian literature. For him there were only two problems. First, he wanted as Secretary of the Department, someone more flexible than Dunk and someone less critical of his style and methods than I. Secondly, he had to fill a rather awkward gap in Moscow, where two earlier Australian Ministers had left different kinds of problems behind them.

The first Australian Minister to the U.S.S.R. had been Mr W. Slater, a Labor Party man with parliamentary and trade-union experience in the State of Victoria. When he passed through Washington towards the end of 1942 to take up his post, we found him pleasant and intelligent. Unfortunately, he went to the Soviet Union under the illusion that his Labor Party and trade-union sympathies would make it easier for him to build up close contacts with Soviet officials and facilitate frank discussion. The contrary experience left him disappointed and frustrated. When to this were added the physical difficulties of finding adequate accommodation, food, transportation and other facilities in war-time Kuibyshev, the result was some form of psychological distress after a few months in the country. He returned to the United States from the Soviet Union far from well, but recovered quickly under Western conditions. However, it was not thought practicable for him to return to Kuibyshev, and he went on to Australia. This short period of service in the Soviet Union was embarrassing to the Australian Government.

The next Australian Minister, Mr J. J. Maloney, also had a trade-union background. He was a Roman Catholic, and had a tougher personality. Maloney served in the Soviet Union from 1943 to 1946 and made some impression upon British diplomats there for courage in holding up his end in difficult circumstances. However, his actions during his period of service had not always been diplomatic, and his strong anti-Communist views had become known to the Soviet authorities.

In these circumstances Evatt may have decided to send a career diplomat more likely to keep his personal political views to himself and more inclined to treat the difficulties of living in a particular foreign country as part of the diplomatic game.

I told Evatt that I raised no objection to being posted to Moscow. Then I added that, while choice of a Secretary of the Department was of course a matter for him and for Cabinet, I felt bound to express the personal opinion that Burton was neither old nor experienced enough for the position. He was then aged thirty-two, and had never served on the staff of an Australian diplomatic mission overseas. If appointed Secretary at that stage he would take over the most responsible post in the Service with the disadvantage of finding there were other officers who regarded themselves as equally capable. It would therefore not be easy for him to establish his authority.

This comment must have made some impression on Evatt, as he asked me subsequently to make a formal recommendation to him stating that, in my judgment, Burton was the best qualified to succeed Dunk. This I refused to do. When the announcement was made of my appointment to Moscow and Burton's appointment as Secretary, Evatt took the unusual course of coming to the Department and speaking to a gathering of senior officers. In doing so, he made it clear that he expected everyone to give the fullest support to the new Secretary.

4

SOVIET UNION

April 1947—February 1950

ERHAPS it is as well that the full and precise consequences of decisions
taken can never be foreseen at the time; otherwise, many people would
be less adventurous.

My wife and I expected difficulties during our time in the Soviet Union,
and if these did not always take the anticipated form, were able to adjust
ourselves so far as they affected us directly. What proved much more
difficult to accept were the consequences for our four children.

We had hoped to be able to keep control of the Wynes house with their
consent while the Wynes were still posted overseas, and to sub-let it to a
young External Affairs family who would allow Alan and John to remain in
the house. This proved impracticable. The only arrangements we could make
were for them to sleep in a nearby house run by an elderly widow, and to
have their meals at the Wynes house sub-let to a more senior friend attached
to another Department. In the event, the widow demonstrated the worst
landlady instincts, such as monitoring the amount of hot water used for
baths. It was an unhappy arrangement while it lasted.

Alan was due to matriculate at the end of 1947, and St Paul's College
at Sydney University generously agreed to accept him as a boarder to start a
Science course in March 1948. My wife and I felt it would be unfair to
leave John on his own in Canberra after Alan's departure to Sydney. He
was therefore booked in as a boarder at Toowoomba Grammar School in
Queensland as from the beginning of 1948, mainly because my sister and her
doctor husband had moved to Toowoomba, where after further overseas
training the husband had developed a practice as a specialist in radiology.
Health and educational problems for one or other of the two elder children
developed after we left Australia.

The Department's Post Report on Moscow stressed difficulties regarding
accommodation, food, transportation and clothing. The Soviet Union had
barely begun to recover from the desolation and shortages of war. Supplies
were scarce, expensive and of narrow range. For the Head of Mission and

his family there was a rented house, the ground floor of which served as a Chancery and the second and third floors as a residence. An official car was provided. This reduced the immediate problems to clothing and supplementary food supplies. Further supplies would take at least six months to order, process, despatch and arrive from Australia.

We ordered from Canada a heavy fur coat for my wife and a long winter overcoat with large lapels for myself, together with a fur hat and a fur cap with ear-flaps. After discussion with health authorities in Canberra, I ordered in Australia a large amount of supplementary foodstuffs—powdered milk, fruit juices, canned vegetables and fruit, coffee, tea and other goods chosen to widen the limited diet available from Russian sources. All the Australian members of the Legation staff ordered similar goods from Australia, but the system then in force was very unsatisfactory and in many ways unfair. No action would be taken in Canberra to procure goods ordered by officers in Moscow until a cheque was received in advance for each. There was insufficient supervision of the process of ordering and ensuring urgent despatch, with the result that a member of the staff might be transferred from Moscow to another country before his Australian goods arrived. I was able to change this system in due course.

We had to gamble on clothes for the twins. For overcoats, caps and hats we took with us warm material from Australia, including sheepskins, intending to have overcoats at least made up in Moscow. My wife selected shoes of different sizes for growing children to cover a two-year period, hoping that her guesses would not prove wildly inaccurate. Additional clothes for all of us would be bought in London during a three-week stay there en route to Leningrad. I insisted on travelling to London by ship, both in order to have my first real holiday since 1940 and also to ensure that all our baggage, and food supplies for my family and for members of the Legation staff, arrived in the Soviet Union at the same time as we did.

My salary as Minister was set at £2,500 per annum, and I was to receive in addition a further £2,500 from which to meet all expenses for servants and for Legation entertainment. It was quite impossible to estimate in advance whether this supplementary sum would be adequate, taking into account Moscow prices. Clearly, however, it would be cheaper, as well as desirable, to take with me from Australia an assortment of Australian wines.

Unfortunately my salary and allowances began only when I took up duty in Moscow. In the meanwhile I had to pay for the goods ordered in Australia and abroad. After selling my car at short notice and with the customary capital loss, I found I was £1,000 in the red. An understanding bank manager gave me an overdraft of £1,000, to be repaid gradually after I arrived in the Soviet Union.

At that time bookings to London by sea were difficult to obtain. Eventually two two-berth cabins were secured on the R.M.S. *Orion*, an Orient ship making its first post-war passenger voyage from Australia to England and carrying, for the most part, tourists who had booked months if not years before. Unfortunately, the only available cabins were separated from one another by several decks. As the twins were seven years old, we could not leave them isolated on their own, so my wife and daughter occupied a reasonably comfortable cabin on a higher deck, while my son and I took over the cabin in the bowels of the ship. Special permission had to be obtained for the passenger ship to carry the food and wine as cargo, but in securing this I had the ready assistance of the businessman who had turned down the offer of appointment to my post.

Farewells from children are not the most attractive feature of the diplomatic life. When we said good-bye to the elder boys at Canberra Railway Station, the younger looked rather lost as he realised suddenly that we would soon be thousands of miles away. The night in Sydney was spent repacking our numerous suitcases and trunks, so as to separate out the articles we would need in England from those which need not go through the English Customs. Aboard ship I buried myself as much as possible for the first week, as John had caught impetigo at school and transmitted it to me. My face was heavily marked and I looked as though I had the plague. It was not until we had crossed the Great Australian Bight and were heading out from Fremantle into the Indian Ocean that I felt I could bear to be seen, and that both my wife and I began to prepare for the future rather than to remember the past.

Neither of us knew any Russian, but we had brought aboard grammars and dictionaries and started regular study. Unexpectedly, we were given some help in spoken Russian by one of the passengers who discovered where we were heading. My wife, being much the better linguist, progressed faster than I. In addition, I began to read an English anthology of Russian literature which she had given me in Washington in 1945.

The anthology included a wide range of extracts and some complete works, from the Lay of the House of Igor—late twelfth century—to post-revolutionary verse and short stories. I was already familiar with the main works of Dostoevsky, Tolstoy and Turgenev, but was glad to be introduced, inter alia, to Krylov's Fables, the verse of Pushkin and Lermontov, Gogol's play The Inspector-General, Belinski's famous Letter to Gogol, Chekov's Three Sisters, and Zoshchenko's ironic short stories.

The voyage itself was uneventful. We found the artificial gaiety of a tourist ship unattractive, but we were too busy to be disturbed. My wife was looking forward to our short stay in England, which she had never visited. Her ancestry is English, with a dash of French, and she had been inclined to suspect that my letters to her from England at times betrayed my wholly Scottish descent. As it happened, we struck three weeks of perfect Spring weather. The parks of London opposite where we were staying were at their best—full of burgeoning trees and gardens lined with tulips of every shade. The twins made the acquaintance of Peter Pan in Kensington Gardens, and revisited him when they passed through London again, regarding him as a personal friend of the family. We all spent a day in Oxford, partly to see my old college, of which David Ross was now Provost. He escorted us personally through parts of the college, walking hand in hand with Mary through the Library and gravely answering her unsophisticated questions.

In London I made contact with the Soviet Embassy, which insisted on sending two junior officials to see us off on the *Sestoretsk*, which was to take us through the Baltic Sea to Leningrad. The ship was not due to leave until 3.30 p.m., but we had to vacate our rooms early—the hotels were still over-full. We had breakfast, packed, and were driven to the wharf. Our first surprise was to learn how small the ship was on which we were to travel. The *Orion* was a fairly large ship, and one climbed to its decks up a steep gang-plank. When Mary saw that she had to walk down a gang-plank to board the ship she showed signs of uneasiness which began to clear when we found that our adjacent cabins were much bigger than those we had occupied on the *Orion*.

We checked carefully to see that all our baggage was aboard, and then went to the dining-room where the Embassy officials were waiting for us. Unfortunately we had had no lunch, and had not yet discovered that Russian hours for meals were quite different from ours. Vodka was produced, however, and we had to drink toasts on an empty stomach. The officials were extremely polite, spoke fair English, and did their best to make us feel at home. Eventually they left the ship, some food was made available to hungry parents and famished children, we drew out from the wharf and moved slowly down the Thames. Although a few of the passengers were Western Europeans travelling to Stockholm, Helsinki or Leningrad, most were Russians and the general atmosphere was already entirely Russian.

The journey across the North Sea was rough and unpleasant, and we were glad to enter the sheltered waters of the Kiel Canal. Once through, we had calm weather for the rest of the trip and enjoyed it greatly. The twins soon made friends with Russian children and joined in their games without any apparent linguistic embarrassment. In no time they had learned their Russian numbers skipping, and by the time my wife and I could repeat the words from one to ten, the twins were teasing us by counting backwards. The Russian stewardesses were friendly although the passengers, mostly officials, were more cautious and stand-offish.

A voyage in the Baltic Sea is an enlightening experience for an Australian. From my schooldays I had seen the world as depicted in a Mercator's Projection map, and when I thought of Asia or Europe instinctively looked up. Experience overseas had corrected this outlook to some extent, but it was in the Baltic Sea that for the first time I began to look down on Europe, as a Russian or a Swede presumably does. The point of view is very different.

We found sharp contrasts between Stockholm and Helsinki. Sweden had escaped the ravages of war, and Stockholm gave every outward sign of affluence. Practically everything could be bought there if one had the foreign currency, and food and service in hotels were far better than in London. In Helsinki we were impressed by three things: the architecture, the paucity of goods for sale and the courageous spirit of the people. Parliament House put the temporary counterpart in Canberra to shame, despite the greater Australian population and resources. Goods in the shops were extremely limited in range and quality. Yet in the market-place near the ship's berth there were many flowers for sale, and people were buying them.

The approaches to Leningrad are not at all impressive. The pallid northern sun could easily be confused by an Australian child with the moon. Low-lying shores, shallow waters, the fortress of Kronstadt and a few artificial islands—there are no distinguishing features of mountain or contrasts of light and shade to mark contact with the vast Russian Empire. Indeed, even in summer when access to the port is not inhibited by ice, the foreigner with a minimal knowledge of history cannot help thinking of the terrible human cost of the creation of this Czarist capital city amidst marsh and swamp, due to the iron determination of Peter the Great.[40]

The establishment of the new city of St. Petersburg was visible evidence that Peter had indeed 'wrenched Russia westwards, for good and ill'.[40] Over the years foreigners have been attracted by its broad avenues and the many European-style buildings constructed in due course. But even today one is struck by the inadequacies of the site as a port, taking into account shallow waters, winter ice and the risks of flooding in spite of all the granite-lined canals designed to discipline the flow of the river Neva. In certain conditions of wind and tide, the Neva banks up and overflows—with consequences vividly described by Alexander Pushkin in his poem 'The Bronze Horseman'.

As the *Sestoresk* edged slowly into its berth, Mary pointed to a Russian soldier in rather unkempt uniform who took up a position near the gangplank. In her clear, childish voice, Mary asked the first of many questions about the Soviet Union:

Q. 'What's that man got on his shoulder?'
A. 'A rifle.'
Q. 'Why does he need a rifle?'
A. 'Because he is a soldier.'

In the circumstances, other explanation was impracticable.

As a foreign diplomat taking up his post as Head of Mission in Moscow, I was accorded every courtesy by the Russian Immigration and Customs authorities and was passed quickly through their hands. We were met in Leningrad by the Australian Chargé d'Affaires, Noel Deschamps, who escorted us into rooms at the Victoria, a European-style hotel furnished in nineteenth century western fashion. As usual, the children were famished when we arrived after mid-day, so we ordered 'breakfast' and, during the lengthy time while it was being prepared, unpacked what was necessary and cleaned up.

On the dressing-table there was a hairbrush and Mary picked it up to use. My wife had looked at it earlier, and said 'Don't use that, it's dirty'. She then took a brush out of her bag and gave it to Mary. Later, after we had been out of the room, we found that the brush had disappeared. It was a first reminder that whatever we said while in the Soviet Union was likely to be heard, unless we were in the open air. I found it difficult to conceive that anyone could be so stupid as to put us on notice for such an irrelevant reason. But the Russians are extremely sensitive regarding any adverse comparison between conditions in the Soviet Union and elsewhere. Perhaps the intention had been to replace the brush before our return, although this too we would probably have observed.

Deschamps had arranged for us to travel by train to Moscow next

[40] See *Survey of Russian History*, by B. H. Summer (Duckworth, London, 1947), p. 265.

evening by the Red Arrow, which left Leningrad about 11 p.m. As I was anxious to see as much of the city as possible, and to hear from him all the latest news about Legation and staff problems, he and I went for a long walk during the afternoon.

We inspected the impressive area near the old Czarist Winter Palace, crossed a few bridges over the Neva, admired the Admiralty spire from a distance, and walked through the Cathedral of St Isaac, whose massive, gilded dome later became a signpost of the city whenever I approached it by air. Like other capitals which had deteriorated under the stresses and dislocations of war, many of the buildings looked rather shabby and in need of paint or repair. But this did not substantially diminish the sense of amplitude of planning and achievement in this city of architectural style, broad boulevards and impressive squares.

Deschamps' conversation, however, related mainly to Legation administrative problems. Food, accommodation, transportation; food, accommodation, transportation. How often I was to hear these words during the next three years, and how much time and energy had to be devoted to the problem of ensuring that members of the Australian staff and their dependents survived in reasonable comfort and with a reasonably optimistic outlook in a country of harsh climate where war-time shortages still persisted and a tradition of low standards of living for the bulk of the population still survived.

Darkness had not yet fallen when, after thirty-six hours in Leningrad, we ensconced ourselves in a four-berth *wagon-lit* compartment of the Red Arrow Express. I had little inclination to sleep. My eyes focussed upon every detail of the sombre landscape until about midnight. Then I dozed, but was awake again when dawn came about 3 a.m. Soon peasants could be seen emerging from simple huts, moving out to work in the fields while the short summer lasted. When Mary woke, she pulled out pencil and paper and began to draw what she could see through the window. She had a keen eye, and some gift for drawing. With her simplicity of approach what she drew revealed more of the Russian countryside and the living conditions of its inhabitants than she realised.

At the railway station in Moscow we were met by other members of the Australian staff. My family and I climbed into one of the two maroon-coloured Legation Buicks, after being introduced to the Russian chauffeur. We were then whisked away to the Australian Legation, followed by members of the staff in the other car. It proved to be a small, three-storey building fronting a very wide street—Sadovaya Samotechnaya—which ringed the city and which at one time had served as a fortification. At the entrance a Russian policeman, who saluted smartly, was posted.

On the ground floor was the Legation Chancery, with barred windows and combination lock safes to keep cyphers and secret documents. The second floor consisted of a dining room, two smallish living rooms, a breakfast room and two bedrooms. On the third floor were two attic bedrooms, in one of which lived a Russian maid, Paulina. It was a great relief to unpack and stow away our substantial baggage, secure in the knowledge that it had reached Moscow. As for the several tons of food brought for family and staff, we had ensured that it had reached Leningrad. After that there was nothing to do but possess our souls in patience until the Russian railway authorities admitted in answer to regular questioning that the goods had reached Moscow—as they did, several weeks later.

By the standards of diplomatic missions in other countries, the Legation building met only minimal requirements and had a number of disagreeable features. No Head of Mission would choose to live in the same building as the Chancery if he could avoid it, as the privacy of his family is inevitably reduced. Moreover, this meant that my family and I were in a significant sense the permanent watchdogs of the confidential information below. There was no permanent Australian guard and the staff lived in various parts of the city—often miles away and with access made difficult because of snow and ice during the long winter. In principle, it was my ambition never to leave the building without one adult Australian occupant. But this meant that, if my wife and I had an evening engagement away from the Legation, we had to bring a member of the Australian staff to the building during our absence. There is a human limit to such unofficial duties, which tend to cause resentment if imposed too frequently. As a result, there were times when my wife and I refrained from going out to theatres or concerts—our main diversion from the strains of Moscow living—in order not to test too far the patience and loyalty of other Australians who had their own problems and needed their own diversions.

The dining and living rooms, with their decorated, somewhat pretentious ceilings, were rather small. Yet we soon came to realise how much better off we were, for purposes of private living and official entertainment, than those foreign Heads of Missions who had acquired or been assigned no building of their own, but had to live in hotels.

One awkward feature of the house was that the kitchen was on the ground floor and removed from the dining-room by a flight of stairs, so that food tended to be cold by the time it was served. As hygiene was important, not least because our young children were with us, my wife began a rather hopeless attack upon the cockroaches she found in the kitchen, while I tried with indifferent success to minimise the effect of summer flies. After considerable delay, and at a cost of some £80 from my own funds, I had fly-screen doors made and erected at appropriate points, but we had a perpetual battle with the servants who found them inconvenient and tended to prop them open.

The Soviet Union sends its own nationals overseas to act as domestic servants and chauffeurs, but the Australian Treasury regards the costs of sending Australians overseas to perform equivalent duties as unjustified. So we had to engage Russians for these purposes and only those officially approved by the Soviet authorities could be employed. We had no doubt that they were all called up from time to time for interrogation as to our habits, conversation and policies, but they were simple, untrained people who certainly derived no pleasure from reporting on us. Indeed, the domestic servants soon developed a kind of limited loyalty to my family. They were particularly fond of our children, and would have spoiled them if allowed.

We became quite attached to two of the various maids we had during our stay in Russia—Paulina and Lisa. On one occasion Paulina waited on table so badly during a formal dinner party, doing every conceivable thing wrongly, that my wife asked her later whether she had been ill. With some difficulty we discovered that she had indeed been very upset—on our behalf. She thought we had made a mistake in seating the American Ambassador on my wife's left, and the Belgian Ambassador on her right. Was not the United States a much more important country than Belgium? Was not the American Ambassador a *bolshoi chelovek* (an important person)? In fact, the American Ambassador in question, Admiral Kirk, had arrived only recently and was, according to protocol, junior to the Belgian Ambassador. We could scarcely be angry with Paulina for being concerned for the reputation and dignity of the Australian establishment.

On another occasion Lisa accompanied my wife to the Mostorg in the middle of winter to buy something. As usual, the store was terribly crowded and my wife found difficulty making her way through the throng. Lisa soon sized up the situation, took up a position in front and forced a passage, swinging her elbows in all directions. 'You see', she commented when she got to the counter and paused for breath, 'here in Russia we are very free'.

The two chauffeurs, on the other hand, were rather a nuisance. Ivan was a somewhat reckless Russian, apt to drink too much on occasion and inclined to drive too fast, presuming upon the status of a diplomatic flag flown from the car on official occasions. He was friendly enough, and sufficiently interested in self-improvement to keep a copy of Tolstoy's *War and Peace* in an accessible place while waiting for us to come out from some function. But the last thing I have wanted in any foreign country—least of all in the Soviet Union—was to run over a pedestrian, who could easily slip on icy winter roads.

One of the earliest words I had to learn was the Russian for 'slow' and 'slowly', but Ivan could never keep his foot off the accelerator for long. On one occasion he was drawing into the curb to deliver us at a Foreign Minister's reception. There was a diplomatic car ahead of us, from which the Dean of the Diplomatic Corps was alighting. Ivan thought the Dean was taking too long, and tooted the horn to hurry him up. I had to apologise to the Dean and arrange for someone who could speak better Russian than I to tick off Ivan and threaten dismissal if a similar incident occurred again. Eventually Ivan beat up one of the domestic staff during a drinking bout, and had to be dismissed.

Victor was more intelligent and quieter than Ivan, but less reliable and lazier. Keeping cars in running order in the winter climate of Moscow involved a considerable amount of work. Victor did only as much work as he was forced to do, and seemed not the least concerned if I were late for an appointment, or if some member of my staff failed to arrive at the Chancery on time.

At the rear of the Legation was a substantial area of land enclosed by an attractive, reddish brick wall about six feet high. In one corner was a double garage, with a few rooms overhead occupied by about fifteen men, women and children. The first sound my wife heard from the garage corner was made by a child who had whooping cough. There lived, amongst others, the dvornik or yard-man and his half-blind, adult daughter Sacha. Amongst other duties, he had to keep the pavement and nearer part of the street in front of the Legation clear of snow and ice in winter, cut wood for the stoves, tidy up the courtyard at the back and attend to a few straggling plants in summer. In winter we used to pity these two, shovelling away snow or picking away at ice with a crowbar in cold we could not have borne for more than half an hour or so.

At the foot of the yard was a 'cultural object', a stone reproduction of Diana the Huntress, with bare legs, broken arms and a short Grecian dress. Even in the middle of summer, she was scarcely credible in a Russian setting, but when in winter the snow covered her feet and ankles and thickened the top of her head she was positively ridiculous. In 1948, returning with my family from a Conference in Geneva, we passed through Paris and took the children to the Louvre, where Mary spotted a bronze statue of Diana. 'Look!' she cried, 'there's Diana and she's got both her arms!'

After we left Russia, one of my successors asked the Soviet authorities for permission to remove Diana from the courtyard. The reply was given that, as she was a cultural object, she must be removed by the local author-ities themselves. Apparently the workmen found great difficulty edging Diana from the soil or rock to which the base of the statue was attached. After several unsuccessful attempts one of the workmen lost patience, picked up a sledgehammer, bashed Diana in the middle and threw the pieces into a truck.

As soon as practicable after my arrival in Moscow an appointment was arranged for me to see the Foreign Minister, Mr Molotov, in order to request a date for presentation of credentials. On guard at the entrance to the Foreign Ministry was a Russian in uniform wearing a blue cap, indicating that he belonged to the M.V.D. or security organisation. As I was about to enter, another Russian in civilian attire came out. I recognised him immediately as someone who had served with me on the U.N. Preparatory Committee meetings in London. Since we had got to know one another fairly well, I smiled and held out my hand; he looked straight through me and passed without a word. It was my first reminder that Russians with whom one had had some official relationships abroad had no ambition to confirm this when they were at home, particularly within sight and hearing of one of the 'blue cap' boys.

My interview with the Foreign Minister was purely formal. He was polite, wished me well, and said he would let me know what date would be con-venient for presentation of credentials. On the prescribed date the Chief of Protocol, Mr Molochkov, appeared at the Australian Legation in full diplomatic uniform to escort me to the Kremlin in a Zis limousine assigned to the President of the Praesidium. My diplomatic staff followed in a legation Buick.

The procession came to a halt at one of the entrances to the Kremlin, where most cars are usually searched, but we were waved through. After a short drive within the walls to the relevant building, we were shown into an ante-room. The Chief of Protocol explained the procedure, and we were ushered into the presence of the President of the Praesidium, Mr Shvernik.

H

Although at that time Stalin was absolute master of the Soviet Union, he did not hold the title of Head of State, which was an honorific post without great influence. I did not once meet Stalin during the whole of my time in Moscow, although I was present at a few special outdoor ceremonies, such as the May Day parade in the Red Square and the annual Air Display which he attended. Once or twice when we were at the Bolshoi Theatre it was rumoured that he had been sitting for a time at the back of a box next to the stage which seemed empty, entering only after the lights had been dimmed and leaving again before they came on. He certainly showed no desire to mix with others in enclosed spaces, and was accessible to only a very few members of the Diplomatic Corps—for the most part, the British, American and French Ambassadors.

At the credentials ceremony my short, formal speech was delivered in English, as my knowledge of Russian was elementary. The text, in accordance with diplomatic custom, had been transmitted to the Soviet Foreign Office well in advance, and Shvernik's reply took account of what I had said. Photographers were then allowed to come in with cameras and movie cameras. By the time they had finished I felt that no Russian official would have any difficulty in identifying me in the future. And indeed, when my wife and I left our first formal Russian reception, an officer charged with the responsibility of calling diplomatic cars needed no prompting from me as to the name of the country I represented.

After the credential ceremony Molochkov accompanied me back to the Australian Legation, where we offered him the traditional glass of champagne. He was a friendly and efficient man, who spoke fluent French and was always helpful when approached by me or any other Head of Mission. He had the respect of members of the Diplomatic Corps, combining politeness with dignity.

I was now officially Australian Envoy Extraordinary and Minister Plenipotentiary, with a Foreign Office identity card certified by a Deputy Foreign Minister and the Chief of Protocol and the right of access to the Foreign Minister and his subordinates. Contrary to common belief, the task of advancing the interests of one's country as a diplomat is both complicated and exhausting, particularly in a country like the Soviet Union, where privacy is minimal and political, as distinct from physical, security a matter of constant concern. One is never off duty.

The Head of an Australian Mission in Moscow has not only his own problems and those of his family; the personal problems of members of his staff can affect their stability and produce highly embarrassing results. An unimaginative administrative decision in Canberra about such matters as salary, allowances and leave may be the last straw. One has to steer between sympathy on the one hand and mollycoddling on the other, but to ignore such problems is dangerous. I soon found that no more than half of my time and energy was available for policy matters and representational duties, including contacts with other diplomats; the rest inevitably had to be devoted to administrative problems if the Australian team were to survive in reasonable health and with a sensible outlook towards their work.

Visits to the Foreign Office were not frequent as representations regarding matters of high policy were rare and informal discussion of the kind I had enjoyed in Washington was impracticable. Such visits never took place before midday, as Stalin's habits of work affected the whole bureaucratic machinery. Only on some special occasion would I seek to see the Foreign Minister, who was dour and uncommunicative, though polite. Most interviews were with Deputy Foreign Ministers, of whom Vyshinsky was the senior. If at all possible, I arranged an appointment with him rather than Gusev or others, who were likely to say only 'Your representations will be considered'.

Vyshinsky, on the other hand, was not typically Russian. His name suggests a Polish origin, but in any event he was voluble, rather proud of his capacity to make ironic jokes, and easily angered. When one left Vyshinsky one at least had some vague idea of his reaction, and could guess as to the probable reply. In the Soviet hierarchy he had no power. At international conferences he was merely the Russian 'voice', but at least the ideas he expressed were intelligible to a westerner. Though an unpleasant personality, as his activities in the purge trials of the 1930s make clear, I much preferred official dealings with him to dealings with more typical Russian bureaucrats who never smiled, never expressed an opinion, but maintained a frustrating silence until a decision was taken elsewhere. Not that one expected tolerant or generous treatment from Vyshinsky: he knew quite well that he was living dangerously from day to day, and that he could be dispensed with or disposed of at any time if he failed to conform strictly to Soviet policy laid down from above.

In the Moscow of 1947-50, contacts with the Diplomatic Corps were vital. I could expect to obtain no confidential information from any Soviet official. It was therefore all the more important to seek information and views from Embassies with far larger and more specialised staffs, greater experience, somewhat closer contact with Russians, and higher prestige. For an Australian, this meant primarily contact with the British and American Embassies, although certain other missions were important. As soon as I had presented credentials, I began my round of calls—a time-consuming business in a city of some fifty diplomatic missions.

In recent years, as representatives from newly-independent Asian and African countries have swollen substantially the numbers of the Diplomatic Corps in some important capital cities, Heads of Mission from such countries have tended to resent the alleged waste of time involved in following the practice of calling upon their older colleagues. Some have pressed for abolition of the old system, and argued that it would be sufficient if a new arrival gave a party for the Corps as a whole and, so to speak, completed calls in a single day. In Tokyo, at a later date, the Corps agreed to abolish the traditional return call, in order to save time and energy, but I strongly opposed any change in the system of the initial call.

In Moscow, Tokyo and Bonn, I found my own calls on individual senior colleagues of very great value. It makes all the difference to meet a man for half an hour in his own setting, to begin the process of tapping his experience and views and those of his country, and of making known to him the special interests and outlook of Australia. Such a call is not only an act of courtesy; it identifies the visitor and the person visited to one another, and is an essential basis for more serious conversations later. To meet at one function all the members of the Corps—even if they accepted such an invitation—would be to identify no one; it would be impossible even to recognise most at a later date.

In this frame of mind, I called upon the Dean of Corps, the Ambassador of Nationalist China, and began to make my rounds. It was not long before I found that my most valuable contact in Moscow would be the American Ambassador Lieutenant-General Bedell Smith, who for almost three years treated me with courtesy and friendliness and, after I had obtained his confidence, with frankness.

The British Ambassador, Sir Maurice Peterson, on the other hand, was polite, stand-offish and uncommunicative. Members of his staff, when new Commonwealth Missions were established, were most helpful so far as the practical problems of settling in were concerned. The British Minister, F. K. (later Sir Frank) Roberts, was approachable and gave me wise advice that it was necessary to understand Russia before 1917 before one could judge how much current policy was Communist or flowed from attitudes and policy of much earlier times. It was he who insisted I must read at once *Letters from Russia*, written in 1839 by the Marquis de Custine. His successor, G. W. (later Sir Geoffrey) Harrison, was also friendly, but both men had to work within the limits laid down from above. Sir David Kelly, who succeeded Sir Maurice Peterson in February 1949, was even more remote than his predecessor. Meetings of Commonwealth Heads of Missions, held about once a fortnight in the British Embassy, were rather artificial and not very rewarding.

Few would expect a British Ambassador in Moscow to disclose fully and contemporaneously his negotiations with the Soviet authorities on matters of high policy, with the risk of inadequate security in one or two Missions and, in the case of Australia, of sudden intervention by Dr Evatt in the United Nations. Normally such information would be relayed to Dominion Governments through London, probably after some delay, at a chosen point of time, and after dilution through the British Commonwealth Relations Office.

But background and atmosphere can be conveyed, perhaps bilaterally, to those Commonwealth Diplomatic representatives regarded as capable of handling both without prejudicing British interests. The difficulties in matters of major importance are admitted. Yet it has been my experience in Moscow, Tokyo and Bonn that American Ambassadors felt able to overcome such difficulties and to judge that a greater degree of frankness served a common purpose.

Unfortunately quite a number of senior members of the British Diplomatic Service at European as distinct from Asian posts have their eyes concentrated upon the 'Inner Circle'—those countries, mostly in Europe, which are regarded as important. To them, Australia was unknown, distant and irrelevant, if not just a plain nuisance. It might be useful for Russians and others to know that the cars of Commonwealth countries, flags flying, entered the British Embassy once a fortnight. This contributed to British prestige as a world power. Frank discussion of policy matters inside the Embassy, however, was quite another matter. There were, of course, exceptions, but it was rare to find an Englishman who had not served in Southeast, South or East Asia, or perhaps Washington, who regarded Australian colleagues as desirable and useful partners.

Another valuable contact was the Swedish Ambassador, Mr Sohlman—a shy, cautious man with a Russian wife (*ancien régime*) and a deep knowledge of the Soviet Union. He stayed on after I left Moscow in 1950 and was still there, as Dean of the Corps, when I re-visited it in 1963. From him I received, not confidential information, but guidance as to how the Soviet press and current events should be interpreted. He knew the Russian language well, and his modest suggestions were worth much more than the confident assertions of many other Heads of Mission.

I also made a point of keeping in touch with the two French Ambassadors who served in Moscow in my time, first General Catroux and later M. Chataigneau. Experience has taught me to respect highly the French Diplomatic Service. In different capital cities I have found that inquiries as to the French point of view are appreciated and are a useful check on British and American views.

Our relations with the Canadian Embassy were close and valuable—closer, oddly enough, than those with the New Zealand Legation. In this particular instance, however, the latter was staffed with persons of such different points of view and with so little experience of security problems as to limit the extent to which confidential information could be discussed.

The New Zealand Minister, Mr Boswell, was a member of the Labor Party and a member of Parliament until he lost his seat. When he arrived in Moscow he expected, like the first Australian Minister Mr Slater, that his political background would facilitate frank discussions with Soviet authorities. As this did not happen, he was greatly disappointed. Although he was tougher than Slater, and lasted the distance in the uncomfortable conditions of Moscow, by the time I appeared he had grown very critical of the Soviet Union—much more so than I was or became.

Boswell's First Secretary had not been trained as a diplomat, but as an academic. He was a linguistic genius. A lecturer in the Classics by trade, I have heard him speak fluent French, Italian and Russian. In due course he left the New Zealand diplomatic service and appropriately held a Chair of Russian in England prior to his early death.

There could have been few greater contrasts within one diplomatic mission than that between the New Zealand Minister and the First Secretary. The former was a simple, likeable man, but rigid in outlook and out of his depth; the latter was flexible, interested in comparative linguistics, ready to send his children to Russian holiday camps, untrained in the ways and responsibilities of governments, with something of the academic's scorn regarding the need for strict security measures, always ready to argue with anyone about anything, often for the fun of the thing.

Apart from general training and experience in a foreign service, I had special reasons for taking the utmost care for security in our own Legation. When Mr Maloney left the Soviet Union, Noel Deschamps took an opportunity to have our Legation premises 'vetted' for listening devices. Quite a number were found in the walls, and one was flown out in the diplomatic bag. This discovery embarrassed Dr Evatt. It was impossible for him to take no action in the matter; on the other hand, he did not want it made public, as this could lead to criticism in Australia of the very existence of our Legation in Moscow and complicate efforts in the United Nations to form bridges between East and West. Knowledge of the discovery was therefore limited to the minimum number of officers in the Department, and I was personally instructed by the Minister not to mention the matter to anyone.

It was my understanding that Deschamps was instructed to lodge a formal protest with the Soviet Foreign Office, where he was told that, if listening devices had indeed been found in our building, they must have been put there by the Germans during their attack on Moscow. When I arrived in Moscow the best advice I could obtain from one or two knowledgeable foreigners was that the Germans had never penetrated to our area of the city. I doubt whether the Foreign Office expected their story to be believed. In any event, it was inconsistent with the date of part of a newspaper which had been found near one of the machines, and which suggested that the work had been carried out during a major 'remont' or repair programme after Maloney left.

I soon discovered that I would have to organise public information of the kind readily available in Western newspapers and over Western radios. So far as Russian papers and periodicals were concerned, a number of Western Missions contributed financially to a translation service run by themselves. It was so efficient that a summary of the day's news from Russian sources would appear on my desk at about 4 p.m. the same day. This summary enabled us to keep in speedy touch with what the Russians were saying to their own people and to the world at large.

If an item seemed of particular interest, we would ask our own translators to provide a full text. There were two of these, Mr Valsimakis and 'Volodya'. The former was an elderly Greek who had married a Russian and become more or less tied to the country. He was not a Communist, but had become used to life in Moscow and stayed on, either because he had difficulty in getting an exit visa or because such a visa would have been denied to his wife. Volodya was a young man, son of a Canadian who had left the country of his birth hoping to find the Promised Land in the Soviet Union. There he burned his boats and found it impossible to leave. Volodya spoke excellent English, and Valsimakis very fair English. Neither had access to our confidential documents, but translated formal communications to and from the Foreign Office, while they were useful in our dealings with the various Russian employees of the Legation.

We could be quite sure that *Pravda* or *Izvestia* would contain the full text of a speech by Molotov or Vyshinsky at the United Nations, but their reports of speeches by Western statesmen would be truncated, distorted and slanted for propaganda purposes. Within two or three months, therefore, I had arranged to receive by diplomatic bag copies of *The Times* of London, the Paris edition of the *Herald Tribune*, and the London *Economist*. Each day we received copy of a bulletin of radio news distributed to friends by the

American Embassy. In addition, I wrote to Sir Ernest Fisk, then working in London, for advice about a good radiogram and aerial. He was very helpful, and in due course I imported the necessary articles. From then on we would listen to the B.B.C. in the early morning and about 7 p.m., so that I was well-informed from non-Russian sources of what was happening in the world at large before making any calls or attending lunches or dinners. The radio was designed to give good short-wave reception and enabled me, on rare occasions, to hear with difficulty broadcasts from the Australian Broadcasting Commission. On one of these I listened to the broadcasting of Australian federal election results, which I learned as speedily as anyone in Australia.

Problems of administration took up an inordinate amount of my time and energy. In Washington, London and many other posts, most of these would be dealt with, under the supervision of the Head of Chancery, either by specialist officers or individual members of the diplomatic staff, and the Head of Mission would become involved only when general principles had to be decided or pressure brought to bear upon a recalcitrant Department in Canberra. But in the Soviet Union the Head of a small Mission like the Australian was constantly involved.

Accommodation for the staff was a constant worry. As all housing was controlled by the Soviet Government, representations to the Foreign Office or appropriate Soviet authorities had to be made at a high level to overcome difficulties or prevent inordinate delay. It was not that the Russians were unsympathetic or unhelpful, but in 1947 everything was still in very short supply. Standards for their own citizens were low; they were accustomed to the rigours of their own climate and inured over the centuries to hardship. It was not easy for them to understand the psychological and physical strains imposed upon Australian men and women by climate, lack of suitable diet and lack of privacy. There was a constant battle to secure, first, temporary hotel accommodation, and secondly, suitable flats within reasonable reach of the Legation. In the meanwhile, particularly when I was out of Russia at a conference, or my wife had to return to Australia to be with the children during the long summer holidays, the Australian Ministerial Residence housed one or other member of the staff as well.

When the supplementary food I had brought from Australia eventually reached Moscow, there was much joy amongst Australian members of the staff who had placed orders and sent cheques in advance to Canberra. All of us, of course, had Soviet ration coupons which enabled us to buy locally certain foodstuffs, not cheaply, but at a minimum price. Other foodstuffs could legally be bought at peasants' markets, but at a greatly inflated price. The basic Russian diet consisted of good bread, kasha (porridge), potatoes, cabbage and a flavouring of fats, usually in soup. Meat was so expensive that most Russians could afford it rarely—unless they were important members of the Communist Party, the military hierarchy, ballerinas or the like who had special privileges. Australians could not have survived in reasonable health on such a diet, and supplements to basic local food were therefore very important. In due course I managed to persuade the Treasury Department in Canberra to provide a sum of £1,000 to purchase supplementary foodstuffs in Australia which could be drawn upon by the staff in Moscow and paid for by them only when so drawn. No doubt these arrangements were discontinued as more foreign currency became available, enabling orders to be placed in nearer Scandinavian countries, but in my time Australia was the most accessible source of supply. We would import butter from Australia, pay freight to Leningrad, a high freight from Leningrad to Moscow—and still find that it cost us much less than local butter.

But if the Australian staff was pleased with the arrival of the food I had brought, the Russian servants were very disappointed and discontented. Before my arrival a temporary member of the staff, an Australian, had assured them that I would be bringing with me a lot of food and that the servants would get their share. This led them to expect that they would receive not only what my wife and I thought necessary to supplement their Russian supplies, but also that they could buy from us more food at foreign prices. They knew that a number of diplomatic missions permitted this. Such a procedure was, however, a breach of Russian regulations which I had no intention of permitting. I had already heard strong rumours that another temporary member of the Australian staff had bought watches overseas and sold them at substantial profit on the black market. Action of this kind was sure to become known to the Soviet authorities and might well prejudice the activities of the Legation in various directions, raising doubts as to our good faith. It could scarcely help me in my relations with them if one of our servants was discovered selling a tin of Australian vegetables on the black market—a considerable temptation at prevailing prices.

Partly as a result of my attitude, however, we had constant trouble with our servants regarding our own food supplies. Whatever amount of sugar or powdered milk my wife put out for the servants, it all disappeared immediately. All of them had relatives in Moscow or elsewhere, and we soon found that generosity on our part merely meant that our supplies were being stretched out to feed an indefinite number of people at a distance. As my responsibility was to provide food for myself and my family, for entertainment, and for the use of our servants only—not the whole population of the Soviet Union—we were reluctantly forced to lock up our supplies and to dole out fixed amounts for the servants at periodical intervals. This was an awful nuisance, and quite contrary to my wife's notions as to how a household should be run.

Transportation was another constant worry, especially in winter. There were only two office cars and a station waggon, and the former were often needed to bring Australian staff into the Chancery and to take them home. We could not have them standing in the snow waiting for buses, freezing to death or liable to catch influenza in the crowded vehicles used for public transportation. But this responsibility made it difficult, at times, to arrange my own movements or to use for necessary family purposes the car supposedly made available to a Head of Mission.

Again, some staff dissatisfaction stemmed from the fact that Moscow conditions called for the exercise of human qualities which did not fit into any categories recognised by the Commonwealth Public Service Board as deserving recognition. Thus, it was important to ensure that goods ordered abroad for official purposes were actually delivered before a calendar year ended. Limits were placed by the Soviet authorities upon the importation of such goods—perhaps because they could bring very high prices if sold on the black market. These limits varied with status, an Ambassador being entitled to bring in the highest amount and his staff lower amounts, in quantities diminishing with rank.

On one occasion we were expecting a new car, a Humber Pulman (Gumber Poolman to our drivers) and regular enquiries as to whether or not the car had arrived elicited only the answer 'Niet' (No). On 30 December, in the middle of winter, a telephone inquiry elicited instead the answer 'Da' (Yes). One of the clerical members of my staff, as a result of unusual pertinacity, some knowledge of Russian, and at the cost of mild frost-bite, managed to clear the car before 31 December—a notable achievement. Because of this, and other local administrative efficiency, I tried to have his salary increased. I was completely unsuccessful.

My main staff problem, however, was how to devise ways and means of alleviating the psychological strains and stresses for Australian men and women living in the Russian communist environment. These were greater for non-diplomatic than for diplomatic officers, as the latter had wider knowledge and experience of non-Australian cultural backgrounds, and at least some knowledge of foreign languages.

Try to imagine the reactions of shorthand typists, who might have been born in Canberra and never been out of Australia, posted overseas for the first time and finding themselves temporarily marooned in Minsk by fog or snow on the way into Russia. To them, the strange new world of language, climate and food must have seemed like a sudden descent into an icy version of hell, with all the difficulties of verbal communication and fear of the unexpected. (Similarly, a Russian arriving in a Western city for the first time in his life tends to expect to see a capitalistic octopus crawling round the next corner.) In such a case, our first task would be to make telephonic contact with them from Moscow, explain that Russian money was being forwarded to cover their needs, informed them that they could telephone the Legation for assistance, and explain that they would be met on arrival in the capital.

Even in Moscow, all was strange and different. The Russian language seems forbidding in itself, because the Cyrillic alphabet is different from the Latin and the words could not even be spelled out, let alone understood, until after a period of study. One could not hop into a bus, drop into a shop for a purchase, or buy movie or theatre tickets without difficulty and without help. The feeling of isolation from the world in which one has lived was strong, and a sense of uncertainty fostered a degree of resentment or even fear, exaggerated by problems of accommodation, food and transportation.

To minimise these effects upon the staff, I managed in due course to persuade the authorities in Australia to agree that every Australian, irrespective of status, should be provided with the means of getting out of Russia for one month in every year, preferably during the winter. After a year in Moscow in my time there, any Australian was likely to feel an impulse to assert his nonconformist individuality by shouting out criticism of the system in a public place, or by throwing a brick into a plate-glass window of a shop in Gorky Street to protest against some of the artificial food products exhibited there, or the prices one had to pay inside.

But the recuperative effects of a few weeks in Stockholm, for instance, were remarkable. In those days foreign airlines were not permitted to operate over the Soviet Union, or to land there, except when special permission had been obtained for a delegation to arrive for purposes of political or trade negotiations. Leaving Moscow for Sweden, one travelled in Russian planes, without air hostesses and without food other than that brought by the traveller. At Leningrad all passengers had to leave the plane while passports were collected and scrupulously examined. Even then, one was still on Russian territory and within Soviet control until disembarkation at Helsinki, in Finland.

The atmosphere in the Swedish plane between Helsinki and Stockholm was utterly different. A tall, blonde, Swedish air-hostess would place an unnecessary pillow under one's head, offer with a smile some titbits of food unprocurable in the Soviet Union, and engage in careless conversation with a freedom which seemed striking. On disembarkation in Stockholm, one drove to a hotel where there was no one on guard to check movements in and out and where one found an amplitude of food disastrously designed to upset a stomach conditioned to Soviet diet. New arrivals in Moscow contracted 'Moscow tummy' before they settled down; it was irritating to have to endure the reverse process in Sweden.

In Stockholm one could wander around the streets, walk up to someone to ask the way or the time of day, order goods at Nordiska Kompaniet for transmission to Moscow, and browse through a range of unforbidden books in numerous bookshops. After a week, the impulse died to look over one's shoulder before talking to anyone. In three weeks, the sense of isolation, lack of privacy and general frustration more or less disappeared. After one more week, one returned to Moscow with a reasonably cheerful outlook on life, ready to finish the current winter or serve one more year before transfer out of the Soviet Union.

I also succeeded in getting approval from Canberra for funds to cover the costs of at least some Russian language lessons for every member of the Australian staff. This was obviously desirable for Australian diplomats, but it took some time to convince Canberra of the desirability of enabling a typist, for instance, to learn something of a language in which she would never become proficient.

My case stressed the need to minimise the strangeness of Russia, the uncertainties and perhaps suppressed fears of the unknown. An Australian girl walking down a Moscow street would see a long Russian word or phrase at the entrance to a building, and would have little idea whether it designated the Headquarters of the Secret Police or a place to buy pencils. If she knew the Russian alphabet, she could spell out the word, look it up in a dictionary, relieve her mind of uncertainty and develop a sense of interest and confidence. In addition, relationships with Russian servants or employees became so much easier when one knew simple words and phrases in daily use. All this helped keep one normal and stable at a post where it was very easy to run off the rails.

There was one problem of great concern to myself and my wife which we did not succeed in solving—the education of our two younger children. While the Australian material which we received from the Correspondence School run by the New South Wales Department of Education was valuable, we were too far away and communication with Moscow was too difficult to permit the quick return of prescribed work done by the children and the return of corrected work to make the system practicable in our case. At that time all private letters to and from Australians posted in Moscow were included in the diplomatic bag, to ensure safe and uncensored arrival. But the bag took a fortnight to arrive. This meant that work sent back to Australia by the children could not be returned corrected for at least six weeks, and possibly longer—by which time the children had lost interest.

For a time my wife took over the responsibility of correction, but this procedure also proved impracticable. We considered the possibility of procuring a governess from England, but the expense involved, together with the need to find accommodation and food for someone who might not in the end prove suitable ruled out this possibility. The only alternative was to try to send the twins to Russian schools. They had picked up a considerable amount of Russian during the summer vacation, and the experiment seemed worth trying.

At first I applied for Mary to be enrolled in the Ballet School, and Peter in the Music School. These were specialist institutions, with selected personnel and students, where special training benefits seemed possible and a number of risks, including health risks, might be minimised. Both applications were refused, but we were told the children could attend ordinary Russian schools if desired. Eventually, after discussion with the children, we agreed. We told the twins that it was an experiment which might or might not work. If successful, they would have the unusual opportunity of acquiring a new and important language; if, on the other hand, they found the work in Russian too difficult, or were unhappy in their schools for whatever reason, they would be withdrawn immediately.

Peter's hair was clipped very short, like all the Russian boys, and he began to attend a designated school for boys only. I think that every effort was made by his teachers to help him settle in, but he did not like the school and was rather unhappy. After a few weeks we withdrew him. Mary had a happier and more successful experience at her designated school for girls. Less individualistic that Peter, and more gregarious, she remained there for about six months. We had been informed that the Soviet authorities preferred that she should not arrive at school in a diplomatic car. This seemed reasonable enough to us, so my wife used to take her to school on foot. During the winter months, this involved a half-mile walk through snow.

On the way to school some of Mary's class-mates would catch up, take her arm, call her 'Marshenka' (the Russian diminutive of her name), and encourage her in winter to slide, like the other children, on icy sections of the pavement where the snow had been hardened by foot-traffic. She managed to keep up with her class, and on one occasion gained the highest mark for handwriting. This did not seem to please a visiting inspector, and Mary never again achieved a comparable mark. Her teachers were friendly and helpful. We did not encourage Mary's playmates to enter our Legation, though a few did, because all entries would be noted by the policeman on duty, and we feared that interest in a foreign child might prejudice the future of her friends or their families.

Eventually, however, health reasons made it necessary to withdraw Mary from school. During the severe winter both she and Peter became ill, probably with scarlet fever. This experience forced us to change our plans to keep the children with us in Moscow. While they remained, they attended classes given by an English governess brought in by friends at the British Embassy to look after their own children.

During our first Moscow summer my time was very largely taken up with the usual problems of settling in. There were calls to pay upon about fifty Heads of Missions, return calls to receive, lunches or dinners arranged by a number of friendly Heads of Missions to attend, and return hospitality to give. Walking, or driving we saw something of the city. The Kremlin area, the Red Square dominated by the garish, twisted spires of St. Basil's Cathedral, the Bolshoi theatre and other impressive buildings, Gorki St and its (apparently) well-stocked shops—these are the things which a foreigner on a short visit is shown and remembers. But we had only to walk a few blocks away in any direction to see the older and more typical Moscow. Apart from a few well-preserved old houses decorated with charming wood carving, the general impression in those years was one of dilapidation— leaking gutters, peeling plaster and poorly lit rooms.

One of the first lessons I learned was the realisation that most generalisations about the Soviet Russia are misleading. Contrasts were tremendous, and the answers to so many questions turned out to be both 'Yes' and 'No'. Are the Russian Communists inefficient? 'Yes and No.' I bought a small children's bicycle, with hard rubber tyres, for the twins to ride in the courtyard. The back wheel proved to be out of alignment with the front wheel. A foreign friend commented: 'These Russians, they are hopeless with machinery'. But when I attended the annual Air Day Display, there seemed no inefficiency about the military aircraft flying overhead.

Again, many books were printed badly on poor paper. No doubt wartime restrictions upon the use of scarce resources were partly responsible. Yet I was able to buy in the second-hand shops a limited edition of the Lay of the Host of Igor, magnificently printed by Communist authority on splendid paper, with coloured Palekh illustrations of unusual quality. This was a national monument, published to increase Soviet prestige and develop Russian pride.

In short, if the authorities decided that something was sufficiently important to the State, finance and other resources would be made available and efficiency of achievement demanded—whatever the deprivations in other directions.

Again, the foreigner taken to inspect a special, show-piece collective farm where conditions and results seem excellent is unlikely to be shown average and less efficient farms. This attempt to conceal has a long tradition in Russia. Centuries before the Communist Revolution the Czarist authorities were expert in preventing foreigners from seeing what they were not wanted to see. Indeed, local conditions were concealed even from the Czarist Head of State. The Potemkin villages built in order to deceive Catherine the Great on tour were designed to mislead her into thinking that the conditions of the serfs were better than they were.

What is seen by the visitor to Russia depends, of course, not only on the access he is given to people and places, but also upon his own temperament—what he is predisposed to find. Today it seems incredible that specialists on social conditions like Sidney and Beatrice Webb could have written on conditions in the Soviet Union in such an uncritical and optimistic manner. Western Europeans frequently refused to believe in the existence of labour camps on a vast scale during the Stalin era, despite the published evidence of a number of Russians and of foreigners who had been detained in them. Yet the basic facts are incontrovertible.[41]

Secrecy, of course, has been used by Czars and by Communist leaders alike not only to conceal from the foreigner what it is thought he should not know, but also to prevent Russian citizens learning facts about the outside world which might disturb them and lead them to question the benevolence of their own governmental system. 'The motive of the Czars was essentially the same one which has animated their Communist successors—namely, to protect a hierarchic society against what they deemed the debilitating ingress of the outside world.'[42]

We soon learned to appreciate the unusual degree of camaraderie amongst members of the Diplomatic Corps in Moscow. Common experience of difficulties engendered a degree of sympathetic interest and support which I did not find elsewhere. Whenever one met in later years someone who had served in the Soviet Union, particularly during one's own period of service, there was immediate recognition of a mutual bond. It was almost as if all such people felt that they wore the same old-school tie.

One illustration of mutual support in Moscow itself was the farewell accorded to members of the Corps who had completed their term of service. I have been present on occasions when friends saying good-bye at the railway station, for instance, seemed almost to take temporary command of the station. At times they would sing some ironic doggerel, in Russian, set to a well-known tune, ignoring completely the disapproving faces of Soviet officials on the station who seemed puzzled at the significance of what was taking place and unable to devise any practicable means of stopping it.

When the train moved off, with cheers, and tears in some eyes, those left behind would return to their places of residence to gossip over a drink. One of the many Moscow stories I heard on arrival dealt with such an occasion, when an American who had farewelled a colleague at the station commented to friends over a subsequent drink: 'Oh! well. It was time for Bill to go. Moscow had got him down. Not like me, of course. I'm quite

41 See *The Great Terror. Stalin's Purge of the Thirties*, by Robert Conquest (Macmillan, London, 1968).
42 *Peace and War in the Modern Age*, F. R. Barnett, W. C. Mott, J. C. Neff (Eds) (Doubleday, New York, 1965), p. 55.

all right.' As he spoke, he ran his hands through his hair, rolled his eyes, gesticulated wildly, and reached for another drink.

At the end of August 1947 I was instructed from Canberra to proceed to New York as one of the Australian delegates to the second regular Session of the United Nations General Assembly, which opened on 16 September. This meant that my wife, after only a few months in the Soviet Union, would be left in Moscow to look after two young children for a period of three months, and that the Legation would be left in the charge of a Third Secretary, as Noel Deschamps had been transferred elsewhere. Fortunately the Third Secretary in question, John Rowland, was a future Australian Ambassador to Moscow, and handled Legation problems more competently than one would expect from someone of his age and experience. So I left for New York via Leningrad, Helsinki and Stockholm on the same plane as the recently appointed first Indian Ambassador to the Soviet Union, Mrs Vijaya Lakshmi Pandit, sister of Prime Minister Nehru.

In New York I suggested to Dr Evatt that I should be assigned once again to the Third Committee, dealing with Social, Humanitarian and Cultural Matters. Although my primary interest was in political and security questions, which were handled by the First Committee, it did not seem to me to make sense to become involved in public disputes with Soviet Representatives in that Committee—which was more or less unavoidable for the Australian representative—and then to return to my post in Moscow to try to do business with the Russians.

Dr Evatt agreed, but a good deal of my time was taken up drafting one of the three Oliver Wendell Holmes Lectures on the United Nations which Harvard University had invited Dr Evatt to deliver. This first lecture dealt with the Charter Conference held at San Francisco in 1945, and was to be followed by a lecture on the operation of the United Nations, drafted by Alan Renouf. Renouf was a member of the Australian Diplomatic Service, attached temporarily to the United Nations Secretariat, but released for a period for Dr Evatt. A third lecture on the future of the United Nations was planned, but I had nothing to do with that and I do not remember who drafted it.

In my draft I devoted a fair amount of space to the 'domestic jurisdiction' clause of the Charter (Art. 2 (7)) which, in my judgment best reflected Dr Evatt's influence at the Conference. To my great surprise, Dr Evatt deleted much of what I had written about this particular clause and, in effect, mentioned it only in passing. Yet during his speech in the House of Representatives on 30 August, 1945 moving the second reading of a Bill to approve the United Nations Charter, the Minister had stressed the importance of the clause he had succeeded in having included in the Charter protecting 'Australia's own vital interest'. 'In particular', he said, 'it assures the retention of the general principle that it is for each nation to determine for itself—without outside intervention—the composition of its own population'.[43]

I came to the conclusion that whereas in 1945 Dr Evatt had wanted to emphasize Australia's right to determine its own immigration policy, later he found it embarrassing to apply such a strict interpretation of domestic

[43] Current Notes, Vol. XVI, No. 6, (1945), p. 187.

jurisdiction in certain issues affecting other countries. Commenting upon the changing attitudes of Evatt towards Art. 2 (7), Professor Norman Harper and Mr David Sissons have written as follows:

> Reviewing the policy of the Australian Labour Government generally on the matter of domestic jurisdiction, it is difficult to find a basic consistency. At San Francisco, Australia claimed that inclusion of the promotion of human rights and the full employment pledge as principles of the United Nations did not withdraw such matters from domestic jurisdiction. In the next two or three years Australia tended to support the reference of issues of competence to the International Court; but such support was often hesitant and unenthusiastic. Yet in the Indonesian, Spanish and religious trials issues, Australia actively attacked the claim of domestic jurisdiction.[44]

It must be admitted, therefore, that Australia contributed to the process in the United Nations which, especially under the pressure of new Asian and African members, narrowed substantially the range of operation of the domestic jurisdiction clause—a process which can still have important consequences for Australian dependent territories.

During the Assembly Session the Soviet Union tabled a resolution condemning 'reactionary circles' in the United States, Greece and Turkey as 'war-mongers'. The Soviet representative, Mr Vyshinsky, used very vituperative language in pressing his Government's case, which was strongly opposed by the United States and other representatives. Evatt decided that the debate was having harmful consequences and tabled a resolution designed to mediate between accuser and accused. The Australian resolution urged *all* members of the United Nations to take positive measures, excluding censorship, to encourage fair and accurate reporting of foreign affairs and to promote the dissemination of information reflecting the desire of all peoples to avoid a third world war.[45]

In the result, neither the Soviet nor the Australian resolution was approved. In their place a resolution jointly sponsored by France, Canada and Australia condemning all forms of propaganda in all countries designed to provoke a threat to the peace or act of aggression, and requesting all member States to take appropriate steps to promote friendly relations among nations based upon the purposes and principles of the Charter, was carried unanimously. The Resolution, as adopted, also referred to the Conference on Freedom of Information and the Press which was to be held in Geneva in 1948.

On this occasion the Session of the General Assembly ended on 30 November, 1947, and I was able to return to Moscow in time to be with my family for Christmas. My wife and children met me at the airport, where I saw Mary and Peter in their winter clothing for the first time. In their heavy overcoats they looked almost as wide as they were tall. I had bought some presents for the servants in the United States. Although Christmas is not recognised as a time for celebration in the Soviet Union, New Year takes its place. When New Year arrived, I was astonished at the similarity of the festivities to those we have at Christmas. Decorated pine-trees with presents

44 Harper and Sissons, *op. cit.*, p. 164.
45 See Keesing's Contemporary Archives, p. 8935.

hanging on them, a gentleman called Grandfather Frost dressed remarkably like Santa Claus—and, of course, deep snow all around.

During my absence in the United States Rowland had several awkward problems to handle. The first related to an Australian Jewish family—husband, wife and children—who, like Volodya's parents, had come to the Soviet Union expecting to find Utopia. They had been sent to the Jewish settlement of Birobijan, where they found living conditions terrible. Somehow or other they managed to take train to Moscow under the subterfuge of passing through to a Soviet border city, and walked unexpectedly into the Australian Legation hoping to obtain help in securing exit permits, so that they could return to Australia.

As they still had Australian passports, Rowland did everything he could for them, and there was an unconfirmed report, hardly credible, that after continuing to the border town they did manage to leave the Soviet Union eventually. Rowland obtained from them a detailed report on Birobijan which was the first direct information on this subject available to the diplomatic community in Moscow. I still find it difficult to believe that anyone who knew from personal experience the precise conditions in Birobijan would have been granted an exit permit.

Secondly, the Legation truck, a vital piece of equipment, became snowbound in the countryside outside Moscow during the long Russian winter. As winter approached, the servants begged my wife to send out the truck to forage for potatoes, cabbages and carrots. As she had come to realise the importance of these for the Russian staff as a whole, she agreed and Rowland approved. Supplies were difficult to procure, and the truck was sent out, in charge of two Russian servants, on three occasions. During the last excursion, snow fell heavily. After considerable delay the servants returned, explaining that the truck had been left at the house of a relative until the roads cleared at the end of the winter.

Old Moscow hands laughed at the simplicity of Australians, who had not learned that work and profit was available in the countryside for men with a truck when vegetables were being gathered in the fields. We will never know whether our servants deceived us regarding their activities in the countryside. But there was no doubt about the bill which they presented to me covering some living-expenses while they were trying to return to Moscow, and their train-fares from the nearest country station.

The most serious problem which Rowland had to face while I was in New York was the insufficiency of Russian roubles to meet the requirements of the Legation and staff until 31 December, 1947. On my return to Moscow I had to give this matter urgent attention.

When I first arrived in the Soviet Union I learned that all Diplomatic Missions had to make formal application to the Foreign Office for the amount of roubles estimated to be necessary to run their respective establishments in the forthcoming calendar year. One reason why Soviet approval had to be obtained was that foreign missions were entitled to a diplomatic rate of exchange which was more favourable than the ordinary rate.

Wages and other Legation accounts were paid in cash, not by cheques, as amounts placed in Soviet banks might simply be withheld during some emergency. Foodstuffs and other goods were also paid for in cash, as there were no credit accounts. In these circumstances it was necessary to keep far more currency in our Legation safe than the Department of the Treasury would have allowed in Australia.

The application for roubles for 1947 was made by Noel Deschamps towards the end of 1946, when there was no Australian Minister in Moscow and the date of arrival of a new Minister and the size of his family were unknown. The amount of roubles sought by Deschamps was thus lower than the sum proved necessary after my appointment and arrival.

When I left Moscow for New York in mid-September 1947, the adequacy of our rouble allocation was still unclear. As the end of the year came closer, however, Rowland saw that we would not have enough to see us through, and arranged an interview at the Foreign Office to explain the circumstances and to seek an additional allocation. While he was not promised a favourable reply, he had the impression that the official with whom he discussed the matter realised that we had a strong case.

As time passed without an answer he arranged another interview and pressed for a decision. On this occasion he was told that the Legation's application had been refused. The situation was explained to me as soon as I returned from New York, and I took up the matter with Vyshinsky immediately. Our case was completely justified, and I argued it with confidence. Vyshinsky made no promise, but said that the matter would be looked at again. To my surprise and irritation we again received a negative answer.

The Soviet authorities rarely give relevant reasons for their decisions, and this was no exception. One can only guess what was in their minds. Presumably they knew that an announcement of devaluation of the currency was about to be made. It had been rumoured for months, and many Russians who had roubles hidden away went on a buying spree, purchasing food or drink which they could consume, or books, lamps or other property which they might hope to sell without too much loss after devaluation. So far as foreign Missions were concerned, it was not their business to worry about the effects of devaluation upon Soviet citizens; nor was it thought likely that devaluation would be so handled as to prejudice the value of roubles held by Diplomatic Missions.

The blow fell on December 14, 1947 when Moscow radio announced a currency reform which included devaluation of the rouble and abolition of rationing. For every ten roubles held by Russians and foreigners alike, only 1 new rouble would be exchanged. This scale of devaluation was varied in respect of roubles held in bank accounts, smaller accounts suffering less than larger accounts, but as the Australian Legation had no rouble account in any bank, such provisions did not affect us.

The effect of this decree upon foreign Missions was serious. The American Embassy, for instance, held large sums in old roubles which lost ninety per cent of their value overnight. Our losses were less, because we were so short of roubles. Nevertheless, we had to face the situation that, until the New Year came and a new allocation was received, there would not be enough

I

local currency for the Australian members of the staff to buy food and other necessary commodities.

In these circumstances there was only one thing to do. Until 31 December, 1947 we drew upon our reserves of Australian food to cover staff needs as a whole. I took comfort from the fact that I had ignored the views of some of my friends as to the quantity of supplies to take from Australia. In due course I found that the representations I had made to Vyshinsky helped us to obtain a far more adequate allocation of roubles for the year 1948. These, however, were made available at the new diplomatic rate of thirty-two to the pound sterling instead of forty-eight. In other words, the costs of foreign representation in Moscow rose considerably, and the Australian tax-payer, through the Department of the Treasury in Canberra, had to pay the higher bill.

The Diplomatic Corps in Moscow was very annoyed that the Soviet authorities had not excepted diplomats from the effects of devaluation, and the British Ambassador took the lead in urging a collective protest to the Soviet Foreign Minister. At that time the Dean of the Corps was the Chinese Ambassador, representing Nationalist and not Communist China. Sir Maurice Peterson pressed him to call a meeting of the Corps to discuss the question, but the Dean showed no inclination to follow this advice. As Peterson was next in seniority, he took the bold course of calling a meeting of Heads of Mission which I attended. First in English, then in French, the British Ambassador put a strong case for protest, and seemed at first to be carrying the well-attended meeting with him. I had authority from Canberra to join in a collective protest if there was substantial support for such action within the Corps.

But the Russians had sent in their Eastern European colleagues to prevent any such protest, and they did this with great skill. One challenged the right of the British Ambassador, who was not the Dean, to call the meeting. In any event, he added, a meeting of the Corps was not an international conference, where decisions might be taken by majority vote. Each Head of Mission represented an independent sovereign government, and could not be bound by any such majority, large or small.

Both these points were well taken, and might have been sufficient in themselves to prevent any decision on the matter. But then another Eastern European diplomat arose and said, in passing, that it would be a pity if, after any such collective protest, the Soviet authorities were forced to disclose publicly the names of those diplomatic missions or members of their staffs who for long had been operating illegally on the black market, to their own substantial benefit. Even a newcomer like myself had heard strong rumours to that effect about a number of Missions. Whether the rumours were true or not, it soon became obvious that a majority would not support a collective protest, and the meeting closed without any decision being taken.

The effect of the currency reform upon Soviet citizens is well illustrated by the comments of the American Ambassador, General Bedell Smith:

> Except for bread, and a few other staples, prices remained at the same high level as before the currency reform. Thus, the ability of the indi-

vidual to acquire more food or more goods hinged on his ability to earn more money, and to earn more money he had to turn out more work.

Few persons in the United States realise how hard a Russian already had to work for the little he received, and what a great strain was put upon his physical and mental resources in being forced to increase the duration and speed of his labor. At the time the currency changed, we calculated that a Soviet worker had to work 4 hours and 57 minutes for a dozen eggs, 14 hours and 5 minutes for one pound of coffee, 1 hour and 10 minutes for one pound of wheat bread, 1 hour and 10 minutes for one pound of sugar, 2 hours and 4 minutes for a package of cigarettes, 104 hours and 30 minutes for a pair of men's shoes, 107 hours and 30 minutes for a pair of women's shoes, 580 hours and 15 minutes for a man's wool suit, and 252 hours for a woman's dress.

His counterpart in the United States worked 38 minutes for the dozen eggs, 22 minutes for the coffee, 6 minutes for the bread, 5 minutes for the sugar, 9 minutes for the cigarettes, 7 hours and 15 minutes for the men's shoes, 5 hours and 32 minutes for the women's shoes, 28 hours and 4 minutes for a man's wool suit, and 12 hours and 52 minutes for a woman's wool suit.[46]

It was only after I returned from New York that I learned what winter means in Russia. By that time my wife was an expert, having seen winter start. As the cold season approached, the double windows in houses were sealed up and only a tiny section, the fortka or fortochka, opened for a brief interval each day to let in some fresh air. In Moscow, snow lies on the ground for about five months, from November to March inclusive, although sometimes it begins earlier or ends later. Sunshine is the exception rather than the rule, and hours of daylight are extremely limited. Warmth becomes as important as food, for without either one dies.

As winter settles in, traffic in the streets slows down, trucks sometimes fail to start, and the weary pedestrian battles cold and wind, wrapped in the warmest clothing available. Most wore valenki—felt boots rising to the calf of the leg, with a rubber underpiece for those who can afford it to keep out water or moisture. The traditional women's headgear is a shawl, wrapped around the head to cover the ears, and spreading over the shoulders. Men wear caps with flaps which can be turned down to cover the ears—fur caps for those who can afford them. Overcoats are long, especially the sleeves, so that hands can be withdrawn as far as possible inside.

In winter the policeman on duty at the entrance to our Legation was warmly clad, but nevertheless worked only a four-hour shift. When a ray of sunshine shone through my window—which was rarely enough—I would try to go outside immediately for a short walk. Wrapped in a long, wool-lined coat with wide fur collar buttoned up under my chin, my hands buried in long fur gloves and a Canadian fur cap with ear-flaps on my head, I could last no longer than half-an-hour tramping through the snow in the bitter cold. Even then, I had to hold a handkerchief over my nose most of the time.

Inside the house we could make do during the autumn with Russian stoves

46 *My Three Years in Moscow*, by Walter Bedell Smith (Lippincott, New York, 1950), p. 139.

set in walls to heat two rooms at once when stoked with wood—a major operation. But when the winter came we relied upon central heating from a furnace in the basement. Unfortunately it was impossible to regulate the furnace in such a way as to distribute warmth equally throughout the building. If the Chancery on the ground floor was kept reasonably warm, we froze upstairs; if the residential section of the house was kept warm, the Chancery was cooked. Much wood had to be sawn in the courtyard to keep the large kitchen stove and the furnace working. A dissatisfied dvornik or servant charged with responsibility for the heating can easily make his meaning clear by sending up inferior wood or failing to attend properly to stove or furnace.

In our time it was a constant battle with domestic servants and other Russian employees to survive. In Russian terms, all foreigners were rich and all diplomats had unlimited resources to call upon. Why not then press them, with all the skill of Russian peasants, for maximum consideration by way of salary, allowances, privileges, food, imported clothing and all the rest for the employees themselves, their children, and their grandmothers, aunts and other relatives, within the compound, in Moscow, or far afield?

Our general relations with the servants were good. They had their little ways and sometimes had to be disciplined, but they also had many attractive human qualities. They wished us no particular ill or inconvenience. But the conditions of their life were so hard, and the battle for existence so severe and traditional, that each individual or family felt justified in pursuing immediate interests without sentimentality or qualms.

Winter inevitably reduces all outside activity. To compensate, there has to be a splurge of activity during the long summer months. One does not repair a street, or change the tram-lines during the winter if one can possibly avoid it. If something goes wrong during the winter this is much more serious than the same misfortune during the summer. In our Legation broad stairs led up from one floor to another, covered by a light-well with double glass at the top. Once we had the walls of the light-well repainted, at considerable cost and trouble. When winter came my wife and I went to the theatre. When we returned and walked up the stairs we found to our astonishment two bricks and scattered glass resting on the stairs. On looking up, it was obvious that they had come through the glass covering the light-well, which was now open to all the rigours of the weather. The bricks, no doubt, had come from a tall, unfinished building on the adjoining block, either blown off by a strong wind or accidentally pushed off. The next day we made the strongest representations to Burobin, the Russian agency which dealt with repairs, for urgent replacement of the glass, but it took three weeks of constant pressure before the work was done. Once again, it was not that the Soviet authorities were unsympathetic; there just wasn't enough glass to go round. While we waited for the repairs, the snow poured into the light-well, the newly-painted walls were streaked in all directions, and the temperature inside the building dropped substantially.

The Russian theatre was the biggest factor in keeping us sane and cheerful during the long, dark winter months. At that time there were about twenty-five theatres in Moscow, all, of course, run by the Government. As a Head of Mission I was entitled to two seats at the most elaborate of these, the Bolshoi Theatre, on all occasions except when the whole theatre was taken over for some special purpose. The seats were not dear, when compared with the price of other commodities. Every ten days a theatre programme was published, and we would pore over this to decide what we wished to see. Often I had conflicting engagements, but there were more than enough times when I was free to gain a fair impression of the quality of Russian productions as a whole.

During the first year we tended to concentrate upon the Bolshoi, which was the most elaborate and splendiferous of all the theatres. There the lavishness of the entertainment contrasted violently with the drabness of surrounding Russian life. The building was of European style, with a large interior similar to opera houses in the West. The stage, however, was enormous, extending right across the interior at its widest extent. When opened to full depth, the distance from the footlights to the back of the stage seemed almost as great as from the footlights to the serried tiers of boxes beyond the farthest seat of the Stalls. Thus a performance of Swan Lake took place on a stage which contributed a sense of amplitude which I have not experienced in any other theatre.

The scenery and dress was striking. When Boris Godunov strode on to the stage in the Moussorgski Opera of that name, his clothing and adornments seemed no less impressive than those of a real Czar of all the Russias. On backdrop scenery there were extraordinarily realistic images of Kremlin Churches, or the Red Square. In mass scenes a couple of hundred people might be on the stage, moving about while artificial snow filtered down from above. The contrast with poverty and deprivation outside the theatre was so great that one wondered how the Soviet authorities dared to put on such a show, lest riots be provoked.

But the theatre was an expression of national pride, both for the Government and the audience. For the latter, it was also a form of escapism from the harsh realities of normal life. The Bolshoi was a show-place to which visiting foreigners were taken. The audience would include diplomats, high-ranking Soviet officials, Party members and members of the Armed Forces, together with representatives of the proletariat, such as Stakhanovites who had exceeded prescribed norms of work. Their tickets were a reward for helping put government policy into effect.

My first reactions to the Bolshoi were overwhelming. Here was colour, light, movement, grace and interest in a drab and dreary world. But in time one became more critical. The lavishness was overdone; socialist realism demanded that a horse be brought on to the stage when it would have been better for his rider to have dismounted in the wings; political twists of famous nineteenth-century Russian literary works became somewhat irritating.

Yet I have rarely been more deeply moved by theatrical productions than by the performances at the Bolshoi of *Romeo and Juliet* in its ballet form, with the prima ballerina, Galina Ulanova, in her prime, playing the part of Juliet; or by the same ballerina in the ballet version of Pushkin's poem, *The Fountain of Bachiserai*.

Boris Godunov stirred me for different reasons, both in the form of the original Pushkin play and its operatic adaptation. So much of Russia, past and present, flowed through its lines that I saw the opera four times, half expecting it to be taken off at any moment when the authorities realised the nature of its message for a European—and perhaps for a Russian.

Boris had come to the throne by arranging for the rightful heir to be disposed of at Uglich. He was quite an effective Czar, but however many battles he won against a Pretender who had no legitimate claims to the throne, he could not defeat the myth that there was some Pretender with a better claim than Boris. To me the moral to be drawn was that they who live by the sword will eventually suffer defeat, but the Soviet authorities obviously did not interpret the story in this way. While they doctored the Pushkin version by exaggerating the part played by the 'people' in the downfall of Boris, they actually left in the section where the holy fool publicly accuses Boris of his crime.

They also failed to excise the unforgettable scene where the monk Pimen, writing in his cell, bears witness to his responsibility to record historical truth:

> One more, the final record, and my annals
> Are ended, and fulfilled the duty laid
> By God on me, a sinner. Not in vain
> Hath God appointed me for many years
> A witness, teaching me the art of letters;
> A day will come when some laborious monk
> Will bring to light my zealous, nameless toil,
> Kindle, as I, his lamp, and from the parchment
> Shaking the dust of ages will transcribe
> My chronicles, that thus posterity
> The bygone fortunes of the orthodox
> Of their own land may learn, will mention make
> Of their great Czars, their labors, glory, goodness—
> And humbly for their sins, their evil deeds,
> Implore the Saviour's mercy. . . .[47]

When we became somewhat tired of the lavish background of the Bolshoi, and our knowledge of the language had improved, we spent more time attending performances at the Little Theatre and the Art Theatre. Here the style was more subdued, the audience less official, the acting excellent. In due course I saw there Chekov's *Uncle Vanya*, *The Three Sisters* and *The Cherry Orchard*. Before I reached Moscow I had developed little interest in Chekov, regarding his work as rather sentimental. In the Moscow setting, however, I found his plays infinitely poignant, reflecting the passing of an old society.

Other outstanding performances were given of Griboedov's *The Misfortune of Being Clever*, Gogol's amusing play *The Inspector-General* which is still relevant in Communist Russia, and a dramatic version of Gogol's *Dead Souls*. Indeed it was the theatre, together with some instrumental

[47] *Poems, Prose and Plays of Alexander Pushkin*, A. Yarmolinsky (Ed.), (Modern Library, New York, 1936), pp. 342-33. Translation by Alfred Hayes.

music, which did most to keep foreigners sane by taking their minds off administrative detail, drab surroundings and daily frustrations.

Within three months of my return to Moscow from New York Mary and Peter fell ill. For some time my wife had noticed in both of them some general inability to adapt themselves to the rigours of the Russian winter. Every effort was made to get them out of the heated house into fresh air for exercise and sunshine, but there was so little sun that it often disappeared before the children were rigged out in their heavy winter overcoats and other protective clothing. We had bought an excellent sledge for them in Sweden, and my wife took them out whenever practicable to near-by parks where they could slide down small hills, emulating the skills of surrounding Russian children.

Russian doctors were called in after we had decided to keep the children in bed, but there was no agreement on the diagnosis. It is our belief that they had scarlet fever, which in Moscow was a notifiable illness requiring transfer of the patient to a Russian hospital. While we had every confidence in the goodwill of Soviet authorities and the desire of the doctors to look after the children as best they could, we had no wish to see Mary and Peter disappear into a Russian hospital for up to a month, where they would be in strange surroundings, out of our control and subject, perhaps, to rather antiquated treatment with inadequate facilities. While in bed at the Legation, Peter had been given 'cup' treatment which was painful, distressing and, in the view of an English doctor, utterly ineffective.

It was fortunate, therefore, that the children's illness was not diagnosed as scarlet fever—whether on medical grounds, or out of a desire to allow us to keep Mary and Peter at home we will never know. Gradually their condition improved, but they were both very run down and Mary had to give up attending her Russian school. It became increasingly clear to my wife and myself that neither child should stay in the Soviet Union through another Russian winter.

While they were still recovering, I received instructions from Canberra to lead the Australian Delegation to a United Nations Conference on Freedom of Information and the Press, which was to open in Geneva on 23 March, 1948. As I had been away from my family in New York and the children were ill, I had not the slightest desire to go. My objections, however, were overruled in Canberra.

Fortunately, someone had told me that a Swiss trade delegation was in Moscow negotiating with the Russians, and that they had come in a Swiss plane—a rare occurrence. When I rang the Swiss Ambassador about a visa, I asked when the plane was due to return to Switzerland. As the probable date fitted in with my obligations in regard to the conference, I asked tentatively whether there was any room on the plane for me. The answer was a friendly 'Plenty of room. We shall be glad to help.' A sudden inspiration made me ask on the spot whether, in that case, there might be room also for my wife and two children, who needed to recuperate in a climate different from Moscow. The answer was in the affirmative. It did not take my family long to decide to seize this opportunity as a gift from heaven, whatever the cost in Geneva. So it was arranged.

One morning in March 1948 we joined the comfortable Swiss plane, which rose from a snow-covered aerodrome and headed for East Berlin. All of us were happy and excited and a difficult landing in Berlin with very poor visibility did not depress us. During the late afternoon we were flying in clear sunshine along the southern end of Lake Geneva. The tidy city, surrounded by high mountains, looked like Paradise. As we passed through the Customs, Swiss citizens turned to look at us. Their curiosity was scarcely surprising, as we were still in our heavy Russian winter garb and must have looked like bears or wolves down from Arctic regions. I had booked accommodation at the Hotel de la Paix, where the Australian delegation was to stay during the conference. At breakfast next morning the children chattered away, finding great pleasure in the sight of fresh, crisp bread rolls, ample butter, honey and spotless white serviettes. The psychological change was just what they needed. In three weeks they were well again.

When the conference began I became extremely busy and pre-occupied. My wife and I decided that it would be best—and far less expensive—if she and the children moved to a quieter spot. I found accommodation for them at the village of Celigny, about fifteen miles north of Geneva, and saw them only at week-ends. They were more than happy there, spending much time out of doors, walking in the nearby hills or idling on the pebbly beach of the small hotel where they were staying. Mary was struck and somewhat puzzled by the tidy accommodation which many Swiss fowls seemed to enjoy, walking up a kind of miniature gang-plank to covered shelter which seemed scarcely inferior to some of the isbas she had seen in the Soviet Union.

In 1946 the U.N. General Assembly had declared that 'freedom of information is a fundamental human right and is the touchstone of all the freedoms to which the United Nations is consecrated'.[48] The conference in Geneva in 1948 was designed to spell out the rights, obligations and practices which should be included in the concept of freedom of information. During debate it soon became clear that, as stated by the President of the Conference Carlos P. Rumulo of the Philippines, 'While the West insists on as wide a freedom as possible, Eastern European countries stress the responsibilities that go with freedom. While the West defends the right to criticise, Eastern European countries consider that criticism too often turns into slander.' The main spokesmen of these two divergent points of view were the United States on the one hand, and the Soviet Union on the other.

In the event, the Conference drew up three draft conventions, namely, on the gathering and international transmission of news, on the institution of an international right of correction, and on freedom of information.

My main responsibility was to try to bring the Russians and the Americans together on anti-warmongering resolutions and in this the Australian Delegation was successful. We were helped by Professor Dehousse, of Belgium, and Leo Mates, of Yugoslavia. In the process, I had to take upon myself the responsibility for immediate decisions in dropping some clauses in draft resolutions tabled on behalf of Australia and approved by Canberra, and in

[48] For an account of the Conference, and the part played by the Australian Delegation, see article in Current Notes, Vol. XIX (1948), pp. 492-502.

accepting amendments of other clauses. There was no time to obtain instructions from Canberra regarding the most important of these decisions, and after I reported it I half expected a peremptory cable from Dr Evatt charging me with exceeding my instructions and commanding me to re-open discussion. However, the unanimity of the final votes on two resolutions apparently assuaged my master, and by the end of the conference I learned indirectly that he was not displeased with the results.

At the end of the Conference I was completely exhausted and made plans to travel back to Moscow slowly, taking in Paris, London and Prague en route. Before leaving Moscow I had asked a colleague in London to inquire as to bookings on an Orient ship for my wife and children to return to Australia as soon as the Conference in Geneva ended; John Burton had been informed of these arrangements. Passing through Paris, however, I received a telegram from Burton stating that he had discussed my family plans with Evatt. Telegrams from the Secretary not infrequently failed to make clear whether the contents expressed the views of the Minister, the Secretary, or both. I interpreted this particular telegram as meaning that both Evatt and Burton 'would like' me 'to take family back [to Moscow] at least until next winter', basing this attitude on certain broad political developments and favourable reaction of Soviet authorities to my work, to my wife, and to the fact that the twins had attended Russian schools. I agreed to do this, but in a telegraphed reply to Burton said 'I see no possibility of children remaining Moscow beyond September'.

In London I cancelled the reservations aboard ship and after some medical check-ups and shopping all four of us boarded a plane for Czechoslovakia. We spent three days in Prague and found it a lovely but sad city. Our enjoyment of the Castle area, the stained glass windows in the Cathedral, the series of impressive bridges, and general evidence of past achievement and prosperity was dampened by the obvious distress of a population which had suddenly found itself behind the iron curtain. After the Communist coup d'état of February 1948, Jan Masaryk, Foreign Minister and son of the first President of the Republic, had committed suicide; purges were still proceeding and Czech citizens could not leave the country. We felt no urge to stay long in Prague, so I called at the local office of Aeroflot to arrange for a quick flight to Moscow.

To my astonishment, the Russian personnel in charge of the office demanded payment for three tickets in American dollars. I offered to pay in pounds sterling, but this was refused. Then I said I would arrange for our Legation in Moscow to pay in Russian roubles, but this offer too was rejected. In desperation, I sought advice from Ronald McDonald, an old friend of Washington days who was Canadian Chargé d'Affaires in Prague. He did his best on my behalf, with the same result. Without authority from Ottawa, he then advanced me the necessary money in Canadian dollars, which Aeroflot graciously accepted. I hesitated to agree to this kindly act, being far from certain that the Australian Treasury would see fit to re-imburse him in the same currency on payment of my cheque in Australia. But the alternative was to return to London and travel by way of Sweden and Finland, at considerable cost and with much delay. Even then, I was uncertain what currency would be demanded for the fares from Helsinki to Moscow. I was much relieved to learn in due course that the Australian Treasury had re-imbursed McDonald in the appropriate currency.

THE BERLIN CRISIS 1948

Soon after I returned to Moscow I found myself involved in important political work for the first time since my posting there. After the Second World War, and pending signature of a Peace Treaty with Germany, an Allied Control Council for Germany was established on which were represented the United States, Britain, France and the Soviet Union. To each of these countries was assigned a zone of occupation.

The city of Berlin was well within the Russian zone, which comprised what is now described as East Germany and omitted those areas of the old German Reich now under Polish administration. Berlin, which had been the capital of the Reich, was thus isolated from the American, British and French zones. Within the city itself four sectors were carved out, of which the Russian sector was in the east and the American, British and French sectors were in the west. Although there were Allied military forces in each of the Western sectors, they, and the German civil population of what is now called West Berlin (comprising the three Western sectors) were in a geographical situation almost ideally suited to Soviet pressure whenever desired. The Soviet authorities could hold up supplies and communications by road or rail, and interfere with access through established Allied air-corridors if they were willing to take risks of accident.

For some three years the Western Allies had done all they could to secure the effective political and economic unification of Germany but had been frustrated, mostly by Soviet intransigence. The Soviet Union had no intention of permitting a strong, prosperous and unified Germany to develop. Indeed, having consolidated the position of communists in Eastern Germany, including East Berlin, the Russians began to interfere in the political life of the Western zones to such an extent that the Western Allies decided that they must take steps 'to rally the German people, unless they were to see a passive, inert and despairing Germany taken over by a small group of Russian puppets'.[49] The Allies therefore took various steps, both political and economic, to avoid such a situation developing, with remarkable results in West Berlin.

In these circumstances Stalin, who had perhaps become a little dizzy with success after the Communist coup in Czechoslovakia, decided to impose a blockade upon West Berlin. He had strong grounds for thinking that he could starve the West Berliners into submission, freeze out Western military forces from what should seem an untenable position, and incorporate Berlin as a whole as the capital of East Germany. This plan was frustrated by the brilliant and courageous execution of what at first sight seemed a hopeless plan to supply Berlin by air with enough food to keep the population alive and enough coal to keep industry at least ticking over.

[49] *The Hard and Bitter Peace*, by G. F. Hudson (Pall Mall, London, 1966), p. 58.

On 20 March, 1948 the Russian delegates walked out of the Control Council, and on 1 April the blockade began. Restrictions were not lifted until 12 May, 1949. The period between was one of crisis, particularly during the earlier months of the blockade when the effectiveness of the air-lift seemed uncertain. 'It was the unforeseen success of the air-lift, combined with the effects of the counter-blockade on the Soviet zone and the morale of the West Berliners, which ultimately provided the West with a diplomatic victory.'[50] More important from Stalin's point of view, 'The experience of the Berlin crisis . . . left a deep impression of Russian ruthlessness and malevolence'[51] and on 4 April, 1949 an agreement to establish the North Atlantic Treaty Organisation (NATO) was signed by twelve countries, including the United States and Canada.

During the crisis, Moscow was a key post. It was my responsibility to keep Canberra informed regarding the Soviet point of view and to comment on the degree of risk involved during the blockade. In doing this, no help could be expected from the Soviet authorities themselves. Stalin was inaccessible to an Australian Minister; Molotov would probably regard any intervention by Australia as irrelevant if not impertinent; Deputy Foreign Ministers and less exalted personnel would have no discretion at all to say anything which could not be read in the Soviet Press.

In these circumstances, contacts with the American, British and French Embassies—especially the first two—were even more important than usual. No doubt the Australian Embassy in Washington and our High Commission in London would report upon information obtained from American and British authorities, but estimates of Russian attitudes would be based largely upon the views of British and American diplomatic representatives in Moscow.

Before the imposition of the Berlin blockade, my reports to Canberra had discounted any Western Press speculation that Soviet policy could lead to war. After my return from Geneva, however, I began to stress the real risk of war. There are rare occasions when the Head of a Diplomatic Mission who has not sufficient information on which to form a sound judgment has to decide in which direction he should err. Should his reports be optimistic, equally balanced, or pessimistic? For a month or two I was pessimistic in the sense that I argued that the risk of military conflict should not be under-estimated. Stalin's position on Berlin seemed to me unusually strong. By blockading West Berlin he could bring about near-starvation of its inhabitants and seriously incommode Western forces—without having to fire a shot. To break the blockade, Western forces would have to fire the first shot—on behalf of a defeated enemy which had committed outrageous crimes under the Nazis. Would public opinion in Britain, France and America support such action, however much they might sympathise with the plight of the West-Berliners?

I was far from being alone in the disbelief that enough food and coal could be brought to Berlin by air to sustain West Berlin. It seemed to me,

[50] *British Foreign Policy*, by F. S. Northedge (George Allen & Unwin, London, 1962), pp. 88-89.
[51] Hudson, *op. cit.*, p. 162.

therefore, that the Russians had only to sit tight on their blockade until the onset of winter made the sufferings of the West Berliners intolerable. At that moment of time the Western Allies would have to give way, with tremendous loss of face to themselves and loss of hope not only in West Berlin but also in West Germany, unless the decision was taken for American, British and French forces to take the grave risk of shooting their way through the blockade.

Gradually, however, my pessimism diminished. When the Western powers accepted the Russian demand to discuss German problems as a whole and not merely Berlin, and when the three Western diplomatic representatives began discussions in Moscow with Stalin, I thought that the situation had eased. My urgent task then was to try to discover what was happening at these discussions. This proved to be one of the most frustrating experiences of my diplomatic career.

Although my contacts with the French Embassy were comparatively slight, relations with the American Embassy were good and those with the British Embassy reasonably satisfactory. As the British Ambassador, Sir Maurice Peterson, was ill at the time, Frank Roberts, who had been his Minister on my first arrival in Moscow and who had returned to London after completing his tour of duty, was sent back specially from London to act on behalf of the British Government. My relations with him were closer than those with Peterson. In short, I fully expected to be able to ascertain how the negotiations were proceeding.

The first interview with Stalin took place on 2 August, and the whole Diplomatic Corps in Moscow was agog to know what had happened. I asked to see Roberts, but found him so imprecise and evasive that the interview was useless. As other Commonwealth representatives had similar experiences, I came to the conclusion that he was under instructions not to disclose the substance of the discussions. I thereupon cabled Canberra to warn the Minister for External Affairs that I did not expect to get any confidential information from the British Embassy about these vital talks unless pressure were applied from Canberra on the British Government. An additional reason for my cable was my lack of success with the American Ambassador as well.

I thought it only fair to tell Roberts what I had done and why. He was rather upset, and replied that it was his understanding that Commonwealth countries were being informed of the course of the conversations through London. Two days later he told me he had checked with London and received confirmation of this.

I know of no evidence that Dr Evatt took up the matter with the British government. Certainly, I myself received no advice from Canberra that this had been done or, indeed, that my reactions to this unusual lack of Commonwealth consultation on the spot were shared by the Minister or his Department. Later I learned, but not from Canberra, that the three Western powers had agreed not to disclose to diplomatic representatives in Moscow the substance of the negotiations with the Russians. I thought it very odd that a British Government should enter into an agreement with two foreign powers limiting the scope of consultation between Britain and other members of the Commonwealth of Nations.

During my periodic visits to the American Ambassador, I deliberately conveyed the impression that, while I did not question the right of the three Western Governments not to disclose to other representatives what was happening during discussions with Stalin, I felt in a personal way the implication that I was not to be trusted to handle in a discreet and responsible manner such important information.

Shortly after I had made this point indirectly, Bedell Smith rang and invited me to an evening film show at the American Embassy. I accepted the invitation. Before the programme started, he took me on one side and said that, as soon as the lights were out, he wanted me to follow him out of the room to have a talk. Somewhat mystified and intrigued, I did this and he led me to his study. There he said that I should not take his failure to discuss with me the Stalin talks as evidencing lack of trust in me, but rather as the carrying out of an undertaking to his British and French colleagues not to reveal the substance of the talks to members of other diplomatic missions in Moscow. He said he was prepared to tell me about the talks, on condition that I did not report what he told me to Canberra.

In normal circumstances I would not have felt able to accept his condition, but the situation was unusual. I had advised Canberra not to expect to receive such information from me; I had been assured formally by Frank Roberts that London was keeping Canberra informed; Canberra had shown no sign that it was dissatisfied or disturbed by my position in Moscow. I therefore agreed, and Bedell Smith told me what had happened to date. This was valuable background against which to focus my comments to Canberra, without revealing what I had been told by one of the negotiators.

In the event, two interviews by the Western representatives with Stalin raised hopes of a peaceful settlement which were subsequently dashed during further negotiations with Molotov and between the four military commanders in Berlin. The Russians were playing for time, expecting Berlin to collapse at latest during the winter season. That their expectations were not unreasonable can be inferred from the comment of Bedell Smith in his book *My Three Years in Moscow*, published in 1950 after his retirement as Ambassador:

> I must say . . . that at the time the situation did not look too hopeful to me. . . . I had serious doubts whether we could feed and supply a huge city by air for a prolonged period, especially during the winter months, when flying conditions in Eastern Germany were notoriously uncertain. Nor was I by any means sure that the morale of the German people would stand the strain.[52]

Yet Bedell Smith had been told by the American commandant in Berlin, General Lucius Clay—whom Smith regarded as a genius in the realm of supply and statistics—that if necessary he could build up the airlift to 10,000 tons a day.

The airlift, in which Australian aviators participated, has rightly been

[52] Bedell Smith, *op. cit.*, p. 242.

described as a miracle. While the blockade was in force no less than 1,592,287 tons of fuel and food were flown in to West Berlin, at a cost in lives of forty-five Allied airmen. On 5 July, 1948, 362 planes brought in 3,000 tons in twenty-two hours. In December the average daily tonnage was 4,500, climbing to 5,500 during the next two months. By the Spring of 1949 the average tonnage reached 8,000 a day, the total during one record day in April rising to 12,941 tons brought in by 1,298 planes which landed every 61.8 seconds.[53]

The morale of the West Berliners was no less impressive, despite cold, hunger and heavy unemployment. If one must pay tribute to the skill and bravery of the crews of the aeroplanes, recognition must also be given of the dogged courage of the Berliners and of their readiness, through plain hard work, to clear the cargoes of the planes in the minimum of time.

The success of the airlift enabled the Allies to avoid responsibility for firing the first shot. 'It was now Stalin who had to take the initiative in belligerency. To stop the airlift he would have to shoot down Allied planes. His nerve was not so strong. . . .'[54]

As the months passed my fears of a sudden crisis subsided. Meanwhile the Soviet and Australian Governments agreed to raise the status of their respective diplomatic Missions to Embassies. During the U.N. General Assembly Sessions in New York in 1947, Dr Evatt had given some thought to this question, and it is my impression that he discussed the matter at that time with Molotov. In any event, formal agreement was reached in 1948, both governments deciding to elevate their current Heads of Missions in Canberra and Moscow from the rank of Minister to that of Ambassador. On 22 May, 1948 I presented new credentials in Moscow naming me Ambassador.

Once again I was collected by the Chief of Protocol, Mr Molochkov, in the official Zis limousine whose exterior looked remarkably like an American Packard. Members of my staff followed in our Buicks. At the entrance to the Kremlin the Zis stopped while Molochkov spoke to the guards, and then refused to start. The Russian chauffeur, perspiration pouring from his brow, tried again and again to get the car moving, without success. After about one minute Molochkov looked at his watch and then asked me whether we could transfer to one of our Buicks. He was well aware of the split second timing required on a formal occasion like this, and of the undesirability of keeping the President of the Praesidium waiting. I, of course, agreed and we left the Zis, stepped into the nearest Buick, which pulled around the Zis and proceeded to the appropriate building. History does not record what happened to the unfortunate chauffeur. Soviet authorities do not take lightly a loss of public face even of this kind.

On the same evening I foretold for the children that our maid, Paulina, would say the wrong thing when she came to tell us that dinner was ready. The normal procedure was for Paulina to throw open the doors to the dining-room and say, in Russian, 'Mr Minister, dinner is served'. This time,

[53] *The Death and Life of Germany*, by Eugene Davidson (Jonathan Cape, London, 1959), pp. 208, 218.
[54] Hudson, *op. cit.*, p. 62.

however, she should say instead 'Mr Ambassador'. When Paulina entered the living-room and uttered the usual formula the twins burst out laughing. Poor Paulina blushed, wondered what brick she had dropped, and was quite upset. It took us some time to explain the situation and for her to recover her composure. In retrospect I blamed myself for not having told her the new formula in advance.

As the summer advanced, my wife and I were faced with a decision about the children. Although the last thing we wanted was to separate them from ourselves, we eventually agreed that a combination of health and educational problems made it necessary for them to go back to Australia. This meant that my wife would have to take them and try to make satisfactory arrangements for them to board at preparatory schools. Her own return to Moscow was quite uncertain. Bookings were made for the family to leave Leningrad by a Russian ship towards the end of August, and to proceed to Australia via London on an Orient Line vessel.

The children were delighted at the thought of returning to Australia, but we decided not to tell them that they would not be coming back to Moscow until after they reached London. To tell them earlier would inevitably mean that they would convey the information to all and sundry, and this would lead to speculation among both Australians and Russians as to whether my wife would be returning to the Soviet Union, and perhaps even about my own possible movements.

I had ordered from Stockholm a magnificent Swedish bicycle with everything which opened and shut. It was to be a surprise birthday present for the twins. Three days before the family left Moscow we produced it. They had a lot of fun learning to ride it, and the bicycle helped to distract their attention from the strains of departure. Vorva, a child of one of the Russian employees living over the garage, managed to damage it slightly. He had never ridden a bicycle and the sight of this shiny machine was just too much for his eager curiosity. He cadged a ride and crashed it into a fence at the bottom of the yard. After the family left, English friends offered to buy it from us for their children, but I could not bear to sell it—least of all to friends whose governess had helped Mary and Peter after they left Russian schools. So I sent them the bicycle as a gift.

I accompanied the family to Leningrad and tucked them into the Soviet ship, returning to Moscow with a somewhat heavy heart, although I hoped to see them briefly in London if I were nominated as a member of the Australian Delegation to the Third Session of the U.N. General Assembly, due to open in Paris on September 21. On this occasion they found the voyage through the Baltic very unpleasant, as the ship struck rough weather all the way.

U.N. GENERAL ASSEMBLY (PARIS—21 SEPTEMBER TO 12 DECEMBER, 1948)

In due course I received instructions from Canberra to proceed to Paris to act as an Australian Delegate to the U.N. General Assembly. As I was entitled to leave and wanted to see my family safely aboard ship in London, I left Moscow for London via Berlin on 9 September, 1948. Two days before departure I sent a telegram to the Australian Military Mission in Berlin, notifying them of the time of my arrival by Soviet plane at an airport in East Berlin, and requesting them to send a car to meet me. This was necessary, as the car would be flying a flag which would enable me to pass through the Soviet sector to the British sector without hindrance.

When I landed in East Berlin, however, there was no Australian car to meet me. I concluded that my telegram had been held up either in Moscow or Berlin by Soviet authorities. This was highly inconvenient, as I was pressed for time to get to London before my family left there, while there had been tension both in the Russian and Western sectors of the city which might make my journey from the airport in any conveyance other than an identifiable official car more difficult. It was not my business to become involved in some incident which might embarrass the Australian Government.

So my first thought was to telephone the Australian Military Mission and arrange for a car to be sent out at once to collect me. I asked for a telephone book, but was told there was no such book. Under pressure I was presented with a battered exercise book in which were written a few telephone numbers. The Australian Mission was not listed, but I found a number for the British Military Mission and telephoned it fifteen or twenty times. Mostly I got a wrong number; otherwise an engaged signal.

I was left with no alternative to trying some unorthodox expedient. Seeing an East-German postal waggon nearby, I asked the German driver if he would drive me to the British sector for $U.S.20, which I always carried with me for emergency use if I ran into currency difficulties. He hesitated, but agreed, for this sum was a fortune to impoverished Berliners. So I placed my luggage in the van and climbed into the waggon alongside him. My black Homburg was uncomfortably conspicuous alongside his battered cap, and I expected the Russian sentry at the exit from the airport to stop the waggon and investigate. Only the fact that I carried a Soviet Foreign Office identity card, certified by a Deputy Foreign Minister and carrying a photograph of me, emboldened me to take the risk of investigation and delay.

The Russian sentry let us through the barrier with never a second look, and there seemed reason to hope that I could arrive at my destination without incident. After we had driven for about twenty minutes, however, I began to sense that something was happening in the city. Questions to the driver en route had made me doubt whether he knew where the British Military Mission was, so I made him stop once or twice while I asked passers-by for directions. But the closer we came to the centre of the city the greater were the crowds of people, and my inquiries seemed less and less welcome. I drew the conclusion that there had been some disturbances, and that inquiries were only drawing attention to myself. So I stopped asking questions, and told the driver to get me into the American or British sectors, anywhere, anyhow, and to stay there.

While we were still in the Soviet sector, a young German came running alongside, jumped on the entrance step and asked the driver to let him stay there. He was dishevelled, and my instinct was to refuse, but when he added

'Take me with you. The Russians are after me, and they'll get me if you don't. I wrestled with my conscience, told the driver to let him stay for ten blocks and then to get rid of him. After ten blocks he seemed relieved and ran off into the crowd.

Suddenly I saw an American jeep occupied by military police. I thought my troubles were over, but a little later I discovered that we were back in the Soviet Sector again. I berated the driver and ordered him to get into the British sector immediately. Eventually he succeeded and after a few inquiries we found our way to the headquarters of the British Military Mission.

At the door I found an English 'bobby', calm, cheerful and helpful. Having explained my predicament, he steered me to a telephone which I used to make contact with the Australian Mission. My troubles were over. My Australian colleagues confirmed that they had received no telegram from Moscow and explained that I had chosen to arrive on the day when some 200,000 or 300,000 West Berliners were demonstrating in front of the burned-out Reichstag to express their resentment at organised provocations taking place in East Berlin. Subsequently West Germans had torn down the Red flag from the top of the Brandenburger Tor, and the Russians had made arrests. There had also been serious incidents in East Berlin.

At that time Berlin seemed largely heaps of rubble. In later years a German Ambassador in Tokyo told me that he had had a home in Berlin, but after the end of the war he was unable to find the street, let alone the house. This may have been an exaggeration, but certainly there were ruins every-where.

During my brief stay in Berlin I was shown around parts of the Western Sectors, entered the ruins of Hitler's Chancellery and saw nearby the water-logged bunker in which he committed suicide. Berlin was an unhappy city, with signs of poverty and distress everywhere. As we walked along some of the streets we were plagued by obviously well-educated Germans trying to sell us American cigarettes or other commodities acquired on the black market.

On 11 September I left for London from Tempelhof airport, where Allied planes were landing every three to five minutes. It was an incredible sight. The corridors out of Berlin were so thick with planes that I was not sorry when we left the confines of our corridor.

In London I had a very unpleasant interview with Dr Evatt, who was obviously opposed to my family returning to Australia. He came close to accusing me of being jittery and unsuited to service in the Soviet Union, and hinted at a transfer to another post. I assumed that he had found it politically convenient to be able to say that my children were attending Russian schools, with the implication that suspicion of the Soviet Union in the West was exaggerated.

I had to remind him that at no time had I raised any question of my own transfer from Moscow. The decision that the twins should not remain in the Soviet Union had been based primarily on health grounds. Even if they had stayed on in Moscow they would be unable to attend Russian schools again, as they had fallen too far behind in their work. I had complied with Burton's cabled request after the Geneva Conference to cancel bookings I had made for the family to return to Australia then and to keep my wife and children in Moscow at least until the next impending winter. Finally, I pointed out that my wife's future movements were uncertain: if she could make satisfactory arrangements for the twins in Australia, it was conceivable that she herself could return to Moscow.

When the Minister saw that I had made up my mind about the children and that pressure would not move me on this issue, he calmed down somewhat. So I accompanied the family to their ship at Tilbury Docks, where I tucked them into their cabins, finding to my satisfaction that on this occasion they had adequate accommodation. We had had only one night together in London before they left.

In Paris I was not in my happiest frame of mind, as my personal situation was uncertain and my financial position became very difficult. I discovered that my Moscow allowances had been cut off immediately after my departure, apparently because the Secretary of the Department of External Affairs wanted me transferred from that post. I can only assume that he reacted adversely, like Evatt, to my decision to return the children to Australia. This made it impossible for me to make proper financial arrangement for the Chargé d'Affaires in Moscow, prevented me from making plans for my wife and children, and yet left me with the financial responsibility for my family's fare to Australia. To add insult to injury, I received advice from London in November informing me that I was not entitled even to the ordinary delegation allowance at the Assembly, and that retrospective deduction was being made covering the allowances I had already received. This was none the less embarrassing because it was utterly ridiculous, but the matter took a considerable time to straighten out. In answer to my protests, the Department of External Affairs informed me that the London instruction had been a mistake, but until the instruction was rectified I was simply short of cash.

During the first half of October I was informed that B. C. Ballard was to be transferred from Paris to Moscow 'for at least six months'. He was a senior officer, of Counsellor rank, with linguistic capacity and considerable experience. Though not quite suitable for Moscow requirements, I welcomed the decision. When I checked with Evatt about Ballard's instructions to depart for Moscow, he said 'Yes, he is a senior man, and should take over until you get back'.

This was the first evidence I had that the return of the children to Canberra was now regarded as a *fait accompli*, and that the imputation that I was not suited to the Moscow post had been withdrawn. Apparently Burton had put to the Minister another suggestion (and still more suggestions about transfer of several other people) but was told that so many changes were not approved. I wrote to my wife saying that I doubted whether the Minister had ever had any intention of transferring me elsewhere.

Meetings of the General Assembly were held at the Palais de Chaillot, which was not far, by Metro, from the Hotel Continental where the Australian Delegation was accommodated. Arrangements had been made for Dr Evatt and Mrs Evatt to occupy a flat elsewhere.

Our hotel was on the corner of the Rue Castiglioni and the Rue de Rivoli, across which were the glorious formal gardens of the Tuileries, with their carefully groomed trees, their statues and their occasional fountains. Walks in these gardens in autumn were a sheer delight. It is scarcely possible to imagine a greater contrast in capital cities than the contrast between Moscow and Paris. The former had grown up like topsy, and except for a few favoured areas, was at that time run down at heel. From the centre of the Tuileries, on the other hand, one looked in one direction through the Petit Arc de Triomphe to the Louvre, and in the opposite direction up to the distant Arc de Triomphe—a vista of beauty and orderliness. Moreover, this area of Paris had not been touched by the war. During the long, exhausting and often frustrating hours of the Assembly, a short walk in the Tuileries Gardens was a rest for the spirit and a solace for the soul.

I have never been able to eat the meals in a large hotel for longer than a fortnight without my stomach revolting at the amount and nature of the food. After a week or two, therefore, many of us sought out the numerous, cheaper and more cheerful cafes nearby where one could order merely what one wanted and make friends with the proprietor, who would personally supervise the cooking.

The management of our hotel complained to Dr Evatt that we were not eating regularly in the hotel. Perhaps the Delegation had been given a slightly cut rate, which the management expected to recover by way of meals. We received Ministerial instructions to eat more often in the hotel, but complied only to the extent of eating irregular, token dinners there. French breakfasts were inexpensive and time was saved by eating them in our rooms. Lunch was usually obtained in some café near the Place de L'Etoile, as time would scarcely permit return to the Continental. We could always invoke the claim of evening meetings of the Assembly and general pressure of work as excuses for eating out for dinner.

From the point of view of the Australian Delegation, the most significant aspect of the Paris Assembly was the election of Dr Evatt, on the second ballot, as President. He had stood unsuccessfully for this high office in New York in 1947. In that year all members of the Australian Delegation were assigned lists of countries whose affirmative votes they were to ensure ahead of the election. I remember that I was supposed to deliver the votes, *inter alia*, of the Soviet Union and the Netherlands. I had driven miles out of New York to the residence where Gromyko and other members of the Soviet Delegation were staying, and had a longish conversation with him during which he was polite and non-committal. My interview with the leader of the Netherlands Delegation was also polite but brutally frank. Dr van Royen, Netherlands Ambassador in Washington, explained to me rather icily that Dr Evatt's activities in relation to the Netherlands East Indies could scarcely be expected to attract the support of the Dutch government for his candidature. At the Paris meeting of the General Assembly we had similar assignments.

I well remember Evatt's reaction when the result of the second ballot was announced. He drew a long breath, and walked slowly but triumphantly down the aisle to take his seat on the rostrum. In United Nations terms, this was the high-water mark of international prestige. For Dr Evatt it was also an opportunity for the exercise of power and the use of publicity. While taking comfort in the degree of prestige which rubbed off on Australia, and not grudging the achievement of a legitimate ambition, some members of the Australian Delegation hoped that Evatt's responsibilities as President might result in our being accorded rather more discretion than usual in handling our respective tasks. In this we were destined to be disappointed.

My recollections of the events of the Paris Assembly evoke very mixed feelings. At first, I was happy to be in Paris, despite a heavy cold which kept me half out of action for the first week. Access to Evatt at least made it possible for me to discuss the Berlin situation with him in detail. For a time my United Nations work seemed quite secondary, and I recaptured a feeling that my presence in Moscow could still be of use. I was dismayed, however, when without any prior discussion with me Evatt intervened officially in the Berlin situation by despatching on 13 November, 1948 to the Four Powers a communication jointly signed by himself as President and by Mr Trygve Lie as Secretary-General. While Foreign Ministers, not officials, decide foreign policy, I found it difficult to imagine any other Western Foreign Minister taking a similar decision without first seeking the comments of their Ambassador to Moscow. This initiative irritated the United States which, in the words of U.S. Secretary of Defence J. V. Forrestal, '. . . succeeded in giving the impression that, after all, the Russian demands are not so extreme and unmeetable'.[55]

Meanwhile the work of the Assembly dragged on and on, and the chances of finishing the agenda in any reasonable time grew less and less. There were a few unavoidable reasons for the slow pace. The American Presidential elections made it practically impossible for the United States Delegation to do other than stall on some major issues, especially Palestine. In subsequent Presidential election years the Assembly Session was timed to begin later, a wise precaution. Further, the underlying Berlin issue, which the Security Council had failed to solve, scarcely facilitated co-operation between Western and Communist countries on any other matters.

But there were other reasons for delays, stemming directly from Evatt's tenure of the Presidency. First, Evatt was Attorney-General as well as Minister for External Affairs, and in his former capacity he had to appear for the Commonwealth Government before the Privy Council in the 'Bank' case, the result of which could have vital domestic consequences in Australia. Prime Minister Chifley had decided to nationalise private banks, which were fighting tooth and nail in an effort to prove that Commonwealth legislation on the subject was unconstitutional. During the Assembly Session Evatt was absent in London for a time seeking leave to appeal, and before he left Paris his energy was substantially diverted to preparation of his case.

Secondly, I had the uneasy feeling that Evatt at some stage reached the conclusion that it would suit him if the Agenda were *not* completed before Christmas. He had always seemed to me to find more satisfaction in political

[55] *The Forrestal Diaries*, Walter Millis (Ed.), (Cassell, London, 1952), p. 496.

activities overseas than at home, but the length of his absences abroad had drawn critical comment in Parliament from members of the Opposition. If, however, there were a second part of the Assembly Session in 1949, he as President would have an indisputable case for being absent from Australia once again.

At no time did I receive a specific instruction to 'go slow', but a personal experience pointed strongly in this direction and strengthened my interpretation of his attitude.

During the Session my responsibilities were concentrated largely upon the work of Committee III, which dealt with Social, Humanitarian and Cultural matters—for the same reason as during the 1947 Session of the Assembly. The primary concern of this committee was the drafting of a Declaration of Human Rights, but it also dealt with the United Nations Children's Fund and the Appeal for Children. On 13 November I was due to make a speech on the latter items, and one of the Australian officials assisting me prepared a draft speech of fifteen pages. I regarded this as much too long; nor did I like certain aspects of the draft. In these circumstances I saw Dr Evatt about the speech, and told him that I proposed to reduce it to about five pages, changing the style somewhat in the process. He half-closed his eyes and said slowly and deliberately, 'Read every word of it'. He would not listen to my objections, and gave no reasons for his own attitude.

With a heavy heart I carried out instructions and read every word of the speech, the general effect upon proceedings being to delay completion of an item on the agenda until after the lunch adjournment. When I finished, my sincerity of purpose was challenged by some other delegation in a way it had never been questioned before in a United Nations meeting. I felt humiliated, and at that moment decided to do everything in my power to avoid representing Australia at any other international gathering while Evatt was Minister for External Affairs. This I succeeded in doing, more by good luck than good management.

The most important item on the agenda of Committee III, however, was the Universal Declaration of Human Rights. The document eventually approved has often been cited as one embodying the noblest aspirations of mankind, while in later years it has been argued that its contents are legally binding upon Members of the United Nations. At the time it was drafted, however, everyone present knew perfectly well that it purported only to embody a set of agreed principles which, to become binding upon Member States, would have to be embodied in an agreed Covenant or Covenants on Human Rights which would then be opened for signature and ratification by those countries prepared to accept the obligations set out therein.

Membership of this Committee was an illuminating experience. The Chairman was Dr Charles Malik, a Professor of Philosophy from the Lebanon, who later held high national and international offices. Malik was a man of intelligence and integrity, but too polite and trusting to be a good Chairman. Representatives of other countries who played a prominent part in discussion were Professor Rene Cassin of France and Mr Alexei Pavlov, Soviet Ambassador to Belgium. Cassin was a lawyer of high status in his own country. He was somewhat dogmatic and vain, and held strong views on such matters as education. Pavlov was an able tactician, who managed to convey the impression that human rights in the Soviet Union were amply protected by its constitution, which I knew to be largely ignored in practice. He was a past master at 'running interference', and when the Chairman tried to close interminable discussion on particular paragraphs of the Declaration, had a habit of taking points of order, during which he would invariably re-open discussion of matter which the Chairman had declared closed. Poor Malik was reduced at times to saying 'Mr Pavlov, I can only hear you at this stage if you are taking a very genuine point of order'. Whereupon Pavlov would confirm the genuineness of his point, only to launch again shamelessly into general debate.

The contrast between the humanitarian arguments advanced by representatives of Eastern European countries and the actual conditions to be found there can be illustrated by reference to an impassioned speech by the representative of Czechoslovakia in favour of inclusion in the Declaration of a clause prohibiting imposition of the death penalty. On the following morning French newspapers carried a news item to the effect that two Czech citizens had been condemned to death in their own country. When a member of some other delegation referred to this at the next Committee meeting, the Czech representative boldly admitted that in his country the death penalty was still in operation, but added imaginatively that he had that day sent a telegram to his government recommending its abolition. In the event, when the final vote took place approving the Declaration, all the Communist countries of Eastern Europe registered abstentions.

During the long debate on the Declaration I gained some unjustified reputation for being able to intervene with serious arguments relating to a wide variety of paragraphs. My comments, though not necessarily approved, were listened to with some attention. I should now confess that my continuing preparedness to intervene was due to a simple diplomatic trick, backed by hard work when the Committee was not sitting. As the day wore on the Chairman, in an attempt to hasten discussion, would ask representatives who still wished to speak on a particular paragraph to hold up their hands, so that their names could be noted and an estimate made of the time required to finish the item. By withholding my hand until sufficient names had been taken to see out the day, I was able to gain a night in which to prepare my own contribution.

As chief Australian representative on Committee III, however, I had one unusual embarrassment. For reasons best known to himself, Dr Evatt had included in the Australian Delegation two 'Advisers' for assignment to my Committee. They were Bishop Burgman (Church of England) and Bishop Eris O'Brien (Roman Catholic). These two worthy and learned gentlemen sat immediately behind me, with the result that I was occasionally uncomfortable when carrying out, under their direct eyes, instructions which were based upon political considerations rather than those of religion or morality.

Not that they importuned me to act contrary to my instructions. It was necessary, however, for me to spend much time and energy explaining my instructions. As my explanations could not always be convincing, this was a considerable burden. They were very ready to help in any way, but it was not easy to devise relevant means of assistance. Dr O'Brien, whom I had never met before, though a scholar of repute, was incredibly modest and never stood on his dignity as a bishop. He would offer to slip off to a library to check a reference or look up some point, but I had junior officials available who could do this. I grew to like him very much, though I doubt whether my official performance would have justified a testimonial for entry into heaven.

The psychological and physical strain upon members of Delegations to a General Assembly Session who take their responsibilities seriously need to be better known. A letter to my wife dated 13 December, 1948 contains the following comment:

> The Assembly ended yesterday. We are all exhausted, and for the moment it is not easy to make plans, or even write a letter. As usual, it will take several days to unwind, and there is not much sleep to be got in the process.
>
> This Assembly has been longer and we have worked harder than any other Assembly. The pressure has been impossible for the last few weeks, and we have treated ourselves as we would not treat dogs. Meetings have lasted until at least midnight, and frequently until 2 a.m. and occasionally until 3 or 4 a.m. This can not go on for ever, and I only hope that the procedure will be revised before next year.
>
> Yet we have not even finished our Agenda! There is to be a second part held in New York on 1st April. I shall do my best to escape that Session. . . . I can think of nothing better . . . than 6 uninterrupted months in the snows of Moscow . . .

The Paris meeting was the last United Nations Conference I ever attended. This was due largely to the accident of circumstance, as other responsibilities were thrust upon me. Yet my keenness to attend had been blunted. The sheer verbiage of Assembly Sessions; the sharp contrast between ideals expressed and action taken by governments; the exhaustion incurred in securing results of limited value; my latest experience of a Minister instructing me to read a text drafted by neither of us which I knew to be too long and inappropriately phrased—all this depressed me. It came therefore as a considerable relief that henceforth I was to be involved only in 'private' diplomacy and in international conferences which were not under United Nations auspices. Unfortunately, I found that the latter bring, at least for the representative of a Middle or Small Power, other frustrations of a different type.

One experience in Paris, unimportant in itself, burned into my mind the need for attention, in carrying out diplomatic functions, to what might be regarded as insignificant practical detail. Thereafter I quoted it frequently to members of my staff.

The British Ambassador to France decided to invite Assembly Delegations and others to an elaborate evening reception at the British Embassy. Winter had set in, and one thousand guests arrived clad in heavy overcoats, which they handed over to a receptionist in exchange for a ticket with a number on it. It was a very pleasant evening, with everything well arranged—except in one respect. The receptionist omitted to place the overcoats in numerical order. When the guests began to leave, their coats could be found only after long delays. Eventually an absolute shambles developed with guests entering the cloak-room to look for their own coats; Foreign Ministers, Ambassadors and Delegates began pushing from behind; tempers grew short, and there were muttered imprecations. The effect of the whole evening was spoilt by this one simple mistake.

Time and again I found in different parts of the world that my junior staff could or would not realise the importance of this example. They regarded my continuing requests to 'Make sure that the microphone works', 'See that the plug fits the machine', 'Check the voltage', etc. as hopelessly old-fashioned and pedantic. There were several occasions, unfortunately, when their over-optimistic attitude was shown to be unjustified.

Three incidents arising out of the Paris Meeting throw light upon the personality of Dr Evatt. At the Palais de Chaillot the Secretary-General of the United Nations, Mr Trygve Lie, had arranged a substantial room for the President of the Assembly just behind the stage on which he sat during proceedings. He could retire into it whenever desired for interviews, while one of the Vice-Presidents acted in his place. The adjoining room was most convenient, because the President could return to the stage at short notice to take charge again whenever necessary. But when the Australian Minister for External Affairs discovered that the Secretary-General had what appeared to be a more adequate suite in a distant part of the same building, Dr Evatt insisted on Trygve Lie vacating it for the use of the President.

Secondly, there was a shortage of coal in France in 1948, and electricity supplies in Paris were rationed. During much of the day there was no heating. Dr Evatt instructed the Australian Embassy to make representations to the French Foreign Office with a view to ensuring that heating was available for his flat whenever required. This involved turning on the electricity supply for a whole block of flats, thus giving the occupants more favoured treatment than other citizens. After some hesitation the request was granted.

Finally, Dr Evatt accepted a decoration from the French Government —the Grand Cross of the Legion of Honour. It is Australian Labor Party policy not to approve decorations except for members of the Armed Forces. The public explanation given was that the French decoration was given not to the Australian Minister for External Affairs, but to the President of the U.N. Assembly. When Lt Col Hodgson, then Australian Ambassador to France, was transferred to Tokyo in 1949, he reported to Canberra that the French Government wished him to accept a decoration before departure. He was instructed to refuse this, under the general British rule, followed by Australia, that diplomatic representatives overseas should not accept foreign decorations.

LAST YEAR IN THE SOVIET UNION

After a few days in Paris completing my section of the Delegation's report I went to London where I intended to take a fortnight's leave. I spent

Christmas Day with Peter Heydon and his family, pleased to be with Australian friends and children when my own family was far away. On the return journey to Moscow, I decided to travel by train via Ostend, Stockholm, Helsinki and Leningrad. I left London on 31 December, 1948 and found the train journey for the most part comfortable and enjoyable.

The British Minister in Helsinki had asked me to stay with him, so I spent a couple of days in his residence. The Russian train from Helsinki to Leningrad left at two-day intervals. I had booked a two-berth compartment to myself, partly for privacy and partly to ensure that all my luggage travelled under my direct supervision. The British Minister sent a Third Secretary to the station to see me aboard, but we were told that no bookings had been made for me in a wagon-lit. I could, however, have a 'soft' four-berth compartment in an ordinary carriage to myself.

The Third Secretary protested, produced the tickets and explained that the British Legation had booked them. He was then informed that, unfortunately, the wagon-lit carriage sent up from Leningrad was shorter than usual by one compartment, namely, mine. Clearly my reservations were being used for some other purpose—probably demanded by a Soviet General or other high Soviet personnage. As my experience in Russia had taught me that it was unwise to accept a situation of this kind without protest, I refused the 'soft' compartment and we returned to my unfortunate host, who nobly invited me to stay on with him until the next train left. He was annoyed with the Russians, and next day telephoned to the Intourist Agency himself, registering his dissatisfaction and demanding for me a compartment in the centre of a wagon-lit carriage on the next train. Asked why he wanted a compartment in the centre, he replied with some acerbity that it was necessary to take precautions in case the carriage sent up from Leningrad was shorter than usual at either end of the carriage. The tickets were duly supplied, and I left by the next train without any further hitch.

On returning to Moscow on 9 January, 1949 I found that the Russian servants had been making hay while the sun of new or temporary masters was shining, and had to be brought back again to some sort of discipline. Half the Australians were sick. One had a skin disease he could not get rid of; his wife was thin and in the doctor's hands. Another had a large boil on the back of his neck. A third had stomach trouble. Although still rather tired by the work at the Assembly followed by considerable travel, I seemed almost the only fit Australian around. As for the Russian employees, Victor had developed a stomach ulcer and left. We were one chauffeur short, but the second car was out of action in any event, and spare parts we had ordered had not arrived.

On 26 January I gave the customary 'Australia Day' party with considerable trepidation as my wife was not present to supervise the domestic servants and preparation of food. The following day I sent her a somewhat flippant account of the party which conveys its atmosphere:

> I had no means of knowing until the last moment whether all the things Valya was going to cook would in fact be cooked or could be eaten if cooked. However, I went through with her the list of what she had to buy, and discussed what she had to cook—then went away to pray and

to see to the liquor. In the event things turned out all right, but standing here on my own to receive guests without you alongside made me feel like a child alone in the jungles of Africa wondering what would happen next.

Last year's experience had taught us a little. We opened up my office as a subsidiary 'bar', and only started to usher people into it when the 'bolshoi salon' got choked. I organised all the Australians ahead of time —Ballard to catch the guests as passed on by me, and to help look after the 'specials'; North in charge of the National Hotel waiter who was supposed to be in charge of the main bar in the dining-room; Hanfield in charge of the second waiter in charge of the bar in my study; Mrs Hanfield, Miss Turton and Miss Swain (all Australians) moving round in charge of our servants supposed to be in charge of circulation of food and drinks. We had Paulina, Lisa, Varia, Zena and Paulina from downstairs all on deck, and all the extra hands made it possible to circulate food and drink more smoothly.

We asked all Heads of Missions and wives and counsellors and wives; all British Commonwealth; all Americans down to First Secretaries, and the French Naval Attache as an extra; Russians—Molotov and wife, 4 Deputy Foreign Ministers and wives, two from Protocol, Head of 2nd European Division, Head of Consular section, Mr. Burobin and Mr. Intourist; all the foreign press correspondents, including your old friends Mr and Mrs Stevens, whose party you are missing this month.

The Diplomatic Corps did its duty nobly, only those being absent (wives or husbands) who had colourable excuses—but practically all were there; most of the foreign press rolled up; Ballard lost a bet that we would get only two Russions. I was just beginning to calm down when the unexpected happened—the arrival of a real, live, Deputy Foreign Minister in the person of Mr Zorin, cum wife.

I then had to improvise. Ballard was shot downstairs to bring up Valsamakis, as Zorin speaks no English; meanwhile I took the two in tow (not a pun), sighing for my absent wife to help particularly to look after Mrs Zorin, and shepherded them into the study-bar, which was minus the waiter, who had to be found. By that time Ballard took over with Zorin and Valsamakis, while I dashed back to the receiving 'line' (consisting of myself) to welcome a bevy of Ambassadors and wives who chose to come at that moment. I ushered most of these into the study so that they could take over part of the job of entertaining Zorin, and eventually saw to my relief that the wife of the Swedish Ambassador (minus husband, who was recalled for Scandinavian Conferences) engaged in chatty conversation with the Zorins.

When the flow of Excellencies subsided, I took Zorin in charge (minus wife, unfortunately, as she had disengaged herself somewhere) and kept some conversation and liquor flowing. He was more than polite, both in conversation and in the length of his stay.

When he left, about ten to eight p.m., I dashed round the other guests, who mostly melted away about the right time except the inevitable hard-core boozers, whom we couldn't get rid of till about 10 p.m. This consisted of . . . . The (representatives of one Commonwealth country) had a field day.

The end of the show was annoying, but not fatal. All the main guests had left before it became obvious that a few had had too much. It was a nuisance for the servants, who wanted to start their own *prazdnik* [party], and for the Australian women, who were dead tired and needed some food. At length, Valya and Paulina managed to scramble together some cold food for all eight of us Australians—4 men, 4 women—and by the time we finished . . . it was midnight and everyone went home. I didn't try to sleep most of the night, but I was relieved that I had fought my way back into Moscow 'sassiety' again, at a time when most people have forgotten me. . . .

In terms of Soviet protocol and practice, the attendance of Mr and Mrs Zorin at the Australia-Day party was an act of grace. The Soviet authorities, of course, had no illusions that Australia could be counted as a Communist or a pro-Communist country; nor did they regard Australia as important from their point of view. However, the decision that Zorin instead of a mere Chief of Protocol should attend our national-day party was evidence that Australia and its Embassy in Moscow had 'registered'.

When my wife left Moscow for Australia with Mary and Peter I was uncertain when I would see her again. The twins were of an age when they had first call upon her, and it was essential that there should be no further interruption of their education. Moreover, the uncertainty as to my own situation after my interview with Dr Evatt in London and Burton's action in cutting off my Moscow allowances made it impossible for any plans to be made other than for my wife to remain in Australia with the children.

However, after I had gathered in Paris that the Minister was assuming I would be returning to Moscow, I cabled my wife to let her know that transfer to another post now seemed improbable and suggesting that she should return to Moscow in February 1949 and remain there until the following September, provided satisfactory arrangements could be made for the twins in Australian boarding schools. She would then return to Australia to be with the children again during the long summer holidays. By the time these were over my own period of service in the Soviet Union should be drawing to a close and Australian federal elections would have been held. No further plans could be made until after my own position clarified.

She received my cable aboard ship off the Australian coast, and telegraphed back agreeing to return to Moscow in the circumstances mentioned. She had written ahead to Frensham School at Mittagong, New South Wales, where Mary had been booked in for her secondary school course, explaining the new situation. The school authorities could not have been more helpful, or more prompt in reply. They offered to take Mary in to the junior school at once, and to keep her at Frensham until her secondary course was due to start. This generous gesture was a great relief, as it meant that Mary would have continuity at the school we had already chosen for her to attend later.

Arrangements for Peter, however, were not so easy. He too had been booked into the Sydney Church of England Grammar School for his secondary school course. Informed of the new circumstances, the Headmaster proved quite rigid in his approach and unimpressed by the fact that I was posted abroad as a representative of the Australian Government and that Peter's illness in Moscow made it impracticable for him to stay there. So my wife had to look elsewhere.

Eventually it was decided to book Peter in at a preparatory boarding school at Toowoomba, Queensland. The headmaster was well and favourably known to my sister, whose home would be open to him. John would be nearby, as a boarder as Toowoomba Grammar School. John was very unhappy there at first, and although in due course he settled in and matriculated well, his hearing became drastically impaired. As a child of three he had had a double middle-ear operation, before the time when sulpha drugs were available. At Toowoomba Grammar School he was a member of the School Cadets, and was placed in a machine-gun section. The noise left his hearing very much worse than it had been, and no medical treatment in subsequent years was able to ameliorate the condition.

During the summer holidays my wife took a house for the family at Hazelbrook, on the Blue Mountains. All the children were with her, including Alan. With school arrangements for Mary and Peter settled, she made air-bookings from Australia, leaving there in February 1949.

I decided to meet her in Stockholm. We had been separated for so many months that I did not relish our meeting again for the first time in the setting of perennial Moscow problems. In due course I flew to Stockholm from Moscow via Leningrad and Helsinki and booked in at the Grand Hotel. As my wife walked from the plane through the deep snow towards the airport building, wrapped in furs and clutching tensely a large handbag bulging with all the paper paraphernalia of travel—passport, traveller's cheques, medical certificate and the like, I realised at a glance the strain she had been under, both in Australia and during the journey back. When she saw me she began to relax, but it took some time before she became her normal self again.

During the remainder of 1949 there were no special developments at the Moscow post. On 12 May, the Soviet authorities lifted the Berlin blockade. While in later years Berlin remained a significant problem and again reached a crisis stage when Khrushchev was in power, for the time being tension in Europe between East and West eased considerably. To my substantial relief, I was not called upon to attend the second half of the Third Session of the U.N. General Assembly in April. It became practicable for me to move out of Moscow a little, accompanied sometimes by my wife.

In May we both journeyed to Tiflis (Tblisi) in Georgia. We had wanted to call en route at Rostov on the Don, but permission was refused by the Foreign Office on the alleged ground that it was a security area. When we reached Tiflis we found we could have arranged to visit Rostov from there (the Soviet authorities in Tiflis not having heard, presumably, of the proscription in Moscow), but developing digestive problems made it necessary to return direct to Moscow.

We had chosen Tiflis for a number of reasons. The journey by train lasted three days, and would give us an opportunity to see a lot of Russia outside Moscow; Georgia was Stalin's birthplace; moreover, Georgia was not Russian by cultural tradition, but a near-Middle-Eastern country which had developed a significant literature long before Russia. We felt that the visit to Tiflis would give us something of the 'feel' of a constituent republic of the Soviet Union whose people did not speak Russian as a first language.

We had a separate compartment in a clean and comfortable wagon-lit. At first we took our meals in the restaurant-car, hoping to have some contact with non-diplomatic Russians; but it soon became clear that the powers-that-be preferred us to be served meals in our compartment, despite the additional trouble involved. No doubt contacts were not encouraged, but there was an element of politeness as well in the decision. A Russian long-distance train is like no other I have experienced. As the journey proceeds, the train, or rather the people in it, 'warm-up'. Russians are a gregarious people, and tend to become increasingly 'matey' on a train, particularly after some of them have exchanged ordinary clothes for pyjamas, which seems the conventional thing to do, and have imbibed a little or a lot of alcohol. In the restaurant-car talk would be likely to become noisier and more boisterous; table cloths would get dirty; good crockery was in short supply; food ordinarily served would not have been deemed appropriate for the head of a foreign mission and his wife. By serving us in our compartment we could be offered the best food, linen and crockery available, without arousing comment from less favoured patrons.

After we left Moscow, the immensity of Russia spread before us—endless fields, clusters of villages with unimpressive izbas (peasant huts), the only building to stand out being an occasional church; poor soil merging, as we moved farther south, into more fertile black soil. The Donetz Basin was industrialised, with inevitable chimney stacks, mountains of slag, dust everywhere. In mountain areas the material for houses improved, as stone and pebble was available.

During the second day we reached the Black Sea which, on this occasion at least, was as blue as Sydney Harbour on a clear summer afternoon. The train stopped for no obvious reason, and all the passengers left their carriages and walked to the water's edge. To Russians who do not live on the coast merely to watch the sea is an experience—just as the first sight of surf breaking on the beach at Manly, a sea-side suburb of Sydney, is a sheer delight to children brought each year from the 'far West'. One of the Russians carelessly divested himself of his clothes, stepped over the narrow strip of shingle, entered the water and swam for awhile, apparently indifferent to the possible departure of the train without him. He then emerged, dried himself somewhat ineffectively with a handkerchief, dressed, stepped up into the engine, and the train resumed its journey.

For half-a-day the railway-track ran along the coast, at times seeming almost to hang over the sea. We passed through countless tunnels, all guarded by armed soldiers—with good reason, for the opportunities for sabotage of the line seemed immense. The train stopped at Sochi, a well-known holiday town whose platform was decorated with an honour board containing photographs of 'The best people in Sochi'—presumably officials, high party members and Stakhanovites. Another resort town, Sukhumi, where the train did not stop, had pleasant avenues with palms and seemed well-lit at night. After the lath and plaster houses of Moscow, in poor repair, the buildings seemed almost lavish. Among them were concrete palaces, with swimming pools, arcades decked with wisteria, and statues. Here the specially-favoured of the land could relax in a friendly climate on the so-called Russian Riviera and forget for a time the harsher realities of ordinary life in the Soviet Union.

Eventually the train turned inland behind the Caucasus and began to wind and climb through pleasant villages. There were flowers in the fields, and occasional glimpses of snow-capped peaks. At wayside stations children were selling rhododendrons and azaleas, wall-flowers and lily-of-the-valley. For my wife, who had grown up in a home whose gardens provided flowers all the year round, they were a sight for sore eyes.

On arrival at Tiflis we were met by an Intourist woman who took us in charge, organised our luggage into an old car and deposited us in two adequate hotel-rooms. She refused to speak Russian, as she wanted to practise her English, which was not very good. We were tired, dirty and hungry, and for the moment wanted no more than baths and breakfast, both of which took time to organise. There was no hot water until midday, and no plug in our bath, but in due course we were able to get reasonably clean and assuage our appetite. From our window we could see a small, stone Georgian church across a quiet street, with people entering freely to worship, and some passers-by pausing to cross themselves on their way past. In the distance were mountains wrapped in a blue haze.

We thoroughly enjoyed our stay in Tiflis, despite the constant ministrations of the Intourist guide and the occasional availability of a car which tended to break down. The city lies around a river bed, with bare hills nearby on whose vantage points were to be seen solid churches and ruined battlements. Tiflis has had to defend itself since the 4th century A.D. from attacks by Persians, Arabs, Mongols, Turks and Russians, and bears the scars of these encounters. Wandering along some cobbled streets, we investigated the old town where silver-smiths were at work in their booths; watched women washing clothes in water from the famous sulphur springs; and entrusted ourselves with some hesitation to a funicular railway which took us past the monastery of St David to the top of a hill laid out in ornamental gardens, with playing facilities for children and blue-cap boys on guard armed with rifles. From this latter vantage point we had an excellent view of Tiflis as a whole, with its river-valley, hills on either side and snow-capped peaks in the distance. In some ways this general view of the city made it seem less attractive than at close range, for tree-lined boulevards were blurred by a haze caused by industrial smoke.

In the newer parts of the town there were some modern stone buildings. Good shops seemed cleaner and better-equipped than in Moscow, and the people in them were better dressed. Many different racial types were represented and the women were often beautiful, with an air of intelligence and breeding. Children in neat school uniforms darted out of school looking clean, alert, sparkling and vivacious. No doubt they had not suffered as much as those in Moscow or Leningrad from the privations of the war; their health had been sustained by local fresh fruits and vegetables and dairy products. Yet health was not the only contributing factor. One sensed the presence of the Middle East, and the influence of ancient civilisations.

One of the main streets of Tiflis was named after Shota Rustaveli, a Georgian poet who flourished in the early part of the thirteenth century A.D. In a well-stocked book shop, I bought an English translation of one of his longest and best-known poems, *The Knight in the Tiger's Skin*. At the theatre we were impressed with Georgian-style dancing. The men were extremely active and vigorous, scenes often depicting preparation for war or actual combat which sometimes seemed physically dangerous for those performing. Women in long dresses, on the other hand, floated around the stage, the movement of their feet often being quite invisible. The general atmosphere was aristocratic rather than proletarian, the man playing the part of the chieftain and leader, the woman providing beauty and elegance.

While in Tiflis we felt we should pay our respects at the grave of A. S. Griboyedov, whose play *The Misfortune of Being Clever* we had so much admired in Moscow. Born in 1795, he was killed in Teheran at the age of thirty-four. He had been sent to Teheran as Minister-Plenipotentiary to supervise the execution of a treaty, and he died during an attack upon the Russian Embassy by Persians who resented refuge from Persian harems granted by the Embassy to Russian subjects. After the attack Griboyedov was identified only by a mark on a finger, as the victims were terribly mutilated. I had read in Moscow Pushkin's account of Griboyedov's premonition of impending death before he left for Persia. Pushkin relates how, while travelling through Georgia himself, he had encountered a cart with a coffin, travelling in the opposite direction. He asked the name of the dead person, and was told 'Griboyedov', whose body was being returned to Tiflis for burial in the monastery of St David. This was appropriate, as Griboyedov had spent some time in Georgia, and married a Georgian woman.

On this occasion we walked up a steep path, which wound like a zig-zag up the hill. As I sensed that we were being followed, I motioned my wife to a seat just after we had turned a corner. Shortly afterwards two men appeared and showed some embarrassment when they saw us staring at them. They were very inefficient sleuths. After momentary hesitation, they continued up the hill where, in the monastery garden, they were viewed with obvious disfavour by an elderly Georgian with a rifle slung across his shoulder who appeared to be the local guardian.

A service was in progress when we entered the Church, and many people were present. In an alcove an old priest dressed in gorgeous but somewhat grimy garments was officiating before an altar brightly lit with candles, and there was restrained singing. There were no statues, but we saw many old paintings and ikons. Outside the church was a ledge of rock on which were several graves, including that of Griboyedov.

In the train returning to Moscow I had time to reflect upon Georgian problems. For centuries the country had been a crossroads between East and West. This brought cultural benefits from both directions, but also regular invasion, hardship and the frustrations of submission for a small but proud and vigorous people. In the middle ages Georgia was free of foreign domination for over a hundred years, and reached its peak of power and influence in the days of Queen Tamara (1184-1212). It is this period which the poems of Rustaveli reflect, particularly his epic poem *The Knight in the Tiger's Skin,* which is full of adventure, doughty deeds and chivalrous attention to the needs of lovely maidens in distress.

The extension of Russian influence over Georgia, first by the Czars and later by Russian communists, was an exercise in imperialism. Ironically enough Stalin, who had master-minded communist control, was born in Georgia, as was Beria also. Perhaps there was poetic justice in the fact that if it was Stalin who was determined to bring Georgia under Russian Bolshevik Party control, it was he too, a Georgian, who was to dominate the Soviet Union, including all the Russians, who suffered greatly under his terrible purges. Although Georgia had been allowed to keep its language and the trappings of its ancient culture, the Army, the Police and the Party were under Russian control. Any Georgian who aspired to high office in the Soviet Union would have to be able to speak fluent Russian.

Situated where it was, perhaps it was unavoidable that Georgia had to submit to foreign domination, although during the 1950s and 1960s many countries became independent and sovereign members of the United Nations with far less claim, from the point of view of population and of economic and cultural resources. It was difficult to believe, however, that this brave and lively people could do other than resent Russian communist domination, or fail to long for the independence it had once enjoyed.

I had also bought in Tiflis an *Anthology of Georgian Poetry,* translated into English by Venera Urushadze. The translatress, obviously Georgian in origin, had a wide command of the English language, although the rhymed verse is at times somewhat forced in English. During the long journey back to Moscow I read a number of the poems. Two-thirds of them are pure Georgian in substance, sentiment and outlook; but communist authorities must have decided that the last third of the book must contain poems with a political purpose, designed to prove the beneficence of the All Seeing Little Father, Joseph Vissarionovich Djugashvili, alias Stalin. The prize poem of the last one-third of the book, which can be reproduced without comment, is an 'Ode to Stalin' by one Kolau Naridadze:

> He rises with the dawn. His eyes behold
> The face of Lenin lit by morning rays.
> And he who makes our lives a joy looks up
> And meets approval in his teacher's gaze.
> Lenin, the guiding light, the hope of all
> Oppressed mankind, smiles down at him with pride,
> At him who holds on high the flaming torch
> That floods the world with light both far and wide.
>
> Our life, our welfare are his constant care.
> He never rests but guards us day and night.
> He meets those kindly eyes with conscience clear
> For he has kept the trust undimmed and bright.
> He slowly lights his pipe. His humble home
> And Georgia's vales arise before his sight.

After spending a few weeks in Moscow to catch up with current problems,

I flew alone to Stalingrad for a three-day visit. The Battle of Stalingrad had become legendary as a turning point in the Russo-German war of 1941-45 and as the symbol of Russian tenacity and courage. In Czarist days the town had been known as Tsaritsyn, but when it had held against White Army attacks after the Revolution of 1917, it was renamed in honour of Stalin. When Stalin died and Khrushchev made his famous speech in 1956 criticising Stalin, it was decided to change the name of the city again and it is now called Volgograd.

When I made my visit I was conscious mainly of devastation, for reconstruction had scarcely begun. Facilities were few, but a battered Intourist car enabled me to move from my hotel to the highest point on the west bank of the Volga, and to the banks of the river itself which, at this point, was about one-third of a mile wide. The land on the East bank was very little higher than the river itself, but on the western side the river bank rose to a height of fifteen to twenty feet. Here the Russian defenders had dug in, although there was also bitter house-to-house fighting in the buildings on the west bank. The Germans penetrated almost to the highest nearby hill before being thrown back. This was a dramatic setting, and I was moved by the visible relics of the heroic defence.

By chance I saw a notice in my hotel indicating that a film on the battle of Stalingrad was being shown during my stay. The performance was in the open air, presumably because no suitable building of sufficient size was still standing and available. Some hundreds of people were present, sitting on hard benches, with a number of the audience behind the screen. There was trouble with the electricity supply, which ceased for fifteen minutes on one occasion. This enforced interruption of the entertainment was accepted by those present in complete silence—in Australia there would have been stamping and whistling before the first five minutes had elapsed. Perhaps the subject-matter of the film restrained the audience, for the sufferings of the defenders of the city had been such that a mere interruption in the electricity supply might well seem to most a pleasant interlude. The film itself, though exaggerated after the manner of other heroic Soviet films, stirred the emotions deeply because of the surrounding evidence of human courage amidst physical destruction.

Later, my wife and I spent an elongated week-end in Leningrad, where we wandered along the quays of the canals, inspected bookshops in the Nevsky Prospect, attended a magnificent performance of the *Bronze Horseman* ballet, and travelled some distance out of the city to visit the Peterhof Palace with its formal gardens and gilded statues glistening with water from the fountains. I also paid a pilgrimage to Pushkin's small study when he was a schoolboy at the Czar's Summer Palace. By that time I had become familiar with most of his writings available in translation (and a selected few in the original). I had also read Troyat's two-volume biography of the poet in a French edition which I had picked up in Paris at a stall on the banks of the Seine on the way back from the conference in Geneva. It was Pushkin's genius which demonstrated, in prose as well as in verse, what the Russian language could be and do. He had absorbed European culture through the French language, and it was his example, more than any other's, which pre-

L

pared the way for brilliant Russian literary achievements during the nine-teenth century from which many European writers, in their turn, drew inspiration.

Unlike Moscow, Leningrad had a persistent European flavour. In the Hermitage Museum, we noted the number of busts of Voltaire, which reminded us of the links between Voltaire and Catherine the Great.

Nearer to Moscow we went on a few short trips by car to permitted places. The most interesting of these was a visit to Zagorsk, called Sergievo in pre-revolutionary times, a little town some seventy kilometres from Moscow where there is a walled monastery which has played an important part in Russian history.

The Monastery of the Trinity, founded by St Sergius in the fourteenth century at a time when Tartar raids were forcing Russian settlement north-ward, gradually became famous, rich and a centre of pilgrimage. Its association with the Czars was close, and Boris Godonuv is buried there. Strongly fortified, it held out against a protracted siege by a Polish army during the Time of Troubles which followed the death of Boris. It was the recipient of large bequests, and by the end of the eighteenth century owned half a million peasants.

After the revolution of 1917, the Soviet authorities turned it into a museum, and sought to maintain and repair it as a national monument. When we visited it, however, the Uspenski Cathedral within the crenellated walls surrounding the monastery buildings was still allowed to function as a church, and the faithful were in attendance. At the entrance to the Cathedral silent beggars held out caps or tins for alms; inside, Soviet artists were endeavouring to restore the ancient frescoes.

The museum section of the monastery was filled with rich religious vestments, ikons, enamelware and peasant wood-carvings. It was the carvings which attracted our attention more than the jewelled garments, or even the finely-worked peasant embroidery. All the objects of everyday life—horses, boats, dogs and human beings—had been carved with skill and humour, and bespoke the basic occupations, needs and interests of simple men and women the world over.

Travel within the Soviet Union, though stimulating and useful, was never a holiday. As the year drew on my wife and I began to make plans for annual leave outside Russia, prior to her return to Australia to be with the children during their summer vacation. The continuing psychological strain of living behind the iron curtain, with its lack of privacy, political insecurity and daily frustrations had begun to take its toll. One night when we were attending a performance at the Bolshoi Theatre, we went out to the front entrance during an interval to get some fresh air. Seeing no Russians near, I began to speak flippantly and critically of the country to which I was accredited. My wife told me she thought it was time for me to leave the country. She was right.

I wrote to Canberra saying that I wanted to take three weeks' leave in Italy, which neither of us had visited, and was astonished to receive a reply from Burton that my leave should be taken in the Soviet Union. His argu-ments were entirely unconvincing and I came to the conclusion that, for some reason or other, he or the Minister or both wanted to keep me behind the iron curtain. This attitude made me angry and I prepared to fight. There was no political reason why I should remain—many members of the Diplomatic Corps were taking leave outside the country—so long as I stayed within the Soviet Union the responsibility for all staff and other administrative problems would remain mine. I wrote or cabled to Canberra expostulating in strong terms.

Eventually I received an instruction, quite contrary to the last, to proceed to Stockholm, Oslo and Copenhagen on an official mission. At that time Australia had no diplomatic representation in Sweden, Norway or Denmark. This was becoming increasingly embarrassing, as these countries were represented in one way or another in Australia. Canberra asked me to make a brief visit to each of the three capital cities and to report on the practicability of Australian representation at minimum cost. In effect, I was asked to form a judgment on whether diplomatic representation in all three countries was necessary; or whether an Australian accredited in one of the three could also be accredited to the other two, or at least to one other of the three.

I was delighted to be given this mission. My wife and I left Moscow by air for Helsinki and Stockholm on 30 September, 1949 and spent about nine days visiting Stockholm, Oslo and Copenhagen, travelling by train between them. In each capital I made a courtesy call on the local Foreign Office, without disclosing the reasons for my visit to the countries in question, and sought the frank advice of relevant members of the local Diplomatic Corps, particularly those of the British and American Ambassadors. As this advice proved unanimous, I felt encouraged to make firm recommendations to Canberra.

The differences we found between people in Sweden and Norway intrigued us. We knew Stockholm reasonably well, and had come to regard it as a place of refuge from frustrations in the Soviet Union. The Swedish Ambassador to Moscow and his Russian wife were friends whom we respected greatly. Yet we had found Swedish society somewhat formal and protocolaire. When we crossed the border by train into Norway, the Norwegians we met seemed more approachable, responsive and ready to talk. The echoes of the Second World War had not died down. Norway had been occupied by the Germans; Sweden had escaped occupation. It was perhaps natural that Norwegians seemed more interested in their war-time allies than the Swedes.

We found the scenery around Oslo beautiful. The town itself was small, squeezed in between hills and fjord; but it was easy to get out of the city by electric train into forest country, where there were wonderful views of the fjord below and its small, wooded islands. Most of the forest trees were of spruce, but birches and other deciduous trees here and there showed up brightly at that time of the year against the darker background. Trails through the woods down towards the city were perfect for skiing in winter. In Oslo itself we spent some time viewing the vigorous and ubiquitous statuary of the Norwegian sculptor Vigeland, whose works filled a whole park.

The journey by train from Oslo to Copenhagen lasted thirteen hours, the track running down to Sweden, whence one crossed the water by ferry-train. In Denmark the fields looked incredibly green, and the cattle in splendid condition. Copenhagen seemed a solid, prosperous city and its inhabitants perhaps a little too well-fed.

My mission finished in Copenhagen and thereafter we began to enjoy our once-forbidden leave outside the Soviet Union. First we flew from Copenhagen to London, where we had to make the necessary financial arrangements. Unfortunately, sterling currency for travel on the continent of Europe was heavily restricted at that time, and our plans had to take this fact strictly into account. We found that the best way to use the money available to us was to pay in advance in English currency train fares to Venice via France and Switzerland, arrange a tourist trip by char-a-banc from Venice to Rome via Florence (with fixed hotel costs also met in advance), and book return train tickets back from Rome to London. This left us with a small margin in foreign currency to meet the unexpected.

We greatly enjoyed the Italian excursion, despite the fact that my wife's health did not permit full use of our opportunities. During 1949 neither of us had been particularly well in Moscow; in London my wife went down with influenza; the change to Italian food upset her somewhat. But in Venice we found sunshine, and after being snow-bound in northern climes for so long it refreshed our spirits. Coming as we did from the Soviet Union, we saw Byzantine influence everywhere in Venice. Yet the splendours of the city, including the Palace of the Doges and the Church of St Mark echoed the past rather than the present. The great days of Venice were over; much of what remained was decayed or decaying, with the sea encroaching more and more. It almost seemed as though Venice was surviving primarily through tourism, and one wondered how long this situation could continue.

After the interminable, flat Russian steppes, the landscape of Italy was a delight. Constant glimpses of mountain and sea; tidy, well-cared-for fields; hill-tops with village houses built of stone; towns with glorious churches and public buildings, evidence of a long and honourable architectural tradition.

We lost our hearts to Florence, with its buildings, statues, paintings and exquisite sense of proportion. The city was small enough to be comprehensible. From the hillside of Fiesole the eye could take it in at one sweep, before resting upon the balanced bulk and lines of the Duomo with Giotto's Campanile alongside. The treasures of the Uffizi Gallery alone demanded weeks of attention, whereas we had only a few days for Florence as a whole. Botticelli, Andrea del Sarto, Michelangelo, Raphael—all the masters seemed well represented in church or monastery or museum or public place. Ghiberti's doors at the entrance to the Baptistry were a miracle of living bronze.

On the way to Rome we called at Assisi, where we admired the frescoes of Giotto and paid tribute to the humble spirit of St Francis. Rome was too vast to do more than note what on some later occasion, with more time, and usable finance, we would wish to see more thoroughly. But the Forum and the Colosseum provided some of the atmosphere of ancient Rome, while the Vatican and St Peter's bespoke the prestige and power of the Papacy.

We wandered around the interior vastnesses of St Peter's, admiring specific treasures such as the Pieta of Michelangelo, but the inside of the Basilica did not attract us as much as its exterior form. My political interest drew my attention to the large number of confessionals, where priests could perform their duties, apparently, in almost any well-known language. In later years I served in countries where there were Papal Nuncios. These were invariably highly intelligent men, whose views on current affairs deserved careful consideration. One can easily under-estimate the significance of the flow of political information and advice to the Papacy through its diplomatic representatives abroad.

The lift took us to the whispering gallery of St Peter's, and I then left my tired wife on the roof-top overlooking the vast piazza below while I ascended the winding stairs to the top of the dome and climbed ladders to its highest accessible point, whence one can look out over the city. My thoughts turned back towards Moscow where, as a keen student in younger days of Dostoevsky's famous chapter 'The Grand Inquisitor', I had often thought of Rome. Here I reversed the process, thinking of the Soviet Union from the point of view of the Roman Catholic Church.

Both Rome and Moscow espoused the principle of authority, to which the individual must submit. Both inspired faith, though of very different kinds, in true believers as distinct from mere opportunists. Both quoted illuminating texts from sacred scriptures. To me, authentic atheism should imply indifference, so that the militant atheism of convinced Communist Party members suggested rather an inverted form of religious belief or emotion.

But there were great differences as well between Rome and Moscow. The belief in resurrection and a future life for those who were saved made earthly existence far less important for the Christian, and earthly suffering in some sense acceptable. Such a belief was lacking in the Communist ideology, which sought controlled Utopia on earth, and fostered rebellion to achieve it. When Gogol in his later years turned to religion and preached resignation, he was bitterly attacked by Belinski in a famous letter written in 1847, the terms of which could easily have been written by Soviet Communist authorities:

> The resignation preached by you is, in the first place, nothing new and, in the second, smacks on the one hand of fearful pride and, on the other, of the most disgraceful debasement of one's human dignity. The idea of rising superior to all men through resignation can only be the fruit either of pride or of feeblemindedness, and in both cases inevitably leads to hypocrisy, sanctimoniousness, celestial quietism. . . .[56]

Many questions passed through my mind as I mused at the top of St Peter's —far more questions than answers. To what extent was the principle of authority espoused by the Catholic Church identical with that acted upon

[56] See *A Treasury of Russian Literature*, B. G. Guerry (Ed.), (The Blakiston Co., Philadelphia, 1943), p. 248.

by the Communist hierarchy? Did Dostoevski malign the Catholic Church in the answers given to Christ, on his second coming, by the Grand Inquisitor? Was Christ's doctrine, as charged, one for the élite, the chosen few only, whereas the Church, in its greater compassion, took the burden of responsibility from the individual and eased the lot of all who believed? Why did Christ find it unnecessary to answer the charge in words, by argument, but rested his case on a simple, symbolic act? Which is the more important, order, or justice; freedom of the individual to choose, or enforced conformity for the alleged benefit of the community as a whole?

We returned to London in time for my wife to do some shopping before leaving for Australia on 11 November by the R.M.S. *Orion*. A few days later I flew back to Moscow, via Berlin. Fog delayed me for one day in Berlin, and we were lucky to get off the ground on the following day. The Soviet plane was scheduled to land in Warsaw en route, but bad weather led to a change in flight-plan. Near Minsk we plummeted down from 5,000 feet through fog, and when we saw the ground we were only one or two hundred feet above it. After some sharp turns we landed all right—whereupon visibility disappeared and we were grounded.

I was given a room at the airport, but the heating was either not on or not working and I nearly froze, although mid-winter had not arrived. I went to bed in my clothes and overcoat, but was unable to sleep much. Next day the weather was even worse, and I was told we couldn't leave that day. As the weather could stay like this for a week, and I had no local currency, I decided to return to Moscow by train, after making arrangements by telephone with our Embassy for transmission of enough funds to enable me to eat and to buy a ticket.

The reversion to Russian food upset my stomach, and I had to make emergency use of public toilet facilities en route to the railway station. The sight inside beggared description—no privacy and no seats, just holes in the ground. I was glad to get aboard the train, despite the fact that there was no *wagon-lit*. The conductor put me in four-berth, 'soft' compartment and I turned my face to the wall hoping for privacy and without ambition for food or drink.

During the night I heard the door to my compartment slide open, and a cheerful, slightly bibulous Russian voice asking 'Is number sixteen here?' 'No!' I replied, in a tone of voice intended to indicate that the intruder was not welcome. 'Thanks', replied the Russian, entering the compartment and stretching himself easily on a bunk opposite me after closing the door. I slept fitfully, but awoke to the noise of the door opening again. Turning my head, I watched a scene one could scarcely imagine outside an authoritarian country. At the door stood a stern-faced conductress, beckoning to my companion to withdraw from the compartment. The powers-that-be had decided that I was to be left alone, whether out of consideration for me or to sever contact between a foreigner and a Russian I would not know. The cheerfulness had disappeared from the face of the convivial intruder who, with mouth half-open, obeyed the signal to remove himself from my presence. The door was closed after him. I sighed with relief and turned my face to the wall again. Ten minutes later the door opened once more with a click. The conductress came quietly into the compartment and, without a word, retrieved a packet of cigarettes which my companion had left behind him, presumably in order to return it to a complaining owner. There were no more interruptions during the rest of the trip.

The journey from Minsk to Moscow by that particular train took twenty-three hours. After my experience of Minsk and the train, the Australian Embassy seemed a paradise of comfort and convenience. I told the staff not to come back to Moscow from leave through Berlin during the winter months.

Moscow was having more than its usual share of illness and problems amongst the foreigners. Lady Kelly, wife of the British Ambassador who had replaced Sir Maurice Peterson, had had sinus trouble, then laryngitis, then jaundice. The Norwegian Ambassador had had a stroke. Australian and New Zealand wives about to have babies were wondering, after the death in Moscow during child-birth of a foreign child, whether they should not fly outside the Soviet Union for their happy events.

Staff at the Australian Embassy was turning over, and I was having difficulty securing suitable replacements. On 3 December, 1949 Ballard had left at Canberra's request. Although he had been in Moscow only just under a year, I made no effort to hold him. He had acquired a useful knowledge of Russian, but had not otherwise proved suitable. On the other hand, F. E. Blakeney and his attractive wife had been sent to Moscow, and I was very glad to have them. In my wife's absence it meant a good deal to have a senior Australian diplomatic wife at hand. The Blakeneys were somewhat worried about the health of their only child, Sally, who began by catching the usual winter colds.

The Italian Ambassador, Manlio Brosio, was now Dean of the Corps. He had had a difficult time settling in after the war, but he and his wife were much respected by their colleagues. Later he became Ambassador in Washington, London and Paris, and Secretary-General of NATO. Mrs Pandit had left. She had never been happy in the drab surroundings of Moscow, which contrasted with the beauty of her exquisite saris. She had been succeeded by Dr Sarvepalli Radhakrishnan, an Indian philosopher equally at home with Eastern and Western thought and, one would have thought, a somewhat improbable choice as Ambassador. He would leave a dinner-party early without recognition of protocol in order to get back to his Sanskrit texts. Social life bored him, but India had great problems and he made his contribution in an effort to solve them. In due course he gained access to Stalin, and in later years became Vice-President and then President of India. Contact with him in Moscow encouraged me to call upon him whenever I passed through New Delhi.

On 30 November, 1949 elections were held in New Zealand and resulted in the overthrow of the Labor Party Government, which had held office since 1935. This caused some perturbation amongst New Zealand's diplomatic representatives in Moscow, as the National Party had advocated abolition or reduction in strength of the New Zealand Legation in the Soviet Union.

But the biggest event of the year for my wife and myself was the result of the Australian federal elections, held on 10 December. She heard the results aboard ship, somewhere out from Melbourne, while I had my ears glued to receivers of the Embassy radio set, which picked up very faint reports of news broadcast on short-wave direct from Australia. Slowly it dawned upon me that the Labor Party had been defeated by the Liberal-Country Party Coalition team, under the respective leadership of Mr. R. G. Menzies and Mr. A. W. Fadden. This meant one thing to both of us, namely, that Dr Evatt was no longer Minister for External Affairs and that the Diplomatic Service of Australia might again seem an attractive career.

I was not a member of any political party and knew well only one probable senior member of the Cabinet—Mr R. G. Casey who had returned to Australian politics after service for the United Kingdom in the Middle East and Bengal. In a letter to my wife written 15 December I referred to 'the tremendous weight that is off my mind'. The letter continued: 'I have no feelings regarding the change of party—I do not even know whether it is a good thing. But no new Minister can possibly be as difficult as the last.'

At the time I wrote, the new Cabinet had not been named. In the letter I speculated as to whether or not John Burton would remain Secretary of the Department. If he resigned, or were removed, Hodgson, Officer or Stirling might be appointed in his place, but I thought any of these appointments unlikely. If I myself were called back to that job, I would not hesitate to accept it, partly in order to bring the family together again and partly to help develop an organised *departmental* foreign policy for the consideration of a Minister and improve departmental morale as a whole. Finally, I added that the substance of any further contribution I could make regarding the Soviet Union was already on paper in draft form as a historical report on Russia.

Sensing that my days in Moscow were numbered, I rushed around the town on a buying spree. Within the rigid limits of what was available and what I could afford, I purchased a number of books, a couple of pieces of old Russian enamel work, and some sets of recordings of extracts from a range of plays performed at the Little Theatre.

Christmas was in the air in more senses than one, but with my family thousands of miles away once again, I found it difficult to generate the appropriate Christmas mood. What happened on Christmas Day is best described in an extract from a letter to my wife:

> I let it be known that I'd gladly have here (at the Embassy) all Australians who wanted to come, but didn't want anyone to come who preferred to stay at home. Not unnaturally, as we now have 4 families, all preferred to stay at home. I then refused to go through the motions of having a Christmas tree decorated on behalf of the Klavdia's etc. Instead, I decided to get Valya to help me select and wrap food parcels cum cigarettes for all the dozens of Russians, and to organise a party for them all on Xmas day. I didn't know what to give our servants, so gave them cash to buy something for themselves. All the others were given some flour, meat, peaches and odds and ends. In addition, they were given enough light liquor to wash down the food Valya bought and cooked for them. 16 sat down to dinner in the laundry, kids and all.
> Blakeneys invited me to go to their place for lunch, and Trueloves to

their place for dinner. . . . However, . . . on 24th. I got an attack of Moscow tummy which made it quite impossible for me to move out (or eat) on 25th—so I didn't go anywhere. I just paced the floor and cursed the world.

As usual, our Russian scamps managed to be just human enough to get under my skin. Even Paulina was upset because I couldn't eat anything on Xmas day. Just before lunch Valya came up and said apologetically that all the boys and girls were down below ready to eat. They were all sorry I was not having a prazdnik myself. They would like me to come down and join them in a toast, but not if I didn't feel like it etc. etc. So I went down below (holding my stomach). They were sitting at some sort of a table spread all over the laundry and when I appeared they all solemnly stood up while I stuttered three words of cheer and sipped a glass of wine I couldn't hold. Then I fled upstairs, thinking against my will that the Russian scalawags in spite of all their 'sins' are really rather more attractive than many of the foreign community here . . .

Over Christmas and New Year there were diplomatic parties in all directions, but I enjoyed none of them for my mind was back in Australia. Mr P. C. Spender, whom I barely knew, had been appointed Minister for External Affairs, but he was to leave almost immediately for a British Commonwealth Conference in Colombo. I was somewhat uneasy lest the new Australian government might under-estimate the importance of a post in Moscow, like the new New Zealand government, so spent much time and energy drafting a telegraphic 'appreciation' of the position in the Soviet Union at the end of 1949. This had to be put into cypher by the Australian staff, whom I had to press almost rudely to get the work done in time to be available before Cabinet met and Spender left Australia. As good Canberra public servants, some of them felt that work during or near the festive seasons should be minimal. This necessary splurge of activity was not helped by partial 'remonts' (repairs) which were being carried out in various parts of the Residence and the Chancery.

In January 1950 the temperatures went down to about 25 degrees Centigrade below zero. Half the foreign colony developed influenza or worse. Mrs Blakeney had to take to her bed for a week with sinus trouble, while her daughter Sally developed a fever for the third time. Some servants were ill and the others had too much to do. A new car arrived from England—without a heating unit. Never had the wearying round of staff problems seemed worse. I found myself trying to track down temporary help in the Chancery from Australians in England and Germany, but nothing developed from these fanciful inquiries.

Shortly after the elections I had sent off to Canberra a formal recommendation that my term in Moscow should not last beyond June 1950, by which time I would have been there three years. No reply came for over a month. While this was understandable in view of the change in government and Spender's absence in Colombo, uncertainty as to my future was becoming more and more embarrassing to my family. If I were to be called back quickly to Australia, it made no sense for my wife to return to Moscow; on the other hand, she had said that she would return even if I remained in the Soviet Union only until June. Arrangements for the children also depended, in some cases at least, upon whether I was to be in Canberra or abroad for most of the year.

About mid-January I received at long last a reply from Anstey Wynes, then Deputy Secretary and apparently Acting Secretary while Burton was on leave. 'The Minister . . . asked me to write . . . a personal note requesting you to hold yourself in readiness to return to Australia "at least for consultation" in about March.' With his customary caution, Anstey added 'I am sorry I cannot be more definite. . . . My own impression is that the Minister will so require, but, of course, this will have to await his return . . . late in January.'

I was tremendously cheered by this news, however vague. It was the first evidence that Spender might have other plans in mind for me, or that, at the least, he understood the need for me to return to Australia for consultation, during which my future would no doubt be discussed. I began to clear my decks for action, destroying personal papers which I burned in the chip-heater in the bathroom. In the process I gathered up unwittingly a fine watch which my wife had given me as a birthday-present: it came to a sad end in the heater. I also wrote to Canberra colleagues posted abroad to ask if there was any chance of renting any of the houses they controlled in Canberra.

The servants must have guessed that something was afoot, because they suddenly pressed me for increased salaries, uniforms, overcoats and what-have-you. I had them assembled and, through Valsamakis, informed them that I was getting too many complaints and demands. If anyone was dissatisfied, he or she should leave immediately. This procedure was a somewhat risky bluff, but it had a salutary effect.

Mildred cabled saying she was quite ready to fly back to Moscow even if my stay there were no more than a month after her arrival, but in reply I strongly discouraged any such action, however much I appreciated the spirit of the offer. On 2 February, 1950 the heavens opened. I received a cable from Canberra instructing me to return to Australia 'as soon as convenient to report . . . you will have opportunity to take leave and may not return to Moscow. Mildred informed.' I made plans to be in London fourteen days later, and in Australia in a further week.

I was now able to discuss plans freely with Blakeney, who would become Chargé d'Affaires. When he expressed surprise at the proposed speed of my departure, and doubt whether I could complete arrangements in time, I told him that, of the many things I had learned in the United States, one of the most important was 'When you see a green light, step on the gas'. Only one thing could delay my programme; namely, failure to secure a Russian exit visa in time. I asked him to take up this matter personally at once and press it hard. The public ground of my departure must be that I was returning on leave and for consultation: no farewell parties would therefore be acceptable.

I am afraid that few of my diplomatic colleagues, upon some of whom I paid farewell calls, believed my story or expected that I would return to Moscow, but as I had no authority to hint that I might not be back, I was firm in resisting invitations to celebratory parties. The New Zealand First Secretary, however, took no notice of my objection, and arranged an informal gathering of a few friends which I did attend and during which he predicted with assurance that I would not be returning.

On the last day I said farewell to the Russian servants with real regret. From time to time they had been naughty, but circumstances were extremely hard for them and for their relatives and it was not for me to criticise. Moreover, they had shown spontaneous affection for our children, and developed a certain kind of loyalty to the Australian establishment.

All the Australians accompanied me to the airport, scarcely identifiable in their winter overcoats, caps or hats. Saying good-bye to them, I found it difficult to maintain my composure. On many occasions during my time in Moscow I had been to the railway-station or the airport to farewell friends, and had held no conscious grudge against them for their cheerful faces and expectations. Yet as I walked to the plane, mounted the steps and waved back from the door, I viewed with emotion the thin line of Australians who waved back, isolated in a country so different and so far from their own. In a few minutes I would be in the air, heading for home and normality; they would return to their flats to continue to bear all the frustrations and tribulations of daily existence. Was I running out on them, deserting them, leaving them to their fate? If I were re-posted to Canberra, were there ways in which I could help them?

Fortunately one cannot live in the past when one is busy with the present and the future draws one on. When I left the Russian plane emotional reactions to the experiences of the preceding three years began to fade. It had been a tough assignment, but one I would not have missed for anything. I counted myself unusually fortunate to have lived in the United States for five years, and in the Soviet Union for approximately three years. These were the two countries likely to dominate the immediate post-war world, competitors for leadership, power and influence. Henceforth I would not have to read Karl Marx or Lenin to know what it was like living in a communist country, or rather, in a country of communist ideology: I would now be able to sense the presence and activity of communism through the pores of the skin, even in persons who were not Russian. True, Soviet citizens were as much Russian as communist, and that too was an important lesson. My early reading of 19th century Russian literature had not been wasted. Dictatorship in Russia was pre-communist as well as post-communist, while national patriotism was a significant aspect of both eras. What was necessary now was to put this invaluable experience of the Soviet Union into world perspective, and to try to induce Australian political masters to take this perspective into due account in determining Australian policy.

5

CANBERRA

Three

Breathes there the man, with soul so dead,
Who never to himself hath said,
    This is my own, my native land!
Whose heart hath ne'er within him burn'd,
As home his footsteps he hath turn'd
    From wandering on a foreign strand![57]

MANY times in my life have I returned to Australia from overseas, but on no occasion have I been more conscious of my nationality than when I returned from Russia. I had left Moscow when it was snow-bound. There I had felt isolated, land-locked and on the wrong side of an iron curtain. Some ten days later I was strolling along the esplanade at Manly with members of my family, eyes screwed up to reduce the glare of the brilliant summer sunshine, watching the breakers pounding towards a magnificent beach, admiring swimmers and surf-board riders who seemed to have not a care in life. These were two different worlds.

My friends told me that my skin was as white as a sheet and that too many diplomatic dinners had led me to put on weight. I was also accused of continuing to look over my shoulder before making any critical remark. When I commented, now and again, that someone in the Sydney area was speaking Russian, doubts as to my sanity arose, although it was not my imagination leading me astray: one hears what one is tuned to hear. It was noticed that when I read in Australian newspapers outspoken criticism of some governmental decision in Canberra, I winced visibly—as if I thought it wrong for such things to be said in a newspaper.

I reported to Canberra, was sent on leave and joined my wife and Alan at Balgowlah, up the hill by bus from Manly, in a small cottage which Mildred had found with much difficulty over the holiday season. It was far

[57] 'The Lay of the Last Minstrel', by Sir Walter Scott.

from satisfactory, and after scurrying around I found a pleasant flat in a new, three-storey building in the same suburb, with a verandah looking out over a golf-course. There we ensconced ourselves until Alan's University term began. John, Mary and Peter had all returned to their schools at Toowoomba or Mittagong. Mary joined us during school holidays, but before she arrived my wife and I flew to Toowoomba to see the two boys, staying with my sister for a few days. John steered me to a tennis court and there produced a booming service, developed in my absence, and ran me all over the court—much to my wife's amusement at this turning of the tables.

In Canberra I had found that no decision had been taken about my future. Spender told me to take leave for the time being, and then to help him on the side-lines at the meeting in Sydney of the British Commonwealth Consultative Committee on Economic Aid for Southeast Asia, held between 15-20 May, 1950 at Admiralty House, Sydney, This meeting set the stage for the formal establishment of the Colombo Plan.

As Minister for External Affairs of the host country, Spender was elected Chairman of the Conference. A considerable tussle developed between him and the Leader of the British Delegation, both using the Sydney Press as a means of furthering their respective points of view, and each being critical of the other for so doing. The British Delegation, concerned about the sterling-dollar problem, was cautious about any immediate financial commitments. Spender, on the other hand, felt that the Plan would never get off the ground unless there were some urgent action. He was able to overcome British hesitation in regard to a Technical Assistance programme, but not in regard to an emergency fund of £15 million designed to help meet priority capital needs of Asian Commonwealth countries. Agreement on the latter was delayed pending preparation by each recipient country of a statement describing its economic situation and development requirements, to be considered at a further meeting in London later in the year.[58] Future experience was to show that Spender's pressure regarding technical assistance was well justified, this aspect of the Colombo Plan having proved an undoubted success. Under the Technical Assistance programme many thousands of trainees from Asia have studied in Australia, and hundreds of Australian experts have visited developing countries to give advice. Naturally, in a programme of this size a number of important problems have arisen, including the question whether many might not be more cheaply trained in their own countries with Australian assistance, and settle more easily into subsequent work in their own milieu.

When I returned to Canberra after the Conference, Spender told me that John Burton had asked for six months' leave of absence without pay. The Minister told him that he could take the leave if he insisted, but in that event a new Secretary of the Department would have to be appointed. Burton took the leave, and retired temporarily to the country property not far from Canberra which he had acquired—and run—while Secretary.

In later years the story was put about that Burton had been dismissed from office by the Liberal-Country Party government, because his sym-

[58] For the Final Communique of the Conference, see Current Notes, Vol. XXI (1950) pp. 350-51.

pathies were with the Labor Party. I know no evidence to support this rumour. Menzies was doubtless critical of Burton, but Spender at no time suggested to me that he had wanted to get rid of the Secretary. The initiative for requesting six months' leave came from Burton, for reasons which he alone knows. Presumably these included disagreement with important government policies as they later developed, but some of these were obvious during the six months he had chosen to stay on as Secretary after the change of government. While on leave he would still remain a member of the Commonwealth Public Service, and as such would be entitled to some senior appointment when his leave expired.

When Burton had made his decision, Spender raised with me the question of my appointment as Burton's successor. The Minister told me frankly that he did not know me well, but he had discussed me with Casey, who had given him a good report. Spender said he was prepared to recommend me to Cabinet, unless I preferred to continue service overseas.

I accepted the offer immediately, for a variety of reasons which have already been made clear. I had no qualms about Burton's reactions, as he had had none about my appointment to Moscow at a time when my seniority and experience gave me much stronger claims than his to appointment as Secretary in 1947. On 19 June I was formally appointed Secretary, Department of External Affairs.

Burton's career as a public servant does not end here, and needs to be rounded off as an element of departmental history. Perhaps this is the best place. Towards the end of 1950, when his leave was about to expire, I raised with the Minister the question of Burton's future employment. I suggested that he should be offered the post of Australian High Commissioner to Ceylon which was then vacant. I argued that it would be invidious for an ex-Secretary to serve in Canberra under his successor; that he needed experience in an overseas diplomatic post; and that, as he had a keen interest in Asia, in some aspects of economics and in the Colombo Plan, a post like Ceylon would be appropriate. Spender agreed and made the offer, which was accepted.

Burton left Sydney for Colombo on 2 February, 1951, and remained there less than two months. Over the years it has been my habit to listen to radio news reports in the early morning, before breakfast. One morning I was startled to hear a news item stating that Burton had arrived in Darwin and had there publicly criticised Australian government policy. He was still High Commissioner to Ceylon, and had not sought from the Minister for External Affairs or from me permission to leave his post. Federal elections were impending, following a rare double dissolution of Parliament which the Governor-General had granted at the request of the Prime Minister. Burton had simply decided to stand, as a Labor Party candidate, for a seat in the House of Representatives. In the event the Liberal-Country Party won a majority in both Houses, and Burton was defeated in the seat for which he stood. Under the Commonwealth Public Service Act, he was still entitled to apply for re-appointment to the Public Service within a prescribed period.

I was outraged by Burton's conduct which, in my opinion, disqualified him from re-appointment to the Public Service in general and the Department of External Affairs in particular. He could easily have requested permission to return to Australia on the ground that he wanted to stand for parliament, resigned as High Commissioner to Ceylon, and then expressed whatever views he wished. Instead, he had flouted every rule necessary for the operation of a Diplomatic Service. I therefore had discussions with the Solicitor-General about the possibility of some penalty being imposed. These proved singularly unhelpful. Meanwhile the Government decided, for political reasons, not to pursue any course which might have made Burton seem a martyr. I thereupon collected all the relevant papers and sent them to the Public Service Board so that its members would at least be fully aware of the facts if Burton should apply to re-enter the Service.

In the event, he did not apply for re-appointment within the prescribed period. Had he done so, I have no idea what would have happened. Personally, I was much relieved, as I could think of no relevant position in the Department of External Affairs to which, in the circumstances, a person of his seniority and background could be appointed.

When I became Secretary, it was clear that I would remain in Australia for an indefinite number of years. My first responsibility was to find a home in Canberra for my family. By great good fortune, Peter Heydon's house in Tennyson Crescent, Forrest, became available. He himself was still overseas and his tenant, another officer of the Department of External Affairs, had just built his own home. Peter let me occupy his furnished house as tenant. It was pleasant, with substantial grounds, situated in an attractive area, and we could expect to continue to use it so long as Peter was posted abroad. In the meanwhile I would have time in which to look around with a view to buying or building a house, if I could find the necessary capital.

My salary as Secretary was determined by the Public Service Board, of which Bill Dunk was Chairman. I was aghast when he told me the salary would be £2,250 a year—the lowest salary in the Heads of Departments range. This was the salary paid to John Burton when, at the age of 32, he was appointed to the post. I was now 49 and my range of responsibility and experience at home and abroad was very much wider than his had been when he took over the post.

So far as my family was concerned, my financial responsibilities were at their maximum. We had no home of our own, but were renting a furnished house. Alan was still at St Paul's College; John was due to matriculate at the end of the year under the Queensland educational system, and could not be moved back suddenly to Canberra at that stage, while during the following years he too would be at St Paul's College; Mary had settled in at Frensham, and we were loath to interrupt the continuity of her schooling. There was every reason to bring Peter back to Canberra as soon as possible as he had begun to think of my sister as his mother rather than as his aunt, but this would be a delicate operation which must be based upon his own wish to return to the fold. Finally, I simply had to have a new car, inexpensive as regards petrol, for use at all times of the day, night and week-end. I was doubtful if I could make ends meet on the salary available.

From the point of view of the Public Service Board, all these considerations were apparently irrelevant. It was only when I told Dunk that my salary as Ambassador to Moscow had been £2,500 and that a lower salary as Secretary must therefore be interpreted as involving a demotion that he sat up and took notice. He had not taken my recent income into account, and agreed to raise my new salary to the same figure of £2,500. I still believed that this amount was too low, but by then I had become so busy as Secretary that there was neither time nor energy left to argue.

I remained Secretary, Department of External Affairs, until 24 January, 1954 when, with the assent of my new Minister, Mr Casey, and in accordance with my own wish, I moved overseas again. This was the most interesting, but also the most exhausting position I held while a member of the Commonwealth Public Service. It is difficult for anyone other than senior members of that Service to realise the physical and psychological strains of the job. No doubt different individuals approach such work in different ways, and some find it less wearing than others. Some are primarily administrators, who seem able to clear their decks of files every day and lay aside official problems as soon as they leave the office unless recalled in emergency; others are more interested in policy than in administration and find it more difficult to shut out policy problems from their minds when they leave the office. I belonged to the latter rather than the former category, although all Secretaries have to be active in both fields.

Here I shall summarise the administrative problems I met,[59] before dealing with the more significant problems of policy which arose during my tenure of office.

For almost six months I made no important administrative changes, except that the post of Deputy Secretary was, in effect, allowed to lapse on the transfer of its occupant overseas. It seemed to me that, under my predecessor, the primary function of the Deputy Secretary had been to ensure that the decisions of Dr Evatt and of Burton were carried out, not to have any views of his own or to relieve the Secretary of the burden of some of his work. During this period too many problems came up to me personally for consideration, but in this way I was able to get the 'feel' of the Department as a whole. Towards the end of the year, with Spender's assent, I submitted to the Public Service Board a recommendation that the position of Deputy Secretary should be abolished, and that three Assistant-Secretaryships should be created, two dealing with matters of policy and one with administrative questions. Of the former, one Assistant-Secretary would be responsible for all United Nations matters and also for economic questions, including the Colombo Plan; the second would deal with all other political problems, especially those related to the Pacific area. The Assistant-Secretaryship (Administration) was designed to ensure that a senior diplomatic officer, who had himself served overseas, would have responsibility for all 'housekeeping' matters. His experience abroad should enable him to argue more effectively with Treasury and Public Service Board officials whose expertise tended to be based upon the conditions they knew to exist in Australia.

[59] For my account of the Australian Diplomatic Service (1935-65), see *Australia in World Affairs 1961-65*, Gordon Greenwood and Norman Harper (Eds), (Cheshire, Melbourne, 1958), Chapter II.

The Public Service Board approved these recommendations. I thereupon promoted A. H. Tange to the position of Assistant-Secretary supervising United Nations and economic matters, and L. R. McIntyre to the 'geographical' Assistant-Secretaryship dealing with Pacific and other policy questions. These two officers, who subsequently had distinguished careers in the diplomatic service at home and abroad, contributed greatly to the establishment of a habit of orderliness of approach in the handling of problems, including consultation inside and outside the Department with officers whose opinions it was desirable to know. They were of the greatest assistance during the period when the Japanese Peace Treaty and the ANZUS Treaty were being negotiated, and while the Colombo Plan was at an early stage of development and implementation.

J. C. G. Kevin was appointed Assistant-Secretary (Administrative). He had not been my first choice, but the latter person had been snatched from me by the Minister for valuable experience elsewhere. For several years Kevin held this thankless post, dealing with such mundane matters as salaries, allowances, movement of staff, housing, leave, health, family educational problems etc., sensitive handling of which is of primary importance in the creation and maintenance of a foreign service which feels itself to be a team and not neglected in remote parts of the world. No one in this position ever achieves fame or glory; indeed, he is lucky if he keeps any friends amongst his colleagues, despite the fact that the final responsibility for decisions rests upon the Secretary. He can only do his best and await the day when he will be given an interesting post abroad, where he can join the critics of his successor.

Though I have few illusions about myself as an administrator, there were two principles of administration which I tried to follow and which I still believe are of great importance: first, to find the right man for the job and give him the opportunity to develop it, unless it becomes clear that he is not the right man; secondly, to appoint as soon as possible a capable 'backstop' who can step up when the needs of the Service and fairness for future career prospects require the senior man to be moved on elsewhere.

In any large organisation some personal problems are likely to arise which take up far more time and energy than their intrinsic importance would appear to merit. Where a government department is concerned, the Permanent Head, who has certain statutory powers and responsibilities, can scarcely avoid handling these himself. One reason for this is that they are likely to attract publicity affecting the Department as a whole, to say nothing of parliamentary questions addressed to the Minister for External Affairs.

During my period as Secretary, I had to give a lot of attention to the handling of four officers, and of one officer's wife. The circumstances in each case were quite different. One senior member of the staff, whose views tended to disagree with those of the government, persisted in arguing them after the point of Ministerial decision had been reached. In most circumstances this is just a nuisance and an impermissible waste of time. When a Minister has instructed the Secretary to send off a telegram embodying a particular line of policy, one can not hold up the telegram because the person whose responsibility it is to draft the telegram disagrees with its content. The time for argument is before the decision has been reached. This particular officer continued to question a number of such telegrams, which involved delay and insufficient attention to other urgent problems. Eventually, with the Minister's assent, I arranged for the officer to be posted overseas, where over the years he has represented Australia with great credit.

A more junior officer was eventually transferred to another government department on security grounds. This was a major operation, as the Public Service Board is loath to act except in the clearest possible case, the kind of case where available evidence would if produced in a Court of Law inevitably lead to a conviction. Such concrete proof may not be available, yet the risk of secret information falling into enemy or prospective enemy hands may be too great in some rare case to permit a particular officer to continue to have access to it. Eventually the Public Service Board agreed to transfer the officer in question when he himself assented.

A third case concerned a very young officer who did not seem to be able to get on with anyone. At a time when he should have been sent to an overseas post for experience, I found he was still in Australia and asked the Assistant-Secretary (Administration) for an explanation. When I was told the reason, I called the junior in to my office, told him that I was going to send him overseas to a particular post despite his past record, and added that if he failed to get on with his colleagues and associates there, he would be brought back to Australia and there would be no future for him in the Department. After six months I was forced to bring him back and discussed with the Public Service Board whether he could be dismissed. However, under Public Service Regulations, he would have been entitled to a hearing, to be represented by a barrister, and to cross-examine those who gave evidence against him. As the main evidence would have had to come from the Under-Secretary to the Department of External Affairs of another Commonwealth country—which would have been quite impossible to arrange—I had to content myself with fining him £1 and marking his file 'Never to be sent overseas again'. I understand that he is still in the Department, and served overseas again after I ceased to be Secretary. I can only hope that his temperamental weaknesses disappeared in course of time.

A fourth case involved questions of health and efficiency. While I had no doubt that the officer in question could not carry out in the future responsibilities apppropriate to his rank, I was unable to insist on his retirement from the Public Service, owing to the rigidity of regulations which seemed designed to protect the individual almost irrespective of the cost to the community of retaining him in employment. I have never felt that the Head of a Department should have the right to 'sack' a particular officer, but I hold strongly to the view that a Committee of, say, three senior Public Servants should have the power to do so in such a case. They should be chosen from different Departments, to avoid the possibility of victimisation of someone who is not liked by his Permanent Head.

Finally, I was haunted by the wife of one officer whose marriage had gone astray. I would be telephoned or visited at home, waylaid as I left the office after a long day, or forced to explain to Prime Ministers or Ministers for External Affairs to whom she had written about her husband. When the latter was posted overseas to an important position, she visited the relevant diplomatic representative in Canberra to ask that the foreign Mission should refuse to issue a visa to her husband. At long last I decided to call it a day. Waylaid again at the door, I agreed to see her once more and told her to tell me everything she wanted to, because I would never talk to her again. I never did.

These were some of the tiresome aspects of my responsibilities as Secretary, but there were great compensations. Outside of Cabinet, I was in the centre of policy discussions, recommendations and decisions on foreign policy. The Department of External Affairs was the channel of communications for all confidential cables, inwards and outwards, for all Departments. With rare exceptions, such as a personal cable from the Prime Minister of Australia to the Prime Minister of the United Kingdom meant for the eyes of these two alone, all telegrams despatched and received passed across my desk. By paying close and immediate attention to these, I could keep my finger on the pulse, widen distribution inside and outside the Department of External Affairs where necessary, take the initiative to secure further relevant information overseas, and generally speed and co-ordinate action.

Few realise the importance of the time element in handling problems of foreign policy. Cables come in throughout the day and night from the four quarters of the globe. If marked with sufficient priority, they are decoded in the middle of the night. Answers may have to be sent before a meeting on the following day if Australian influence on the course of events at, say, a United Nations Conference is to be effective. Jack Walsh, the Head of our Cables Section, was extremely reliable. He or his deputies would keep in touch with me at night or over week-ends, at home or in the Department. If the subject-matter seemed important, I would be told of it at once and could decide whether the cable should be processed out-of-hours, or wait until normal working time.

Walsh soon got to know the kinds of matter I regarded as urgent, and sometimes would bring me an important cable in its earliest form, before being typed and duplicated. I could read it in full and warn the Minister or relevant staff what was coming up the ladder, so that background material could be prepared immediately. The Minister might be asked a question in parliament on some overseas development reported on the radio. Saving fifteen or thirty minutes in providing him with official information from abroad might make all the difference in his decision merely to ask that the question be put on the notice paper, or to reply at once.

The most important task of a Secretary of a Department, however, is to try to develop and maintain good working relationships with his Minister. Their outlooks on policy and on life may differ substantially, but this need not prevent frank discussion or the growth of mutual respect.

Spender was my Minister for only nine months before he moved to Washington as Australian Ambassador. I think we worked reasonably well together, although I cannot say that we were in any sense close. There was no doubt about his native intelligence or his tenacity in pursuing ends he thought important. As a young man he had come up the hard way, securing first-class honours in Law at Sydney University, but having to fight to build up a practice at the Bar without family financial support or relations with solicitors to ease his way. When I was Associate to Halse Rogers he was beginning to make a name for himself as a barrister, not especially popular with his colleagues; thrusting, ambitious and somewhat impatient for success. In Court he spoke fluently and easily, although he had a tendency to perorate which did not always go down well with a jury.

Spender was no starry-eyed idealist but a realist who liked to regard himself as a 'man of the world'. He had found life, including law and politics, a tough game, and was not averse on occasion to in-fighting of a kind which the Marquess of Queensberry might not have approved. But I admired his capacity for initiative, his courage in fighting for his policy and his readiness to take an important decision himself in emergency. Seen in retrospect, his contribution during his short period of office as Minister for External Affairs was striking. Before he left for Washington the Colombo Plan was well under way, and the ground securely laid for the ANZUS Treaty.

Casey's appointment as Spender's successor in Canberra was great good fortune for me. As I had served under him in Washington for two years we knew one another well. As Minister for External Affairs he had a head-start over other members of the Cabinet or the Liberal Party, in view of his previous wide experience of international problems and the world at large. These had given him a range of international contacts quite unusual for an Australian politician.

Casey had been born with a silver spoon in his mouth. This made it difficult for him at times to appreciate the trials and tribulations of officers of the Public Service, including myself, who were not so well financially endowed. Though not specially imaginative, he was more sensitive than Spender, and open to suggestion and influence if approached unobtrusively and undogmatically. Many years before I had read Liddell Hart's book *Strategy: The Indirect Approach*, from which I learned valuable lessons, including the desirability of avoiding frontal attacks upon well-fortified positions. These were of substantial use in my relations with Casey. Further, he was an avid traveller who derived much stimulus from seeing new places and meeting new people. I travelled with him to various parts of the world, especially Southeast Asia, sometimes in circumstances of strain and stress for both of us. In my experience it is in such circumstances that a closeness of relationship is established between Minister and Adviser which bears fruit later in the more formal atmosphere of a Ministerial office in Canberra.

I was also fortunate while Secretary of the Department in finding myself in increasingly close relationship with the Prime Minister, Mr Menzies, who sometimes acted as Minister for External Affairs when Casey was overseas. When I had to see him as Acting Minister to obtain decisions I was impressed by his intellectual capacity, his quickness of apprehension and of decision, and his readiness to leave details to advisers provided they carried out the general principles of approved policy.

Few people know the tremendous pressures upon the time and energy of a Prime Minister. I soon discovered that my first responsibility was to reduce to a minimum the number of matters raised, and to refrain from bothering him unless important issues were at stake. In the late afternoon or evening I would enter his offices in Parliament House with a couple of files under my arm. When shown into his room, as often as not I would find a tired man sitting behind a desk, looking somewhat disconsolate. His opening words were always 'Well, Watt, what's the problem?'

Unlike some other Ministers of the Crown, he never fussed about with departmental files; nor did he want to read a submission, long or short, unless this were unavoidable. He wanted an adviser to *tell* him what the problem was, in clear and simple terms. After that, as a skilled cross-examiner, he would ask singularly pertinent questions. Occasionally he would demand evidentiary support for some statement of fact or opinion, and would then glance at a telegram or other document on the file presented for inspection. Then he would pause for a moment and say 'Well, what do you suggest?' After listening patiently to the answer, he would make up his own mind, accepting or rejecting certain aspects of the advice as he saw fit. If the immediate need were for despatch of a telegram, he would say 'Well, draft a telegram along these lines'. His instructions would be in broad terms, leaving it to me to fill in the details. I would go away, draft the telegram and merely send it in for approval. Unlike some Ministers he would never alter the draft merely for the sake of proving that he was the Minister, but only where he felt that his decision had not been expressed adequately. No adviser could ask for a more satisfactory method of dealing with problems of foreign policy by a political master.

As a speaker in the Australian Parliament Menzies was unmatched. Of burly physical frame, his voice was powerful, clear and well-modulated. He never read a speech if he could avoid it, and preferred his advisers to supply him with ten or twelve 'headings', which he would then elaborate in his own way, adapting his words and his wit to the reactions of his audience. He rarely got excited, knew exactly where he was heading and seldom said anything which he had not originally intended. On some occasion when one of his Ministers had made a foolish speech which evoked laughter when delivered and ridicule from a subsequent Opposition speaker, I have heard Menzies slowly but surely regain control of the House in fifteen to thirty minutes. This is a rare gift whose significance most Australians under-estimate.

I accompanied Menzies on three visits to England which involved travel to the United States and other countries as well. Two of these were the occasion of Commonwealth Prime Ministers' Conferences (including one which followed immediately after the coronation of Queen Elizabeth II). To see the Commonwealth in action at the highest level at meetings in 10 Downing St was an invaluable and unforgettable experience. Every such visit provided opportunity for contact and discussion with high advisers in the countries visited and helped me to judge which way the international wind was blowing. Indeed, I came to the conclusion that a Secretary of the Australian Department of External Affairs should make one visit each year overseas in order to do his job back home properly. At no time during my subsequent career in the Public Service did I feel in as close touch with thinking and developments around the world as during the years 1950-54.

Travelling abroad with Menzies was a great contrast to travelling with Evatt. Menzies was a considerate master, though he was always apt to tease his advisers by making some ironic comment. For instance, I carried with me both a raincoat and a heavy overcoat, because I had learned the hard way that flying around the world takes one through all climates and that the adjusted temperature of aeroplanes can be either too hot or too cold. Menzies tagged me as a person who took out double insurance, and kept on finding new ways of expressing this point of view. Apropos of nothing in particular, he would suddenly say 'Watt, do you wear a belt as well as braces?' Returning from England to the United States on one occasion via Iceland, we approached Reykjavik airport in mid-summer about mid-night, when it was still light. The landscape below seemed incredibly bare, rocky, barren, rough and unattractive. Menzies called to Roland Wilson, then Secretary of the Department of the Treasury, and invited him to look out the window. Wilson complied, could see nothing of note, and sought illumination. Menzies replied 'Wilson, you should pay careful attention to this landscape. It reminds me of a Treasury report.'

These overseas journeys also revealed some of Menzies' human frailties. He always chose to stay at the Savoy Hotel which, so far as I was concerned, had only one attraction—closeness to Australia House, from which cables had to be sent. Apparently he liked a suite there which enabled him to look out over the Thames Embankment. In England, he allowed himself to be caught up rather too much in a social round, and this reduced time available for serious work. No one could be briefed in less time before a conference, and few could express themselves more effectively; but it was exasperating to find oneself in a constant battle with his Private Secretary, Hazel Craig, in order to have ten minutes discussion with the Prime Minister before a meeting.

On one occasion I ignored her injunction against seeing him, knocked at the door of his sitting-room and walked in. Miss Craig had told me he was extremely busy, and had left word that he was not to be disturbed. It was late afternoon when I entered, and I found the Prime Minister listening to the radio broadcast of a cricket match. He looked up in surprise when I entered, knew that he had been caught out, motioned me to a chair with a twinkle in his eye and said 'Sit down! Three more overs to go.'

At times the only chance I had to discuss with him the next foreign policy subject-matter at a Prime Ministers' Conference was during the ten minute drive from the Savoy to 10 Downing St. I learned quickly that I must have ready before each meeting a single sheet of paper on which I had summarised the background and noted particular points for an Agenda item. If Menzies had not read it before the meeting because I could not get access, I would put it in front of him as he sat down at the meeting. Usually he had time to read it through quickly before discussion really got under way. No doubt his training as a barrister made it possible for him to assimilate material like this in the minimum time.

His devotion to the Commonwealth of Nations in its older 'British' form and to the Crown left him open to suggestion by British statesmen that he should play a part they themselves preferred to avoid. Prime Minister Attlee, for instance, as Chairman of a Prime Ministers' Conference, showed considerable capacity for silence when some difficulty arose—such as a staged outbreak by Nehru (with Kashmir in the background) regarding attempts to get a reluctant Prime Minister of Pakistan, Liaquat Ali Khan, to attend the Conference. Attlee would doodle while Nehru spoke, then look up with an innocent face and ask the Prime Minister of Australia whether he might not care to comment. Menzies seemed to regard it as his duty to respond, despite the fact that he was likely in the process to draw fire upon himself and upon Australia.

The Prime Minister had a keen interest in foreign affairs, and once told me in his office in Canberra that I did not know how lucky I was to be able to concentrate solely upon international problems. Any Prime Minister, he added, had to handle a wide range of domestic matters many of which were dull and boring. Menzies said he would like nothing better than to be able for a time to give his whole attention to foreign policy, for which he felt he had some vocation. Yet when he was his own Minister for External Affairs from January 1960 until December 1961, after Casey's retirement, Menzies was not particularly successful in his handling of this portfolio. Of course, he was still Prime Minister and doubtless overworked, but a second factor may have been the strength of his attachment to British parliamentary and legal traditions, which tended to make him less sympathetic to Afro-Asian points of view.

He had strong reservations regarding the United Nations Organisation in its political and security aspects, finding the posturing, exhortation, moralising and occasional vituperation of some of its members offensive to pragmatic common sense. On one occasion when in New York I urged him to call upon the Secretary-General, Mr. Trygve Lie, to demonstrate publicly an interest in the Organisation. He agreed somewhat reluctantly. When we left the massive Secretariat Building, he expressed amazement that countries were willing to contribute funds for such a lavish building, where the international staff enjoyed conditions of work which most governments, including Australia, could not afford to provide for public servants in their own countries.

There seemed to him to be a strong element of fantasy and unreality in the United Nations where many members, though themselves militarily and economically weak and deficient in according fundamental human rights to their own citizens, were outspoken in their criticism of Western countries which, in their opinion, failed to live up to their international responsibilities. For Menzies, a decision to refer a matter to the United Nations for its consideration was not a policy in itself; before such a decision was taken, it was necessary to consider carefully what was likely to happen in the United Nations if the matter was so referred. He believed that Australian interests were often better served by relying upon the support of 'great and powerful friends'—a description which he readily applied only to Britain and the United States.

Travelling with Menzies provided an occasional opportunity to attract his serious attention to some important problem which required far more time than could be given to it by a Prime Minister in Canberra. Thus, on the way to London in December, 1950, our plane rose from the airfield at Calcutta and headed for New Delhi. The Indian Government had sent to Calcutta an Indian Air Force Dakota. There were no passengers except the Prime Minister's party; no accompanying Press men. I knew that the Prime Minister was locked in the plane for hours, out of telephone contact or other interruption.

I asked Menzies whether he had read Sir Owen Dixon's report on Kashmir. 'No,' he said, and added 'have you got it there?' I produced the report from my brief case, and between Calcutta and New Delhi he read it from cover to cover. He had a tremendous admiration for Dixon, who, I assume, had accepted the thankless appointment as United Nations Mediator on Kashmir only because Menzies had urged him to do so.

Dixon's report greatly stimulated the Prime Minister's interest in the problem of Kashmir, which he subsequently pursued in New Delhi, Karachi and London. In New Delhi he met Nehru, and in answer to my question as to how he found the Indian Prime Minister, replied after a pause 'He uses words to conceal the direction of the blow'. On the other hand, his contact with Liaquat Ali Khan in Karachi was close enough to enable him to play a useful part in London helping to persuade the Prime Minister of Pakistan to fly to London to attend the Prime Ministers' Conference. Outside the conference, and partly through Menzies' influence, there was discussion of Kashmir which, though unsuccessful in resolving the differences between India and Pakistan, nevertheless reflected a substantial effort by Commonwealth countries in this direction.

After I ceased to be Secretary in 1954 and was once again posted overseas, the closeness of my relations with the Prime Minister gradually diminished. While Secretary of the Department, however, I found his personal interest and general support a great encouragement. It also strengthened my authority within the Public Service as a whole.

POLICY MATTERS

By 19 June, 1950 when I was formally appointed Secretary of the Department, Spender had already made a number of important declarations on policy. On 9 March, 1950 he had given his first general review in the House of Representatives of the new Government's foreign policy. I have already summarised this speech elsewhere.[60] Here it is necessary to refer only to his strong advocacy of a Pacific Pact, with the United States as an essential party, and to his support for the concept of a Colombo Plan comprising capital aid and technical assistance for under-developed countries in Asia. In the same speech he had stressed the importance for Australia of 'the island areas immediately adjacent', adding that we were 'vitally concerned with whatever changes take place in them'. 'New Guinea', he said, '. . . is an

[60] Watt, *op. cit.*, pp. 113-15.

absolutely essential link in the chain of Australian defence'.[61]

This was the settled framework of already-announced Government policy when I took over responsibility as Secretary. However, my first serious involvement in policy matters was related to the unexpected outbreak of the Korean War on 25 June, 1950.

SOUTHEAST ASIA V. MIDDLE EAST

For several years after the Menzies Government came to office there was argument and uncertainty as to whether, and if so to what extent, Australia should plan to participate with Britain in the defence of interests in the Middle East. Strong pressure was maintained upon Canberra by London in an effort to ensure Australian participation, and this was accompanied by discouragement of Australian trends towards military involvement in Korea and Southeast Asia, except for the Malayan area regarding the defence of which informal discussions took place periodically between British, Australian and New Zealand Service representatives (ANZAM). The most effective form of pressure was upon the Australian Prime Minister, Mr Menzies, because of his attachment to the British Commonwealth as a whole and his genuine desire that British interests should be given full consideration.

It was my view that this pressure should be resisted. While Australian assistance to Britain in the Middle East should not be ruled out as a bare possibility in some future emergency during which Australia itself was not endangered, it seemed to me not to make sense after the experience of the Second World War, to train troops for desert warfare when all the signs pointed instead to involvement in tropical areas nearer home. I did not consider myself a strategist, but I did not believe that any Australian government could convince public opinion, in another general war, of the virtue of sending Australian divisions to the Middle East or Europe while Britain diverted her own forces from these areas for the defence of Singapore and Malaya. It seemed clear that European colonial powers were on the way out from Southeast Asia. Britain could withdraw from the area, whereas Australia was tied to it by the inescapable facts of geography. Moreover, in the post-war world, only the United States of any then conceivable allies had the power to exercise decisive influence in the Pacific Area and American, as well as British policy, had to be taken into serious account.

OUTBREAK OF THE KOREAN WAR

When the Korean War broke out on 25 June, 1950, the United States decided to intervene in support of the Republic of Korea (South Korea). In the temporary absence of the Soviet representative, the U.N. Security Council asked members of the United Nations to assist American forces. Spender was anxious to comply, and with speed. His main policy objective was to secure a Pacific Pact including the United States. American troops were soon in dire need in Korea. Commitment of Australian Naval and Air Force units to the Korean theatre, though valuable in the early days of he

[61] Current Notes, Vol. XXI (1950), p. 164.

war, did not seem to him a sufficient gesture either in carrying out U.N. requests in a case of clear aggression or in helping the United States in emergency.

The Resolution of the Security Council requesting assistance to repel the armed attack by North Korea was passed on 27 June. The Australian Cabinet agreed to Australian warships in Japanese waters and the R.A.A.F. squadron then in Japan being made available to the United Nations command in Korea, but at that stage a majority, including Menzies but not Spender, did not favour despatch of Australian troops. On 6 July both Houses of Parliament approved the decisions regarding warships and aircraft.

Menzies left Australia for a world tour on 9 July and spent the period from 13-22 July in Britain. On 14 July the U.N. Secretary-General sent a communication to fifty-two members of the United Nations requesting them to consider supplying ground forces for Korea. It is my recollection that Spender cabled Menzies in London supporting despatch of Australian troops; in any event, the Prime Minister restrained the Minister for External Affairs from initiating moves in this direction, pointing out that the British Government was not sending troops and did not think Australia would be justified in doing so.

This was the situation when the Prime Minister went aboard one of the 'Queen' ships to cross the Atlantic. During the morning of 26 July I received a telephone call from James Marjoribanks, Counsellor in the Office of the British High Commissioner to Australia. He asked to see me urgently. When he came to my office he said he felt I should know that the British Government would be announcing at 8 p.m. Australian time that British ground forces would be sent to Korea.

Marjoribanks, a Foreign Office man temporarily seconded to the Commonwealth Relations Office during a period of posting in Australia, was a friend of mine and has remained one in subsequent years. On this occasion, however, the message he had brought made it difficult for me to observe normal courtesies, although I knew he was only carrying out instructions. I thanked him for the information, but felt bound to confess great surprise. It was contrary to the view of the British Government as expressed very recently to the Australian Prime Minister in London. Menzies was now in mid-Atlantic and more or less incommunicado. On the basis of the information available to him when in London, he had told Spender to hold his hand regarding the despatch of Australian troops to Korea. Spender himself was at Moss Vale (more than 100 miles from Canberra) recuperating from an illness. The British Government's decision to change its policy and to announce the change on the day it notified Australia was a matter of great importance to Australia, and I could not answer for Spender's reaction.

As soon as Marjoribanks left my room, I telephoned Spender, told him that something important had happened requiring urgent consideration by him, and adding that I proposed to drive down to see him immediately, bringing the relevant papers. He agreed, and I left Canberra at once by a fast Commonwealth car. When I explained the matter to him in Moss Vale, he strode up and down the room repeating the words 'Watt, it's not going to happen, it's not going to happen'. He meant that he was not going to allow the United Kingdom to cash in on American goodwill ahead of Australia, having helped restrain Australia from acting earlier.

Spender decided that Australia must make a public statement of principle *ahead* of the British statement, indicating an intention to send troops to Korea. There was no time for a Cabinet meeting. He rang 'Artie' Fadden in Brisbane and persuaded a somewhat reluctant Acting Prime Minister to agree to immediate issue of a statement if Mr P. A. M. McBride, Acting Minister for Defence, also agreed. Another call was placed to McBride, who was in South Australia, and he too agreed. As I drove back to Canberra in the early evening, I asked the driver to turn on the radio for the 7 p.m. news, and heard an announcement of the following statement issued in the name of the Acting Prime Minister:

> In response to the appeal of the United Nations, the Australian Government has decided to provide ground troops for use in Korea.
> The nature and extent of such forces will be determined after the conclusion of discussions which the Prime Minister will have in the United States.

In my interview with Spender I had made no attempt to influence him one way or the other. As he might be risking his Cabinet position in acting contrary to Menzies' latest instructions, I felt it would be improper for me to express an opinion as to what he should do. However, I agreed with his decision, and admired his courage.

Before leaving Moss Vale, I suggested to him that he should try to contact the Prime Minister by telephone in mid-Atlantic. It was unlikely that he could get through, but it seemed appropriate for him to try. It was not for many years afterwards, when I was passing through The Hague in 1963 subsequent to my retirement from External Affairs, that Spender, then a Judge of the International Court of Justice, told me that he had in fact spoken to Menzies and informed him of the decision in Australia to send troops to Korea.

When I returned to Canberra it was my immediate responsibility to ensure that cables were sent to New York with instructions that they were to be brought to the attention of the Prime Minister, on his arrival there, before he spoke to any members of the Press.

In the event, Menzies accepted the *fait accompli* without resentment. He could scarcely have done otherwise in the circumstances, for he was greeted in the United States with the greatest good-will, asked to address both Houses of Congress, and succeeded in negotiating a very substantial loan. In his book *Australian Diplomacy and Japan, 1945-51* an American writer, R. N. Rosecrance, comments as follows:

> America was hard pressed in Korea and the offer of Australian ground forces at such a critical time must have been warmly welcomed in all sections of the American government. It would probably be correct to say that Australian-American relations attained a degree of cordiality in the summer of 1950 which they had not known since the days of the Pacific War.[62]

[62] (Melbourne University Press, 1962), p. 184.

It is important to stress that Spender believed that Australian troops should be sent to Korea irrespective of American reactions; at the same time, he believed that such a decision would help towards the negotiation of a Pacific Pact.

Some account of these events was given by Lady Spender but her version omits reference to the attitude of the British Government.[63] Again, Sir Arthur Fadden claims that I telephoned him in Brisbane and that he made the decision 'off-the-cuff'.[64] Here his memory has played him false. It was Spender who took the initiative and who secured Fadden's and McBride's assent, although the actual statement was issued in Fadden's name.

ANZUS

From the Australian point of view, by far the most significant event during my term of office as Secretary was the successful negotiation of the defence treaty between Australia, New Zealand and the United States (ANZUS), which was signed in 1951 and ratified in 1952. The initiative was Spender's and the credit belongs to him; but he and I agreed completely upon the objective, and I did my best to support his moves. Certainly, no other subject took up as much of my time and energy as this. Although most Australians tend now to take the ANZUS treaty for granted, success in negotiation could never have been achieved without a constant battle to overcome difficulties.

Spender has now published his own account of the inside story of ANZUS and in the process has revealed a number of matters which formerly had been confidential.[65] It remains for me, therefore, only to confirm the main points he has made, to fill in some background and to describe my own activities and reactions as an official.

During the Prime Ministers' Conference held in London from 4-12 January, 1951, which I attended as a member of the Australian Delegation, it became clear that no member of the Commonwealth of Nations except New Zealand would support the kind of 'tough' peace treaty with Japan which Australia and New Zealand thought essential. Australia, in the words of Dr Evatt uttered on 17 August, 1947 after a visit to Japan, wanted '. . . the disarmament and demilitarisation of Japan, destruction of its capacity to wage war, and a sufficient degree of supervision under the peace treaty to prevent the growth of war-making capacity . . .'[66]

By 1951, however, the Korean War was in full swing, the Communist Chinese were in control of mainland China, a Communist insurrection in Indonesia had been crushed, and the 'Emergency' in Malaya was at an acute stage, requiring the use of very substantial British military and police forces to withstand and control Communist insurgency in that area. The United States was even more averse than members of the Commonwealth to the imposition of military and economic restrictions upon Japan, and quite un-

[63] *Ambassador's Wife*, (Angus and Robertson, Sydney, 1968), pp. 165-66.
[64] *They Called Me Artie*, (Jacaranda, Brisbane, 1969), p. 114.
[65] *Exercises in Diplomacy*, (Sydney University Press, 1969).
[66] Current Notes, Vol. XVIII (1947), p. 470.

willing to maintain an occupation force in Japan to ensure that such restrictions were put into effect. For the Americans, Japan had come to be regarded as a possible ally rather than a defeated enemy.

In these circumstances, continued Australian pressure for a 'tough' treaty would merely have isolated her from her erstwhile allies without achieving the objectives she desired. Obviously, it was necessary for the Australian government to pursue the broad aim of security against Japan by other methods. Spender fully realised the need for such a change, but had to steer a difficult course between Australian public opinion on the one hand and the policy of the American Administration towards Japan on the other hand. In particular, he had to time his change of policy in such a way as to maintain continual pressure upon the United States for a 'tough' Japanese Peace Treaty until he was able to demonstrate to Australian public opinion that, if such a treaty were unobtainable, an acceptable substitute had been found which would ensure the security of Australia if Japanese militarism should in the future revive.

John Foster Dulles, at that stage a Foreign Policy Adviser to the U.S. Secretary of State assigned to work in particular on problems relating to a peace settlement with Japan, was scheduled to arrive in Canberra on 14 February, 1951. Before reaching Australia, he had visited both Japan and the Philippines. Information from our Embassy in Washington had led us to expect that the primary purpose of his visit would be to secure Australian assent to the kind of Japanese Peace Treaty which the United States wanted, but that he would also be prepared to discuss some form of security arrangement which would include Australia and New Zealand. As to the latter, we knew that the United States had come to no decision; the onus would rest upon Australia and New Zealand to convince Dulles of the need for such an arrangement, in which case he would have to report back to President Truman.

Here it is necessary to say something about relationships with New Zealand. As already indicated, during my journey across the Pacific in 1940 I had travelled from Auckland to Wellington, on my own initiative, to make contact with the New Zealand Department of External Affairs, and had then met Alistair McIntosh, who had appreciated the interest shown. In Washington and in Moscow my relationships with the New Zealand diplomats had been easy and fruitful. Yet I was always conscious of some underlying feeling of distrust of Australia by New Zealand officials, centred largely around the personalities of Dr Evatt and of John Burton. At San Francisco in 1945 Dr Evatt seemed to get on reasonably well with the New Zealand Prime Minister, Mr Peter Fraser, but New Zealand officials felt with much justification that Dr Evatt wanted always to be in the centre of the spotlight, and to take all the credit for himself. Nor did they regard Burton as a co-operative colleague.

In 1943 McIntosh became Secretary, Department of External Affairs, while in 1945 he also became Permanent Head, Prime Minister's Department. In these key positions he played a valuable and central part as adviser to Prime Ministers of different political parties over many years. He was thus my opposite number when I became Secretary in 1950. During my tenure of that post we kept in close touch with one another, particularly in regard to the negotiation of the ANZUS Treaty.

Both Spender and I were somewhat uneasy about the firmness of the New Zealand position during these negotiations. While the British Government had a strong influence upon Menzies, it had little or none upon Spender. In New Zealand, on the other hand, there seemed almost an instinctive tendency to accept the British point of view. During the Second World War, Australia withdrew its military Divisions from the Middle East after Pearl Harbour; New Zealand, on the other hand, kept its Army contingent in the Middle East. After the War, New Zealand was more ready than Australia to accept commitments to help Britain in the Middle East, and only changed its policy when Britain eventually (and reluctantly) accepted as inevitable the Australian view that the area of probable future Australian military involvement was Southeast Asia.

Before the arrival of Dulles in Canberra, I had inferred from discussions with Marjoribanks that Britain was opposed to Australia and New Zealand entering into a military Pact with the United States which involved mutual obligations between all the parties. This was never stated directly in so many words, but was the obvious conclusion to draw from comments that Britain would *not* be opposed to a unilateral declaration by the President of the United States of readiness to assist the two Dominions in the case of aggression against them. This was the position in relation to Canada. On 18 August, 1938 during a visit to Canada President Roosevelt had said publicly: 'I give you the assurance that the people of the United States will not stand idly by if the domination of Canadian soil is threatened by any other Empire'.[67]

During preliminary discussions with the New Zealand Delegation to the Dulles talks in Canberra the New Zealand Minister for External Affairs, Mr Doidge, seemed prepared to accept such an American declaration of support as sufficient, if a formal treaty could not be obtained. This attitude stemmed partly from the fact that such a declaration would meet British views and partly from New Zealand reluctance to accept additional commitments in the Pacific. Her overall capacity was limited, and she felt that by planning to help Britain in the Middle East she was helping to strengthen the North Atlantic Treaty Organisation (NATO) in that area. If there were to be a Pacific Pact, she wanted Britain to be a party. On the other hand, she would be opposed to any 'off-shore' arrangement the Americans might have in mind which might include Japan and the Philippines.

I shared Spender's view that a Presidential declaration was inadequate. In the first place, the geographical situation of Canada was utterly different from that of Australia and New Zealand, as President Roosevelt had made clear to Casey when the latter presented his credentials in 1940.[68] Roosevelt had the support of Cabinet and Congress in making his statement about Canada. On the somewhat doubtful assumption that President Truman was prepared to make a similar declaration about Australia and New Zealand, what guarantee was there that Congress and American public opinion would support it?

[67] *Keesing's Contemporary Archives*, p. 3190.
[68] Casey, *Personal Experience, op. cit.*, pp. 10-11.

After the First World War, Congress had refused to follow the lead of President Wilson in regard to the League of Nations, created substantially as a result of his own initiative at the Versailles Conference. The most significant factor in the failure of the League had been the refusal of the United States to become a member. In later years, President Roosevelt had experienced the greatest difficulty in changing the outlook of 'isolationist' America, which had been forced into the Second World War by the Japanese attack at Pearl Harbour. If Japan were accorded a 'soft' Peace Treaty, and should in the future adopt again an aggressive, militarist policy, what real security would a favourable Presidential declaration provide for Australia and New Zealand? At the very least, our first objective during the talks with Dulles should be to seek a formal guarantee by Treaty, even if—as a last resort—we were forced in the end to accept a Presidential declaration.

Australia, like New Zealand, would have preferred Britain to be a party to any such Treaty, but this would depend upon American willingness to accept her as a party. Relationships between the United States and Britain were very close; they were both parties to NATO; but American support of Britain in Europe was a very different matter from American support of Britain in the Pacific, involving as it would obligations to defend British colonial territory at a time when European colonies overseas were on the way out.

Moreover, the United States would doubtless be embarrassed in relation to France and the Netherlands, both Allies in NATO, if, for instance, she gave guarantees for Malaya and Singapore and not for Indo-China or Dutch New Guinea. On the other hand Australia, like New Zealand, could not agree to any 'off-shore' Pact including Japan, for public opinion in the two countries at the time would simply not accept such an arrangement. In all these circumstances, from the Australian point of view, a tripartite Pact between the United States, New Zealand and Australia seemed the best solution if this could be obtained.

Spender has described in his book how Dulles, during the first day of the talks in Canberra, argued with great skill in favour of a 'soft' Peace Treaty with Japan, and eventually made it clear that the United States, while ready to listen to Australian and New Zealand views on the subject and anxious to give effect where practicable to the opinions of war-time allies, must in the final result take its own decision.[69] In short, while ready to accept minor amendments to the American proposals for the Peace Treaty, the broad lines of the American draft would be retained, whether Australia and New Zealand liked them or not. In particular, American military occupation forces would not be made available to enforce a 'tough' Peace Treaty.

When Dulles had finished his exposition of the case for a Peace Treaty along the lines of the American draft, the Australian and New Zealand Delegations expected him to broach the subject of a Pacific Pact. To their astonishment and dismay, Dulles said nothing at all about the Pact. It fell to Spender to raise the issue, and to grasp the labouring oar.

[69] Spender, *Exercises in Diplomacy, op. cit.,* p. 125.

It was not until the second day, during a private conversation with Dulles on the way to lunch, that the Australian Minister for External Affairs learned for the first time the reason for the visitor's silence on this issue. In reply to Spender's insistent questioning, Dulles revealed that when he left Washington he had in fact intended to discuss in Australia the possibility of an 'off-shore' security arrangement; however, in view of the 'violent objection that had been expressed by the U.K. through Gascoigne in Tokyo',[70] he had decided not to pursue the matter further.

Sir Alvary Gascoigne was at that time the United Kingdom Political Representative in Japan, with the personal rank of Ambassador. The fact that, presumably on instructions from London, he had intervened with a view to preventing Dulles raising in Canberra a matter of vital importance to Australia came like a bombshell.

My own reaction to this intervention was strong and critical. Britain, of course, was entitled to follow her own interests. Equally, however, Australia was entitled to do likewise. But the method adopted by Britain could well have resulted in the defeat of the primary objective of the Australian Government's foreign policy at that time by depriving Australia of the opportunity of discussing the issue with Dulles and without informing Canberra of what she had done. This seemed to me ungenerous treatment of a Commonwealth country whose citizens had volunteered in their hundreds of thousands during two World Wars, both of which had broken out in Europe.

I tried to analyse the reasons for the British intervention. For Britain, Europe was central and the Far East now peripheral. Presumably she feared she might be dragged into some war in the distant Pacific—a 'wrong war against the wrong man in the wrong place', as Sir Anthony Eden was to say in 1954[71]—because of Dominion treaty obligations to support irresponsible Americans thought to lack Britain's judgment and experience. But was no account to be taken of the fact that Britain (and Canada) were both members of NATO, whereas Australia and New Zealand were not, and that the two latter (as two World Wars had shown) could easily be dragged into a war arising out of NATO obligations without any really effective voice in the decision? Was there also perhaps an element of wounded pride involved? Was it felt to be humiliating for a Great Power to find a Member of the Commonwealth party to a security treaty with a foreign power, however friendly to Britain, without Britain also being a party?

Of course, we had only Dulles' account of the conversation with Gascoigne. Conceivably, Dulles might have invented the whole conversation; if so, we had no means of checking. We could scarcely have cabled London asking for confirmation of the fact that Gascoigne had acted behind our backs in a manner directly prejudicial to Australian vital interests.

My own view, from circumstantial evidence, is that some such conversation did in fact take place in Tokyo. We knew from Washington that Dulles had intended to discuss a Pacific Pact in Canberra. In the event, he was silent on this subject, until prodded into a readiness to listen and then into speech. Something important and unexpected must have happened after he left

[70] *Ibid.*, p. 124.
[71] *Full Circle*, by Sir Anthony Eden (Cassell, London, 1960), p. 102.

Washington. We had reason to believe that the United Kingdom approved no more than a unilateral Presidential declaration. It therefore had a sufficient motive for intervention. If the course of action taken did not seem to follow Marquess of Queensberry rules, there was the precedent of the British decision to send troops to Korea. In short, if this was the way the game was to be played, Australia had to fight to defend her vital interests.

Spender's handling of the difficult situation in which he found himself deserves praise and public recognition. Australian public opinion, and both political parties, wanted a 'tough' peace treaty with Japan which was no longer a practical possibility. To press too hard in this direction would have risked antagonising the United States, besides being ineffective. The only alternative likely to satisfy public opinion was to obtain a security treaty with the United States which the latter had to be persuaded to accept and which Britain was trying indirectly to prevent. New Zealand, though ready to support Australia in efforts to secure a tripartite pact, would settle if necessary for a Presidential declaration—as would also the Australian Prime Minister, Mr Menzies, who had warned Spender to be careful not to over-play his hand.[72]

The fact that a draft ANZUS Treaty was completed before Dulles left Australia on 19 February and that this Treaty, with minor amendments only, became the actual Treaty which entered into force on 29 April, 1952 was due primarily to Spender's courage, pertinacity and skill. He refused to agree to a 'soft' peace with Japan unless a security treaty for Australia and New Zealand were associated with such a peace. When pressed by Dulles, he agreed without prior Cabinet authority to the inclusion of the Philippines in such a Pacific Pact if the United States Administration should so insist, although he argued strongly for a tripartite pact only.[73] When in 1951 he became Australian Ambassador to Washington, his close relationships with Dulles and continuing initiatives in Washington contributed towards American official acceptance of such a treaty, which Dulles had had no authority to indicate when in Canberra.

This is not to suggest that Spender was solely responsible for the treaty. His efforts would have been in vain had it not been for the favourable political climate created in the United States by common American, Australian and New Zealand suffering in the Second World War and the effect of speedy Australian support in the Korean War. New Zealand, too, made a significant contribution to the final result, while the Australian Cabinet supported the position Spender had achieved at the Canberra Conference with Dulles and the British Government, on reflection, raised no formal objection to the Treaty.

The Australian Department of External Affairs also played its full part in the negotiation of the Treaty. Before Dulles had arrived in Canberra, its senior officers had studied closely comparable security treaties and one officer, Ralph Harry, had produced a draft treaty which was of considerable value during the discussions with Dulles. It had to be amended substantially to meet points raised by the American Delegation, but it formed a solid

[72] Spender, *op. cit.*, p. 118.
[73] *Ibid.*, pp. 127-28.

N

basis for argument and provided evidence that the Australian Delegation knew what it was talking about.

The British Government sent to Australia Sir Esler Dening (a senior British diplomat and a Far Eastern expert who had enlisted in the Australian expeditionary forces during the Second World War), in order that he should be present in Canberra during the Dulles talks. Later he became British Ambassador to Japan, where I had regular contact with him in later years when I myself was posted to Tokyo. No British representatives attended the talks themselves but, on Spender's instructions, I went to see Dening in the Canberra Hospital where he was recuperating from an illness. I told Dening precisely what had happened. He thanked me for the information and did not appear to object to the tripartite proposal or even to hold the view that the possible inclusion of the Philippines would be unacceptable to the United Kingdom. Of course, he did not commit himself to British Government approval of the draft.

The next task was, in Spender's words, 'to clear the draft treaty with the British Government at the highest level'.[74] The full text was cabled to London, but clearance took a considerable time, during which cables were exchanged in both directions. We did not expect the British Government to express formal disapproval of an agreement regarded by the governments of two Dominions as vital to their interests, but we did not rule out heavy indirect pressure from London designed to arouse governmental and public apprehension in the United States, Australia and New Zealand of undesirable effects from such a treaty. In Australia and New Zealand many people would be disturbed by the fact that Britain would not be a party.

While consultation continued, I thought I could detect in the Australian Press, here and there, articles and comments strikingly similar in content and tone to conversations I had had with senior members of the staff of the British High Commission in Canberra. The Australian government could do little or nothing to counter these, because at that stage the fact that a treaty had been drafted during the Dulles visit was highly classified information. As Dulles had no authority to approve such a treaty in Canberra, it would have been disastrous for Australia to reveal the extent of progress made, before Dulles had reported to President Truman and his Secretary of State, and before the necessary soundings had been taken with members of Congress.

From recollection, it was some three weeks before we received the first official reactions of the British Government to our report on the Dulles talks. I do not remember the precise contents of the first messages to Canberra and to Wellington, but they must have raised a number of awkward questions, including the possibility that the Philippines might be a party. On this last point both Australia and New Zealand welcomed any assistance the United Kingdom might give them in Washington designed to ensure that U.S.-Philippines problems should be dealt with outside the ANZUS Treaty. Eventually the American Administration decided to enter into a separate

[74] *Ibid.*, p. 162.

security treaty with the Philippines, along lines similar to ANZUS, and the British Government may well have played a helpful part in this decision.

When the first British message was received, my main concern was not the drafting of an Australian reply, which did not seem to me to pose any real difficulties, but the probable reaction of the New Zealand Government. Britain's special place in New Zealand affections and overseas policies; the unavoidable but awkward situation in which Britain would be placed publicly if she were not a party to ANZUS; New Zealand's readiness before the Dulles talks to settle for an American Presidential Declaration—all these factors made me wonder whether the New Zealand Government would stand firm. If it did not, the extraordinary progress which had been made towards an ANZUS Treaty would be undermined, and an opportunity which arises once in a generation if at all might be lost and never recur.

Since I had become Secretary, I had on a few occasions been in touch with McIntosh by telephone. By using this less orthodox means of communication, I had been able to consult on some matters in ways impossible to follow in formal cables. On receipt of the first British reply, I told Spender of my concern regarding New Zealand reactions at the political level, and asked his permission to fly across to Wellington, without any publicity, to explain in detail the Australian attitude before New Zealand views crystallised. From Wellington, through our own High Commission, I would be able to let him know what our sister Dominion was thinking, and thus put him in a position to send to the New Zealand Minister for External Affairs any message he thought desirable or necessary. Such a trip, however, would first have to be cleared with McIntosh by telephone; otherwise my arrival might be regarded as unwarranted interference and work in the opposite direction to that intended.

Spender assented to my proposal, and I telephoned McIntosh. He told me that he personally would welcome such a visit, but would have to sound out his political masters. Shortly afterwards I received from him the 'all-clear'. To my great satisfaction I was invited to spend a few days in Wellington as the guest of the New Zealand Government. I thereupon left Australia without anyone being aware of the fact except Spender and the two Assistant-Secretaries, Department of External Affairs.

My reception in Wellington could not have been more friendly. In effect, I was temporarily incorporated as a member of the Department of External Affairs, where I had the frankest discussions with McIntosh and with Foss Shanahan, who had accompanied Doidge to the talks in Canberra with Dulles. I explained Spender's reactions to the British message, and the points he was likely to make in reply. It quickly became clear that, so far as New Zealand officials were concerned, there was no significant difference between the New Zealand and Australian outlook. The testing point, however, would be reactions at the political level. McIntosh said his department would draft a reply to the London message for the Prime Minister's consideration, and invited me to participate in the drafting process.

The end result was that the Prime Minister accepted the basic points of the departmental draft, and I flew back to Canberra with a copy of his approved telegram in my pocket, knowing that Spender would agree with its contents. He was pleased with the telegram, but commented a little testily that New Zealand had already appropriated most of the arguments he wanted to use himself.

It was some time after my return to Canberra before Australia and New Zealand received official approval from London of an ANZUS Pact. Reading between the lines of the London telegrams, it seemed clear that, at the political level, Britain found distasteful a security treaty between the United States and two Commonwealth countries to which she herself was not a party. At the same time, realistic reflection upon the importance of the issues to the two Dominions led the British Government to accept it, perhaps in the hope that in future years she herself might become a member of ANZUS. The Conservative Party, then in Opposition in London, clearly did not like the agreement. When the Attlee government fell and was succeeded by a Conservative Government under Churchill, the issue of British membership was raised, but without success.

I was still on tenderhooks about ANZUS until the Treaty was publicly initialled in Washington on 12 July, 1951. By that date we had heard from our Embassy there that the question of inclusion of the Philippines had been dropped, while two comparatively minor amendments to the Canberra draft would be necessary. Britain, too, had indicated its assent.

When the news of the initialling came through I was in Melbourne. In the early evening I went to a small cafe for dinner. Four young men entered the cafe and sat down at the table next to me. One of them carried a newspaper under his arm which had a banner headline containing the word ANZUS. I was all agog to know what the headline said, but did not feel like asking.

Having given his order, the young man with the paper turned to the football news on the back page and read it with great attention. Eventually he turned the pages one by one until he came to the front page which, I was now able to see, had the words 'ANZUS TREATY SIGNED' splashed across it. As I drew a breath of relief, I heard the young man say to his companions 'Anzus Treaty Signed. Huh! The Americans know they need us!'

Formal signature of the ANZUS Treaty, as distinct from initialling an agreed text, did not take place until 1 September, 1951, on the eve of the Conference called to discuss the Peace Treaty with Japan, which was signed at San Francisco on 8 September, 1951. A Bill to ratify the ANZUS Treaty was introduced into the Australian House of Representatives by Mr R. G. Casey in February 1952 and approved after considerable debate which even today makes unhappy reading.

The Menzies government, of course, made the most of its success in negotiating ANZUS, partly because it believed that this treaty was of vital importance for Australia, and partly because the Japanese Peace Treaty, which was before the House at the same time, did not contain the restrictions upon Japanese re-armament and economic development which most Australians still thought desirable.

Members of the Labor Party strongly criticised the Peace Treaty, claimed that a 'tougher' Treaty could have been secured, and argued that the Peace Treaty was too high a price to pay for the security guarantee by the United States contained in ANZUS. The Opposition formally voted against ratification of the Peace Treaty. Against this background, senior Labor Party spokesmen minimised the importance of ANZUS which, though formally accepted by the Opposition, was either damned with faint praise or denigrated as unimportant or unnecessary.

While it is true that the attitude of the Labor Party was adversely affected during the debate by references from the Government Benches to Dr Evatt's alleged mishandling of the Manus Island question during his own term of office, nevertheless the reaction of the leader of the Labor Party and of his senior colleagues was ungenerous. Many years later one of Dr Evatt's Cabinet colleagues when the Labor Party was in power, Mr John Dedman, published an 'inside' account of the American approach to the Australian government for base rights on Manus Island after the war which makes a strong case for Evatt's handling of the question.[75] What still remains unexplained is why Evatt never made as good a case for himself in Parliament. If Evatt had disclosed what Dedman has now made public, Government criticism of Evatt on this issue would have been ineffective.

But irrespective of the rights and wrongs of charges about the handling of the Manus Island question, there is no doubt in my mind that had Dr Evatt been in office when the ANZUS Treaty became a practicable possibility, he would have grasped the opportunity with both hands and, if successful in negotiating the Treaty, would have acclaimed the result as an achievement of the first order.

When Sir Robert Menzies retired from the Prime Ministership and from Parliament in 1966 he said that the two most significant achievements of his long term of office were the formation and development of the Liberal Party in the domestic field, and the ANZUS Treaty in the field of foreign policy and defence.

CLOSER RELATIONS WITH SOUTHEAST ASIA

When Mr R. G. Casey took over from Spender as Minister for External Affairs in the first half of 1951, he discussed with me the desirability of his making an overseas visit to increase his understanding of current international problems and to make personal contact with political leaders in other countries. Casey has always been a great traveller, someone who likes to go places, see things and meet people. He once told me that he never knew what weight to give to the contents of a telegram unless he could visualise the person who sent it.

Within the Department of External Affairs we held the view that any new Minister, however able, took about one year to settle in. He would take over his portfolio with certain preconceived ideas, many of which were impracticable in the immediate international situation in which Australia found itself. It was not until he had been 'processed' through London and Washington, and attended one Session of the U.N. General Assembly that he became sufficiently aware of the attitudes of other relevant countries, and began to focus more accurately the areas of policy in which Australia might be able to take initiatives with prospects of success.

[75] See *Australian Outlook*, Vol. 20, No. 2 (August 1966), 'Encounter Over Manus', pp. 135-53.

Casey, of course, was no newcomer to the international scene. His past Cabinet experience, his period of service as Australian Minister to the United States and British Minister of State in the Middle East, his long years as Australian Political Liaison Officer in London, and his unique appointment as British Governor of Bengal—all of this gave him a background far more relevant to his new portfolio than that of any other member of the Cabinet. But he had not been directly involved in day to day handling of international problems for many years. In particular, the problems of Asia and the Pacific had grown more and more important. A good-will visit of the kind he had in mind seemed to me an excellent introduction to his new responsibilities, and I supported it strongly. But when I asked Casey what countries he thought he should visit I found he had it in mind to journey towards and end his visit in the Middle East. This seemed to me mistaken, even dangerous. It would demonstrate a special Australian interest in the Middle East and arouse expectations both abroad and at home at a time when, in my judgment, Australia should be indicating that commitments in that area belonged to the past, not the future.

I put this point of view to my Minister and suggested that he should make a good-will visit to Southeast Asia instead, thus drawing attention within Australia to the serious problems of this area and proving to political leaders there by his presence and inquiries Australia's interest in their difficulties and desire to help where practicable. He accepted this suggestion and decided to pay short visits also to Hong Kong, Japan and Korea. The Korean War was raging, and he felt that a Ministerial visit to Australian troops in the field was desirable, as well as discussions with President Syngman Rhee. In view of the importance of Japan and the history of its relationships with Korea, a few days in Japan en route to Korea would be valuable. Moreover, there were Australian occupation forces in Japan.

So it was decided, and the Minister asked me to accompany him. We left Australia on 20 July, 1951 and returned on 22 August, spending on average about four days in each of Djakarta, Singapore, Saigon, Bangkok, Tokyo and Manila, and shorter periods in Hong Kong, Pusan and Seoul. It had been Casey's wish to visit Rangoon as well, but transportation difficulties and lack of time did not permit him to do this. So far as I am aware, the Minister had never before visited Asian countries north and east of Singapore, and this journey stimulated in him a personal interest which resulted in many later trips to Southeast Asia during his term of office. For me, it was an illuminating experience and destined in due course to affect my own future postings.

On the return journey from Tokyo and Manila we called again at Singapore where Mr Malcolm MacDonald, British Commissioner-General for Southeast Asia, put us up at Bukit Serene, on the Jahore side of the Causeway. There we reflected upon the lessons of the journey, discussed various aspects with MacDonald, and wrote up a summary of impressions and conclusions which formed the basis for Casey's subsequent report to Parliament on 27 September, 1951.[76]

I have always regarded this good-will visit by Casey as a kind of water-

[76] Current Notes, Vol. 22, No. 9 (September 1951), pp. 511-17.

shed in the attitude of the Australian Government towards Asia, especially Southeast Asia. If one studies carefully the terms of the Minister's report, one finds many phrases which were repeated over and over again in later years.

Direct discussions with political leaders in Southeast Asia and with foreign diplomatic representatives posted there—particularly British and American diplomats—opened Casey's eyes to the difficulties which the countries he visited had to overcome in recovering from the 'devastation and chaos caused by the war with Japan'. These, he felt, had been insufficiently realised in Australia. 'New governments have had to be established, new administrative machines built up, production re-organised and markets found —all this amongst populations, many of whose lives had become accustomed to the use of force as trained guerrillas. In the light of the situations that have existed in the countries of South-East Asia . . . they have done very well indeed in all the circumstances'.

The Minister reported that the most important single result of his trip had been the realisation of the great significance of Indo-China and Burma to the security of Malaya, and indeed of Southeast Asia as a whole. In private conversation with me he had commented upon the necessity of 'lifting our sights'. By this he meant that Australian interest in the security of Singapore and Malaya was not enough: there must also be interest in the security of areas to their north whose stability substantially affected the security of these two British colonial countries.

He became convinced that the political, economic and military situation in the countries of Southeast Asia was of the first importance to Australia, and informed Parliament that he proposed in the near future to recommend to the Government a review of Australian representation in the area. 'It is essential', he declared, 'that we should have our own posts reporting quickly and directly to Australia so that we can follow developments and be in a position to take diplomatic and any other action which appears appropriate and practicable. As Singapore is clearly the central point of this area, the nature and scope of our representation in Singapore will in particular receive the urgent attention of the Government'.

The general lines of Casey's report and recommendations were received favourably by Government, Parliament and Press, and for some years Australia gave much attention to the build-up of its diplomatic representation in the area, within the limits of available finance and man-power. When the good-will visit was made, Australia had no diplomatic representation in Burma, Vietnam, Cambodia or Laos. In Bangkok there was a Consul-General, while in South Korea the Australian representative on the United Nations Commission for the Rehabilitation and Reconstruction of Korea (UNCURK) had to double-up in practice, though not formally, as Australian diplomatic representative to the Republic.

In Japan, as no Peace Treaty had yet been signed, there were no formal diplomatic Missions, but the British Commonwealth Representative on the Allied Council for Japan was Colonel W. R. Hodgson, who had been Secretary of the Department of External Affairs. The Australian 'Commissioner in Malaya', based in Singapore but with loose responsibility for covering developments in Malaya and the British Borneo Territories also, was not an officer of the Department of External Affairs and had been chosen primarily with a view to keeping an eye on trade possibilities. Yet the British Government regarded Singapore as a centre for regional advice on political as well as economic matters, and for regional military recommendations and action.

Malcolm MacDonald had held U.K. Cabinet Office and high overseas appointments before becoming British Commissioner-General for Southeast Asia. He had at his disposal impressive resources at 'Phoenix Park', including senior Foreign Office and Colonial Office advisers. In addition, he was Chairman of the British Defence Co-ordination Committee, which included British Service Officers in charge of Army, Navy and Air Force contingents in the Far East. MacDonald, who had a roving commission enabling him to view the problems of Southeast Asia as a whole, also had the right of direct communication with the British Prime Minister. His position was one of considerable delicacy as well as importance, as he had to maintain friendly relations with British Governors, High Commissioners and Heads of Diplomatic Missions while exercising a wider responsibility than any of them. Though he avoided direct interference with the way in which they carried out their tasks, he could not but question through London their handling of issues if he felt that wider considerations had not been taken sufficiently into account. Casey was particularly impressed by the range of MacDonald's responsibilities and the need for Australia to tap at the source the information at the latter's disposal, without waiting for it to be filtered back to Canberra through London.

In planning his journey to include Japan, the Minister for External Affairs had no desire to stir up delicate problems relating to a Japanese Peace Treaty. But by this time the ANZUS Treaty had been initialled, and it was clear that the Peace Treaty would be of the 'soft' variety. When our plane rose from the airfield at Hong Kong and headed for Tokyo, Casey suddenly realised that in a few hours Japanese Press reporters would be questioning him about Australia's attitude to Japan. In the plane a new formula was devised which, in general terms, was less antagonistic than past statements and which looked to the future rather than to the past. It ran as follows: 'It would be idle to pretend that Australia has forgotten the war; but if Japan by her *actions* demonstrates that she has broken with her aggressive military traditions, Australia will be glad to meet her half-way'.

The few days spent in Tokyo were quite valuable both in forming first impressions of post-war Japan, and in reminding us of problems which would arise when the Peace Treaty was signed. Arrangements were made for the Minister to meet Prime Minister Shigeru Yoshida at his country residence in the hills near Hakone. Yoshida proved to be a man of outstanding intelligence and ability, shrewd, and with a sense of humour. His daughter Mrs Aso, who acted as his hostess, had social grace and charm. I began to realise that not all Japanese were militarists and that some were unusually sophisticated.

There was also evidence of a desire by other Japanese to be friendly in a distinctly personal way. Somehow it was discovered that I had an interest in tennis and I was invited to the Tokyo Tennis Club. I was collected in a small, battered car by the Marquis Matsudaira, who had been and I think was still then Grand Master of Ceremonies in the Imperial Household. He was polite, pleasant and attentive. At the courts a few people were playing and the Japanese insisted that I should join in a game. This I was very reluctant to do as I was tired, out of practice, without tennis clothes and without a racquet which suited me. My protests were overridden and clothes, shoes and a racquet of some kind were found. Although I played atrociously my efforts were roundly applauded—in short, I found it impossible to be angry with the first Japanese with whom I had ever had any real personal contact. Some six years later I found myself, to my own astonishment, President of that Tennis Club and, while posted in Tokyo, played many games there with Japanese and foreigners. These contacts proved to be a valuable adjunct to my diplomatic responsibilities.

Clearly, some change would have to be made in Australian representation in Tokyo when the Peace Treaty was signed. Colonel Hodgson was a man of courage and wide experience, but he was a military man at heart, direct and blunt in style. Past membership of the Allied Council in Japan was scarcely the best background for an Australian Ambassador to Tokyo. A clean break with the past was desirable, and a different kind of person should be sent to try to develop a new relationship between the two countries. In 1952 such a change was in fact made, though it involved overriding Hodgson's own wish.

During the good-will visit I was concerned, as Secretary of the Department, to familiarise myself with detailed aspects of our diplomatic representation in the area as a whole, including the quality of our representatives and the adequacy of their accommodation and general conditions of service. Gaps and weaknesses became obvious in various directions.

First, we were far too dependent upon British help and advice in Indo-China. Early Australian diplomatic representation in Saigon at least was essential. While it was not unreasonable to call upon the British Ambassador in Saigon to cover one post-war visit by an Australian Minister for External Affairs, involving assistance with accommodation, transportation, arrangement of interviews, entertainment and the like, such expenditure of his time, energy and available finance should be regarded as exceptional and temporary. Yet costs of establishing a diplomatic mission in Saigon were high, and it would not be easy to induce Treasury to provide the necessary funds.

Secondly, funds were also needed to improve the living and Chancery quarters for our Ambassador in Djakarta, where the tropical climate and general complications of ordinary life imposed heavy strains upon Australian staff. In Singapore, the Australian Commissioner's residence had excellent grounds and a good site, but the house itself was highly inconvenient, rather like a large, run-down club. It was the target for constant attack by Australians living in Singapore, who were strongly critical of the Australian Government for not providing a house which could be utilised with efficiency and which was at least roughly comparable with other official residences.

Conditions in war-time Korea were inevitably poor. Our representative on UNCURK, J. (later Sir James) Plimsoll, did not complain and was obviously carrying out his responsibilities well; but Australia was operating in Korea on the cheap. Plimsoll should be able to slip across to Japan whenever practicable for reasons of health, consultation and recreation, and establishment of an Australian Mission to the Republic of Korea was desirable in due course.

In Tokyo, on the other hand, the residence of Colonel Hodgson was excellent, but we only had it on lease. Nor could the Chancery arrangements be regarded as other than short-term. Substantial capital would be required to put our long-term representation in Japan on a satisfactory basis.

Nor was I happy about the quality of Australian representation at all posts in the area. Weaknesses of temperament or personality were apparent in two high quarters, and transfers seemed desirable when they could be arranged. This would take time; meanwhile, staff would have to be found for new Missions or for existing Missions whose responsibilities were to be increased. Such staff requirements, and consequent increase in costs, would also tend to reduce personnel and finance available for our representation in other quarters of the globe.

RELATIONSHIPS WITH THE DEPARTMENT OF DEFENCE

My main energies as Secretary were concentrated upon foreign policy in relation to defence. This was not because I had any special expertise in the latter field, but rather because defence and foreign policy were inextricably mingled and of primary importance to Australia during my tenure of office.

After taking up my duties, I soon found that relationships between the Department of External Affairs and the Department of Defence were at a low ebb. Put bluntly, the Department of Defence did not trust External Affairs. How far past events had justified this attitude I do not know, but in a speech in Parliament on the Report of the Royal Commission on matters arising out of the Petrov spy case, Mr Menzies referred to '. . . the Australian Security Intelligence Organisation . . . set up by the late Mr Chifley in 1949 after there had been a serious leakage from the Department of External Affairs between 1945 and 1948'. This statement was repeated by Sir Robert Menzies in 1970. In 1972 Burton repeated earlier denials of such charges.[77]

When Dr Evatt was Minister and John Burton was Secretary, the distrust was reciprocated. To both of them Sir Frederick Shedden, Secretary, Department of Defence and the three Chiefs of Staff seemed stuffy, old-fashioned, rigid, unduly attached to British traditions, inadequately Australian, and unprogressive. In turn, the Defence Department regarded Evatt and Burton as unpredictable and insufficiently concerned about problems of security. Even during my Washington days it seemed clear that American Service officers were somewhat reserved about confidential information being sent to Australia through External Affairs channels, and preferred transmission through Australian Service channels.

[77] *The Measure of the Years*, (Cassell, Melbourne, 1970), p. 190; *Canberra Times* 15/2/72.

Clearly positive efforts had to be made to remove this mutual distrust, and to create an atmosphere of confidence and co-operation between the two Departments. A significant opportunity came to move in this direction when, a year or two after I had become Secretary, Cabinet decided that the Secretary, Department of External Affairs or his senior representative should be invited to attend meetings of the Defence Committee when items on the agenda involved problems of foreign policy. At that time the Defence Committee sat in Melbourne. Its Chairman was Sir Frederick Shedden, civilian head of the Department of Defence, while the Chiefs of Staff of the respective Australian Armed Forces were members. This enabled me to make regular contact with Shedden and the Chiefs of Staff. Attendance at meetings in Melbourne took up more time and energy than I could easily spare, but I found them very much worth while. Shedden made me feel welcome and the Chiefs of Staff began to understand that I was not trying to butt in with amateur opinions on technical matters they alone were competent to handle. I learned a lot about their points of view and the problems they had to meet.

Relations of confidence between the two Departments gradually improved until, under my successor as Secretary, the stage was reached when a senior External Affairs officer became Chairman of the Joint Intelligence Committee. Eventually the Chiefs of Staff were transferred to Canberra, where they should have been many years earlier, together with ancillary planning and other staff. At the time of writing, an ex-Secretary, Department of External Affairs—Sir Arthur Tange—is Secretary, Department of Defence, while two senior External Affairs officers have acted in succession as Head of the Defence Department's expanded and co-ordinated intelligence activities. This is a far cry from the mutual suspicion of the 1940s.

ILLUSTRATIONS OF VARIED ASPECTS IN THE LIFE OF A PERMANENT HEAD

Many other aspects of foreign policy required consideration while I was Secretary, including such important matters as the Colombo Plan, the problem of Dutch New Guinea and relations with China. I have omitted any further reference to these, as I can add no new information to that I have already published elsewhere.[78]

One of the most important and difficult functions which the Secretary of the Department of External Affairs has to perform consists of interviews with foreign Heads of Missions. The latter have to keep the Australian Government advised of relevant policies of their own governments, and to keep the latter informed of developments in Australian foreign policy. Naturally, they prefer to discuss both with the Minister for External Affairs himself, but he is an extremely busy man who is simply not available at short notice to every Head of Mission, except in regard to some urgent and important issue.

The Head of the Department is the next target of the diplomats, particularly when they want informal discussion. Some Ambassadors think it

[78] See, *inter alia*, relevant portions of Watt, *Australian Foreign Policy*, op. cit.

beneath their dignity to seek appointments with other senior officers of the Department, although the latter would frequently be adequate for the purpose. As a result, the time and energy of the Secretary tends to be burdened with diplomatic interviews. In self-defence, I had to insist with a few Heads of Missions that I would not see them on the day when the interview was requested unless I had an assurance that an urgent, current matter was to be raised. Unless they gave such a guarantee, I suggested a senior officer should be seen instead if they wanted an appointment that day.

Such interviews require much experience and good judgment as to the precise extent to which the Australian Government's policy—which may only be evolving in a particular direction—can be revealed to a foreign representative. The reactions of the latter to information disclosed may also be of considerable use to the Australian Government when policy is actually formulated.

Accurate recording of the substance of such interviews is also important. It is not only necessary to place a copy on the relevant file, but also essential that a copy should be sent to the Minister to ensure that he is aware of the discussion before meeting the foreign envoy himself. When I became Secretary I was not satisfied with the adequacy of such records of past conversations, and made it a rule to dictate a summary either on the day of the interview, or if that proved impracticable, on the following day. I also kept in my own files another copy of the summary, so that I could turn it up quickly without having to call for the file itself. When in March 1954 I was again posted overseas, I found that my own set of copies comprised three separate files.

Today there is a strong tendency to write-down the importance of the work of Ambassadors, and almost to assume that modern communications, together with frequent visits to his jurisdiction by Foreign Ministers and other Cabinet members, makes the Ambassador almost irrelevant. The role of an Ambassador in the twentieth century has certainly changed. But his presence in and understanding of the country and its people is still of the highest importance, if only in advising his Minister whom to see, what not to say and how best to say what must be said.

Actually, of course, these are not his only functions. An unsuitable Ambassador can do his country much harm in a very short time; an able man can be a significant influence on relations between the two countries. One illustration of such an able man was Mr Haruhiko Nishi, the first Japanese Ambassador to Australia after the Peace Treaty came into force. His position was more delicate and difficult than that of any other foreign Head of Mission in Australia. Yet, although he had to deal with contentious issues such as Japanese pearl-shell fishing on the Australian continental shelf, he performed his functions with distinction and gained the respect of all of us as a man of integrity.

Depending upon the personality and attitude of a particular Minister for External Affairs, another important function of the Secretary may be consultation with the Minister regarding appointments overseas as Heads of Diplomatic Missions. Most people have little conception of the difficulty of finding suitable men for such appointments, or of the obstacles which may have to be overcome if they are to be posted in the right places. So far as career officers are concerned, many factors have to be taken into account which are known in detail only to the Secretary and the senior official dealing with personnel matters. These include such items as health, length of service at difficult posts, family matters, and claims of other officers already posted overseas who can not be shifted at short notice. For every person appointed, the names of several others will usually have been considered.

Appointment of non-career men presents different problems. No capable man in mid-career is likely to be willing to interrupt his professional or business occupation for a temporary appointment of several years. Moreover, although there is a case for such outside appointments in particular circumstances, general regard has to be given to the reactions of career officers, whose morale is likely to be affected if what are regarded as 'plums' are handed out indiscriminately to non-career men. It is rare to find among the latter group individuals ready to be posted to a country with a difficult language and an exhausting climate. If recruitment of officers to the Department of External Affairs is to be maintained at a high level, so that the best people are attracted to the diplomatic service, there must be confidence that ample opportunity for appointment to important posts will not be denied to them, provided they prove themselves competent, in order to find a convenient niche for a 'political' appointee.

In my time as Secretary, Washington and London were still regarded as posts for politicians who had served as members of Cabinet, and only in very recent years has this policy been modified by the appointment of successive career officers (Sir Keith Waller and Sir James Plimsoll) as Ambassadors in Washington. While there is a case for appointment of ex-Cabinet Ministers to the United States and to the United Kingdom, this policy should at least only be followed when appointees have the right qualifications for the positions. This, regrettably, has not always been so.[79]

Taking into account the persons available while I was Secretary, the qualifications of some of those whom the appointees succeeded as Heads of Mission, and the subsequent record of their service, I take some satisfaction in the selections made. The responsibility for choice, of course, was that of the Ministers for External Affairs then in office, in consultation with the Prime Minister and subject to approval by Cabinet. Proposed appointments, however, were discussed with me and my advice either as to individuals or location, though not always followed, was taken seriously into account.

In 1952 two important decisions were made regarding our representation in Tokyo and Singapore. When the Japanese Peace Treaty came into force, Hodgson was transferred from Tokyo to Pretoria, where he held office as Australian High Commissioner until his retirement from the service. Dr (later Sir) Ronald Walker, an economist by training, was appointed to Tokyo in Hodgson's place, but with the new title and function of

[79] See *The Australian Quarterly*, December 1964 (Vol. XXXVI, No. 4), article on The Ambassadorial Issue pp. 11-18, by Watt.

Ambassador. Fortunately the support of the Australian Prime Minister, who had seen the leased residence in Tokyo of the Australian Head of Mission, made it possible to secure Treasury approval for purchase of the property. At the time of purchase the price was not high, and the value is now many times greater.

In September 1952 McIntyre was sent to Singapore as Australian Commissioner in Malaya. His work in Canberra as Assistant-Secretary dealing in particular with Japanese Peace Treaty and ANZUS problems had been invaluable and his departure overseas left a substantial gap in the Department, but he was the best available officer to maintain liaison with the British Commissioner-General for Southeast Asia. In December of the same year Tange was sent to Washington with the rank of Minister to serve under the Ambassador, Sir Percy Spender. This decision was another blow, for the time being, to the effective work of the Department, but in Canberra it was felt desirable to have an experienced official in Washington, partly to remind the Ambassador if necessary that he was no longer Minister for External Affairs and to ensure fullest consultation with the Department.

For the rest, Professor W. R. Crocker was appointed High Commissioner to India (March, 1952); A. R. (later Sir Roden) Cutler High Commissioner to Ceylon (April 1952); Major-General W. J. (later Sir Walter) Cawthorn High Commissioner to Pakistan (April 1954); John Quinn Minister to Vietnam, Cambodia and Laos, based in Saigon (November 1952); C. T. Moodie Minister to Burma (March 1954); B. C. Ballard Minister to Thailand (April 1952)—to mention only South and Southeast Asian posts.

No wide series of diplomatic appointments can be perfect in all respects, for reasons mentioned earlier. Taken as a whole, however, our diplomatic representation in Asia was strengthened considerably, while the creation of diplomatic Missions in Burma, Thailand and Indo-China was public evidence of increased Australian interest in Southeast Asia in particular.

The appointment of John Quinn was made with some hesitation. In many ways he was ideally suited to Saigon. His French was excellent, while his experience in Singapore would be useful. However, his treatment by the Japanese after the fall of Singapore made one wonder whether it was fair to send him back to Southeast Asia, where acute memories of the past were likely to be revived. Generally speaking, an officer of the Department of External Affairs has no choice regarding his posting, unless special family circumstances or health reasons provide sufficient grounds for re-consideration. In this instance Casey authorised me to speak to Quinn in advance in order to make it clear that, while the Government wished him to go to Saigon, he should regard himself as completely free to refuse the post. Quinn did not hesitate, but indicated at once his readiness to go to Indo-China, where he served Australia well.

On one occasion I accompanied Casey to Saigon when Quinn was Minister there. A few hours before attending a formal dinner of welcome to the Australian Minister for External Affairs, Casey suddenly announced that he was going to make a short speech in French. He jotted down a few key phrases and asked Quinn for comments. I can still see Quinn's pained expression as he tried to explain what was wrong with the Minister's French.

Despite my own and Quinn's apprehensions Casey, who while young had picked up a certain amount of French and German as a result of private tuition, made his speech and was roundly applauded at the end. His instinct was sound—the effort was taken as a mark of courtesy and goodwill, whatever grammatical flaws the members of the Académie Française might have found in it. I learned the useful lesson that to be able to communicate directly in another language can help establish a personal contact which may not be possible even through the world's best interpreters.

There is little more to report about my period of service as Secretary of the Department of External Affairs, except to try to convey to others some sense of the constant psychological and physical pressures of the job and to explain how I came to leave this post and move out again into the field.

While in Australia, no day of the week was my own to do with as I liked. Telegrams came in on each of the seven days, and if they were urgent they had to be dealt with at once. Over the week-end there was of course a duty officer, but if the matter was important I was likely to be involved. Every Sunday morning I went to the office to read the inwards telegrams. No week-end passed without Casey ringing me from his home at Berwick, Victoria, if I had not already rung him.

From time to time speeches had to be prepared for the Minister to deliver in Parliament. Material was supplied by the various divisions of the Department, tidied up by the Assistant-Secretaries, and approved by me before submission to the Minister. During debates in the House of Representatives on foreign policy, attendance in the House was necessary in case the Minister needed some information or advice regarding matters raised during the debate.

In addition, it was necessary to keep an eye on the preparation of material in answer to parliamentary questions, as an inaccurate or inadequate answer could be seriously embarrassing to the Minister. Departmental correspondence was voluminous. Despatches and memoranda from Australian Missions overseas had to be read by someone with sufficient experience to evaluate them. Consultation was necessary with other relevant Departments at various levels. Staff transfers between the home office and overseas posts—and vice versa—constantly took place. Promotions were made and appeals against promotions attended to. Briefs had to be prepared for Australian Delegations to international conferences—in particular, the annual Session of the United National General Assembly. Much of this work, of course, was done down the line, supervised by Heads of Sections or Divisions under the watchful eyes of the Assistant Secretaries, but if anything went wrong the responsibility came back to the Secretary himself. He has to keep his finger on the pulse, press for action where necessary, intervene at times and generally act as departmental co-ordinator and chief adviser to the Minister.

When the Secretary goes overseas, accompanying the Prime Minister or Minister for External Affairs or by himself, there is never any let-up—only a different kind of strain. At every Australian post he passes through the Head of Mission will want to discuss his own special problems, hoping that by personal discussion with the Head of the Department he can cut through departmental red tape or reduce delay often experienced in obtaining replies through normal written channels.

Some idea of the pace of overseas journeys can be gained from a few factual extracts from letters to my wife:

March 31, 1952. Singapore. 'I am back again at long last at a point where contact with Australia is possible again. My schedule was knocked about because of 4 unexpected days delay at Bangkok waiting for a French plane to come through from Paris. (There is no such animal as Portuguese Airways). If I had known how long the delay would be I would have returned to Singapore and flown from there to Saigon.

At Saigon our hotel bookings had disappeared and no others were procurable—at least while a French tourist ship was in town. So the poor old British had to take us in. I stayed with the Minister and Rowland with his staff. We used their cars, borrowed their money and generally took up their time. They were very nice, but it is the last occasion when this sort of thing can happen.

After some uncertainty, we managed to fly to Hanoi for 2 days, and one late afternoon flew in a tiny biplane at 500 feet to Haiphong and round some of the perimeter fortifications. This gave me a better idea of what the military problem is than anything else. Then His Majesty Bao Dai decided to see us, and with great difficulty we flew to Dalat (a mountain resort) and cadged a lift back the same day in a small French official plane which happened to be there. This made it possible for me to leave for Singapore on March 30—otherwise I would have been sunk as regards collecting my thoughts before meeting Casey here on April 2.'

June 9, 1952. London. '. . . the London visit is more or less over. We leave for The Hague tomorrow morning; moving on to Paris on the afternoon of 11th; back to London on 13th. The (P.M.'s) party will stay there a little longer than expected, but I may have to go to Bonn and to Berlin on 14th., returning to London on 16th. Eden wanted Menzies to go to Berlin to cheer up the locals, but the P.M.'s time-table made this impossible. Then it was suggested I should go. Partly in order to relieve him from presure, I agreed to go—although from the public point of view it makes no sense. I don't imagine the Berliners will decide to stand firm because I have arrived on the scene. In addition, there are departmental reasons for going. . . .'

March 15, 1953. New York. '. . . although I recommended coming home via the Pacific, Casey has asked me to return via the Middle East. For him, this means primarily Cairo—although he also wants me to spend a day or two in Djakarta. If I am going that way, I must see Walter Crocker and Jim McIntyre. If I go to Delhi, I have to go to Karachi. In short, I can not now be home before March 31, and may not be home until April 2 or 3. . . . Tonight I leave for Rome via Boston, the Azores, Lisbon, Barcelona and Nice. A day in Rome; then to Cairo via Beirut; 3-5 days in Cairo (bookings are difficult from there). Leave Cairo probably 23rd. for Karachi; arrive Delhi probably 27th.; leave Delhi about 29th.; one day in Singapore; one or two in Djakarta.'

On rare occasions overseas visits involved experiences unique in themselves
—such as presence at the Coronation of Queen Elizabeth II, which I
described to my wife as follows:

1.6.53. Savoy Hotel, London. 'It is Coronation eve and time to go to
bed—10.30 p.m. We have to rise at 5.30 a.m., breakfast at 6, leave at
6.30 by car for the Abbey, be in our seats between 7 and 8 a.m., await
the arrival of the Queen about 10.30 a.m., sit through the ceremony, get
some refreshments in Westminster Hall somewhere about 1 or 2 p.m.
and leave the area not earlier than 2.30 p.m.

There is no other thought in London or the British Isles at present
except the Coronation. Crises in Korea; dangers in Egypt; the troubles
in Kenya—all are forgotten. The streets are decorated and crowds of
people, cars, buses etc. press through the central areas. Many are sleeping the night in the open to try to view the procession.

There is an emotional fervour which has to be experienced to be believed. In some respects it is good. After two World Wars, a couple of
depressions and the dead monotony of austerity in the post-war years,
this country has gone on the loose. A sense of national pride is around
and a willingness to 'go-it-alone', i.e., to shake off the Americans, however impracticable such a policy may be. Conferences held in this atmosphere are somewhat dangerous.

The trip to London was too quick and therefore tiring. Half-a-day
in San Francisco; a night-flight to Washington; one day in Washington;
a day train to New York; a night flight to London via Scotland. It took
us a couple of days to recover.

We ran into a Garden Party at Buckingham Palace—with 6,998
others. The only royalty we saw was dusky, with gaudy umbrellas held
on high. Then a terrific 'do' at the National Gallery attended by gentlemen laden with ironmongery and an unusual proportion of lovely ladies
and lovely dresses—cum tiaras where appropriate. Unfortunately the
arrangements for cars after the event were so bad—the traffic in London
is hopeless at present—that an impressive evening was spoiled. I met
the Brosios, who send their love, and the Dixons, who did likewise. My
Thai buddies . . . were there too.

Yesterday we went 20 miles to Hatfield Hall, seat of the Marquess of
Salisbury. There the Queen mother was at least visible, and I saw Lady
Dixon presented. . . .'

2.6.53. London. 'It is midnight on Coronation Day. The tumult and the
shouting is dying away. Tomorrow, work begins. Knowing that a
serious crisis on Korea may well occur this week, I'm afraid I couldn't
quite catch the Coronation mood.

Heather Menzies, Brigadier Pollard and I got off to an early start
about 6.45 a.m. Despite a circuitous route, we were at the Abbey in 20
minutes. We were sitting in different parts, so we separated and I entered by the Peers' door! This was because I was sitting in the back row
behind about 2 to 300 peeresses.

The Abbey was about half-full already when I entered. You would
not have recognised it. Masses of built-up seats, draped in elaborate
materials. I could not see the altar or the proceedings near it, but I
looked straight down an aisle at the throne and had a better seat than
I could have expected. . . .

197

I had mixed reactions to the glitter and pomp. I am glad to have seen it once. I doubt if any country can do it better. But I am not sure that Orders and uniforms are still in place in this atomic world.

The Queen was rather stiff and strained. How could she be otherwise? She only had to trip once with the Crown on her head to wreck the show. The Duke of Edinburgh did his stuff well, although he showed a few traces of concern for his wife's ordeal.

I think the crowds in the streets were perhaps more significant than the ceremony. They sat—thousands of them—through a cold, wet night. Their support for the Royal family was unmistakable. It did them good to go on an emotional bender after years and years of restraint.

At night we saw the procession outside the Abbey on television. It must have been impressive—in spite of some heavy rain. Late tonight we have been sitting in the Menzies' suite—minus the Menzies—looking out over the Thames at a fireworks display. Some of the others have gone to a cabaret show at the Savoy, but I am off to bed. . . .'

But if there were compensations, there were also serious disadvantages, from the family point of view, in the kind of life I was leading. The demands of my work in Canberra, and frequent absences overseas, threw an altogether disproportionate burden of family responsibilities upon my wife. These were not made any easier by an operation, while we were still in Heydon's house, which left her with a continuing digestive weakness. My salary was inadequate, and I simply did not have the financial resources to buy land and build. The house we had owned in Hunter's Hill was eventually sold, but realised only enough to cover first and second mortgages, so that we lost whatever equity we had in the property. Efforts on my part with the Department of the Interior to secure a rented house proved fruitless. My children needed to feel that some particular house was their permanent home, and I felt keenly that I was letting them down through my inability to arrange this.

Eventually, somewhat in desperation, I wrote to Hodgson to tell him that I proposed to ask Interior to transfer the tenancy of his house to me. I regretted doing this, but saw no alternative. While Secretary he had enjoyed the advantages of a good house in Forrest, together with a considerable entertainment allowance denied to me. There was no real prospect of his returning to Canberra: his children were more or less grown up and he was merely drawing rent from some tenant whose responsibilities and claims were far less than mine.

Naturally, Hodgson was not amused at my proposal, and strongly opposed it. The Minister of the Interior supported his attitude, and my application was rejected. In these circumstances Casey should have given me the strongest backing—either to secure Hodgson's house or some other. But although my general relations with him were excellent, he seemed to have a blind spot regarding my family difficulties. At any rate, he never seemed to realise the unfair burden which lack of a house, inadequate salary and frequent absence was imposing upon my family. These were not matters which I cared to press upon him, but he should have been aware of my general situation.

My discomfort reached the point of positive anger when telegrams passed across my desk from and to a senior Australian overseas whom the Government wanted to return to carry out special functions for a few years. He agreed, but raised stiff conditions as to salary and housing. Both conditions were unreasonable, and the demands as to salary were reduced after strong telephonic resistance by the Secretary, Prime Minister's Department. On the other hand, he was given a specific promise of a house in Canberra as soon as he returned, although his case was far weaker than mine and he would be enjoying a privilege in breach of current regulations or practice. It was so outraged that I determined to raise my housing problem with the Prime Minister himself.

The opportunity came when Casey was overseas and Menzies was Acting Minister for External Affairs. One afternoon, after we had dealt with some official matters, I asked leave to raise a personal problem with him. I said I was loath to do so, as a Prime Minister's time and energy should be devoted to more important matters, but that all other approaches had failed. He listened carefully and sympathetically to my account of my housing problem and its cumulative effect upon my family. When I finished he said he would certainly see what could be done to help, because he believed that the claim of the Secretary, Department of External Affairs, to a satisfactory house in Canberra ranked only after those of the Prime Minister and the Minister for External Affairs, taking into particular account the relationships between the Secretary and foreign Heads of Mission. He could foresee some difficulties, because of the precedent which might be created, but he would give the matter full consideration and do his best to assist me. I greatly appreciated his attitude.

In the event, a house became available to me before Menzies had had time to deal with the problem. An officer of the Department of External Affairs, then overseas, was transferred to another post where he was likely to remain for a further three years. He had lived in a house in Forrest which he had rented to someone in the expectation that he would be taking it over again after a two or three year posting. As he was now to be out of Australia for a further three years, I applied to the Department of the Interior for permission to lease his house and my application was approved. It had many disadvantages, including poor design and significant cracks in the dining-room, probably due to soil subsidence, but it was a house, in a pleasant suburb, reasonably close to my office. I jumped at the opportunity, although I was overseas when the approval came and my wife had to arrange the actual transfer from Heydon's house and purchase additional furniture.

Despite its disabilities, this house became our first real home in Canberra. Some months later I was able to enter into arrangements with Interior to purchase it on long terms. I was greatly relieved when the transfer to my name went through, as henceforth the house would be under my control, whether I was posted at home or abroad. In fact it made a great deal of difference to the children, who came to regard it as their home while away at boarding school or university college. It remained in my hands until

199

shortly after my retirement from the Commonwealth Public Service in 1962, when I sold it and bought a new and more adequate house in Red Hill.

Oddly enough, it was during the very year that the problem of a permanent home in Canberra was being solved that I began to wonder how long I would remain Secretary of the Department, and based in Canberra. There were a number of reasons for this, but my mind was first directed to the possibility of my moving into the field again when, to my surprise, I found that Cabinet had approved on 18 February, 1952 a number of recommendations by Casey regarding overseas appointments, including my posting in Singapore for a three-month trial period while still holding the office of Secretary.

As indicated earlier, during his visit to Southeast Asia in 1951 the Minister had been greatly impressed with the work of the British Commissioner-General for Southeast Asia and his roving commission to cover the area as a whole. Casey felt that the establishment, on a much smaller scale, of a similar Australian office with a roving Commissioner, who would also maintain close contact with Malcolm MacDonald, would be of considerable importance to Australia. He had discussed this possibility with me in general terms on occasion, but I had not taken it very seriously, as we had enough difficulties on our hands finding manpower and finance for our expanding diplomatic representation in particular countries of the area. In any event, to establish a permanent office for an Australian Commissioner for Southeast Asia was one thing; to send the Head of the Department of External Affairs to Singapore for a limited trial period, while remaining Secretary, was altogether different. In Southeast Asia he would be neither fish nor flesh—neither a Diplomat posted overseas with specific functions, nor a Permanent Head merely making a visit. After one general tour he would become a plain nuisance both to our local Missions and to the foreign Governments concerned. To remain overseas for a period of three months would also tend to undermine his authority as Secretary at home.

Casey, however, found the unorthodox, in war and in peace, peculiarly attractive. He was always looking for someone with new and bright ideas who was neither 'dull' nor 'boring'. For a man of his width of experience he was too susceptible to novel suggestions which had not been thought out properly, and somewhat impatient to take short-cuts which might be dangerous.

One notion which he expounded to us (and to Anthony Eden) which I did my best to discourage, was that the solution of international problems would be facilitated if a 'top-man' spent a lot of time travelling on short visits between—for instance—London and Washington. He felt that some Englishman could spend, say, three weeks in Washington, tell the British Ambassador just what people in London were really thinking, make personal contact with important Americans and return to London to tell the Foreign Secretary what people in Washington (including the British Ambassador) were really thinking. In fact, of course, such a person would become an infernal nuisance. He would get in everybody's hair, the Ambassador might well resign, the Foreign Secretary protest that he himself was quite capable of telling Washington just what people in London were thinking, and the wife of the peripatetic visitor try to divorce him. At the senior level in the Department such proposed permanent travellers and messengers were referred to somewhat irreverently as Casey's 'flying angels'.

The decision to send me to Southeast Asia, based upon Singapore, for a period of three months was one which I felt I could not flatly oppose. To do so would not only have put me in conflict with Casey but also involve reversal by Cabinet of action taken on a formal recommendation by the Minister. I came to the conclusion that the only course to follow was to agree to make one round trip to the countries of Southeast Asia, operating outwards from Singapore, to warn Casey in advance that the three-month proposal was unworkable, and to force the issue after my round trip had been made. I expected it to take about a month. It did not appear to cross the Minister's mind that my absence from Canberra for three months would also have family implications.

This is how things turned out in practice. On returning to Singapore from a round of useful visits which on this occasion included Rangoon, I reported to the Minister who passed through Singapore in early April that another such round was utterly impracticable for at least six months if not longer. I added that I had exhausted whatever information I could obtain from Malcolm MacDonald and that to stay on in Singapore would be embarrassing to our local representative and a waste of my time. On reconsideration Casey allowed me to return to Canberra.

During the following twelve months I gave much thought to the desirability or otherwise of my continuing indefinitely as Head of the Department of External Affairs. Gradually I came to the conclusion that I should stay in that post for a strictly limited period only, for a variety of reasons.

By April 1953 I was fifty-two years old. It was inconceivable to me that I could last as Secretary for another eight years, the earliest date when retirement from the Service was permissible and practicable. Secondly, my individual contribution to the work of the Department had already been made. Broadly speaking, my function had been to cover the transition from the Evatt-Burton regime to the regime under Casey; to reorganise the Department on what I believed sounder and more objective lines; to help get able officers in appropriate positions both at home and abroad irrespective of private political views; to share in the re-orientation of Australian policy towards Southeast Asia and Japan; to help improve relations with the Department of Defence; and to participate in the ANZUS negotiations.

By chance my work had tended to concentrate on Defence matters, and these seemed inexorably to be propelling me towards the Southeast Asian area. The next step after ANZUS was to try to obtain a wider security pact covering Southeast Asia as a whole. Australian relations with Singapore and Malaya raised important issues as to whether Australian troops should be stationed there, to help in handling the 'Emergency' and to play a part in maintaining stability during the movement towards independence of these two territories. While Australia had strengthened substantially its diplomatic representation in Southeast Asia, this would take some time to settle down, and in the meantime there was room for a senior Australian diplomatic presence charged with the task of viewing the area as a whole. Such a presence, however, could not be on a short-term, temporary basis only.

I had never served in Asia, and I had few illusions that short visits to Asian cities lasting three or four days could be regarded as a substitute for actually living there. My Moscow experience had taught me how misleading impressions of Russia could be, based upon visits of one or two weeks during which a conducted tour would provide the newcomer only with evidence of the most impressive aspects of the country. Although in Asia one could go off the beaten track to some extent, understanding of such ancient and different civilisations needed basic study, time, and day-to-day experience of local realities.

It did not take me long to decide that, if I took an overseas post again, I would want to go to Asia. I had served in Washington and Moscow, spent years in England as an undergraduate and visited the continent of Europe. The major posts in Asia at that time were Tokyo and India, but these had already been filled in 1952. Nor was India or Japan specially relevant to current Australian Defence problems. It seemed to me, therefore, that circumstances pointed to Southeast Asia, with headquarters at Singapore. For a limited period prior to Malaya and Singapore becoming independent there was room for an Australian imitation of the British Commissioner-General for Southeast Asia. Although there was no precedent for such a person to be based in British colonial territory, and it would not be easy to fit an Australian in, this did not seem impossible. He might not be welcome to the British colonial authorities in the field, but any resistance on their part might be overcome by the growing desire of London to secure Australian military help and political and economic support in British Southeast Asian territories, especially as it had now become reasonably clear that Australian ground troops were unlikely to be committed to the Middle East.

Nor was I unconscious of the possibility that my honeymoon days with the Minister for External Affairs would not last for ever. In Washington we had learned that Casey had a tendency to develop a 'crush' upon some person he had newly met which diminished with the passage of time. Having drawn from such an individual all the 'bright' ideas he could produce, Casey would come to feel that he was not such a first-class man after all, and switch his interest to someone else. After my experience with Evatt, I had learned to appreciate my relations as Secretary with Casey, but I had no desire to stay beyond the point where he might begin to find me 'dull' or 'boring'.

Transfer overseas would, of course, raise family problems again, but the position had changed considerably since our days in the Soviet Union. Alan had spent three years at Sydney University and his problems there would not be closely dependent upon the presence in Australia of my wife and myself. John had embarked on a Science course at Sydney University and had entered St Paul's College. He had won a Canberra Scholarship on matriculation, and seemed to have settled in at the University. The increased detriment to his hearing could not be affected by our remaining in Australia—he was in the hands of the best available specialist. The twins were now at secondary school. Mary was happy at Frensham, and continuity there seemed best for her. Peter had decided to return to Canberra from his preparatory boarding school in Toowoomba, and had gradually become part of the family again. He was then at the Canberra High School, as we had thought it necessary to cancel his booking for 'Shore', in order that he should be at home with us again for as long as possible. Finding a niche for Peter in a good boarding school would be the most serious complication.

My wife's preference would have been to stay in Australia to be near the children. But I was conscious of the fact that life for a Canberra house-wife with a family and limited financial resources—to say nothing of a husband tied to the busiest job in the Department and constantly vanishing overseas, could scarcely be regarded as ideal. While difficulties experienced abroad, especially in Moscow, were in many ways worse than in Canberra, there were substantial compensations of contact with others sharing in-terests beyond the round of daily household chores. In any event, my wife had never tried to restrain me from choosing work where I felt I could be most effective, and had accepted the changes of the diplomatic service as part of the game.

These reflections, which I have summarised together, took place gradually and over a considerable period of time. Towards the end of 1953 Casey put the specific proposition to me, asking whether I would go to Singapore as Australian Commissioner for Southeast Asia, with the personal rank of Ambassador. I would be 'accredited' to the British Authorities in Singapore, Malaya and the British Borneo Territories, but would also be expected to visit other countries in the area with the permission of Canberra and the assent of local governments, and to exercise a somewhat loose co-ordinating responsibility for our posts in Southeast Asia as a whole while they were being built up. These Missions would be instructed to send me copies of their reports to headquarters, and I could comment upon them if I thought fit. I would not, of course, be entitled to instruct other Heads of Mission what to do or what to say—that was a matter for Canberra.

I accepted this proposal, and on 15 November, 1953 the Minister announced my appointment to the new post and the promotion of A. H. Tange as my successor to the Secretaryship of the Department. Tange reported that it would take a little time to wind up his affairs in Washington and return home; on the other hand, I was anxious to hand over my responsibilities at the earliest practicable date, and at latest by the end of the year. My authority as Secretary would diminish from the day of the public announcement of my posting overseas, both with departmental staff and Heads of Foreign Missions. As well, one's mind inevitably moves for-ward to problems connected with new functions. Casey, however, held me in Canberra as Secretary until 24 January, 1954. After winding up my affairs in Australia and placing Peter in Geelong Grammar School—the only School which agreed to take him at short notice, my wife and I travelled to Singapore on an Italian ship, arriving there on 23 March, 1954.

As I drove home from my office in the late afternoon of my last day in Canberra as Secretary, I suddenly realised that I had driven for half-a-mile without being conscious either of the route I had taken or of any street or vehicle passed on the way. I took myself in hand and drove slowly and carefully until the car was safely in the garage. My mental condition was a reaction to the strains and stresses of some three and a half years as Secretary, during which I had been stretched to the utmost. If I had any leave during that period, I do not remember it—except a fortnight in Sydney when I went down with influenza.

During the final week at home I had mixed feelings of relief at handing over responsibilities to someone else and a sense of deep loss as well. It took some time to adjust myself to the new situation. Ideally the position of Head of the Department of External Affairs should come at the end of one's public service, as it does in the United Kingdom, so that when one leaves the post it is in order to retire. In my day, however, the Australian Diplomatic Service was too recent and too undeveloped for service as Secretary to end in immediate retirement. Even many years later, my two successors in office have been posted overseas on completion of their terms as Secretary.

Yet, despite a considerable number of frustrations during the eight subsequent years I served abroad, I did not come to regret my decision. I had had my run, had made what contribution I could and it was time for others, with a different approach to make their own different contributions.

The Prime Minister, Mr Menzies, was incredulous regarding my transfer from Canberra. On two occasions before the decision was formally made he called me aside and asked 'Do you *really* want to go to Singapore? Casey's not just trying to get you out of the way?' I assured him that I wanted to go and tried to explain, but he did not really comprehend my attitude and shook his head in wonder and surprise.

The San Francisco Conference to establish the United Nations, 1945. Dr. H. V. Evatt is shown addressing the Sub-Committee on Regional Arrangements. The author is sitting on Dr. Evatt's left (*photo United Nations Conference Secretariat*).

The United Nations Preparatory Commission, London, 1945. The Australian Delegation of Officials (from left to right) are, A. H. Tange, K. H. Bailey, the author, W. R. Hodgson (leader), T. Glasheen (deceased), A. P. Renouf and P. M. C. Hasluck.

R. G. Casey and the author arriving in Saigon (1951) by R.A.F. plane from Singapore.

A photograph taken before a lunch for the Australian Prime Minister given by the Prime Minister of India in December, 1950. In the front row of the group are (from left to right), Heather Menzies, R. G. Menzies, Mrs Menzies, Jawaharlal Nehru and the author (*photo Indian Government Press Information Bureau*).

The Australian Prime Minister at United Nations Headquarters, New York, in 1952. The group (from left to right) includes W. D. Forsyth, Permanent Representative of Australia to the United Nations; the author, then Secretary of the Australian Department of External Affairs; Prime Minister R. G. Menzies; and United Nations Secretary-General Trygve Lie (*photo Unations*).

The author arriving at the Palace in Tokyo to present his credentials (1954).

In 1961 Prime Minister Menzies held a meeting of Heads of Australian Diplomatic Missions in Europe and the Middle East at Geneva. The group includes (left to right) L. Arnott, B. Ballard, the author, A. H. Tange, J. K. Waller, L. J. Lawrey, [R. G. Menzies], J. Quinn, E. McCarthy, N. St. C. Deschamps, H. A. McClure Smith and J. M. McMillan.

Willy Brandt, Governing Mayor of Berlin, presenting a memento of Berlin to the author during the latter's farewell visit in 1962.

6

SOUTHEAST ASIA

March 1954—April 1956

THE fortnight spent at sea between Sydney and Singapore was a god-
send for me. I have always loved the sea, with its restlessness, its
indifference and—for the passenger aboard ship—its sense of isolation.
Nowhere else in the world than during a voyage have I found it easier to
forget, for the time being, the time of troubles in which we all now con-
tinually live. To gulp in fresh sea-air instead of city smog, see flying fish flip
from the top of one wave to another or lean over the bows to watch them
crash down to release a flood of foam which, in the right latitudes, is
specked with phosphorus—in circumstances like these I can recover quickly
from the psychological strains of a busy life and adjust myself to new and
very different situations.

It was a wrench to leave all the childlren behind. Our main concern had
been finding a suitable niche for Peter. An application to re-open his earlier
booking at Sydney Church of England Grammar School was summarily
rejected. Peter would have been far happier in a New South Wales School
as, apart from Canberra, all our associations had been with Sydney. However, there was no alternative but to look elsewhere. I tried to get him
accepted by Melbourne Grammar School. The Head Master was extremely
helpful, but unable to take Peter for a year. He suggested trying Geelong
Grammar School, where Peter was in fact accepted. This was the most
expensive school in Australia, but I would not have minded that if he had
been happy there. On the whole it was not a successful experiment. Peter
enjoyed his first year at Timbertop, in the country; for the rest, his musical
interest was developed to the point where he finds relaxation playing the
flute. It was not until his later days at Sydney University that he developed
fully, physically and mentally, and found his metier, after a Science course,
as a computer scientist.

Before leaving Canberra I had spent some capital improving the house.
This was facilitated by an increase in my salary from £2,500 to £3,250 a
year. On being posted to Singapore we let the house, furnished, to a British

Commonwealth diplomat who left it much the worse for wear. After that experience, I decided against any further diplomatic tenants, and took less rent from Australians.

Family considerations were very much in our minds. But there was nothing more we could do about them and I turned my thoughts gradually towards the problems of Southeast Asia. The first need was to catch up on basic reading. Before reaching our destination, I had read the remarkable if pedantic book by G. Coedes entitled *Les Etats Hindouisés d'Indochine et d'Indonésie*, and a history of Malaya.

In due course we reached Singapore and unpacked our belongings in 'Glencaird', the residence of the Australian Commissioner in Malaya. By then the house had been substantially re-constructed with the funds obtained from Treasury, and was now very well suited as a Head of Mission Residence. It was in a pleasant area, not far from the University; the site and grounds were adequate. The only disadvantage not due to unavoidable climate resulted from the fact that Treasury had exacted, as its price for providing funds, External Affairs' consent to construction of a flat on one side of the house for an Australian member of the Diplomatic staff. This saved money, but destroyed the possibility of free movement of air across the building. Moreover, it is never desirable, if avoidable, to include the families of a Head of Mission and a member of his staff in the one house, even where both have separate entrances. I could not grumble, however, as the residence was functional for its purpose and, in its new form, approved even by the ever-critical Australians who lived in Singapore.

We were quickly introduced to the racial problems of the area through our servants. The house servants were Chinese, living for the most part in the basement. Those working outside the house were Malays. My driver, Dawad, was Indonesian, a person of simplicity and charm if not necessarily of innocence. He and his family lived by the garage, which was separate from the house. He was quiet, unobtrusive, and watchful on behalf of my wife whenever she took a walk on her own in the late afternoon near the 'Gap'. As she walked downhill he would follow her at a distance with the engine switched off, turning one corner just before she was about to reach another corner, forever keeping an eye upon her personal safety. He kept the outside of the car spotless, drove well, but was utterly useless if the engine needed attention. Then, of course, we had to seek help elsewhere, either from a Caucasian or a Chinese. We became very attached to Dawad, despite a few quirks and a degree of racial fecklessness. Thus, once a year he would approach me shyly seeking a loan to enable him to get his wife's jewellery out of pawn and to celebrate Hari Raya in an adequate fashion. Subsequently the loan was repaid, without protest or ill-will, by monthly deductions from his wages.

In days before the Second World War, Chinese servants in Singapore used to be famous. But in our time the prestige of European colonial masters had been damaged irretrievably and the quality of available servants had begun to deteriorate. The 'Number One Boy' in the house on my arrival proved unreliable. He drank and the sounds of domestic strife in the basement were all too obvious. In due course he was dismissed. His replacement turned out to be tubercular and could not be retained. Eventually we engaged Ah Fong, an elderly Chinese who had reduced his age by ten years or more in order to secure the job and was one of the old school—trustworthy and capable of combining independence and dignity with loyalty to the establishment. He brought his own team of womenfolk with him, and ruled them as the head of a Chinese family should. His efforts to control my wife in the same way were not as successful, but I don't think he resented her refusal to conform—after all, Caucasians have funny ideas about women and tend to spoil them.

We found the climate of Singapore extremely oppressive. For Europeans not born there the working hours of Canberra or London are unsuitable. The old tradition of large rooms, open verandahs, ceiling fans and a long afternoon siesta made much more sense. Nor is modern air-conditioning a sufficient cure, particularly that minimal degree of air-conditioning which the Australian Treasury, in those days, could be induced to approve. Our vast bedroom had an air-conditioner of ancient vintage which made a noise like an engine entering a tunnel. When we turned it on, the noise made sleep difficult. When we turned it off and opened the windows, we stifled. On the whole, I preferred the noise to the humidity; my wife preferred the reverse situation. Gradually we adjusted ourselves to local conditions and made our mutual compromises, but not without a deterioration in energy and patience. Eventually when all my books, which had been stored in Canberra, were sent to me by mistake—I had asked for a selected few—I bought a more modern and quieter air-conditioner for my study, largely in order to prevent the books mouldering away. This gave me a reasonably comfortable room in the residence in which to work.

The offices of the Australian Commission in the city area were unsatisfactory as regards size, comfort and security. In due course I managed to rent the top floor of a new building which, in normal working hours only, was completely air-conditioned. In the new offices all the Australian staff could be brought together, including those dealing with trade matters, and this improved both efficiency and morale.

Shortly after arrival in Singapore I called upon the British Commissioner-General for Southeast Asia, Mr Malcolm MacDonald, and upon the Governor of Singapore. Relations with the former and members of his staff proved easy and valuable. I had known the Commissioner-General since Oxford days, and he and his staff knew that the Australian Government had not sent me to the area to try to interfere with British colonial administration. The Governor of Singapore was correct in his dealings with me, but not exactly responsive. In Kuala Lumpur, on the other hand, the British High Commissioner, Sir Gerald Templer, gave me a warm welcome which, unfortunately, was not sustained under the regime of his civilian successor. The reasons for the attitude of the British colonial authorities will be elaborated later, as during the first six months after taking over my new responsibilities I was caught up in world and regional rather than local affairs, and spent a considerable amount of time outside Singapore and Malaya.

At the Conference of Foreign Ministers of the United States, France, the United Kingdom and the Soviet Union, which opened in Berlin on 25 January, 1954, it was decided that two conferences should be held in Geneva as from 26 April, one on Korea and one on Indo-China. Australia was invited to attend the conference in respect of Korea as one of the countries which had contributed armed forces to resist the North Korean incursion in 1950. Although she regarded herself as an 'interested state' entitled to be present in respect of discussions on Indo-China, she refrained from pressing this claim, in order to avoid over-weighting the number of countries present. If Australia had pressed her claim, so also would countries like Thailand, the Philippines and perhaps Burma. Nevertheless Australian interests were thought by the Government to be so involved in the future of Indo-China that it was decided that the Minister for External Affairs should at least be present in Geneva at the commencement of the Conference, so that he could be in close contact with Sir Anthony Eden, leader of the British Delegation, and with representatives of other Commonwealth countries.

On 12 April, 1954, Casey announced that he was leaving Australia immediately for Singapore and Saigon, prior to having talks in London and Paris en route to Geneva. He arrived in Singapore the following day and arrangements were made for me to accompany him on his journey, a bare three weeks after I had taken up my new post. Preliminary talks were held with Malcolm MacDonald and the British Service Chiefs, and we then flew to Saigon to obtain a first-hand and last-minute assessment of the situation in Indo-China.

The situation as viewed from Saigon was not reassuring. Bao Dai, the Head of State, was in France, whither he had gone to take personal charge of negotiations with the French for a new Treaty between France and Vietnam under the terms of which Vietnam would acquire additional powers. Ngo Dinh Diem had not yet been asked to form a government, and was still abroad. The impressive personality of General de Lattre de Tassigny, whom we had met in Saigon during an earlier visit and who had raised French morale in Indo-China by his determination and initiative, was missing: he had died in France some two years earlier after a severe illness. French forces were under heavy North Vietnamese pressure at Dien Bien Phu.

After discussions with Vietnamese leaders and with Australian, British and American representatives, Casey came to the conclusion—as he reported to Parliament on 10 August, 1954—that one must look for a negotiated, political settlement of the problems of Indo-China.[80] At that time there was much discussion between American and French representatives of the possibility of American intervention from the air, primarily to try to save Dien Bien Phu. Casey formed the opinion that such intervention would be a mistake. 'It would not have the backing of the United Nations', he told Parliament. 'It would probably embroil us with Communist China; it would wreck

[80] See Current Notes, Vol. XXV (1954) pp. 574-82.

the Geneva Conference; and it was most unlikely to stop the fall of Dien Bien Phu.'[81]

On 19 April we reached London, touching down at Calcutta and Karachi en route, where the Minister had short discussions with the Australian High Commissioners to India and to Pakistan respectively. In London Casey saw Churchill, Eden and other governmental leaders and told them of the conclusions he had reached. These fitted in with the views of the British government which, having learned recently of the enormous destructive capacity of the hydrogen bomb tested by the United States, was determined not to associate itself with any American plans for intervention in Indo-China.

Despite this concurrence of views, the Australian and British positions at Geneva were not identical. There was agreement that American or Allied intervention from the air would be mistaken; but it was Australian policy to establish some Southeast Asia Treaty Organisation, including the United States, at the earliest practicable moment and to avoid any adverse American reaction which might result in a loss of American interest in Indo-China and the writing-off of Vietnam, Laos and Cambodia to the Communists. Britain, on the other hand, fought tooth and nail to resist any talks on a new Southeast Asian Security Organisation until after the conclusion of the Geneva Conference, where Eden hoped to secure both Communist and non-Communist guarantees of whatever settlement emerged. For Britain, what happened in Indo-China was peripheral and unimportant as compared with what happened in Europe and the Middle East. This was a judgment which any British Foreign Secretary was entitled to make, but it did not follow that other countries, including Australia, must inevitably reach the same conclusion.

The Australian Delegation settled in at the Hotel de la Paix where the Canadians, led by Secretary of State for External Affairs Lester Pearson, were also accommodated. Canadian, New Zealand and Australian officials met practically every day with British officials to discuss latest developments. The Conference on Korea opened on 26 April and ended inconclusively, without agreement, on 15 June. Most interest, however, centred upon the discussions regarding Indo-China, which opened on 8 May. By that date Mr Casey had left for Australia, where federal elections were to be held on 29 May. His departure left me in temporary charge of the Australian Delegation until he returned to Geneva on 13 June, the Liberal-Country Party having been returned to office.

It is a somewhat invidious responsibility to be in charge of an overseas delegation during an election campaign at home, as Governments are very disinclined to take imaginative initiatives in the international field in such circumstances. While I knew the general lines of Government policy, positive instructions on Indo-China issues came only after the first Cabinet meeting following the elections. Meanwhile my task was to gather all the information I could, report it to Canberra with comments, refrain from Australian commitments, and generally try to hold the fort pending the Minister's return.

[81] *Ibid.*, p. 576.

The results of the Conference on Korea, which were minimal, can be described in a few words. On 15 June, the day when this Conference ended, a joint statement was issued by the delegations of the sixteen non-Communist States represented at Geneva, describing the continuing differences between the contending parties as follows:

> 1. We accept and assert the authority of the United Nations. The Communists repudiate and reject the authority and competence of the U.N. in Korea, and have labelled the United Nations itself as the tool of aggression. . . .
> 2. We desire genuinely free elections. The Communists insist upon procedures which would make genuinely free elections impossible. It is clear that the Communists will not accept impartial and effective supervision of free elections. . . .[82]

Continuance of these differences was neither surprising nor unexpected, but much time and energy was spent before the non-Communist countries came to the conclusion that further discussion would be useless, and that the Conference on Korea must be terminated. To do this without creating the public impression of lack of patience if not of actual bad faith was far from easy. Before the final session, the representatives of the sixteen non-Communist States met alone to discuss how to end the Conference. Anthony Eden was in the Chair.

I have never been an admirer of Eden, even as Foreign Minister, let alone as Prime Minister. Amongst other reservations, I have always disliked a British technique (perhaps a Great Power technique) which involves sitting back while smaller fry commit themselves to points of view (sometimes at British suggestion) until the broad course of a debate becomes clear—whereupon a British representative introduces some compromise proposal as if it had been British policy from the start. In the meantime criticism of some more extreme proposal has been diverted towards the representatives of Small or Middle Powers.

At the private meeting of the sixteen, Eden suggested from the chair that, at the final plenary meeting, the Foreign Minister of Belgium might take the initiative by proposing that discussions on Korea at Geneva be terminated. M. Spaak, whom no one could accuse of being unsympathetic or unresponsive to British proposals, was taken somewhat by surprise. He said that he hoped that Belgium would never be found wanting in performing its international duty, but he was a little apprehensive that, if he took such an important initiative, people in his country might interpret his action as an attempt to arrogate to himself the responsibility of the Foreign Secretary of a Great Power.

When he made this reply, one could have heard a pin drop, and Eden flushed. However, Spaak then agreed to the Chairman's suggestion, saying that he would do his best. In the event he moved in plenary session for an indefinite adjournment of discussions upon Korea—and drew upon himself the very effective wrath and criticism of Molotov and Chou En-lai in the process.

[82] *Ibid.*, p. 576.

The Geneva Conference on Indo-China filled me with inspissated gloom. There were three main reasons for this. First, as Australia was not a direct participant its influence was inevitably marginal. Secondly, it was my first experience of what was in effect a Great Power Conference where important decisions were reached during secret discussions in private villas between two or more of four men—Eden, Molotov, Chou En-lai and Bidault (later Mendes-France); at conference sessions such agreements were merely registered. Between 1945 and 1948 I had attended United Nations Conferences, and had become wearied by verbiage, iteration and the contrast between high-falutin' principles expressed and national self-interest pursued in practice. To my own surprise, I found that I was reacting strongly against the lack of publicity accorded to Great Power discussions at Geneva, which made it impossible for public opinion in relevant countries to learn what was going on. Thirdly, I feared that any settlement reached at the Conference would be a kind of confidence trick played by the representatives of Great Powers upon world public opinion.

In a letter to my wife dated May 2, 1954 I wrote as follows:

This Conference is different from any I have ever been at—and worse than any other. I sometimes think the old League of Nations spirit haunts Geneva. Or perhaps this is an 18th. century Conference. The formal proceedings . . . are a mere facade. Everything has been decided beforehand and formal proceedings merely register positions worked out between 2 or 3 or 4 powers—usually Great Powers. The Press are excluded from the Conference. No speech can stir the Press and, through publicity, modify a Great Power attitude.

This is corridor diplomacy, hotel diplomacy, private villa diplomacy. Press Conferences are used by Great Powers to score quick advantages through breach of confidence. Small powers, like Australia, have great difficulty in learning the basic facts before decisions are actually made.

We have had some small influence. In British Commonwealth meetings we have raised doubts, made it clear there are different points of view etc. In 16 power meetings on Korea, Australia has taken an initiative and gradually helped make vocal a bloc of liberal opinion—instead of chiming in with one voice after the South Koreans and the Americans. In a Conference speech, Casey seized the psychological moment for a reasoned and liberal speech which had the support of most small power delegations.

But it would be futile to delude oneself into believing we have much influence. Now that I have to act as Leader of the Delegation, and Bedell Smith has arrived, I personally will have more responsibility and, perhaps, more influence. But the problem of Indo-China is so real, so difficult, so dangerous, that I fear a Far Eastern Munich which could have most serious consequences for Australia.

Our own elections hamstring any substantial initiative we can take on policy. The Petrov case and subsequent closing of Embassies in Moscow and Canberra seriously limit our ability to influence Russia, and perhaps China. We can not act as Chairman, or become member of a Committee, because Russia will object. Any influence must be indirect —on the Americans or the French. I despair of influencing the British. . . .

I have never before been more conscious of how many people's lives can be put at stake, now or later, by such few people. Those who know the facts can almost be counted on the fingers of two hands. Hypocrisy, dissimulation, *suppressio veri* are the order of the day. . . .'

Only once while I was still in Geneva did my personal gloom lift slightly. Before Casey left for Australia to contest elections there, an unpublicised ANZUS Council meeting was held on short notice. Those present included Dulles (who was about to return to the United States), Bedell Smith (who had just arrived to take over from Dulles), Casey and myself and, from recollection Alistair McIntosh (representing New Zealand). General discussion of the prospects for an 'acceptable' settlement in Indo-China did nothing to dispel pessimism. Subsequently there was some discussion of what might be done to help prevent a deteriorating situation in Indo-China getting worse. Here the Australian Delegation took the initiative in pressing for early military staff talks.

In his report to Parliament on 10 August, 1954, Casey described this meeting as follows:

In the course of the early stages of the Conference, a meeting of the ANZUS Council was held at Geneva. I took the opportunity . . . to push the proposal that a meeting of military representatives of relevant countries at the highest level should be held as soon as possible so that we might have established by the most competent military authorities whether a lasting solution in Indo-China could be reached by continuation of the fighting. We also wanted to have a military evaluation of the situation that would confront us in South-East Asia if no negotiated settlement was reached at Geneva. I also pursued independently with Mr. Eden this question of a meeting of high military representatives.

These military talks eventually took place in Washington on 3rd. June, and resulted in a report which has been of considerable value to the Governments concerned. . . .

In view of rigid British opposition to any discussions, prior to a Geneva settlement on Indo-China, designed to establish a Southeast Asia Treaty Organisation, Five-Power Military Staff talks in Washington between representatives of the United Kingdom, the United States, France, Australia and New Zealand were the maximum procurable in the circumstances. They constituted at least one step in the direction of healing the serious breach in British-American relations, symbolised by the different attitudes of Eden and Dulles towards the Geneva Conference and their mutual distrust of one another, which greatly disturbed the Australian Delegation at Geneva.

I have analysed elsewhere the nature of the Accords formulated at Geneva and the extent to which, if at all, the participants were bound to observe them.[83] Here it seems relevant only to mention some additional facts and to make some comments upon the part played by several political leaders.

The new Australian Cabinet met on 4 June, 1954 to discuss the question of Indo-China. Before it met, the Australian Delegation at Geneva exerted

[83] See my *Vietnam, An Australian Analysis*, (Cheshire, Melbourne, 1968), especially Chapter 3.

itself to the full to telegraph all available information about the Conference and to assess its probable results.

The decisions upon Australian policy made by Cabinet were cabled to me immediately after they had been made, and I was instructed to convey them to Eden. He received me at his private villa, and read the telegram through carefully. Although he found its contents broadly satisfactory, Harold Caccia was called in to read and comment upon the telegram before the Foreign Secretary committed himself to any official reaction. Caccia too had no special criticism to make, and I was able to report to Canberra that Eden welcomed the general policy lines communicated to him. The only basic difference between the two governments at this stage related to the timing of efforts to establish a Southeast Asia Treaty Organisation.

In my opinion Casey's decision to return to Geneva after the Australian elections was a mistake. Talks on Korea were about to fold up, while the outcome of discussions on Indo-China was quite uncertain. I was afraid that when the Minister returned there would not be enough work to do to occupy his time and energy as, when the Korean question was adjourned indefinitely, there would be no Conference meetings for him to attend. I thought it more important for the Minister to remain in Canberra, where decisions on foreign policy and defence seemed likely to be required.

My own ambition was to leave Geneva at the earliest possible moment after his return. I felt that in Singapore and Southeast Asia there was a job for me to do, whereas nothing I could do in Geneva would have any noticeable effect. However, it took me about a week after the Minister's arrival to secure his permission to leave.

Casey himself did not stay in Geneva until the end of the Conference on Indo-China. By the end of June he was in the United States, where he attended another ANZUS Council Meeting. As late as 17 July Eden himself still felt it 'prudent to prepare for the possibility that the conference might fail'.[84] It was only during the last week, while time was running out for the new French Premier, M. Mendes-France, that the log-jam began to move. Mendes-France had undertaken to resign if a settlement were not reached at Geneva within one month of his assuming office, and only as this date-line approached did Communist governments make concessions which France felt were acceptable. The Accords were completed on 21 July, 1954. Unfortunately the main participants evinced little desire to explain and clarify their meaning and significance; instead, there was a general attempt to gloss over their ambiguities and to minimise the extent of disagreement amongst those who attended the Conference.

The part played by John Foster Dulles in relation to the Geneva Conference has been much misunderstood. Many have accepted unquestioningly Eden's critical attitude towards Dulles. A stereotype picture of the Secretary of State has been built up showing him as a rigid man of moral fervour ready to take all the risks of 'brinkmanship' in order to contain or beat back 'Communism'. Somewhat inconsistently, Eden seems to have felt that he was unpredictable, if not actually untrustworthy.

[84] Eden, *op. cit.*, p. 141.

P

My experience of Dulles has been much more limited than that of many others, but, for what it is worth, this is not my picture of the man. At the San Francisco Conference in 1945 I thought he showed much skill in judging and handling Dr Evatt. During the ANZUS talks in Canberra in February 1951 he demonstrated outstanding ability as a negotiator, determined to insist on what he thought vital to the interests of the United States, but always ready to listen to any reasonable argument and to give serious consideration to ways and means of protecting Australian interests within the limits of overall American policy. His manner was dour and unsmiling, but he was highly intelligent, and his approach to problems struck me as far more pragmatic than moralistic or missionary.

He had never wanted a Conference on Indo-China, fearing that it could result in a concealed sell-out to the Vietminh. His reluctant assent to the Conference was probably given in the hope of bolstering the French Government and sustaining French support for ratification of proposals to create a European Defence Community. Having agreed, however, his aim was to strengthen the hand of the French, who had few cards to play. Hence the continuing noises off-stage about possible American intervention, and his refusal to participate personally in the Conference on Indo-China.

One of the most exhaustive studies of the Geneva Conference is that made by Robert F. Randle—several years too late, unfortunately, to have any significant influence on world public opinion. The author, who had access to the private papers of Dulles, formed the following views:

> 1. President Eisenhower and Secretary of State Dulles concluded, no later than the first or second of April 1954, that the United States should not become militarily involved in the Indochinese War unless the Chinese intervened. Both men adopted a policy of caution, to which they adhered throughout April and throughout the period of the Conference. Mr. Dulles' real policy was masked by an ostensible policy of threats and warnings of United States, and possibly Allied, intervention.
> 2. Dulles's responses to the Indochina crisis and his approach to allies and adversaries in the world arena and within the United States were, for the most part, characterized by astuteness and an acute sense of political realities and the limits they imposed and the possibilities they offered. My study of Mr Dulles has led me to conclude that accounts that picture the late Secretary of State as an inflexible exponent of his own, puritanically inspired views of world politics are probably inaccurate and grossly oversimplified. Such assessments are certainly not correct in respect of his performance in 1954. I believe . . . that a fresh approach to Mr Dulles as Secretary of State is required.[85]

Despite the concessions eventually made by Molotov and Chou En-lai at Geneva and forced by them upon the North Vietnamese, it is very unlikely that such concessions would have been made if the U.S.S.R. and Communist China had not feared that further intransigence might lead to a complete breakdown of discussions at Geneva and, conceivably, to American intervention in the Indo-China war. It is also arguable that Eden's statement in plenary session on 10 June that the conference might have to admit to the

[85] See *Geneva 1954*, (Princeton University Press, 1969), p. ix.

world its failure had far more effect upon Molotov and Chou En-lai than his extraordinary patience and ingenious suggestions for compromise. Certainly it was followed, within a week, by indications from both Communist leaders of readiness to make some concessions.

The personality of Chou En-lai greatly interested non-Communist Delegations, whose leaders had not previously had an opportunity to judge his capacity. We all quickly became aware that he was a man of intelligence and ability. Though tough he did not leave the impression of complete intransigence, perhaps partly because at that time it suited Peking to build up an impression of sweet reasonableness and moderation in expression which reached its peak a year later at the Bandung Conference.

Two countries showed particular interest in maintaining close contact with Chou En-lai on a somewhat personal basis, namely, India and Canada. India, which had contributed no forces to the Korean war, was not officially represented at either of the Geneva Conferences, but Mr Nehru sent his *alter ego*, Mr Krishna Menon, on visits to Geneva where he operated persistently on the side-lines. During Casey's absence in Australia I received a message asking me to call upon him. I had never met him before, and was intrigued by his spare, ascetic-looking figure and the number of cups of tea he drank during a conversation lasting about fifty minutes. During that period he must have talked for forty minutes, I for ten. His conversation was so indirect that I had to cudgel my brains to try to understand what he was driving at.

Eventually I realised that he had summoned me, as an Australian and therefore a stooge of the Americans, in order to stress that the Western Powers should not make the mistake of thinking that Korea was a secondary problem for Peking. He wanted me, no doubt, to warn my American masters that they had better make some real concession on the Korean issue.

Once I had gathered Menon's real purpose, my response was easy to decide. I said I could not anticipate any change in the Australian or allied position on Korea, which seemed completely justified. I felt, however, I should tell him in confidence (hoping he would inform Chou En-lai) that Peking should not underestimate the risks of failing to reach a sensible agreement on Indo-China. As someone who had lived five years in the United States I was bound to say that I had found the Americans peculiar people who tended to be apathetic about international problems until the point came when they thought they were being pushed around. They did not like this, and their subsequent reactions were apt to be unpredictable and somewhat violent.

The Canadian Minister for External Affairs had included in his Delegation a senior official, Chester Ronning, whom he used to maintain informal contact with Chou En-lai. Ronning had been born in China, of missionary parents and spoke Chinese before he spoke English. He had a close sympathy for all things Chinese. During the 1950's I had crossed swords with him passing through Ottawa when, outraged by reports that General MacArthur was about to bomb the Yalu Dams, he had made the mistake of expounding to me what Australian foreign policy should be.

Ronning knew Chou En-lai personally and was able to chatter informally in the latter's own language. Casey was impressed by this and, with his inherent fascination for the unorthodox, played with the notion of Australia emulating the Canadians. After the elections he telegraphed me from Canberra saying that he was thinking of bringing back with him to Geneva Charles Lee, an Australian citizen of Chinese ancestry who was a member of our diplomatic service. He felt Lee could be useful for contacts with Chou En-lai.

My reaction to this proposal was adverse. It seemed to me merely imitative of the Canadians, and might only make our delegation seem silly. Lee had been born in Australia, not China, and had never met Chou En-lai. It was perfectly possible that the latter might refuse to see Lee; in any event, he was very unlikely to talk freely to Lee even if he agreed to one interview.

While I was meditating ways and means of convincing Casey, without seeming rude or officious, that it would not be a good idea to bring Lee, I passed Ronning in a corridor of the Palais des Nations. Suddenly I had a brain-wave. Ronning would be sure to oppose Lee coming to Geneva, not only because it did not make sense, but also because he would not want any competition in this field. So I turned back, caught up with Ronning, drew him aside and said I wanted to ask his advice. I explained what Casey had proposed and added that I was doubtful whether this would serve any useful purpose; but he knew China and Chou En-lai and I would be grateful for his opinion. Ronning strongly opposed Lee being brought to Geneva and raised no objection to my quoting him in my reply to Casey.

I hastened to send a telegram to Canberra stating that I had taken the liberty of discussing the matter with Ronning, who had raised a number of objections to the proposal which I set out in detail. Casey, I knew, would not welcome receiving these comments, placed on the record which others in the Department would see, but I could think of no other way of influencing the Minister's attitude towards his plan. In the event I received no reply; I heard no more of the proposal and Charles Lee did not leave Australia.

Before leaving Geneva for Australia for the election campaign, Casey had had an urge to call upon Chou En-lai himself. At the time I had made discouraging noises. We were not a member of the Conference on Indo-China; Australia did not recognise the Peking regime. To meet Chou En-lai accidentally coming out of a Session on Korea would be one thing: it was quite another thing to seek a personal interview with him, which the Chinese Delegation might well arrange to be photographed for world-wide propaganda purposes.

When the Minister returned to Geneva he said to me somewhat belligerently 'I'm going to call upon Chou En-lai'. I guessed that, remembering my unwanted intervention about Charles Lee, he understandably felt it was time to exert his Ministerial authority. So I said simply 'Yes, Sir'. Shortly afterwards a meeting with Chou En-lai was arranged and Casey went to see him, taking with him a junior member of our Delegation. When he returned he told us that Chou En-lai had 'a reassuring sort of face'. This phrase was added to the Department's informal Treasury of Quotations—stimulated, perhaps by the fact that *Time* magazine published during the same week a photograph of Chou En-lai looking like the devil incarnate.

During the last four days of the Conference the Communist Powers at Geneva made the vital concessions regarding the 'temporary' dividing line between North and South Vietnam at the seventeenth parallel, the two-year period before elections for Vietnam as a whole, and the constitution of the Supervisory Commission which made possible the Geneva Accords. By then I had been back in Singapore for weeks and the Minister was back in Australia. In effect, the Australian Delegation to the Conference had been disbanded, although L. R. McIntyre had been sent from London to Geneva to keep his eye on the closing stages and R. L. Harry, as Australian Consul-General in Geneva, was also there to report.

The pace of developments during the last few days, however, was so hectic as the deadline set by Mendes-France approached that it would have been difficult for the British representatives to keep Australia and other Commonwealth countries fully informed, even had they so wished. In fact, the participants were in no haste to disclose the precise nature of the Accords. As late as 10 August, when the Minister for External Affairs made a full statement on the Geneva Conference to Parliament, Casey indicated that some of the final documents had still not been made public. It seems clear from internal evidence to be found in the comments made by the Australian Prime Minister after a Cabinet Meeting on 24 July that the Australian Government had not been able to focus accurately the precise nature of the settlement.[86]

To me the vital next step after the Conference was the creation of some Southeast Asian Treaty Organisation which might help stabilise the situation in Indo-China. The speed with which such an organisation (SEATO) was in fact established—the treaty was signed a mere seven weeks later in Manila —reflected strong fear that the seventeenth parallel chosen at Geneva as the dividing line between North and South Vietnam would prove but short-lived, and that the whole of Vietnam (to say nothing of Laos and Cambodia as well) might come under Communist control. Although on 4 June, 1954 Bao Dai had once again called upon Ngo Dinh Diem to form a government in South Vietnam and the latter had accepted, arriving in Saigon on 26 June, I was far from being alone in wondering whether Diem, who must face enormous difficulties in exercising effective authority, would last longer than one or two years.

MANILA TREATY CONFERENCE (SEATO) 1954

By 30 August, 1954 I was in Manila as Leader of the Australian delegation of officials who, as from 1 September, were to have preliminary discussions regarding a security pact for Southeast Asia. The countries represented were the United Kingdom, United States, France, Thailand, Philippines, Pakistan, New Zealand and Australia. The Foreign Ministers of these countries were to meet in Manila about a week later to consider the recommendations of their officials, and to decide important outstanding issues.

[86] See Watt, *Vietnam*, *op. cit.*, p. 64-65.

My team of advisers included a number of senior people from Departments other than External Affairs, namely, A. D. McKnight (Assistant-Secretary, Prime Minister's Department), S. Landau (Assistant-Secretary, Department of the Navy), and Brigadier T. J. Daly (Director of Military Operations and Plans, Department of the Army). Their presence and their helpful advice reflected the closer and warmer relations which had developed between their respective Departments and the Department of External Affairs.

Critics of SEATO today rarely remember the atmosphere of the time, or the policy statements made during the month preceding the Conference by Australian political leaders. These need to be recalled if the terms of the treaty itself are to be understood.

In a major foreign policy statement by Mr Menzies in Parliament on 5 August, 1954, the Prime Minister strongly condemned 'Communist aggression' which used 'cunning or bloodshed, fraud or fury, with callous indifference to all moral and spiritual considerations'. He said that it was 'foolish, superficial, and dangerous to speak of the conflict in the world as a contest between two economic systems, capitalism and communism.' Indeed it was 'desperately important that the world should see this as a moral contest; a battle for the spirit of man'.[87]

In the past, the Prime Minister added, it had been one of the traditions of the Australian Government that commitments were not accepted in advance. In two world wars Australia had an opportunity to decide what it was going to do and enough time to assemble, train, equip and despatch armed force. We could not gamble on that being our position any longer. The time had come when we must present a common front backed by a common power. 'We must accept military commitments. . . . for us . . . to expect our great friends to accept commitments while our own attitude remained tentative and conditional, would be utterly inconsistent with the intelligence, character and record of our country.'

In becoming a party to ANZUS and a Southeast Asian Treaty Organisation, we were not contracting ourselves out of the old world; rather were we about to contract ourselves into a regional defensive arrangement which would give strength not only here but also in Europe itself. '. . . The decisive battle for Australia may be fought far away, in Malaya, over the great oceans, over the cities and fields of England.' 'Communist aggression must be resisted at the right time and in the right places.' While it 'would be a great crime to have created a war which was unnecessary', it would also be 'a great crime to have preferred peace to justice and freedom'. Freedom could not be purchased cheaply; nor could it be defended by one-sided goodwill. It was not our business 'to convert the Communist powers away from Communism by force', but it was our business to help to see that free countries, including our own, were not converted to Communism by force. The sacrifices of two wars had taught us grim lessons, the greatest of which was that we could not live alone. '. . . We stand or fall with our great associates in freedom.' It was essential to try to shore-up the non-Communist States of Indo-China, lest we find ourselves '. . . forced to

[87] See Current Notes, Vol. XXV, (1954), pp. 568-74.

regard the Communist frontier as lying on the southern shores of Indo-China, within a few hundred air miles of the Kra Isthmus'.

On 10 August the Minister for External Affairs reported to Parliament on the Geneva Conferences on Korea and Indo-China.[88] Australia, said Casey had had two main aims regarding Southeast Asia. The first was 'a negotiated settlement in accordance with the realities of the situation—which did not unfortunately make practicable a solution at all closely in accord with our wishes'. The second aim was the achievement of a collective defence for Southeast Asia, while avoiding action in this direction which might have been seized upon by the Communists as a pretext for breaking off the Geneva negotiations.

The Five Power Military Staff Talks held in Washington, which Australia had pressed for at the ANZUS Council meeting held in Geneva, had helped to give a common basis for the military judgments of a number of the countries which were ready to participate in a Southeast Asian Defence arrangement. Another important step had been the agreement, during the visit of Churchill and Eden to Washington in late June, to set up a joint American-British study group to make preliminary examination of the political and other implications of such a defence arrangement. That study group had met for about ten days in July and made considerable progress in pointing up the main issues involved in the negotiation of a pact. 'Australia and New Zealand were associated through direct consultations with the United Kingdom on the one hand, and through the ANZUS relationship on the other.' A meeting of the ANZUS Council had been held in Washington immediately after the Churchill-Eisenhower talks, and this had been attended by Casey. In short, 'the Australian Government's agreement with the Indo-China settlement was taken in the light of the knowledge that a collective defence would be established in the Southeast Asian region to support that settlement and to deter any breach of it by the Communists'.

Such a pact, said the Minister, should pay attention to economic as well as to military factors, although, in a separate statement issued on 10 August, he made it clear that economic provisions in the proposed Treaty should not be designed to supersede the Colombo Plan.

I have quoted at some length from these two speeches in order to underline the fact that, when I arrived in Manila, the Sino-Soviet split had not occurred, 'Communism' was regarded as 'monolithic', under Soviet leadership, and the Australian government was deeply concerned regarding the stability of countries in Southeast Asia.

It was the task of the officials who met in Manila to work over the draft treaty which had been drawn up in Washington as a result of consultations there, leaving major points of difference for decision at the ministerial level. On the second day of our sessions light was thrown upon the difficulty of establishing a security organisation in a Southeast Asian setting when the full text of the Washington draft, which was a confidential document, was published in a Manila newspaper.

Amongst the officials of other delegations were three whom I was to meet again elsewhere. Contact with them in Manila proved very valuable

[88] Ibid., pp. 574-82.

later. The first was Douglas MacArthur II, a relative of General MacArthur. Subsequently he became United States Ambassador to Japan when I was posted to Tokyo as Australian Ambassador. Second and third were two members of the Philippines Delegation, namely, Raoul Manglapus who was then official Head of the Foreign Office, and Felino Neri, who also became Ambassador to Japan during my time there. In 1966 Manglapus came to Australia to deliver the annual Dyason Lectures sponsored by the Australian Institute of International Affairs.

At Manila the major problem was the desire of some delegations, particularly that representing the Philippines, to include in the SEATO Treaty the NATO declaration that an armed attack upon any one of the parties should be considered an attack upon them all. This declaration, as I have written elsewhere, is 'psychologically comforting and politically reassuring. . . . But the important point . . . is not what an attack is considered to be, but what each party is bound to do when an attack on one party comes. If one examines the text of the NATO formula, it is clear that . . . each party is bound under the terms of the treaty itself to take only "such action as *it* (emphasis added) deems necessary".'[89]

Australia had already learned during Dulles' visit to Canberra in 1951 that the United States Administration was unwilling to use again in a security treaty a phrase which had given rise to much debate in the Senate when ratification of NATO was under consideration and which seemed to some Senators to diminish Congressional powers. During the ANZUS discussion we were quite satisfied with the formula drafted in Canberra, according to which each party, in the event of an armed attack, declared that it 'would act to meet the common danger in accordance with its constitutional processes'. We understood perfectly well that ANZUS could not commit any party automatically to a declaration of war if an armed attack occurred—a situation which had advantages for Australia as well as disadvantages. At Manila, therefore, the Australian officials were satisfied with the American proposal that Article IV(1) of SEATO should follow the ANZUS rather than the NATO formula. Indeed, we could not understand why the Philippines Delegation, which had accepted the ANZUS formula in the U.S.-Philippines Security Treaty of 1951, should now try to resurrect the NATO formula.

The Australian and American officials held private discussions on this issue. MacArthur convinced us that, from the legal point of view, parties to SEATO would acquire no more rights under the NATO than under the ANZUS formula, and that a repetition of the NATO declaration would simply not be accepted by the American Senate. In these circumstances we argued the American case in full sessions, relieved some of the pressure from the United States, and gained some American good-will in the process.

This good-will was demonstrated later on a different point. Australia wanted firmer machinery for military planning than the United States thought practicable; but the American delegation supported a re-draft of our own proposal on this issue, which was eventually incorporated in the Treaty. Article V contains the sentence 'The Council shall provide for

[89] See Watt, *Australian Foreign Policy, op. cit.*, p. 126.

consultation with regard to military and any other planning as the situation obtaining in the treaty area may from time to time require'. This at least enabled Australia to argue in the future, if it so wished, that military planning should not be limited to what the United States thought fitting, but should depend upon whatever the actual situation in the area 'required'.

However, the most crucial issue had to be dealt with by the Foreign Ministers themselves. The United States was prepared to give a security guarantee to its partners only in respect of 'Communist aggression'. For this reason its delegation wanted to include that phrase in the text of the Treaty itself. Asian countries in particular objected, because they felt that other Asian countries, such as India, would be likely to find the phrase unnecessarily provocative. Moreover, although the most immediate danger was believed to be Communist aggression, other forms of aggression could occur.

Eventually the United States agreed to delete the word 'Communist' from the text of the Treaty, provided there was appended to its text a special American reservation making it crystal clear that the *United States* would be bound to 'act to meet the common danger' only in the event of 'Communist aggression', although it was prepared to *consult* with the other parties to the Treaty in the event of other kinds of aggression. This meant, however, that the remaining parties to SEATO would be undertaking wider obligations under the Treaty than the United States. The Australian Prime Minister in Canberra was opposed to such a situation.

The bare words of treaties are never in themselves sufficient to explain how they came to be signed and ratified. SEATO is no exception. Casey's signature of the SEATO Treaty at Manila was an act of political courage which could conceivably have cost him his portfolio.

Dulles came to Manila with a committed programme which allowed him only three days there. On the fourth day he had to be in Taipei. Three days was too short for the Ministerial meeting. In particular, it was impossible for the Australian Delegation to communicate and consult adequately with Canberra. The Australian Legation in Manila had to send confidential telegrams to Canberra in hand cypher—a slow and tedious process, both as to despatch and receipt. On the last day of the Conference a crisis developed.

It had been decided in private session to adjourn for lunch, and to meet again in public session at 4 p.m. for final brief statements, to be followed by signature of the Treaty. At 2.30 p.m. Casey telephoned Australia and asked me to stand by while he explained to the Acting Minister for External Affairs, Mr (later Sir John) Spicer that it was impracticable to carry out the Prime Minister's instructions to go no further than the Americans regarding obligations under the Treaty. The line to Australia was very bad, and Casey had to repeat himself several times to explain his meaning.

Spicer told Casey that Cabinet had decided he was to sign the Treaty with a reservation similar to the American reservation, unless Casey was completely convinced that such action by Australia would stop the Treaty being signed at all. In that case he should sign 'subject to the right of the Australian Government to introduce a reservation on the lines of the American reservation prior to ratification of the Treaty'. Presumably because of the bad line, Spicer got the impression, which he conveyed to Cabinet, that Casey had told him that this latter proposal would be acceptable to the other parties to the Treaty. Casey, however, had made no such statement.

When the Minister for External Affairs discussed the matter with his advisers in Manila, the latter were in a quandary. We had no doubt that if Casey carried out the instructions from Canberra, the Conference would fail and Australia would incur the odium for indefinite postponement of the establishment of a Southeast Asia security organisation. Our current assessment of the situation in Indo-China convinced us that creation of such an organisation was necessary and urgent. But it was not our function to advise the Minister to disobey instructions and, in so doing, to risk losing his seat in Cabinet. The decision he made, therefore, was peculiarly his own.

Casey made an appointment to see Dulles at 3.50 p.m., and when he left us to keep the appointment we did not know what he was going to do. When he returned, with Dulles, the session opened at once. Each Foreign Minister then announced his support for the text, including the American reservation. The Treaty was signed, the Conference adjourned and Dulles flew out of Manila to keep his appointment in Taipei. Above his signature, Casey wrote the following:

> I sign, subject to the right of the Australian Government to review the Treaty prior to ratification, in accordance with Australian constitutional practice. The real purpose of the Treaty is to present a concerted front against aggressive Communism, which presents the free world with immediate problems of security. Our own defence policy is directed to this dominant purpose.

He had gone as far as he could to carry out Cabinet's wishes, but this was not the form which Cabinet had approved.

We all thought that Casey had made the right decision, but were uneasy as to the personal consequences for him. Immediately after the voting and signature, we drafted an urgent telegram to Canberra explaining what had happened. The central fact was that, during the Minister's conversation with Dulles, the latter had said bluntly that it would be calamitous if Australia insisted on appending an American-style reservation or appended a reference to Australia's right to introduce such a reservation prior to ratification. This would start off a chain-reaction, and the Conference would end in chaos.

Before Casey left Manila in the early morning of 10 September on a world tour, he received a cable from Menzies expressing surprise at what had happened and instructing him to re-open the matter with the other signatories. It was impossible for him to do this. The key figure at the Conference, Dulles, had left Manila, while other Foreign Ministers had either left or were about to depart. Even if practicable, such a reversal of what had been done the day before would have had shattering results. So Casey approved a long telegram explaining the situation and setting out at length the reasons for the course he had taken; he then proceeded on his planned trip.

At some early stage, either just before I left Manila or just after I arrived back in Singapore, I was instructed to return to Canberra for consultations about the Conference. I had picked up a heavy cold in Manila which, with the exhaustion of the preceding ten days, had left me almost immobile. Although my only ambition was to get back to Singapore to recover health in familiar surroundings. I would have found it difficult to leave Manila without the medical ministrations of a Canberra doctor who happened to be passing through the Philippines. He dosed me with drugs and got me on the plane, although I doubt whether flying in such a state improved my hearing. In Singapore I recovered gradually, and by 17 September was writing to my wife from Canberra.

The Prime Minister was out of Canberra until 21 September so that, after discussions in the Department of External Affairs, I was able to spend some of the intervening period chasing up scattered members of my family. On the evening of 22 September I was summoned to the Prime Minister's offices in Parliament House, where were assembled Mr Menzies, Sir Philip McBride (Minister for Defence), Senator Spicer (Attorney General and Acting Minister for External Affairs), Allen Brown (Secretary, Prime Minister's Department), Arthur Tange (Secretary, Department of External Affairs), James Plimsoll (Assistant-Secretary External Affairs) and Allan McKnight (Assistant-Secretary, Prime Minister's Department).

Although all those present were well-known and not unfavourably disposed, this was not an experience I enjoyed. In effect I was being asked to report upon the work of my Minister, Mr Casey at the SEATO conference and to explain why he had not done more in carrying out government wishes. I would much have preferred the Prime Minister to discuss the matter personally with Casey himself. Furthermore, Menzies is a skilful cross-examiner, and I had had too much experience of the law to want to appear in the witness-box myself.

Menzies asked me to explain in my own words what had happened at Manila, but his tone was serious and implied that the information he had received so far on the subject was insufficient to justify the final course of action taken by Casey.

In effect, my reply was a defence of the Minister for External Affairs. First of all it was necessary to clear away misunderstanding as to what Casey had or had not said to Spicer on the telephone. Here my statements were given added weight because I had actually been present during the conversation. I was able to say quite firmly that Casey at no time had indicated that an Australian appendage to signature reserving Australia's right to introduce prior to ratification an American-style reservation to the Treaty would be acceptable to other national representatives at Manila. If Spicer had interpreted Casey's conversation differently, this must be attributed to the hopeless telephone connection which had made it necessary to repeat statements several times in an attempt to convey meaning.

This explanation eased the atmosphere somewhat, and I then made the following points:

    1. The Americans were open to criticism in limiting the conference rigidly to three days. Whatever the demands upon the time of a Secretary of State, I doubted whether Australia should ever again accept

without formal objection such a time-table. Three days was simply too short in which to deal with the issues involved. In particular, although the Australian staff in Manila had half-killed themselves drafting, coding and decoding cables to and from Canberra, the facilities available had been inadequate to the circumstances.

2. The Americans had been adamant about limiting their obligations under SEATO to cases of 'Communist aggression'. Congress would not have approved wider obligations. The difficulty, however, had been to prevent some other delegations insisting on following suit. Had they done so this would have wrecked the unity of the Conference and rendered hopeless the chances of inducing other countries, like India, to become parties in the future. The Philippines, for instance, had indicated during the morning of the last day its intention of entering a separate reservation similar to the American. Dulles had found it necessary to have the conference adjourn while he persuaded President Magsaysay to override the Philippines Delegation, which included members of Parliament. Had Australia subsequently insisted on an American-style reservation, the Philippines at least—and probably others—would have followed suit. In these circumstances an acrimonious debate would have occurred, and the Conference could have broken down.

3. In substance, though not in form, Australia had not really accepted wider obligations than the Americans. The undertaking to 'act to meet the common danger' (as with ANZUS) did not involve any automatic commitment to war, or indeed to take any particular form of action— which might be no more than despatch of a diplomatic note. Why should Australia be more sensitive to such a formal commitment than the United Kingdom, which had fewer long-term interests in South and Southeast Asia than Australia and was determined not to become militarily involved. It was inconceivable that Britain would fight India because of an attack by the latter on Pakistan (or vice versa), or supply troops to help Thailand in a war, say, with Burma. Yet Eden had specifically authorised Lord Reading, Leader of the British Delegation, to sign the Treaty without reservation. So far as Pakistan was concerned, there could be no misunderstanding as to the Australian position. I had strongly urged Mr. Casey to inform Zafrullah Khan, Leader of the Pakistan delegation, before the final vote, that Australia did not regard signature of the Treaty as imposing any obligation upon Australia to fight on behalf of one member of the Commonwealth of Nations against another member, and he had done this.

4. Under Article IV (2) of the Treaty the Americans had specifically held open at least the possibility of the United States acting in the event of non-Communist aggression. Although this was only an obligation to consult about measures to be taken, it was far from unimportant.

5. It had been quite impracticable to reconvene the Conference or to re-open this delicate issue with the other parties after the final Sesion on 8 September. By that time Dulles was on his way to Formosa, and the world had the SEATO text.

After some general discussion among those present, Menzies asked my opinion regarding the possibility of re-opening the issue through diplomatic channels before ratification of the Treaty. I thought and said that such a move had no chance of success; there were no new arguments to put which had not already been expressed at Manila. Moreover, an Australian initiative along these lines would scarcely improve our relations with the Americans, and would tend to create in the Communist world the impression of disunity among the parties to SEATO.

Finally, Menzies asked what I thought the reactions of other parties to the Treaty would be if the Australian Government, when introducing it to Parliament, inserted into the Bill or the supporting speech of the Minister for External Affairs a statement to the effect that Australia interpreted its obligations under the Treaty as limited to cases of Communist aggression. I replied that I could only speculate but, for what it was worth, I did not think that such action would prove fatal to acceptance of the Treaty by other parties. Some countries might be rather irritated, but on reflection they would realise, first, that the Treaty was in fact designed primarily to counter Communist aggression and secondly, that any such interpretative statement could scarcely reduce in fact the degree of obligation imposed upon Australia by the actual words of the Treaty.

The meeting then ended, to my great relief. In the event, the Government did include in the Preamble to the Bill specific reference to Communism. In addition Casey, when introducing the Bill, said that '. . . resistance to Communism is the immediate objective of the Treaty and it is for this principal purpose that the Australian Government is prepared to commit itself to this treaty. In fact, we cannot at present see any other circumstances in which we would be obliged to intervene. . . . the Australian Government would never regard itself as being committed . . . to military action against any other member of the Commonwealth . . . The Pakistan Foreign Minister was informed of our position on this point before the Treaty was signed.'[90]

Dr Evatt, Leader of the Opposition, strongly attacked the Government on these two points and, speaking in reply, Casey had to admit that the statement in the preamble to the Bill had 'no legal significance'.

SINGAPORE AND MALAYA (1954-6)

It will be seen from the above account of my activities that during the first six months at my new post I spent most of my energies on regional defence problems and was out of Singapore for much of the time. This was the most interesting and important aspect of my work. After the Manila Conference and my visit to Australia, regional responsibilities became more routine. They included attendance at SEATO Council meetings at Bangkok (February 23-25, 1955) and Karachi (March 6-8, 1956); occasional journeys to Bangkok for meetings of Council Representatives held between SEATO Council conferences; and visits to Vietnam, Cambodia and Laos. In addition, I kept in close touch with Malcolm MacDonald and, by invitation, attended meetings of the British Defence Coordination Committee when Australian interests were specially involved. This latter Committee was chaired by

[90] Current Notes, Vol. XXV (1954), pp. 741-42.

MacDonald as British Commissioner-General for Southeast Asia, until he was succeeded in that office by Sir Robert Scott.

It was only after my return to Singapore following my visit to Australia in September 1954 that I was able to give proper attention to my more specific responsibilities in Singapore, Malaya and the British Borneo Territories. In order to understand the problems which existed in this more limited sphere some background account of developments which had taken place there since the war with Japan is necessary.

The period from March 1954 to March 1956, during which I was posted in Singapore, was one of swift transition from the old colonial system to greater local authority and control. The basic question was whether Singapore and Malaya, singly or together, with or without the British Borneo Territories, would move speeedily through a stage of self-government to independence with a parliamentary system on the Westminster model, or whether one or more Communist States would be established in the area.

This is not the place to describe the complicated constitutional arrangements in Singapore and Malaya following upon the establishment of original British control. Here it is sufficient to point out that, when the Japanese attacked Malaya, Singapore, Penang and Borneo in 1942, they were met neither by adequate Commonwealth forces, properly equipped, nor by a unified, indigenous spirit of resistance to the invader. The result was catastrophic. Churchill himself has described the fall of Singapore as 'the worst disaster and largest capitulation in British history'. European prestige fell to a low ebb.

Japan, locked in a life and death struggle with China, treated the overseas Chinese harshly; Malays, on the other hand, were favoured. The growth of Indian nationalism was encouraged. Continuing resistance to the Japanese was carried out mostly by Chinese, many of whom were Communists, although some British officers from India infiltrated the jungle and helped to keep up pressure upon Japanese units and communications.[91] After the Japanese surrender, it was some weeks before substantial British forces arrived in Malaya. In the meanwhile Communist guerrilla forces avenged themselves upon collaborators with the Japanese, and there were some communal disturbances between Chinese and Malays.

The British Commonwealth defeat in Malaya and Singapore in 1942 led to serious criticism of past British policy. 'It was alleged', writes J. M. Gullick, 'that the multiplicity of governments in pre-war Malaya and the discrimination in favour of Malays at the expense of Chinese and Indians had caused administrative inefficiency and popular apathy, both detrimental to the British defence of Malaya.[92]

The British Colonial Office, realising that Malayan independence could not long be deferred in view of the changed world attitude towards 'colonialism', and regarding unity as an essential pre-condition of independence, decided to act quickly after the Japanese defeat before the conservative Sultans of Malaya recovered their confidence. Under threat of

[91] *The Jungle is Neutral*, by F. Spencer Chapman (Chatto and Windus, London, 1953).
[92] *Malaya*, by J. M. Gullick (Ernest Benn, London, 1963), p. 88.

supersession if a review of their relations with the Japanese so warranted, these Rulers agreed to a plan for a Malayan Union, to include the nine Malay States, together with Penang and Malacca, but not Singapore, which would remain a separate colony under its own Governor. The exclusion of Singapore would retain a majority for Malays in the Union; Singapore, whose population was predominantly Chinese, could continue to be a free port, whereas the Malay States would raise considerable revenue from Customs duties; important naval and military bases in Singapore would be retained by Britain. In the Union, a system of equal rights for all citizens linked with Malaya through birth or a long period of residence would be substituted for the old principle of a privileged Malay community.

This imaginative plan was defeated by the swift development of Malay political organisations, supported in London by sometime British administrators with a pro-Malay bias. In its place was substituted a plan for a Federation of Malaya, under a British High Commissioner with strong financial powers, advised by a federal Legislative Council of official and nominated members. Each of the nine States was to have a chief executive (Mentri Besar) and a State Secretary, both Malays. There were also to be British Advisers, whose powers would be less than those of the old British Residents in the Federated Malay States. Special provisions safeguarded Malay rights; Malay Rulers resumed sovereignty in their own States; and the High Commissioner had to consult a Conference of Rulers on important matters, including immigration. Non-Malays would become federal citizens if both parents had been born and resident for fifteen years in the Federation; local birth and residence also enabled a person to apply for citizenship. Singapore was to be excluded from the Federation, and to move slowly towards self-government by way of elections for some seats in a Legislative Council, voting for which was on a limited franchise.

It is a matter for speculation whether the decision to drop the plan for a Malayan Union and to force through the plan for a Federation of Malaya against the opposition of Chinese, Indians and Communists was a fatal mistake or merely inevitable. Few people who have lived in Malaya can believe that the prolongation of Sultans' courts and powers into the second half of the twentieth century made political sense, or that in the long-term Malaya can survive on any other basis than equal right for all its citizens, whether Malay, Chinese or Indian. Psychologically, the moment after the defeat of Japan was the right time to force through changes, rather than to permit time for ingrained Malay conservatism to regain strength. Whatever the correct decision, the die was cast and the Federation was formed, although independence did not come before Communist revolts tested to the full the capacity of Commonwealth and Malayan forces to contain and defeat them.

The Communist 'Emergency' in Malaya and Singapore began in 1948. On 23 July it was announced that the Acting High Commissioner of the Malayan Federation and the Governor of Singapore, on the advice of their respective Executive Councils, had outlawed the Malayan Communist Party and three affiliated organisations, on the ground that the Party had planned and was superintending 'the carrying out of a campaign of violence for the purpose of upsetting the authority of the lawful Governments in the

Federation of Malaya and Singapore with the object of imposing its will upon the people of the country'.[93]

On August 3, 1948, Mr Malcolm MacDonald broadcast as follows:

> Communist leaders decided in March this year to stage an armed insurrection. To introduce it they planned to provoke widespread labour unrest throughout April, stimulating it by their customary methods of intimidation, such as stabbing trade union leaders reluctant to join them, hurling hand-grenades, and burning factories. On May 1 they planned to hold large political demonstrations to try to impress the people of Malaya with their supposed strength. They expected fairly quickly to establish themselves in regions which they could proclaim as Communist territory. In each of them they would hoist their flag, and in each they would form a provisional Communist administration. The personnel for these petty governments had been prepared. They expected that only a short time would be needed to subjugate Singapore. Instead of issuing decrees from Government House in Singapore, they are in a grievously weaker position, licking their wounds in the jungle following defeats at Batu Arang and elsewhere.

Mr MacDonald went on to describe the build-up of British troops and police forces, referred to a great improvement in the arms situation, with more supplies due from Britain and Australia, and to availability of aircraft and crews. He concluded with a confident statement of ability to protect the civil population and strike at the insurgents.

While the Communists had indeed failed to realise their hopes of a quick take-over, MacDonald's description of the current and future situation was over-optimistic. It took years for the British authorities to organise sufficient military and police forces, to use effectively Emergency Regulations giving wide powers of arrest and deportation, and to devise and implement a counter-guerrilla plan designed to extend effective administration and control of populated areas and to isolate the Communists from food supplies and intelligence sources. Under the Briggs plan of 1950, New Villages were set up in Malaya to which some 500,000 Chinese squatters were removed. These villages were 'enclosed by barbed wire, guarded and provided, eventually, with elementary social services and a form of self-government'.[94]

The years 1950 and 1951 have been described as the 'years of hope' for the Communists, during which the security forces were fighting a difficult war of attrition. The most striking success of the insurgents was the killing in a road ambush of the High Commissioner for the Federation of Malaya, Sir Henry Gurney, on 6 October, 1951. The British Government responded by appointing as High Commissioner and Director of Operations Sir Gerald Templer, Commander-in-Chief of Eastern Command in Britain. Mr D. (later Sir Donald) MacGillivray was appointed Deputy High Commissioner. As a civilian, former Colonial Secretary in Jamaica, it was to be the latter's responsibility to concentrate on problems of administration.

General Templer was not everyone's cup-of-tea, and his work in Malaya has been both praised and criticised. Yet if he was indifferent to the niceties

[93] Keesing's Contemporary Archives, p. 9427.
[94] Malaysia, Wang Gungwu (Ed.), (Cheshire, Melbourne, 1964), p. 157.

of personal relationships in a colonial setting, his active presence and gadfly activities built up morale at a time when it was low. A man of extraordinary nervous energy and drive, he appeared suddenly in the most unlikely places, disturbed complacency, criticised or got rid of the inefficient and fought the Emergency ruthlessly with a single-minded determination to win it. Personally, I found him not at all over-bearing, but receptive and appreciative of Australian contributions to the British effort.

Templer left Malaya on 30 May, 1954. The situation he left behind him had improved sufficiently to convince the British Government that a civilian High Commissioner could take over. Sir Donald MacGillivray was promoted to this post, and Lieutenant General G. C. Bourne was sent out to take over as G.O.C., Malaya. The new High Commissioner was installed on 1 June, 1954 and the stage was set for Malaya's first elections in 1955. When these were held, Malaya was on the threshold of independence, and the Communist insurgents could no longer claim that they were fighting to eject imperialist masters.

This, then, was the local background in Singapore and Malaya during my period of service there. Mine was not an easy task, as I was wearing two hats. As Australian Commissioner for Southeast Asia (although I was not given this actual title for a considerable time after arrival in Singapore) I had to follow developments in Southeast Asia as a whole. These I found intensely interesting and the association with others easy and valuable. But my experiences when wearing the hat of Australian Commissioner to Malaya were not as pleasant or as fruitful.

It was when I tried to inform myself about 'colonial' developments in Singapore, Malaya and the British Borneo Territories that I found at all times reserve and occasional actual resentment. Governors in Singapore and the High Commissioner in Kuala Lumpur after Templer's departure were colonial officials accustomed to running their own shows, subject to over-riding instructions from London. Nothing in their experience had prepared them for association with diplomatic representatives of independent members of the Commonwealth of Nations, which required a different kind of expertise. They knew that London wanted Australian military and economic assistance, especially during the Emergency, and that they must therefore be formally polite to me. But there was nothing spontaneous in their attitudes: if I asked questions, they would reveal as much as they thought they had to, but information was not volunteered, and the general atmosphere was that Australia had no claim to any share in responsibility. Australian troops, air-craft and crews, naval vessels, weapons generally— Yes. But no questioning of policy, please. Their jobs were difficult enough as they were, without outsiders butting in.

As a freeborn Australian, I must confess that I found the imperial-colonial atmosphere of Singapore and Malaya and the Borneo Territories unpleasant and irritating. Had I been born there, I have no doubt that I would have been working for removal of the imperial umbrella in the shortest practicable time. The constant attitude of 'father knows best'; of treating the local population as children; of playing up to the unjustified pretensions of Sultans; of senior and junior British staff treating High

Commissioner or Governor as the Queen herself—all this, against the background of the irrevocable loss of imperial prestige during the Second World War seemed to me a form of rather unsuccessful play-acting.

Personal relations with Governors, High Commissioners, Colonial Secretaries and the like were, on the whole, amiable enough. They granted me access when requested, and accorded me a number of courtesies. Yet I doubt whether they ever understood that my purpose was not to interfere or to be critical. It was certainly my aim to be helpful, while trying to protect Australian interests and to advance Australian points of view where these seemed relevant.

In dealing with the British colonial authorities futile questions of protocol tended to assume an importance they did not deserve. All rules of protocol, of course, are in themselves artificial; yet, in the strictly diplomatic world, rules devised gradually over centuries provide simple answers to questions of prestige and conduct, and their observance saves a tremendous amount of energy and argument.

In Singapore, my personal rank of Ambassador meant nothing at all. I was regarded as a member of the Consular Corps. When, however, I found myself placed rather oddly at gubernatorial dinners, or failed to meet there some individuals I would have expected, I asked my staff to inquire for a copy of the local list of precedence. They were told that no such list existed. I refrained from telling the Governor that I had found a copy of the list in my drawer on arrival; formal or not, it represented gubernatorial practice. Eventually I drew the conclusion that the Governor had to avoid inviting a certain range of people to dinner at one and the same time, because problems of local protocol were too difficult for him to solve. In particular, military representatives in the area were incredibly sensitive regarding questions of prestige, and simply would not sit below someone they regarded as inferior in status or rank. This attitude reached the height of absurdity when, after the first elections in Singapore in 1955 which resulted in Mr David Marshall becoming Chief Minister, a very senior British military officer objected strongly to being present at the airport to meet a visiting V.I.P. if Marshall were to be presented to the visitor ahead of him. It was little consolation for me to read, in a life of Raffles, that he had similar problems in handling the British Commander of the Armed Forces in Java.

The only serious bout I had with Singapore authorities on the question of protocol arose out of procedure at the Remembrance Day celebrations on 11 November, 1954. I found myself placed with all the members of the Consular Corps near a war memorial, waiting for the Governor to arrive. Eventually he came, with a considerable entourage, got out of his car, laid a wreath on the Memorial—and departed immediately. Members of the Consular Corps were then supposed to lay their wreaths, in no particular order, and I found that my wreath was laid just after that of a Japanese official.

This was utterly ridiculous, and I decided to make a stand. I instructed my staff to make it known in the appropriate official quarters that, if the same procedure were adopted on the next occasion, I would not be present.

They were to add that it was my impression that Australia had played a considerable part in the defence of Singapore; that she was an independent member of the Commonwealth of Nations; and that her representative expected that due account would be taken of these facts at any such ceremony in the future.

This message sank home. In 1955, on Remembrance Day, Commonwealth Representatives were asked to stand in line just behind the Governor. They laid their wreaths immediately after his, while he remained on parade. On Anzac Day, of course, Australian and New Zealand representatives combined in a ceremony of remembrance and invited British and relevant Allied representatives to be present; but although British Service officers came readily enough, neither Governor nor High Commissioner was ever present. Presumably this would have been beneath their dignity, as they would not have been the central figures present. It was during my service in Singapore and Malaya that I came to the conclusion that it was a very rare Governor or High Commissioner who was not stiffer on parade than the Queen.

There were protocol problems in the Federation of Malaya as well. The first elections were held in July 1955, and the first meeting of the new Legislative Assembly was a political event of considerable importance for the Commonwealth of Nations as a whole. I was invited to attend, but was given a seat where I was completely lost in the crowd. No one would have known that Australia was represented, or had any interest, or that this was a Commonwealth event. On the other hand, the gaily-clothed Sultans were adulated by the playing of their local anthems, during which the audience stood on nine occasions before the Sultans moved to dominant places in the hall. Last but far from least the High Commissioner arrived, British Service officers sprang to their feet as one man, God Save the Queen was played, and speeches began. As a private individual I could not have cared less where I sat, provided I could see and hear. As the senior representative of Australia in the Federation I was appalled at this failure of imagination and judgment. Representatives of the Commonwealth should have been treated as an important part of the ceremony.

One other question of protocol in the Federation irritated me beyond measure. In October 1955 the annual meeting of the Consultative Committee of the Colombo Plan took place in Singapore. After the sessions ended Mr Casey, who led the Australian Delegation, decided to visit the Federation, accompanied by his wife. In these circumstances it became my responsibility to travel with him, and Mrs Casey asked my wife to come as well. One of the points of call was Penang, the pleasant island just off the north-west coast of Malaya which had become a British colony before the foundation of Australia. On such visits it was customary for the British High Commissioner's staff to arrange for the visitors to stay with the British Resident, in most attractive surroundings. I myself had already been accorded this courtesy, which I had much appreciated.

Arrangements for the visit to the Federation were put in train. My staff was told by an Aide-de-Camp of the British High Commissioner that Mr and Mrs Casey would be staying with the Resident in Penang, but that as a

Ministerial representative from another Commonwealth country, who had attended the Colombo Plan Meeting, would be present in Penang at the same time, it would not be practicable for my wife and myself to stay with the Resident. Other arrangements would be made for us.

I told my staff to inform the Aide that I thoroughly understood the situation; that it would not be necessary to make other arrangements for my wife and myself; and that we would be happy to book in at an excellent hotel on the island. When this message was conveyed, the Aide replied that as we were part of the Minister's group during the visit, the High Commissioner insisted on making arrangements for our accommodation. We were therefore to stay at the home of the British official in Penang second in rank.

This was quite ridiculous. I was far from amused at the assumption that our bodies were at the disposal of the High Commissioner. In other circumstances I would have had a first-class row and flatly refused to carry out such instructions; but my Minister was on a formal visit to the Federation, and such a row would have been embarrassing to him. So I bit my teeth, decided to say nothing for the moment and to conform. At that stage I did not know that the second official on the island was on leave, so that when we arrived at his home the door was opened by servants, who were the only occupants. I decided there and then that, on any future visit to the Federation, I would stay exactly where I pleased and let the High Commissioner know that if he did not like it he could lump it.

A further illustration of some of the absurd complications which an Australian diplomatic representative can face in a British colony relates to a formal visit to the British Borneo Territories in 1955. As Australia had no representative in Borneo, practical arrangement for the tour had to be left in the hands of relevant British authorities. I wanted to call at Kuching (capital of Sarawak), at Brunei and at Jesselton (capital of British North Borneo—now Sabah) for official talks with British officials and the Sultan of Brunei.

The arrangements made for me indicated clearly a deliberate attempt to limit my contacts and to divert me and my wife to the irrelevant. We did not stay in Kuching, allegedly because the Governor of Sarawak was away, and I could meet him in Brunei or Jesselton (which I did, very briefly indeed). In Brunei I was escorted to the Sultan by a British officer who was to translate and thus be in a position to omit or confuse anything he thought delicate. Unfortunately for him neither he nor his superiors knew that I had met the Sultan on a plane returning from London after the Coronation. As I knew he spoke English, it took only a couple of minutes for us to take over from the interpreter, who was relegated to translation of a conversation between my wife and the Sultana, who were getting along quite happily without his help.

We were passed on through Jesselton to spend two days and nights at Sandakan, on the far north-east coast, where we were housed by an English business man. Sandakan is a pleasant enough place, but utterly cut off from the rest of the British Territories. In those days the roads from Sandakan leading north, south and west simply petered out in the jungle after a few miles, the only contact with 'civilisation' being by air or sea.

On the return flight we stayed with the Governor of North Borneo at Jesselton. He sent us out in a motor-boat to some island (which took up half a day). My official conversations with him were scarcely rewarding. At that stage he was enjoying greatly a visit by a daughter of Lord Curzon, who at considerable length was describing why her father had been upset at missing the Prime Ministership. 'It was not *what* was done, but the *way* it was done that upset him.' These and other stories went on far into the evening after dinner. As my wife had caught a severe cold and was literally rocking in her chair, I was not amused at the Governor's complete failure to notice her condition and to permit us to retire from his gracious presence. In short, except for some experience of the countryside, the visit to Borneo was practically a dead loss—as it was intended by its British rulers to be.

From Singapore itself I had reported to Canberra, no doubt somewhat sourly, upon these stupidities, without suggesting at any time that any action should be taken from headquarters. It was with dismay, therefore, that I learned suddenly that the situation I described had angered the Prime Minister's Department, which made some kind of protest to London about the failure to give adequate recognition to my status.

The final page in the protocol story was written when Lord Home, newly appointed British Secretary of State for Commonwealth Relations, passed through Singapore in 1955. The Governor gave a dinner in his honour, and my wife and I were invited to attend. When the date arrived I was ill in bed and had to apologise for my inability to be present, but my wife was asked to go in spite of my absence. She was seated alongside Lord Home, who—made aware in London or Canberra of the Australian Government's dissatisfaction—proceeded to cross-examine my wife about the nature and scope of my responsibilities, in an atmosphere of disbelief. I regarded this procedure as highly irregular, if not actually improper. As an Australian official I was fair game for doubt or criticism and quite ready to defend myself. To bring my wife into the matter did not seem to me a very gentlemanly approach.

In the event, after Lord Home's return to London, some adjustment was made to the listing of myself and Foss Shanahan, who had by then become New Zealand Commissioner for Southeast Asia. This made little or no difference to our standing or activities; indeed, the complaint made by Canberra to London merely made my position more difficult, as local officials naturally assumed that I myself had stimulated the complaint. I was not sorry therefore to be able to recommend, during the second half of 1955, the abolition of the office of Australian Commissioner for Southeast Asia, and my own transfer elsewhere.

With the Federation of Malaya and Singapore moving in separate ways and at different speeds towards self-government and independence, and with the up-grading and settling-down of our diplomatic representation in Southeast Asia (including an Embassy in Bangkok where SEATO had its headquarters) arguments for my continued presence in Singapore no longer had the same force. After the elections in Malaya in 1955, T. K. Critchley was appointed Australian Commissioner at Kuala Lumpur, where it seemed essential to open a separate office.

IMPRESSIONS OF SINGAPORE: 'IT CAN HAPPEN HERE'

The most important developments in Singapore during my time there were the elections held on 2 April, 1955 and the strikes and riots which occurred during the following May.

Following publication early in 1954 of the report of a Commission under the chairmanship of Sir George Rendel to study desirable changes in the Constitution, the British Government accepted its main recommendations. These included the establishment of a Legislative Assembly of thirty-two members, twenty-five of whom would be elected, three ex-officio members holding Ministerial office, and four nominated unofficial members. A Council of Ministers was to replace the old Executive Council. It would be presided over by the Governor, and comprise the three ex-officio members and six elected members chosen by the leader of the largest party (or a coalition of parties). Ministers, under the leadership of a Chief Minister, would determine policy 'in all matters other than those relating to external affairs, internal security and defence'. This represented an important constitutional advance, but fell short not only of independence but also of full self-government in respect of internal affairs.

Before the elections British officials expected or at least hoped that they would result in a majority for the Progressive Party, a non-communal, conservative group some of whose members had served on the Governor's Executive Council where, indeed, they had been groomed to take over political responsibility. This party stood for free enterprise and for gradual political progress towards a Confederation of Malaysia which would include Malaya, Singapore and the Borneo Territories.

To the surprise of most, the Progressives won only four seats in the Assembly, whereas the Labour Front, led by a successful criminal-defence lawyer, Mr David Marshall, won ten seats. For the rest, the People's Action Party won three, the Malay Union Alliance three, and minor parties another five between them. The platform of the Labour Front included as objectives moderate socialism, union between Singapore and Malaya and 'immediate self-government and independence within the Commonwealth'. After the Malay Union Alliance agreed to support the Labour Front, Mr Marshall was appointed Chief Minister. The People's Action Party, led by Mr Lee Kuan Yew, a Singapore lawyer who had had a brilliant academic record at Cambridge University, included extreme left-wing elements. It had campaigned for immediate independence for a combined Malaya and Singapore, and was strongly critical of British imperial controls under the new Constitution.

Marshall was born in Singapore, of Iraqi-Jewish extraction. He was a man of natural ability and mercurial temperament who had qualified as a lawyer the hard way after some preliminary experience in business. He had had few opportunities while young, and had to fight his own way to the front. As a speaker in the Assembly, his style was somewhat melodramatic, but he was effective in addressing a jury. His speeches never suffered from understatement. Once I heard him declaim in the Assembly 'I refuse to act as a chromium-plated bumper-bar for colonialism'. He was dissatisfied with his Ministers' powers under the existing constitution, and aimed at achieving complete independence at the earliest possible moment; but before he had time to settle in as Chief Minister, he was faced with a crisis in Singapore, where there were widespread riots and strikes.

The riots were spearheaded by secondary-school students in Chinese schools who had been heavily indoctrinated by Chinese Communist teachers. During a strike of bus workers, students erected barricades, overturned cars, stoned the police, who replied with batons, hoses and tear-gas. Troops were called out to protect important installations. During the disturbances four people were killed. The Chief Minister, broadcasting on 12 May, charged that 'the pattern of developments . . . closely conforms to the Communist technique of seeking to foment industrial unrest on any excuse'. Later the government stated that it would take necessary steps to deal with the situation in relevant Chinese schools. It introduced new Emergency Regulations and arrested a number of people.

The riots of May 1955 were an illuminating experience. Since our arrival in Singapore we had always been conscious of a degree of tension under the normal 'business as usual' calm. It was not hard for its inhabitants to find causes for discontent: contrasts of wealth and poverty; racial resentments; overcrowding; the economic exploitation which tends to follow a high degree of competition; lack of adequate educational opportunities for the young unless in private Chinese schools whose teachers and text-books came largely from Communist China; the ruthless activities of Chinese secret societies. But the riots were not mere outbreaks of discontent; rather were they deliberately planned attempts to embarrass the first elected government of Singapore and to create chaos and fear.

When they occurred my wife was in Australia. The following extract from a letter to her written on 15 May, 1955 conveys something of the atmosphere:

It looks as if the immediate violence in Singapore is over for the time being. A 'settlement' has been reached between employers and employees . . . and sympathy strikes are being called off. The 'Martyred' student aged 16 has been buried without a further outbreak of violence. Dismissed workers are reinstated, paid in full, and guaranteed new jobs somewhere if an arbitrator decides they are not needed. The Communists and pro-Communists have succeeded in securing another 'bloodletting' in May (last year's student demonstrations were on May 13). The new Labour Front Government has been seriously embarrassed. Four men are dead (including one American press man) and some still seriously injured. Colonialism has been shown to be 'brutal'.

But if violence has stopped—touch wood—the significant proof that 'it can happen here' has been given. On the Chief Minister's own statement, the strikers had no case which was not being given fullest weight. A Court of Inquiry was sitting; the Company offered to continue to pay their wages meanwhile; yet they tried to prevent buses leaving the depot. Running buses were attacked and drivers intimidated. Chinese Middle School students played a most active part—in their hundreds—with encouragement, money, processions, organised movement by lorry etc. etc. Other Trade Unions were quite ready to come out in sympathy strikes. In short, the encouragement to violence and its use were *not* the accidental outcome of a legitimate industrial dispute. It was designed by Communists to weaken authority, discredit the new Government and (perhaps in the long term) to bring about a suitable revolutionary situation in which an organised minority could take over. . . .

This last half-week has been most unpleasant. There has been an underlying tension which could have exploded at any moment. For the only time since my return I was glad you were not here. I instructed the staff to avoid trouble—we have enough troubles of our own about forces etc. already. I had to send the staff home early on one day as a precautionary measure. None of us ran into actual trouble. We avoided passing through the worst areas. Occasionally we had to wait while processions passed, or go through streets not very far from incidents. We went out at night only when we had to.

There are some good features of the riots. The Government has been shocked and would be crazy to abolish the Emergency Regulations just now. Marshall, on the whole, stood up to his responsibilities. The police acted with unusual restraint under grave provocation. Citizens have been shocked into taking the matter seriously. Communist influence in Chinese Schools is clear to anyone who is not blind. The Federation (of Malaya) has had a warning before the next elections. . . .

Mr David Marshall never appeared to me to be more than a transitional Chief Minister, filling the gap between Governor's rule and a locally-born political leader of Chinese race. It did not surprise me, therefore, when Marshall resigned on 6 June, 1956 in a fit of impatience after a conference in London where the British Government refused—with the evidence of the riots before their eyes—to grant immediate self-government.

Marshall was succeeded by his deputy, Mr Lim Yew Hock, a moderate trade union leader who later became High Commissioner to Australia. But he too, though of Chinese race, was a leader of the transition period. At elections held on 30 May, 1959 the People's Action Party, under the leadership of Lee Kuan Yew, won an overwhelming victory. He proved to be less radical in policy and tougher on extremists than might have been anticipated. On 3 June, 1959 Singapore became a self-governing State.

IMPRESSIONS OF MALAYA: CONTRASTS WITH SINGAPORE

During my last year in Southeast Asia I spent more time on developments in Malaya, where constitutional changes were proceeding faster than in Singapore and where the possibility of Australian troops being stationed was a problem of the first importance.

In many ways it was always a relief to visit the Federation. To a person born in continental Australia living on an island twenty-five miles wide and ten miles deep induced a feeling of claustrophobia. In normal times one would have driven across the Causeway to Johore Bahru, on the mainland,

and sped into the countryside for a breath of fresh air. But the Emergency was on, and Johore was one of the most dangerous States. When my wife and I first drove up the peninsula to visit Malacca, Kuala Lumpur, Kuala Kangsar, Butterworth and Penang, the British authorities insisted on my official car being preceded by an armoured car and followed by a truck-full of armed soldiers while we were still in the State of Johore. I could not object to British concern for our welfare, but I was far from certain that the military vehicles would not merely draw attention to our passage and suggest to the insurgents that we might be more important than we were.

There was little to do on the island of Singapore, except play sport by day and bridge by night. Neither of us were bridge-players, while rain was apt to intervene to prevent me playing tennis with any regularity. I bought a small car so that my wife and I could drive, unencumbered by an official chauffeur, in the later afternoon when the oppressive heat of the sun had declined. Usually we drove to the Gap, where we walked for half-an-hour, enjoying the vista of a pale, silver sea lit up by the departing sun. As we passed the comfortable houses, splendidly sited, of Major this and Lieutenant Colonel that, whose way of life was in many respects more ample than it would have been in Britain, the doubt arose in my mind whether Singapore was a military base or a base for the military. So much of the usable land on the island was occupied by British forces, Army, Navy or Air, that it was a disturbing political factor as the local population moved towards self-government. At one stage I wondered whether Labuan, an island off the coast of Brunei with a useful airfield, might someday prove to be a more favourable site, from the political point of view, than Singapore; but it seemed clear even in 1955 that no British Government would ever again find the money to establish a new base on the Singapore scale.

There were no natural resources on the island of Singapore, except its strategic situation, commercial skill and cheap labour-supply. Despite torrential rainfall, even the water-supply depended upon pipes running across the Causeway, perfect targets for sabotage. To enjoy life in Singapore one had to be at heart a business-man, Chinese, British, Indian, or Australian.

Malaya was different. On the peninsula there were mountains to catch the eye—some high enough to enable the visitor to breathe cool air—and the variety of forest land and cultivated fields. Except in some cities, the background was Malay, not Chinese. Over the centuries the Malays had learned not to take life too seriously. If they worked too hard acquiring possessions, some Sultan might wrest them away overnight. Rice was available, bananas and other tropical fruit, fish swam in the rivers and in the coastal waters where traps could be set in which the fish caught themselves. No one amongst the Malays was very rich—the Chinese ran the tin-mines and most commercial activities, while Europeans controlled the rubber plantations— but living was not too difficult. When personal problems arose there were the consolations of the Islamic religion and the philosophy of tidapathy.*

The outlook on life of Kuala Lumpur was utterly different from that of Singapore. In Singapore the thrusting, hard-working, dominant

---

* The words *tid apa*, in the Malay language, mean 'no matter, never mind, what's the use of worrying', an outlook very like that reflected in the Russian word 'nichevo'.

Chinese improved their living standards as best they could, maintaining over generations in the enervating, tropical climate the energy their ancestors had possessed in China. They concentrated upon commerce, and some grew rich. While they took pride in the ancient traditions of China, those who were successful concentrated more upon making money than upon the finer cultural traditions of their homeland—witness the dreadful statuary of the Tiger Balm gardens. Ships from all nations came to Singapore, whose inhabitants were in touch with business in its world setting. As Chinese, their thoughts were of this present life; if government did not provide them with adequate education or protection, they set up their own schools and joined secret societies.

This was not the Malay way of life, which was more gracious, more humane for people of their own race and religion, and more feckless. At Universities most Malays concentrated upon Arts subjects, leaving to the Chinese the more technical and arduous courses in Medicine, Engineering or Science. To the Malays, the Chinese were intruders. Malaya belonged to the Malays. Malay must be the national language; Malays must have special land rights; in the public service and in the Army, Malays were to be privileged. Let the Chinese concentrate on Commerce, leaving politics, administrative control and defence predominantly to the Malays.

In Kuala Lumpur, the British authorities clearly had a pro-Malay bias. Members of the Malayan Civil Service were trained predominantly in the Malay language. The rights of the Sultans had to be preserved. Malay privileges were not regarded as unreasonable. Perhaps in the shadowy future it would be necessary for Chinese to acquire equal rights with Malays, but that prospect was so far away as to affect current policy but little. In any event, during the Emergency the great majority of the insurgents were Chinese. All Chinese were therefore suspect to some extent. To help the Malays maintain control seemed a patriotic duty.

Before the elections took place in Malaya on 27 June, 1955, I made a visit to the Federation to try to form some estimate of what the result would be. It seemed probable that the 'Triple Alliance', consisting of the United Malays' National Organisation (U.M.N.O.), the Malayan Chinese Association (M.C.A.) and the Malayan Indian Congress (M.I.C.) would win, though I did not foresee that it would win 51 of the 52 elective seats. One of my strongest impressions during my visit, however, was of the unsophisticated attitude of the ordinary Malay voter.

I was taken around a number of villages close to Kuala Lumpur by an Australian member of the Malayan Civil Service. He thought that most people in these kampongs would vote as told by the headman. Walking from one village to another, I saw a Malay sitting on his haunches under a tree, with a look of rather vague concentration in his eyes. The thought passed through my mind that he might be wondering about the elections, asking himself whether he should vote for U.M.N.O. and its leader Tunku Abdul Rahman, or for the Negara (National) party, led by Dato Sir Onn bin Ja'afar. Turning to the Australian District Officer accompanying me, I asked: 'What's he thinking? Which party to vote for in the elections?' My guide burst out laughing before replying: 'He's not thinking. He's waiting for the durian to fall.'

The durian, I had had reason to learn, was the fruit of a Southeast Asian tree which contains pulp notable for its fetid smell and agreeable taste. When I had first driven to Penang from Singapore, I was suddenly recalled by urgent business and had to fly back, leaving Dawad to drive the official car on his own to Singapore. That was over a week-end. When on Monday morning I stepped into the car at 'Glencaird' to go to the office, my nostrils were assailed by a vile odour. It reminded me of a smell we had noted while driving in forest country in the Federation and which had been explained as the smell of the durian in the jungle. I glared at Dawad and charged him with having brought a load of durian in the car on the way back from Penang. With some hesitation he sheepishly admitted his crime. There was nothing I could do except instruct him to use every known means of diminishing the smell. In the event, this took about a week, during which I did not dare offer anyone a lift in the car.

The District Officer's reply caught my fancy, and I used the phrase 'Waiting for the durian to fall' as a headline for a memorandum to Canberra on the impending elections. It was intended as a warning that, however inevitable the quick movement towards self-government in Malaya, one should not delude oneself into thinking that democracy was about to spring full-grown from the soil. For the simple Malay under the tree, the elections were far away if not utterly irrelevant. At a certain stage of ripeness, the durian fruit would fall from the tree. He had judged that the time had come, and was waiting to catch or pick up the fruit, in order to sell it. The price would keep him or his family or both in other food for a meal or a day. The only thing in his mind was short-term subsistence, not the pride of nationhood or the game of parliamentary democracy.

After the elections Rahman was appointed Chief Minister. As I thought I should establish contact with him in his new capacity at an early date, I flew to Kuala Lumpur to see him. A new house had been assigned to the Chief Minister, and he had just moved in. I knocked at his door at 4 p.m., the time arranged, and was surprised to find that he opened the door himself. As a younger brother of the Sultan of Kedah, I would have expected him to regard such an act as beneath his dignity. His manner was simple and pleasant. Showing me into the living room, he explained that there had not been time to arrange matters in the house as he would wish. A servant rolled in a traymobile carrying afternoon tea, but Rahman poured the tea himself. One could not help being struck by the human naturalness of his manner, and I began to understand why, although not a person of great intellectual capacity or will-power, he could bind together, as a political leader, people of various temperaments and even races. He wore his attractive Malay clothes with the easy grace of a Malay aristocrat, and talked as he felt at the moment without wondering what the political effect might be of what he was saying.

This simplicity of approach to problems, of course, had its disadvantages. Before he became Chief Minister, and before the Prime Minister of Australia announced on 1 April, 1955 the Government's decision in principle to send a battalion of troops to Malaya, there had been a small recruitment campaign in Australia to enlist fifty Australians as members of the Police Force in Malaya, where the Emergency required large civil as well as military forces. Some minor criticism of this campaign appeared in the Malayan Press, and I became anxious lest this should affect the much more vital question, still undecided, whether Australian troops should be sent to the area.

Without instructions from Canberra, I flew to Kuala Lumpur to sound out the Tunku, then Leader of U.M.N.O. in the Legislative Council. I suggested to him that the recruitment of fifty men in Australia was a comparatively unimportant matter, and added that if criticism of such re-cruitment should increase, perhaps it would be wiser to discontinue the latter. Abdul Rahman appeared to agree, but we both understood perfectly well that no formal proposal had been put by me, or firm attitude expressed by him.

I flew back to Singapore in a Dakota aircraft, bumping through the enormous cumulus clouds which thicken in that area in the late afternoon, and as I had a severe cold, went straight to bed. At 7 p.m. I arose to listen to the radio news and, to my amazement, heard something like the following:

'Speaking in Malay to a gathering in Penang this afternoon. Tunku Abdul Rahman said that the Australian Commissioner had come to see him this morning. He had referred to some recent Press criticism of the sending of Australian *troops* to Malaya, and said that, if there was any more such criticism, he would take steps to see that they did not come.'

I forgot my cold, dressed, dashed to the office and sent a most immediate cable to Canberra making clear that at no stage of my conversation had I discussed the issue of sending Australian troops: I had been talking about recruitment of Australian police. As luck would have it, the crisis which I feared did not eventuate. The radio report apparently reached Australia, if at all, too late for the morning newspapers. By the time the Australian Press became interested, the British High Commissioner in Kuala Lumpur had already been in touch with Rahman who, on his return to the capital, explained that there was no text of his speech and implied that the English report of it over Radio Malaya must have been based upon a mistaken translation from Malay.

There is little doubt that the radio report was accurate, and I am still puzzled as to why he spoke in those terms. It is quite possible he thought, on the spur of the moment, that he was helping me or the Australian govern-ment in regard to the major decision, then pending, about troops. Apparently he was quite unable to appreciate the probable effects of his statement in Australia; nor could he have realised that, if I had in fact said to him what he told his audience, the Australian Government would have been justified in recalling me from my post.

The question of the despatch of troops to Malaya was the most important single Australian issue during my period of service in Singapore. In Aus-tralia itself the issue was highly contentious, as the Labor Party Opposition, under Dr Evatt's leadership, strongly opposed the eventual decision. Before the Government announced that it would send troops, some Australian journalist heightened tension and uncertainty by cabling to the Singapore Press information allegedly gained from official Australian sources that the Government in Canberra had come to the conclusion that troops would be despatched. Extracts from statements to this effect published in the *Straits Times* were then cabled back to Australia to the Australian Press—whereupon the Labor Party criticised the government for announcing in Singapore what it had failed so far to tell Parliament.

It was a great relief to me when Mr Menzies made a public statement on 1 April, 1955 indicating that, having consulted Cabinet, he would propose to Parliament Australian participation in a strategic reserve in Malaya, together with Britain and New Zealand. After referring to Australian aircraft units already in Malaya, he added:

> We will, so soon as is practicable, establish in Malaya, as part of a larger joint reserve—
> Naval forces, consisting of two destroyers or two frigates, an aircraft carrier on an annual visit, and additional ships in an emergency;
> Armed forces, consisting of an infantry battalion, with supporting arms, and reinforcements in Australia; and
> Air forces, consisting of a fighter wing of two squadrons, a bomber wing of one squadron, and an air-field construction squadron.
> These are not in themselves massive forces. But taken in conjunction with forces to be provided by our sister countries, they will be some proof of the seriousness with which we take the Communist threat and will, I have no doubt, serve as some guarantee to the people of Malaya that their present orderly progress towards democratic self-government, a progress which enjoys the deeply sympathetic interest of Australia, will not be interfered with by dictatorial Communist aggression.[95]

It was against this background that the C. in C. of British Air Force Units in the Far East, Air-Marshall Fressanges, decided to fly to Australia for consultations, and offered to take my wife and myself with him in his R.A.F. plane. With Canberra's approval, I jumped at the opportunity both for consultations in Canberra and to see my own children. We left Singapore on 12 April, 1955, so that I was in Australia when the Prime Minister made a major statement in Parliament on Foreign Affairs and Defence eight days later. While this speech still did not clarify the question whether Australian troops were to be used against Communist insurgents in Malaya, Mr Menzies indicated the seriousness with which he regarded potential situations in Southeast Asia when he said that, in the event of a 'hot' war, 'additional Australian forces would be required which would probably be of the order of two divisions'.[96]

During the first week of May I flew back to Singapore with Air-Marshall Fressanges, leaving my wife for a time in Australia with some of the children. To my surprise, I found myself almost popular with the British Commanders-in-Chief. General Sir Charles Loewen, in charge of British Land Forces, Far East though a Canadian by birth, seemed to think that my visit to Australia had really stirred things up and got the Australian

[95] Current Notes, Vol. XXVI (1955), pp. 279-80.
[96] *Ibid.*, p. 289.

Government moving in the direction of Malaya. This was a complete misconception of my role, which had been only to advise, before I left for Australia, whether or not Australian troops would be welcome in Malaya. After soundings, I had reported that in my judgment they would be welcome. Indeed, it was not until 16 June that the Prime Minister announced that the Australian battalion would be 'available for use against Communist Terrorists', though not 'in relation to any civil disturbances or in the internal affairs of the Federation or Singapore'.[97]

It was decided that the battalion would be sent to barracks in Penang, which was close to Butterworth where Australian air-units were stationed and an Australian Air construction unit was to operate in due course extending the runways. In October 1955 the battalion arrived, and I flew to Penang to meet them. During the flight I asked the pilot an impermissible question. Did his flight plan permit him to fly over the ship carrying the troops, together with naval escorts, as they ploughed their way up the Straits of Malacca? He did not reply, but I noticed that the plane veered westward a little.

Soon I was gazing down at a large white ship, with a destroyer or frigate ahead and another behind. I have never forgotten that mental image. To me it symbolised, for good or ill, an involvement of Australia in Southeast Asia of a new kind, an undertaking of fresh and perhaps dangerous responsibilities. It was a solemn moment. That night I had dinner in the Officers' Mess at the new barracks, and the following day watched the troops on parade. They were an impressive group, and I was proud of them.

FAREWELL TO SOUTHEAST ASIA

By the end of 1955 it was clear that there was no longer room for an Australian Commissioner for Southeast Asia. SEATO was in existence and functioning and David Hay, Australian Ambassador to Thailand, was well qualified to carry out the functions of Council Representative at SEATO Headquarters in Bangkok. Critchley had been appointed Australian Commissioner in Kuala Lumpur, and would become High Commissioner when Malaya became independent in 1957. Our other diplomatic posts in the area were well-established. The decision had been taken to send ground forces to Malaya in time of peace. I had recommended the abolition of my office and my own transfer.

In January 1956 I was offered the post of Australian Ambassador to Japan, which I readily accepted. By then my wife was in Australia again partly for a serious medical overhaul and partly to be with the children during the long-holidays. It took some time to complete formal arrangements for my transfer and, as usual, my impatience began to increase as I began to think of problems ahead rather than of those around me. Letters to my wife in Australia reflect this attitude of mind. On February 13, 1956 I wrote as follows:

> It is Chinese New Year—heralding in the Year of the Monkey—and the servants have all gone bush. They left on Saturday afternoon and will return tomorrow—Tuesday morning. Meanwhile I am alone in this

[97] *Ibid.*, p. 419.

mausoleum listening to the damn crackers which have been going off all night and all day. . . .

I shall not be sorry to leave this place. The atmosphere is changing and older groups are beginning to go or plan to go. Sir Sydney Cane (Vice-Chancellor, University of Malaya) leaves this year. The Dean of the Faculty of Medicine hands over to a Malayan in June. Maurice Brown has decided to leave this year. . . . The British get sourer and more introverted as Marshall proclaims that Colonel Blimp has left England and now lives in Singapore. It is all pretty inevitable, but rather unpleasant. The Chinese think Australians are British, but haven't succeeded in converting English people to this point of view. . . .

Before my wife returned to Singapore on February 20 I had time to reflect on the two busy years which had passed.

One has to live in the tropics to understand the physical and psychological pressure of hot and humid climates. I myself have always felt better and worked better in colder latitudes. The oppressive, steamy heat of the tropics causes a gradual diminution of energy and initiative—at least for those not born there. Indeed, one could hardly help wondering whether the underlying racial tension in Singapore and Malaya which may burst out into communal violence is not in some degree related to climatic factors. Is it not possible that, over the years, unbearable tropical pressures build up which lead the Malay to run amok and the Chinese, who tend to count life cheaply, to turn to violence?

Yet it would be absurd to regard climate as primarily responsible for the continuing tension between Chinese and Malays. One must take into account the great differences in their cultural background and their attitudes to life. Could they ever combine and work whole-heartedly together in their common interest? Only, if at all, under enlightened leadership on both sides working to bring about greater commercial opportunity for the Malays and greater political opportunity for the Chinese. In any event, Australian involvement in the area would be a ticklish business, as it was not in Australian interest to take sides with either race against the other. Instead, our task would be to bring whatever influence we had on both races with a view to bringing about closer co-operation between them. Although difficult, this was not a hopeless ambition for persons of European descent, provided they had no pretences to imperialism. I did not believe that I as an Australian was any more different from Dawad than was Ah Fong.

The pleasantest aspect of my posting in Singapore had been relations with the Office of the British Commissioner-General for Southeast Asia. In 1955 Malcolm MacDonald had been transferred to New Delhi as High Commissioner. His place had been taken by Sir Robert Scott, with whom I had had dealings in London when he was Assistant Under-Secretary at the Foreign Office, in charge of Far Eastern Affairs. Scott had been an old China hand. Caught in Singapore after it fell to the Japanese, he had suffered severely at the hands of the latter. He was a man of conspicuous courage, and seemed to harbour few resentments agains his erstwhile captors. His urbanity, tolerance and ability set a high standard. Many years later, I was able to induce him to come to Australia to give a series of lectures for the Institute of International Affairs, during which he proved an effective speaker and demonstrated much skill in discussion.

If relations with British Colonial Authorities had been less happy and more frustrating, due allowance should be made for the fact that they themselves were under considerable strain in both Singapore and Malaya. The handing-over of power to others is never easy; for ex-imperial masters to hand over responsibility to colonial leaders must be difficult indeed. They had enough troubles on their hands without having to take into account the views of independent members of the Commonwealth of Nations, like Australia, particularly during a transition period.

Of course, the Singapore posting had also involved visits outside Singapore and Malaya, and these had been invariably stimulating.

Thailand, substantially independent over the centuries, had a fascination of its own. With considerable skill its rulers had managed to play off one encroaching European power against another and to steer their own way through difficult waters. As a result, Thailand seemed the only country in Southeast Asia where colonial chips-on-shoulder were conspicuous by their absence. Bangkok at that time could scarcely be termed beautiful, but it attracted interest—with its sophisticated elite, its curious temples with multi-coloured tiles and placid Buddhist statues, its shops where the tourist acquires Thai silk, silverware and brassware, its unsavoury 'klongs',* its carefully regulated coups d'etats, its lack of roads and extensive rice-fields, its tough military men and its substantial areas of corruption.

Bangkok was fast modernising, and contrasted greatly with Brunei, where thousands still live in wooden houses set on stilts in shallow waters, many of the inhabitants—so it was said—never appearing on dry land until the day of their funerals. Revenue from oil resources in Brunei did not percolate down to the main section of the population.

Saigon had seemed a French provincial city, with its tree-lined streets, gardens and museums. I had listened there to Ngo Dinh Diem discourse at length on the problems of his country and his own over-confident ability to handle them. Phnom Penh, too, seemed French rather than Eastern. During an interview with Prince Sihanouk I had been placed alongside him on a sofa. He spoke with animation, and when he got excited, tended to bounce up and down on the sofa. The flippant thought had struck me then—What was the correct protocol? To bounce or not to bounce?

A grand dinner in Phnom Penh had laid my wife low in Saigon for days, and she was unable to accompany me to Laos. I had flown to Vientiane with John Rowland to find no single bed available in that highly undeveloped town, so we had to proceed on the same afternoon to the royal capital, Luang Prabang, where beds could be found in a royal guest-house. The flight through high mountains and the landing on a small air-strip with a hill at one end was not exactly amusing. But we received a friendly welcome in this city which seemed utterly isolated from the outside world.

The Royal Palace at Luang Prabang was small but adequate, set on the banks of the Mekong in its higher reaches. There we were presented to the

* i.e. Canals.

elderly King Sisavang, our messages of goodwill being translated from French into Lao by the Crown Prince, the present King of Laos. The replies of His Majesty, we suspected, were invented by the Crown Prince. That evening, while awaiting at the Palace a performance in the grounds of a story from the Ramayana, I had been embarrassed to be present when the Chief of Protocol and a senior military officer entered the room and went down on their knees to the King in a form of kow-tow. They too, I think, were embarrassed, though they would not have been in my absence. On the following day we were taken twenty miles down the Mekong in a dug-out canoe with an outboard motor, and landed to have an alfresco meal on a high bank outside a large cave filled with Buddhist relics. When we had finished, a bunch of serviteurs who had travelled independently squatted on their haunches in a circle to enjoy their own food.

In these surroundings, Australia seemed planets away. Yet had I not heard the Chief of Protocol say, while travelling down the river 'You know, when we received word that Australia was prepared to sponsor the admission of Laos to the United Nations, we were quite excited'. Fearing that I had misunderstood his French, I asked him to repeat what he had said. It was difficult to believe that anyone in Luang Prabang could get excited about anything Australia did, but perhaps our foreign policy was not quite so irrelevant to other countries as it sometimes seemed.

When my wife returned from Australia my private musings on Southeast Asia quickly ended as we became immersed in practical plans for departure. Bookings were made for us to travel to Japan by the French liner *Cambodge*, on which we were provided with the best accommodation we had ever had aboard ship—a comfortable cabin with bathroom, a small sitting-room and a separate verandah outside the cabin from which we could watch the sea in privacy.

There was the usual round of calls, farewell dinners and packing when I returned from a brief visit to Karachi on my last SEATO Council exercise, and we were quite exhausted when the day came to leave. At 'Glencaird' the Chinese servants were drawn up to say farewell. We would miss Ah Fong, with his Chinese dignity, self-respect and obstinacy; also his daughter, with her pleasant manner and natural smile. Dawad drove us to the ship and shyly handed us a basket of Singapore orchids which he could not afford. Alan Dudley, Deputy British Commissioner-General, and his wife came to the wharf to see us off and presented us with a book to read on the voyage. Most Australian members of my staff and their wives were there to say good-bye. Once again, as when I had left Moscow, I had the uneasy feeling that I was running out on them, leaving them to deal with local complexities while I moved to less physically strenuous climes.

In the late afternoon the hawsers were lifted, the tugs strained and the *Cambodge* moved slowly through shallow waters towards the open sea. As dusk fell, the outlines of Singapore's buildings began to fade, and the lights of the teeming city came out. Gradually the shore-line fell away. As it did so, the problems of Southeast Asia grew more and more blurred, for our eyes were set on Tokyo. That night I retrieved from my luggage a history of Japan, and was soon immersed in its contents.

7

JAPAN

1956-59

I n life as in international affairs one should be, but rarely is, prepared for the unexpected. Our call at Saigon en route to Japan substantially complicated our settling in at my new post and, for my wife, involved temporary pain and some continuing disability.

During our stay in Saigon I was busy with official calls and discussions with Australians, British and Americans and she was left more or less to her own devices. On the first day a member of the Legation staff escorted her on a drive in the countryside. For the following day, I had a round of stag engagements, so when the Australian Military Attache (Fergus McAdie) suggested she should accompany him and his wife in the plane of an American Attache on a flight to Siem Riep in Cambodia to visit Angkor again, she jumped at the opportunity. In a note made at the time she wrote as follows:

> Our brief excursion in the previous year to Angkor Wat, the Bayon and Bantei Srei had been the most stimulating experience of our two years in the area. Alan looked a trifle doubtful at my going off without him, but I pointed out that I could hardly have better chaperonage than that of the Australian Army. Taking his movie camera, I set off in the plane with the American Colonel and his American and Australian friends.

Her description of my reaction to the proposal is a considerable under-statement, although I did my best to conceal my hesitation in agreeing to the plan. In fact I was opposed to the trip unless I were with her. Her eye-sight had not improved over the years. I remembered the high, stone steps we had climbed on our previous visit to Cambodian temples, without any hand-rail support—more dangerous when descending than when mounting—so that I had taken care to climb behind her and to come down in front to break any possible fall; an intuitive sense of foreboding overcame me. I thought of our visit to the Bayon in the late afternoon, with the gigantic carved heads of ancient Khmers looking in all directions from high up on the temple, and the racket of invisible cricket-like animals in the forest making a noise like the constant ringing of innumerable small bells. It was an eerie atmosphere, and if she went again, I wanted to be with her.

But I suppressed this superstitious reaction and agreed. I knew well that nothing would give my wife more pleasure than such a trip. I was tied down in Saigon; the opportunity was unlikely to recur; McAdie had a reputation for practical efficiency.

Darkness came, and there was still no news of the return of the party from Cambodia. At 7 p.m. I received a telephone call from McAdie: 'I am sorry to have to tell you that your wife had a fall in the Bayon and broke her wrist. We are at the American Seventh Day Adventist Hospital in Saigon, and the arm has now been set. We will be back at the Legation in 15 minutes.'

I bit my lips and suppressed my anger at myself for not trusting my own intuition, based on past experience. But what had happened could not be undone. My reply, therefore, was limited to two words: 'Which wrist?' 'The left.' 'Thank God for that', I commented, and the conversation ended.

Apparently, in the interior darkness of the Bayon, she had stepped down on a stone which had twisted to one side. As she fell, encumbered by a hand-bag and my movie camera, she put out her left hand to break the fall. When she hit the ground, she felt a bone break. Indeed, it broke in two places. The party led her down from the building with difficulty, and it was three hours before they were able to get back to Saigon. In Saigon she was X-rayed by a Chinese radiologist, given inadequate anaesthetic by the wife of an American doctor, who set the bones but was unable to wrap up the result properly because the hospital had run out of gauze bandages temporarily. When she left the hospital the doctor advised her to have another X-ray in Manila to check the results of his treatment.

When we boarded the ship in Singapore we had noted a beautiful Khmer head, taken no doubt from some Cambodian temple, placed on a ledge set in the last turn of the stairs into the dining-room. The stone was slightly reddish in colour, although in other light it might have seemed violet. The sculptural tradition was Hindu, but the art—and the personality—distinctively Khmer. The face of the King, or noble, or priest wore an expression of self-sufficiency, almost of self-satisfaction. The lips were mildly curved in an inscrutable, Mona Lisa smile.

As I came down the stairs on this particular evening I glanced at the bust. Presumably I was somewhat overwrought, for to me the smile had become a positive leer—mocking and contented. I closed my eyes momentarily, shook my head and sat down at table, but I had no stomach for food. After toying with this and that, I returned to our cabin, where my wife was sitting up stiffly in bed in obvious pain.

Before leaving Singapore I had arranged to call upon President Magsaysay in Manila. Now I was more concerned with getting expert medical attention for my wife. But when the ship arrived, passengers were not allowed to land. We were regarded as a plague ship, because there had been reports of plague outside Saigon. These reports had been highly exaggerated, but the Philippines Press is not noted for under-statement; clearly the government was not prepared to take any risk. Eventually our Ambassador to the Philippines, 'Mick' Shann, managed to come aboard. He undertook to convey apologies to the President, and to cable Hong Kong about Mildred's medical needs on arrival there. In the circumstances, the vivid, tropical colours of Manila Bay impressed us rather less than they would otherwise have done.

By the time the *Cambodge* reached Hong Kong Mildred's arm had stiffened. We were met at the wharf by a representative of the Governor, bearing an invitation to lunch that day, and by Australian officials. Urgent arrangements were set in train to X-ray my wife's arm, and a doctor pronounced the half-expected verdict—the arm had been set badly and it would be necessary to re-break it in order to set it again. I presented my apologies to the Governor for Mildred's inability to attend lunch, and his wife was kind enough to send her flowers. We both appreciated a somewhat unexpected telegram of commiseration from Canberra and indications of readiness there to help in any way. The Australian Government Commissioner in Hong Kong, Keith Ridley, and his wife, neither of whom we had met previously, were a tower of strength. Mildred was placed in a hospital on the Peak in a room with a magnificent view and was operated on the following day.

I had no inclination to proceed to Tokyo by the *Cambodge*, but we deferred a decision until after the operation. When I first saw her she was still emerging slowly from the anaesthetic, looking very ill and far from this world. Eventually she became fully conscious, and I could see a light in her eyes which reflected reserves of strength. Gradually we began to discuss plans, and agreed that I should proceed with all our luggage to Tokyo, where arrangements had been made for me to present credentials at an early date, thus enabling me to function officially and to meet a wide range of people when the Emperor's birthday was celebrated at the palace at the end of April.

The doctor had told us that Mildred must remain in hospital for three days, and not travel for about a week. She could then fly to Tokyo and arrive there not much later than the ship. The hospital seemed adequate and the site splendid. The Ridleys insisted on her staying with them after she left hospital and promised to keep a close eye on her while still there. So I agreed to leave her in their hands.

I returned to the *Cambodge* in the late afternoon. The ship threaded its way out to the open sea, with an ethereal setting-sun tipping hills and buildings and water with incredible shades of pink and red. When I went down to dinner, I glared at the Khmer bust and thought at him as follows: 'Well, you have had your little bit of fun, but failed to achieve the worst. My wife has survived. Do not expect that you or your country will escape punishment for this malicious act.' The only response was a supercilious smile.

Between Hong Kong and Tokyo I had a few days in which to reflect on the nature of the problems ahead of me. No Australian who had lived in Singapore and Malaya in the immediate post-war years could fail to have reservations about Japanese leaders and Japanese policy. Recollections of Japanese treatment of prisoners of war, especially those forced to build the railway from Burma to Siam, were too vivid, to say nothing of the treatment of Chinese in Singapore itself. During my term of office as Commissioner for Southeast Asia I had unveiled in the Singapore Cathedral a memorial plaque to the twenty-two Australian nurses machine-gunned by the Japanese in cold blood on Banka Island. Only one of them survived to tell the tale. How could savagery of this kind occur?

Yet I had lived in too many foreign countries, including Germany and the Soviet Union, to believe that nations can be simply divided into 'baddies' and 'goodies'. If in British countries '. . . the Colonel's Lady and Judy O'Grady' were 'sisters under their skins', so too human beings in all countries have common human experiences and impulses, good and bad. Governments, political leaders, groups and individuals are open to criticism and condemnation, but not peoples. In Canberra we had found that the first post-war Japanese Ambassador to Australia, Mr Haruhiko Nishi, was a man of character and integrity. Clearly the Japanese people would be difficult to understand. Just as obviously, the worst mistake is to approach a country with fixed ideas in one's mind. I did not propose to dissemble my attitude towards Japan's militaristic past; at the same time, remembering our own Australian faults, I must search for common ground.

At Yokohama I was met at the wharf by the Chef de Protocol of the Japanese Foreign Office, representatives of Commonwealth Missions in Tokyo, and the staff of the Australian Embassy. Soon I was seated in the Ambassadorial car (another Humber-Pullman, which broke down at regular intervals) driving through streets tortured with traffic until at length we swung through the high, wrought-iron gates opening into the grounds of the attractive Embassy Residence. The Japanese servants were all drawn up at the door, under the protecting portico, to greet me. There were smiles and bows and curious glances to see what sort of an odd fish I might be. After drinks with the Australian staff, luggage was unpacked, books placed on shelves and I was free to wander around the house and garden which was to be our home—I use the word advisedly—for some four years.

A couple of days later Mildred flew in from Hong Kong, arriving at night. I met her at Haneda Airport and one of the Embassy staff helped clear her quickly through Immigration and Customs. A first glance showed that she was still far from well, but she responded to the warmth of the welcome and sympathy of the Australian wives who met her on arrival, as she did later to the unobtrusive but efficient helpfulness of the Japanese domestic servants. After an unpleasant flight in an American civilian plane where the glamorous air-hostesses had eyes only for male passengers and the only drink available seemed to be champagne, she began to relax in the new surroundings—utterly different from Singapore—which no past description of mine could adequately conjure up in her mind.

It is not easy to say just why we settled so naturally and easily into the Embassy residence in Tokyo. The house and grounds were on a far more ample scale than any we had been accustomed to before.[98] There were two and a half acres of garden, falling away from the house in a series of

[98] For a detailed description, see *Japan: Land of Sun and Storm*, by Mildred Watt, (Cheshire, Melbourne, 1966), Chapter 1.

terraces. It was Japanese in style and feeling, except for a substantial, cut lawn on the top terrace. To the foreigner steeped in Western traditions, Japanese gardens are an acquired taste and their sophisticated beauty is appreciated only gradually. Nothing is accidental—mounds are built up to give privacy; pine trees are placed so that the moon can be seen through them; rocks are chosen for shape and colour, which changes when there is rain; a bright display of flowering annuals would be regarded as vulgar, for effects must be subdued. A path is never constructed in a straight line, or stones placed too symmetrically; a hedge is so constituted with different shrubs that it is utterly different in Spring from its appearance in Autumn; curving lines and a high-developed sense of form impress themselves slowly and unconsciously upon the newcomer, who begins to develop a new standard of taste.

The Embassy garden helped me learn that one of the most effective approaches to the understanding of Japanese is the aesthetic approach. Architecture, gardens, pottery, scrolls—an Australian can find in these much beauty and enjoyment. And if he can not respond easily to the ritual of the tea-ceremony or the artifice of flower-arrangement, it is healthy for him to come to understand that in a good Japanese restaurant the manner in which food is served, and what it is served in or on, are as important as the food itself.

The residence, however, followed for the most part European architectural traditions. The dining-room, oak-panelled, with an arched ceiling, resembled a miniature Oxford or Cambridge college dining-hall and seated twenty guests with ease. All the wood-work in the house was excellent, including stairs which wound upwards to the family living quarters and fixed cupboards and bookshelves more adequate than those in any other Embassy residence I have inhabited. One bedroom was furnished in Japanese style, except for Western bed-steads. From the flat roof over the second floor the tip of Mount Fuji could be seen in the distance on a clear day. During our stay in Japan my wife and I must have walked hundreds of miles on this roof, enjoying exercise and privacy which are not easy to come by in Japan. From there we could watch the effects of changing seasons on the garden below, while keeping a wary eye upon the numerous kites which glided effortlessly round and round looking for prey. At the foot of the garden, concealed from view except from its lower reaches or from the roof, my Australian predecessors had built a good hard tennis court, which had a wooden practice-board nearby. These were a great boon. Regular practice on the Embassy court, and occasional play at the Tokyo Tennis Club, widened my range of local contacts and helped keep me fit.

The worst feature of the residence was use of certain ground-floor rooms for Chancery purposes on the side of the house opposite the garden. Within the first week I became quite dissatisfied with some of the arrangements for handling secret documents. Although we had combination safes and a barred-off area, not all appropriate papers were housed in it. I gave instructions for urgent, makeshift changes in the old arrangements, but felt obliged to recommend to Canberra complete separation of the Chancery from the residence and the building of a new Chancery within the adequate grounds available. The strength of my case could not be disputed, but the cost was substantial. It was not until seven years later, when I passed through Tokyo in 1963 after retirement, that I found such a Chancery in course of erection.

In no other country were we ever so fortunate as regards domestic servants. They all had their little ways, but past sad experience had taught us that, with one exception, these frailties were minor. With a good cook in the kitchen, and pleasant, efficient girls for manifold duties up-stairs and down, the butler was my only real concern.

Shinji San was quite a personality, though not a very attractive one. His English was more than adequate. Always deferential in manner—except on a few occasions when he had drawn too heavily on his privileges as keeper of liquor supplies—he varied in the Japanese fashion his degree of deference according to the place in the hierarchy of those with whom he was dealing. So I was accorded the deepest bow, my wife a little less, and my daughter—when she stayed with us for a year between school and university—noticeably less.

Wherever Shinji was born—and his under-estimate of our memories led him to mention over the years three different locations of birth—he was a born wangler. He could produce anything from anywhere, provided the necessary wherewithal were made available. Extra chairs?—they could be borrowed from the Mitsui Club next door. Cutlery, china, glassware?— we had to stop him arranging the matter, unknown to us, with the New Zealanders or other members of the diplomatic corps. His competence was immense, but greatly exceeded the depths of his doubts as to the propriety of a proposed course of action.

Shinji had a most delicate ear. No conversation which took place in the house, whether between members of the family or with visitors, seemed unimportant. If my wife or I moved from an upstairs room to the front door, somehow or other he knew, and was at the door before us to see us out. If a Commonwealth meeting of Heads of Mission were held in my study, his loving care of the room, before, during and after the meeting, was immense. I will never know whether he managed to place microphones here and there at relevant times and activated them by remote control. Of course, I took counter-measures, giving him the shortest notice of a meeting, and walking with members of my staff or of my family in the garden if I wanted to discuss something particularly confidential.

In the early days I considered sacking Shinji, for nowhere outside the Soviet Union had I felt less 'secure'; but in view of what I regarded as Canberra's insufficient appreciation of the importance of security in my circumstances, and the probability that I would merely exchange a competent butler for one less efficient but equally keen to listen, I kept Shinji during my term in Tokyo. Towards the end he was slightly surly or insolent on occasions when he had imbibed too much liquor, but I left the decision to keep or sack him to my successor, whom I duly warned.

Soon after my arrival in Tokyo I presented my credentials to the Emperor. In those days a new Head of Mission was collected at his residence, together with members of his diplomatic staff, in three ceremonial coaches complete with uniformed drivers and footmen. Preceded by police outriders we drove slowly through the busy, motor-car-ridden streets of modern Tokyo to the palace, where the moat was crossed by the most honorific bridge. Apart from parks and shrines, the palace area was a real reminder of what Tokyo once had been as the seat of the Shogun or dominant military commander in Tokugawa times. Though much of the palace itself had been destroyed during the Second World War, a few distinctively Japanese buildings remained. In any event, the defending walls of the palace, consisting of massive blocks of dark, weathered stone well and truly laid, reflected much of the hierarchical system of Japanese society and the uniqueness and isolation of the alleged descendant of the Sun-Goddess.

Then there were calls, together with my wife, upon the Empress and other members of the Royal Family—the Crown Prince, as yet unmarried; widowed Princess Chichibu, Prince and Princess Takamatsu and Prince and Princess Mikasa. I had not previously served in a country where there was a royal court, well supported in this instance by members of the Imperial Household Board, friendly relations with whom eased the way of the diplomat who soon came to respect their unobtrusive skill.

Tokyo has a large Diplomatic Corps, some of whose members were experienced Far Eastern hands. Although calls and return calls took up much time and energy in the first couple of months, I gained much in the process. First call must be made on the Dean of the Corps, who in this case was Sir Esler Dening, the British Ambassador who had been born in Japan and grown up in Australia. Then the Americans, the French and all the rest, including many Commonwealth colleagues. In Tokyo, as in Moscow though for different reasons, members of the Corps were somewhat isolated from the local population, and there was thus a substantial esprit de corps which had its pleasant features.

Meanwhile, of course, there were visits to the Gaimusho (Foreign Office), which had begun with the first call of all upon the Foreign Minister and was followed up by calls upon the Vice-Minister (Permanent Head of the Foreign Office) and a number of senior officials. As new comers we were also entertained by the older foreign diplomats, and return entertainment became necessary. This was all part and parcel of the settling-in process to which we had become accustomed overseas, but the normal strains and stresses were increased by my wife's disability, which required changing of the cast on her arm and, for some time, daily visits to hospital for physiotherapy. As at other posts, the usual problem arose of mixing official and family responsibilities, especially finding an available car and driver to take my wife to hospital, or to a dress-maker, or a shop, or seeking fresh air out of Tokyo. Here there was no question of her driving herself in our own small car that I had brought with me from Singapore, except in the country on rare occasions when we could take short leave in the mountains at the attractive Embassy house which my predecessors had acquired at Karuizawa in ampler Occupation days. This house, however, was shared with various members of the staff to give them a break from the oppressive summer heat of Tokyo. I myself drove my car in Tokyo itself only on a short run to the Tennis Club, partly to keep my hand in, but largely so that my official car could be available to my wife for a drive to some park for a walk.

An early decision for me was whether or not to try to acquire some proficiency in the Japanese language. Although my linguistic competence is limited, I have always wanted to learn the language of any country in which I have lived.

So when I reached Tokyo I asked my Counsellor, Tom Eckersley, who was the Department's best Japanese scholar, about starting to learn the language. He asked one simple question—'How long each day can you give to study?' 'A maximum of one hour', I replied. 'If that is so', he said, 'put aside the idea of trying to learn it'.

In due course I came to agree that his advice was sound. Japanese, and Chinese for that matter, is so different from a European language that to learn to use it effectively requires an effort of quite different order from adding another European language to what one already knows. Inquiry at the British Embassy elicited the information that their young Japanese language students did nothing else but study Japanese for two years—by which time they could only read the newspapers, the range of whose characters were limited to 1,800 or 2,000. An educated Japanese would need to know at least 5,000 and probably 8,000 characters.

At my age and with my responsibilities, an attempt to learn Japanese would have been futile. I had to rely on my staff, and began to press the Department in Canberra to increase the scarcely-visible incentives to our young men to learn Japanese. My wife, on the other hand, whose linguistic capacity is greater than mine and who had more time than I to pursue private interests, was able to build upon a background of a year's previous study of Chinese and to acquire considerable competence with written characters which gave her some insight into the mysteries of Japanese literature.

It was not easy, during the first few months, to leave Tokyo for the purpose of seeing the rest of Japan. We both read voraciously, as time permitted, books on Japanese history and began to build up a library of translated material, including myths and chronicles, translations by Arthur Waley and Donald Keane, and some modern novels. We prowled around the secondhand bookstores in the Kanda, which could be described as Tokyo's Charing Cross Road, and found there an incredible range of local and foreign material. But it took up to an hour to escape the dust and smog of Tokyo; when one adds the time for the return journey, it becomes clear that one can scarcely drive into the countryside and mountains during a short afternoon.

Yet we did escape on brief excursions, usually limited to a week-end—to Karuizawa at the end of May 1956, to Nikko in early July and to Kyoto later in the same month. This proved to be the right order of visits, designed primarily to spy out the land for later journeys of more extended duration and to learn of possible problems ahead during the planned visit to Japan of Mr Menzies in August.

Despite poor weather and the slow, bumpy passage over the atrocious old road up the mountains, the trip to Karuizawa filled us with happy anticipations of mid-summer leave in the Embassy house there. As we began to climb inland from the coast at Odawara, the changing landscape with its tidy fields, half-hid houses, clear streams rippling over rocks and pebbles, variegated trees and hill-sides lifted our spirits. In our isolated house at Karuizawa we found peace and quiet, no industrial smoke and sufficient unpretentious comfort to enjoy our reading, punctuated by extensive woodland walks. And if the ground on which we trod was saturated and boggy in wet weather, while Mount Asama, reputed to erupt every twenty years or so, hung somewhat menacingly in the sky, we much preferred these vague disabilities to the crowds, the noise and the dust or mud of Tokyo.

Nikko was a different kind of experience. We took little pleasure in the over-gilded buildings and shrines designed to perpetuate the memory of Ieyasu, the first and greatest of the Tokugawa Shoguns, but the combination of mountains and streams and the magnificent cryptomeria (Japanese cedars) were memories to cherish. Nor would we soon forget the remains of the avenue of some 50,000 enormous trees which had lined the road between Utsonomiya and Nikko planted, so the story goes, by a member of the Matsudaira clan who could not afford contributions to the Ieyasu memorials of gold leaf and other materials. The trees were in fact a far more adequate memorial than the contributions of the other feudal lords. And on later occasions we always came with anticipatory pleasure to the hotel at Nikko from which, in a corner room, we could view through the open shoji windows a changing scene of beauty, utterly different in tone and atmosphere during Spring, Autumn, Winter or Summer; moreover, in the hotel grounds were a number of stone relics, worn with age, of samurai or monk or lantern, with the attractiveness of complete simplicity.

It is wise for the foreigner to see the over-ornate Nikko shrines before visiting Kyoto, the old capital where the Emperor held his court for so long before moving to Tokyo after the abolition of the Shogunate system in the mid-nineteenth century. To compare the Nikko buildings with those at Kyoto makes it immediately clear why the latter was for centuries the cultural centre of Japan.

We travelled to Kyoto by train, as the unreconstructed roads of our period in Japan made it impracticable for us to drive such a distance by car. At Tokyo station we were led into the special room for V.I.Ps, and were solemnly escorted to our carriage in due course by the white-gloved Station-Master or his deputy. Once inside the carriage I realised that someone in the Australian Chancery had blundered. I had chosen a night train but instead of the two-berth, private compartment I had requested we found ourselves in a Pullman car of old type with curtains for each bunk and no possibility of opening a window. Only Japanese men were visible, some of them already starting to undress in the corridor. I knew that Mildred, with her arm still in a sling, would have a difficult time undressing and that, as one addicted to fresh air, she would feel stifled. However, before we could collect our wits the train started and we had to make do as best we could.

Mildred took the lower bunk and had a most unpleasant journey. It was late July, scarcely the best season for lack of fresh air. When she had undressed with difficulty, she pulled the curtains aside for a couple of feet and gradually dozed off, only to wake gasping for breath to find that the conductor had pulled the curtains together again. I cursed myself for not checking precisely the details of our bookings.

In modern Kyoto one has to search for the more attractive aspects of the past. We were not pleased with the hotel into which we had been booked; nor did we enjoy the Gilt of the Golden Pavilion whose reflecting pond had, unfortunately, been drained for cleaning, or even the buildings of the Heiean Shrine. But in the Imperial Palace, with its gently-curving, laminated-bark roofs and subdued interior decorations, in the private garden of the Emperors and other gardens of the city, and in certain parts of the Nijo Palace we found beauty, dignity and restraint of a kind which made a lasting impression upon us. During our later years in Japan we never let slip any opportunity of seeing Kyoto again.

After a three-day visit, we hastened back to Tokyo by day. I had recalled our over-night tickets, and substituted bookings in an excellent air-conditioned observation car through whose windows we could watch the attractive country landscape, wooded hills on our left, occasionally the sea on our right. Summer was progressing, and the colour of the rice-fields was deepening. My official car met us at the station, and as we turned once again into the Embassy grounds, we felt that we were coming home. Now there was specific work to do, to try to ensure a successful visit to Japan by the Prime Minister of Australia.

For some time I had been recommending to Canberra a good-will visit by Mr Menzies, both because I thought it would be good for the Japanese to meet a man of his stature, and good for our Prime Minister, who had little inclination for Eastern cultures. All the arrangements had been worked out carefully. The Japanese authorities, who at that stage were heavily engaged in 'visitation' diplomacy, presented me with a hopelessly over-loaded programme, which I declined to accept on the spot but transmitted to Canberra with recommendations as to what should be omitted. Eventually, after quiet but firm resistance on my part to pressure, the programme was suitably reduced. We were to hold various functions at the Embassy, including a garden-party at which a wide range of guests would be able to meet the visitors. During an officially-organised visit to Gifu to enable members of the Diplomatic Corps to view the distinctive sport and art of Japanese cormorant fishing, we had bought a number of lanterns which seemed suitable for use during our garden-party, to enhance the Japanese character of the Embassy grounds.

Last but not least, I had with some difficulty obtained permission from Canberra to fly to Honolulu to meet the Prime Minister, who was returning from London via the United States. Experience in Australia had taught me the hard way that there is nothing more difficult than to obtain the un-divided attention of a Prime Minister for half-an-hour. It was my firm belief that I could convey more to Mr Menzies about the distinctive aspects of Japan during the flight from Honolulu to Tokyo than during a couple of weeks in Japan, where an exhausting programme and constant interruptions would minimise opportunities for conversation.

The totally unexpected happened. On the day before I was due to fly to Honolulu, I received a cable saying that the Australian Prime Minister had to return to London to help deal with the Suez crisis, and that his visit to Japan must be postponed.

There was nothing left to do other than to seek an urgent appointment at the Gaimusho and to explain, as politely as I could, that the whole trip was off. Suez *was* a world crisis, and I did not have to invent reasons for Mr Menzies' decision; but the Japanese, though verbally understanding, were hyper-sensitive in the early post-war years, and could scarcely be expected to understand the hundred per cent support for the Anthony Eden line on Suez which the Australian Prime Minister was giving. As I could not understand it myself, I could scarcely blame them. To Gaimusho officials, and no doubt their political masters, the underlying reality was that cancellation of a carefully-arranged good-will Mission to Japan at very short notice was less important to the Australian Government than personal efforts to help Eden carry out a policy which a sometime British Ambassador later described as 'the crazy gamble of Suez'.[99] I returned to the Embassy Residence somewhat depressed, wondering whether the planned visit would ever take place.

It did in fact take place, some seven months later, but in less favourable circumstances. By the time it was over, I had begun seriously to contemplate early retirement from the Australian Diplomatic Service. During the visit something snapped in the fairly close relationships I had had with Menzies, and I had come to doubt my continuing usefulness in the Commonwealth Public Service.

Perhaps this is the place to say something about Menzies' attitude to the Suez crisis. As recently as 1967, when he published *Afternoon Light*, he persisted in defending it in terms identical with those used in 1956, although this is possible only if, like Nelson on one famous occasion, one puts the telescope to a blind eye.

At the time, on the basis of what I read—mostly in non-official sources— I disagreed with British and Australian policy. Not that I had any sympathy with Nasser's high-handed action in taking over the Suez Canal. If Britain and France, in the absence of American support, could have succeeded in wresting back from Nasser control of the Canal, by force, and in maintaining some form of international control, I would have had no moral qualms. Morality had not entered into Nasser's calculations. But to me, British policy was incredibly ill-conceived and misjudged.

By 1956 it seemed already clear, in the anti-colonial world of the post-war period, that British and French power to employ force to settle the issue had little or no chance of succeeding, at least without the active support of the United States. The joint ultimatum to Egypt and to Israel issued by Britain and France was sure to raise a hullabaloo in the United Nations. Further, the ultimatum made public on 30 October, 1956, was issued at the beginning of the last week of the American Presidential elections, a circumstance which could only irritate the American Administra-

[99] *The Diplomacy of the Great Powers*, by Sir William Hayter (Hamish Hamilton, London, 1960), p. 48.

tion beyond measure. Adverse reactions within the Commonwealth of Nations were entirely predictable. In short, only a swift military victory by Britain and France in seizing the Canal could have kept alive even the bare hope of international success. Instead, military plans made and forces available to put them into effect ruled out any such possibility. Yet Menzies chose to identify Australia whole-heartedly with the Eden policy and in the process to isolate Australia from the Afro-Asian world, including members of the Commonwealth, and to increase tensions with our American ally—although Eden had not consulted Australia before the ultimatum was sent.

It may well be that Menzies did not know the full facts at the time and that the manuscript of his book *Afternoon Light* was in the Press when Anthony Nutting published in 1967 his own account of the Suez crisis.[100] If so, one would have hoped that the Australian ex-Prime Minister would have felt the need, in his subsequent book or elsewhere, to modify his account of what happened in 1956 and to have expressed doubts as to Eden's judgment and conduct.

Anthony Nutting was British Minister of State at the Foreign Office from 1954 until he resigned in 1956, after the Suez landings. He was in a position to know what was happening, and he liked what he knew so little that he chose to sacrifice his political future rather than remain in power. The substance of his account has since been confirmed by Geoffrey McDermott, one of the very few Foreign Office men on the 'inside' of Eden's Suez policy.[101]

From these two books it seems clear that at the time of Suez Eden was a sick man, dependent, according to McDermott, on tranquillising and soporific pills. He concealed from the British Parliament and people what Nutting describes as 'a sordid conspiracy with France and Israel to seize the Suez Canal'[102] and entered upon a course of action which the Minister of State regarded as 'politically insane'.[103] Commenting upon the events of 30 October, 1956, when the ultimatum was delivered, Nutting writes: 'Seldom in Parliamentary history can there have been a more tendentious pronouncement by a Prime Minister purporting to give the facts of a grave international crisis'.[104]

In the light of statements like these, it is difficult to understand Menzies' obstinate support for Eden in 1956 followed by his subsequent silence as the real facts have become publicly known; nor does it seem sufficient to blame President Eisenhower or the United Nations for the failure of the British Prime Minister's policy. The result of the Suez episode was to diminish British prestige greatly and, in Nutting's view, to make Nasser 'a martyr and a hero', and to raise him 'to a pinnacle of power and prestige unknown in the Arab world since the beginning of the eighteenth century'.[105]

[100] *No End of a Lesson* (Hamish Hamilton, London, 1967).
[101] *The Eden Legacy and the Decline of British Diplomacy* (Leslie Frewin, London, 1969).
[102] Nutting, *op. cit.*, p. 14.
[103] *Ibid.*, p. 15.
[104] *Ibid.*, p. 116.
[105] *Ibid.*, p. 171.

I had hoped that the Australian Prime Minister's postponed visit to Japan could take place without much delay, and had made representations to Canberra to this end. As the months of 1956 passed, however, and January and February of 1957 as well, I began to give up hope. Suddenly I learned one day late in March that Menzies was coming in a fortnight's time. Arrangements had already been made in Canberra between the Japanese Ambassador to Australia and the relevant Australian Departments.

I did not find this lack of foresight, and of courtesy to me as Australian Ambassador to Japan, very amusing. A business trip to Osaka which I had arranged to make contact with certain Japanese business men and to inspect factories was hastily cancelled, and I set to work to try to influence the programme as far as practicable at that late stage. A tentative programme had already been drawn up by the Japanese Ambassador, in consultation with the prospective guests, which allowed little time in Tokyo and still less upon Australian Embassy soil there. I cabled suggestions; the Gaimusho raised difficulties and the final compromise, allowing more time in Tokyo, was reached only a few days before the party was due.

Once again I pressed Canberra for permission to fly to Manila to meet the Prime Minister and fly back with him to Tokyo. This seemed doubly necessary in view of the evidence that Canberra clearly had failed to understand that programmes drawn up by the Japanese Ambassador and the Gaimusho would be designed to further Japanese interests, not Australian. The Department, more in sorrow than in anger or by conviction, formally assented, presumably regarding me as a frustrated ex-Secretary who had now been too long in the field. Clearly, however, my proposal was regarded as quite unnecessary, the reply underlining the strong desire of the Prime Minister to have a long talk with me on the evening of his arrival in Japan. Against my better judgment, I did not persist in my plan to fly to Manila—a decision which later I had cause to regret. In the event, at no time during the visit did I have adequate opportunity for a *private* conversation with Menzies about Japan and its people. Had I gone to Manila, I believe that some at least of the difficulties associated with the visit might have been avoided.

The Prime Minister's party included Dame Pattie Menzies, Allen (later Sir Allen) Brown (Secretary, Prime Minister's Department), Jim (later Sir James) Plimsoll (Assistant-Secretary, Department of External Affairs) and a number of less senior officers and aides. Plimsoll was an old colleague; Brown was neither a shrinking violet nor a sensitive plant, but we had worked together amicably enough when I was Secretary of External Affairs. The remaining members of the party were not in my opinion the kind of Australians who would make a good impression abroad, and I was sorry they were coming.

The visitors were accommodated at Geihinkan, the official residence for State guests. In some ways this was convenient for them as a group, but involved minimal security for their conversations with one another and increased my difficulties in maintaining contact with them. The size of the party also made it impracticable for me to include an Australian member of my staff who spoke Japanese, when we all left Tokyo on tour to Kyoto,

Nara and Osaka. As a result, the only persons in the group who could communicate with Japanese in their own language were the Japanese Ambassador to Australia and a representative from the Gaimusho. I would never have chosen to involve the Prime Minister in such a situation, but clear indications were given that none of his Australian entourage was to be left out of official engagements except during formal talks with the Japanese Prime Minister, when only Brown, Plimsoll and myself were present to support Mr Menzies.

A few days before Menzies' arrival our official car broke down and had to have a major overhaul. I had been trying to get Canberra to agree to replacement of the old and inevitable Humber Pullman, without success. In the circumstances, we had to hire a local Cadillac, at considerable cost. It was no satisfaction to me to have been proved right on the subject of the first Embassy car. Apart from losing some face with the Japanese, it is a fact of life that the Head of an overseas Mission is responsible in the eyes of a Ministerial visitor for everything which goes wrong.

After the usual welcome at the airport in cold, dusty and windy weather, Menzies and his party were driven to Geihinkan, and then came to the Embassy for a 'family' dinner which I had been able to insert into the programme. As this was likely to be the only occasion for serious talks amongst the Australians prior to formal conversations with the Japanese the following morning, I was ruthless in asking to the dinner only the most senior member of the Embassy staff and his wife. Tom Eckersley was an old Japan hand, with a scholarly knowledge of the Japanese language and long experience of the country during several postings, both before and after he entered the diplomatic service. His presence was essential. I am afraid the remaining members of my staff scarcely appreciated their exclusion from the dinner, being democratic Australians, but there were sound if differing reasons for not inviting them.

After dinner the men in the party went upstairs to my study where we discussed problems of the tour. This was a useful exercise, but no substitute, in my judgment, for an informal and lengthy private conversation between the Prime Minister and myself. I have always agreed with Robert Louis Stevenson that conversation is a talk between two individuals: the more present, the greater the number of interruptions and distractions and the less ground likely to be covered frankly.

Alone, I would have tried to convey to Menzies some understanding of Japanese history: the position of the Emperor, the Shogunate system, the warrior tradition; the influence of Chinese culture, the aesthetic sophistication of the elite, the significance of 'form'; Japanese courage, pertinacity and patriotism; the sense of hierarchy, of loyalty to one's superior in station, of obligation to family, clan and nation; the stern realities underlying exterior rituals of politeness; the catastrophic effects of defeat in the Second World War by a foreign enemy for the first time in recorded history, and the temporary 'low-posture' while economic recovery was pursued and self-confidence built up once again; the nature of current 'invitation diplomacy'.

Moreover, there were some things which could not have been hinted at in full company, because they might have carried an implication of faint criticism of the Prime Minister. He was leaning rather too heavily upon the very able Ambassador of Japan in Australia as a source of information, although the latter's activities, naturally enough, were directed towards furthering the interests of his own country. Indeed, during the visit Menzies on several occasions publicly praised the virtues of the Ambassador, seemingly unconscious of the fact that the latter might be embarrassed, that his fellow-countrymen might begin to wonder whether he might have become too 'pro-Australian', and that such persistence eventually forced the Prime Minister of Japan to praise me publicly on one occasion as he could not allow a foreign visitor to be more polite than he was himself.

On the following morning, having signed the visitors' book at the Palace, official talks took place at the residence of the Japanese Prime Minister, Mr Nobusuke Kishi; Brown, Plimsoll and myself were present to support Mr Menzies. On the Japanese side Mr Kishi was attended by his Ambassador to Australia and senior representatives of the Gaimusho and other Ministries. During the discussions Menzies performed splendidly, recovering without difficulty from a rather embarrassing situation in which he found himself placed.

Mr Kishi opened with words of welcome and then continued in terms which disclosed a surprising lack of understanding and finesse. He was obviously reading from a piece of paper covered with Japanese characters, a copy of which was in the hand of each of the other Japanese present. He spoke in Japanese, and paused every now and then for an interpreter to translate. What he said can be summarised briefly, if barely and starkly, as follows:

> Since 1945 there have been six matters of importance in Japan-Australia relations. Four of them Australia has been kind enough to deal with satisfactorily. Thank you very much. This leaves two matters, the most vital, namely, trade and pearl-shell fishing. Now that you are here, Mr Menzies, you will no doubt be so kind as to solve these outstanding matters as well. Then we will be able to thank you very much again, and our future relations will be very good indeed.

What Mr Kishi actually said, of course, was much fuller than this, but my interpretation of its substance was as set out above and I found myself reacting adversely. Here was the Australian Prime Minister on a good-will visit to Japan, designed to symbolise the new and better relations between the two countries since the signature of the Peace Treaty. Now his hosts were, in effect, standing him up against a wall and pressing for quick answers to questions of great importance to Australia, whose government had gone a long way, within the limits of Australian public opinion, to improve relations with Japan. The Japanese Government seemed to be taking these past gestures of good-will for granted, and was pressing for more at an inappropriate time. Had it already forgotten that there had been a war during which Australia had been under attack and Australian prisoners mistreated?

I slipped a note to Menzies on which I had written: 'You may wish to remind Mr Kishi that there has been a war'. He read it and looked at me somewhat quizzically—as if to say 'Do you really think it was necessary to remind me of that?' He waited patiently until Kishi had finished and then, speaking without any notes, made the following points.

Menzies expressed his pleasure at visiting Japan for the second time, the earlier visit being in 1950, before signature of the Peace Treaty. In particular, he was glad to have the opportunity to speak frankly to representatives of the Japanese Government, for frankness was the essential basis of understanding. One had to begin by remembering that there had been a war during which Australia had been under attack by Japanese forces. Wars caused bitterness and distrust and it was natural, therefore, that the Australian people had been resentful, and suspicious of future Japanese policy. This attitude had been a limiting factor of importance which no Australian Government could ignore.

However, Australia had signed the Peace Treaty and, in doing so, had not claimed the kind of reparations sought by other allied countries which had suffered more on their own territory. The Treaty inaugurated a new era in relations with Japan and the Australian Government, being peaceful in outlook and not disposed to perpetuate old enmities, had decided to do what it could to help Japan back to its rightful place in the community of nations. So Australia had supported Japan's application to become a member of the United Nations, and sponsored her membership of the Colombo Plan. She was dealing with the problem of war criminals serving sentences in a liberal and civilised way. These decisions had not been welcome to all Australians, and should not be taken for granted. They had required some courage and leadership by the Australian Government.

Mr Kishi had raised two additional issues, namely, pearl-shell fishing and trade. These matters were both complicated and delicate and required the most careful consideration if Australian public opinion was to be kept on side. On pearl-fishing, for instance, he must remind his Japanese friends that quite a number of Australians doubted whether, before the war, Japanese pearling vessels in Australian waters or near the Australian coast had been manned only by fishermen, or that they fished only for pearl-shell. Moreover, Australian pearl-shell interests believed they were entitled to special consideration regarding pearl-shell lying on the Australian continental shelf, which was a long way from Japan. Differences of opinion on the legal questions involved were regrettable, but the outcome was important to Australia—beyond the value of the pearl-shell garnered. The lawyers would have to get together to see whether a case could be worked out for the International Court of Justice. No doubt their opinions would be submitted to him in due course, but it would be quite wrong for him to try to interfere at this stage.

As to trade, this was of vital importance to both countries. But he should make it clear that, while Australia understood Japan's desire to reduce the imbalance of trade between the two countries, it was illusory to think that the natural state of trade between all countries was a mathematical balance between each one of them. There were countries with which Australia had an unfavourable balance; she did not like this, but was content if her

S

overall balance of trade was favourable. Moreover, Australia exported to Japan mostly raw materials which Japan processed and often sold abroad, acquiring foreign currency in the process. Officials from the two countries had had preliminary negotiations for a trade agreement, and he respected their capacity too highly to interpose himself between them. Australia had hopes that a mutually satisfactory trade agreement could be worked out in the near future and, when this was done, the two Governments would applaud the results.

Menzies concluded by stressing that his own visit was essentially a good-will visit, designed to register for both the Australian and Japanese people the Australian Government's desire for friendly relations between them. His Government would be glad to follow this up and he was pleased, for instance, to extend to Mr Kishi an invitation to come to Australia. The Japanese Prime Minister had suggested, during his opening remarks, that there should be an exchange of visits between parliamentarians. This was a good idea and he was ready to agree to it now. Mr Kishi had wondered whether Menzies would wish to consult his colleagues about the matter before deciding. This was not necessary. He knew his Cabinet colleagues' attitude well, and was prepared to speak for them at once. As to par-liamentarians generally—it was his strong impression that Australian parliamentarians were not resistant to proposals for overseas visits. Perhaps the situation in Japan was different.

This last statement brought a roar of laughter from the Japanese present, and Menzies ended on this humorous note. His reply had been a tour de force. He had given nothing away, resisted undue pressure, showed good-will, and ended with laughter.

Not all the rest of the visit of the Ministerial party had as happy an out-come. An Australian silver cigarette box brought as a gift for Mr Kishi was wrongly inscribed in Tokyo where Mr Kishi's first name was mispelt while being engraved. The box had to be discarded. As the Embassy had supplied the name of the engraver, the Embassy was blamed; quite overlooking the fact that one of Mr Menzies' staff, who knew no Japanese, had insisted on leaving the box with the engraver and on giving the instructions for the inscription.

Worse still, the Embassy through a member of its staff failed to carry out a Prime Ministerial instruction relayed through and emphasised by me to refuse a pressing invitation to a dinner at a Japanese restaurant by a Japanese business man who at that moment was in personal correspondence with Menzies regarding business deals in Australia. When we returned to Tokyo after an exhausting and somewhat frustrating visit to Kyoto, Nara and Osaka, Menzies discovered, when the business man in question was passing through the receiving line at an Australian Embassy reception, that the gentleman concerned was expecting the Australian visiting party to dinner that evening. The refusal, we discovered on inquiry, had not been conveyed. Menzies was understandably angry—with us, not the business man, whose invitation he now felt it would be too discourteous to refuse.

The final mis-event of the visit, so far as my wife and I were concerned, was a 'family' dinner given by the Prime Minister at Geihinkan just prior to his departure for Manila. Mildred, Mary and I were invited to attend. The dinner was a careless, care-free affair which would not have mattered much but for the fact that the Japanese Ambassador to Australia and a member of the Gaimusho had been invited at the last minute. Whether they had sought an invitation or been asked to come as a mark of appreciation of their attentions during the tour I do not know. In any event, their presence and our reading of their probable reactions to what they saw and heard greatly depressed Mildred and me.

It would be futile to try to reproduce in detail what happened. Suffice to say that the stories, comments and activities of the Press Secretary were scarcely edifying and that the 'family', listening to better stories by the Prime Minister, sounded more and more like an undistinguished claque. None of the visiting Australians seemed to realise that he or she was in Tokyo, not Australia, or that they were being measured by two highly intelligent and sophisticated Japanese who would doubtless report their impressions in the highest local quarters.

Returning from the airport after the departure from Tokyo of Mr Menzies and his companions, I reflected upon the results of the visit. I had hoped that the Australian Prime Minister might return to his own country with new understanding of the Japanese people and a new feeling for the East which might affect future Australian policy. These hopes I now regarded as illusory, then, or in the future. As our car turned through the gates of the Embassy, I said to my wife: 'This sort of visitation by a group of Australians insensitive to their surroundings makes me want to retire from the Public Service at an early date. I wonder if I should see out my time here, and retire at sixty?'

TRADE AGREEMENT WITH JAPAN

On 6 July, 1957 a Trade Agreement was signed at Hakone, Japan, by the Japanese Prime Minister, Mr Nobusuke Kishi, on the one hand and by the Australian Minister for Trade, the Rt Hon. J. (later Sir John) McEwen, and myself on the other hand. Signature of this agreement, in my opinion, marked a watershed in post-war relations between the two countries. Despite the fears of Australian manufacturers that their own products would be undercut by a flood of Japanese exports, the Treaty proved a striking success and was renewed and extended in 1963. Under these agreements mutual trade increased greatly, and while at time of writing the balance of trade still favours Australia substantially, the ratio of such Australian preponderance fell from approximately 11:1 in 1956/7 to approximately 2:1 in 1969/70.

Although signature of the Treaty was a matter of great satisfaction to me and the most important event during my posting in Tokyo, I can claim no credit for it. Indeed, the manner of negotiation, and my own slight involvement in it, was a cause of frustration and annoyance.

The agreement followed exploratory talks early in 1956 and preparatory negotiations in Canberra from November 1956. I was not kept informed of the nature of these negotiations until the text was suddenly telegraphed to me, with instructions to clear up with the Gaimusho a few minor matters, prior to the arrival of Mr McEwen in Tokyo to sign the Treaty.

Over the years I had grown accustomed to the attitude of the Department of Trade, with certain notable exceptions, to the Department of External Affairs. Broadly speaking, we were regarded as striped-pants diplomats, obsessed with protocol, unable to recognise the basic, material facts of life. The Department of Trade was determined to control Trade policy, subject to occasional fights with Treasury, and under a powerful Minister who knew how to get his way, built up a Departmental establishment with salary ranges which enabled them to lure from External Affairs and elsewhere officers with special economic capacity.

We did not dispute their expertise on trade matters, but still maintained that selling goods abroad involved many non-economic problems which should be taken into account. I have had personal experience of a senior officer of the Trade Department operating overseas exuding self-confidence and substantially unaware of the peculiarities and susceptibilities of the countries he was visiting.

The Department of Trade wanted its Trade Commissioners abroad to have diplomatic privileges, and was thus happy to attach them as Commercial Counsellors to our diplomatic missions where these existed; the Department, however, was disposed to pay only lip-service to the supervisory authority of the Head of Mission over all members of his staff. One such Commercial Counsellor told me that, before being posted overseas, he had been told in his Department that, in general terms, he should regard himself as a member of the Ambassador's staff and should keep the latter informed of what he was doing; if, however, he ran into any trouble with the Ambassador, he should go his own way in the knowledge that he would be fully supported at home.

During my time in the Australian diplomatic service my experience with Commercial Counsellors and Trade Commissioners varied. At a subsequent post in Germany, I found close co-operation and mutual understanding. Unfortunately this situation did not obtain in Tokyo, where I had constant trouble with my Commercial Counsellor which came to a head in a manner which I shall describe later.

Against this background, I had learned to abstain from protest regarding the course of negotiations on which I should have been kept informed, partly because I doubted whether the Department of External Affairs in Canberra was allowed to play any effective part in trade discussions. It is one thing, however, to be kept out of negotiations and to have no responsibility for them: it is quite another thing, having been kept out of negotiations, suddenly to be launched into responsibility for clarifying certain items in the discussions. When I received the text and instructions, therefore, I studied the contents carefully and raised in expensive cables quite a number of questions the answers to which were not clear to me. In Canberra my questions were probably regarded as irrelevant if not impertinent, but at least I had raised issues regarding which I had doubts and received specific instructions regarding them.

Eventually an English text was agreed in Tokyo, and a Japanese text was checked carefully by Tom Eckersley, some of whose suggestions for appropriate translation from English were accepted by the Gaimusho. Mr McEwen then arrived in Japan to sign the Treaty, accompanied by W. A. (later Sir Alan) Westerman, then Deputy-Secretary, Department of Trade. I had asked the Department to excuse me from the rite of counter-signing the Treaty, partly because my own contribution to its negotiation was negligible and partly because the signature of the Australian Ambassador seemed to me to add nothing to the signature of the relevant Minister of State. I was instructed to sign, apparently for reasons of Departmental prestige which I felt could better have been sustained by insistence in Canberra upon a greater voice in the negotiatory process.

Mr McEwen carried out his mission with his customary effectiveness, warning Japanese authorities and business men that the Treaty was in a sense experimental because, if they pressed their new opportunities too hard in certain sensitive areas, opposition would grow in Australia to extension of the agreement. In the event, the Japanese exercised considerable restraint, thereby diminishing Australian fears and helping to facilitate the acquisition of further privileges in 1963.

During Mr McEwen's visit to Japan he was courteous to me, and my wife found him considerate. I can not say the same for his entourage. Westerman showed every sign of minimising any chances I had of speaking to his Minister alone. The only real opportunity for this was during the long drive from Tokyo to Hakone to sign the agreement, made necessary because the Prime Minister of Japan was holidaying there. Westerman obtained his Minister's assent to his driving to Hakone with the Minister in the main Embassy car instead of myself, on the alleged ground that urgent matters had to be discussed. This lowered my standing in Japanese eyes, but I agreed to it, on condition that I drove back with the Minister alone. When we left Hakone, however, Mr McEwen told me that he was tired and would like to get some sleep in the back of the car. We had no conversation all the way back, and I gave up the idea of trying to tell the Minister for Trade something about Japan that he was unlikely ever to hear from officers of his own Department.

VISIT OF THE JAPANESE PRIME MINISTER TO AUSTRALIA

In December 1957 Mr Kishi made a return visit to Australia which could easily have caused a set-back in gradually improving relations between Australia and Japan. He had been a member of the Tojo Cabinet from 1941 to 1943, and after the war was held as a Class A war criminal suspect by Allied Occupation Authorities. Although not tried or condemned as a war criminal, this background did not mark him out as the ideal person for the first visit to Australia after the war of a Japanese Prime Minister. I was brought back from Tokyo to be at hand during his visit, following the equivalent Japanese custom, but as I had little personal association with Mr Kishi and could not communicate in the Japanese language, I was far less successful in occupying his attention in Australia than the Japanese Ambassador to Australia had been with Mr Menzies in Japan.

In the event, the visit passed off without major incident. The President of the New South Wales Branch of the Return Services League of Australia suggested that Mr Kishi should be met on arrival by a guard of honour consisting of Australian war widows. In Canberra the Japanese Embassy had pressed to have included in the visitor's programme laying of a wreath upon the Australian War Memorial, a proposal which raised quite a number of Australian hackles. Had I known about it before leaving Tokyo, I think I could have persuaded the Gaimusho to advise the Prime Minister to delete the item, as far too risky on a first visit after the war by a Japanese Head of Government. But the programme had already been printed before I reached Sydney. In due course the wreath was laid, but immediately afterwards some Australian placed on the flat top of the memorial a copy of the judgments of the War Crimes Tribunal detailing the crimes of the persons sentenced.

I remember with gratitude and appreciation the attitude of the Governor-General of the Commonwealth during the visit. Sir William (later Viscount) Slim had no particular reason to love the Japanese, whom he had fought in Burma, but he was impeccably courteous to Mr Kishi and his entourage during the latter's visit to Canberra. They were invited to stay at Government House and entertained there. The Governor-General also enhanced my status in Japanese eyes when he insisted on my staying at Government House as well.

In short, 1957 was an important year in relations between Japan and Australia. The events of that year described above were followed in January 1958 by a ten-day visit to Japan of an Australian Parliamentary Delegation, led by a Cabinet Minister, and a return visit to Australia by a Japanese Parliamentary Delegation in August-September of the same year.

In March 1959 Mr R. G. Casey, Australian Minister for External Affairs, visited Japan as a guest of the Japanese Government. He was accompanied by Mrs Casey, Gordon Jockell (a senior officer of the Department of External Affairs), a representative of the Commonwealth Scientific and Industrial Research Organisation, and a Private Secretary.

As Mr Casey was not a Head of Government, Geihinkan was not made available for him and his party. They would have been put up at the Imperial Hotel, had he not chosen instead to stay with Mrs Casey at the Australian Embassy, with whose lay-out he was familiar from his visit to Tokyo in 1951. This sensible decision gave me ready and unimpeded access to the Minister during the first few vital days. The Department of External Affairs had compiled a useful brief, and there was time to consider problems privately in some depth before the first serious discussions with the Japanese Foreign Minister.

Some four or five months before the Casey visit, a major difference had arisen with my Commercial Counsellor in Tokyo. The issue was referred to Canberra, where neither the Minister nor Department of External Affairs gave me any support. This was the last straw which broke the camel's back, and was the decisive factor in my decision to leave the Commonwealth Public Service before reaching the age of sixty-five.

I was staying at Nikko for the week-end when one of my staff telephoned for instructions about a telegram which the Commercial Counsellor had handed in for despatch to his Department in Canberra. It strongly recommended a course of action of which the External Affairs staff at the Embassy correctly guessed that I would strongly disapprove. In fact I was outraged at the proposal, conveyed to me over the telephone in deliberately garbled form. I knew it to be foolish. The result, I was convinced, would be the opposite of that intended; it cut across long-term and important activities of my own; it was not something which one would remember with pride.

It is a serious decision to hold up a communication from a senior officer of a Commonwealth Department to his own chief in Canberra. I therefore gave instructions that the telegram should be despatched unaltered, along with a separate telegram saying that the matter had not been discussed with the Ambassador, whose personal views would be telegraphed as soon as he could return to Tokyo. Thereupon I made haste back to the Embassy and sent a long cable flatly objecting to the proposal and setting out reasons. In my considered judgment, then and now, the arguments I put forward were unanswerable.

In due course I received instructions from the Department of External Affairs to allow the proposal to be carried out, slightly modified as to form but not at all as to substance. This was a considerable blow to my self-respect and to my confidence that my continuation in the Public Service, or at least as Ambassador to Japan, was of further use. I considered the question of immediate resignation, but came to the conclusion that the effects upon my family would be so drastic, and the impossibility of giving a frank public explanation for my action so great that this course was not open to me.

The general effect of this incident, however, when added to recurrent frustrations regarding various administrative controls and delays at the Canberra end, led me to the point of planning to leave the Commonwealth Public Service at or about the age of sixty. I was entitled to stay on until sixty-five, and originally my superannuation contributions had been arranged on that basis. My experiences under Dr Evatt, however, had made me decide to increase my contributions so as to make retirement at the age of sixty possible.

Before Casey left Australia I had written to him personally about a planned early retirement, omitting detailed reasons. There seemed no point, after the instruction I had received about the proposal of my Commercial Counsellor, to elaborate what would have amounted to a Bill of Complaints. But I had been closer to Casey than to any other Minister, and when the opportunity for a quiet personal talk with him in my study came unexpectedly after late evening engagements when everyone else was in bed, I took it. I doubt whether he fully understood the reasons prompting an early retirement, but he listened patiently and was not unsympathetic.

Shortly before that time it had been announced publicly that the respective Embassies in Canberra and in Moscow of the Soviet Union and Australia, the staffs of which had been withdrawn after the Petrov case, were to be put in operation again. The request of Vladimir Petrov, a junior member of the Soviet Embassy in Canberra, for political asylum and the intervention of the Commonwealth Government to ascertain whether Mrs Petrov, who was being escorted out of Australia by Soviet security officials, really wanted to return to the Soviet Union, had made world headlines. These events took place shortly after I arrived in Singapore in 1954. The requests for asylum of Mr and Mrs Petrov were granted; a Royal Commission of inquiry into espionage was set up in Australia; Dr Evatt, the leader of the Labor Party Opposition appeared before it as Counsel for some interests until the Commission withdrew permission for him to appear; the Soviet Government felt it had to show its displeasure at the Petrov affair by requesting that all Australian Embassy staff in Moscow should leave the country. Australia then followed suit and asked Russian diplomats to leave.

It is doubtful whether diplomatic relations between the two countries were actually severed, as the Soviet authorities still continued to print the name 'Australia' in their Diplomatic List, with a blank beneath indicating that no Australian staff was serving in Moscow. In practice, however, the effective re-opening of the Embassies had to be negotiated.

Now that the decision to re-open had been taken, the task of finding a suitable Australian Head of Mission for Moscow would not be easy. It had crossed my mind, after the public announcement, that I might be of some use to the Australian Government in that capacity. In principle, I was against an Ambassador returning to the same post for a second time, but the circumstances were somewhat exceptional. Actually, I had been the last Ambassador to the Soviet Union, as the Mission had been kept at Chargé d'Affaires level after my departure in 1950. I was vain enough to believe that relations between the Soviet Union and Australia had been better when I left than when I arrived. In a sense, therefore, I would merely be continuing in Moscow, after a long interruption.

There were additional reasons for my thoughts turning in this direction. By the end of my term in Japan I would have served at Asian posts for six successive years. This experience had been invaluable, but by now I had become somewhat saturated with Asia. To return to the problems of Europe would be a relief. In Russia there would be practically no negotiation; no visits by parliamentarians and few by tourists; I would concentrate upon reporting and interpreting. A couple of years there in decent isolation and obscurity would bring back my early literary interest in Russia which I hoped to pursue in some written form after retirement.

With all these thoughts in my mind, I raised with Casey the possibility of my being transferred to Moscow about the end of 1959, when my term in Tokyo should end. There was no specific request, and no definite reply. As no other relevant posts seemed to be available, the only alternative appeared to be an extension of my Tokyo term for an additional year, after which I would be eligible to retire.

Subsequently I changed my mind about Moscow and wrote to the Minister after his return to Australia informing him that my preference would be to spend two years in Germany if and when that post became vacant. I had sought the opinion of the American Ambassador, Douglas MacArthur II, and he strongly advised me to go to Bonn if that were practicable. I took his advice seriously and came to the conclusion that he was right. His appointment to Tokyo had been a windfall for me, as I had come to know him well during the Manila Treaty Conference in 1954. In Tokyo, he made himself available to me at any time I wished, and gave me valuable information about developments in Japan which an American Ambassador, at that time, was best placed to acquire.

MacArthur pointed out that I had already served in Moscow; that my activities there would inevitably be restricted; that the German problem, in many ways, was the opposite side of the Russian question and that my experience of Russia would be valuable in Bonn; that I was more fitted linguistically to operate in Germany than in Russia; and that the growth of the European Economic Community was of great importance, even to Australia—it would be an interesting and significant subject on which to report. Lastly, but not least, I would be closer to Western Europe as a whole and could learn much about the extent to which that area was likely to integrate.

In the event, the Australian Government considerately offered me the post of Ambassador to the Federal Republic of Germany. Patrick Shaw, our Ambassador there, would have completed four years of service in Bonn by 1960. I could end my term in Tokyo late in 1959, return to Australia for consultation and leave, and take up my new post in Bonn about April, 1960.

For my wife and myself, the final year in Japan was one of quiet consolidation. Despite the administrative frustrations to which I have referred, we had met a wide range of interesting people and learned much about the country and its distinctive history. Signature of the Trade Agreement, coupled with the exchange of visits by political leaders at the highest level, had given me some standing with Japanese officials and in the Diplomatic Corps, of which I had by then become a senior member. Indeed, by the time I left I was Number 4 in the List, and in danger of becoming Dean— an office I have never coveted—if I stayed on much longer.

While in Japan I had tried to build up some other impression of Australia than a vast, empty land occupied as much by weird animals as by under-cultured people. This was not an easy task, either with the Japanese or the Australian Government. I could penetrate the English-language Press on occasion without too much difficulty, but the Japanese Press was not interested in making available space to upset the strongly-held and simplistic convictions of Japanese about Australia and its people.

I had only limited success with Canberra in trying to get adequate financial support for members of my staff keen to learn Japanese; Canberra expected them to be twice as efficient as Englishmen, and to learn Japanese more or less in their spare time, even though the Embassy was under-staffed on the political side. My efforts to secure some financial provision in the budget for cultural activities failed completely. Not a shilling was made available during my term for cultural diplomacy, which in Japan can have significant effect in changing images of a foreign country. Yet Mr Menzies provided £1,000 to assist a *Japanese* exhibition, mostly of modern art, to come to Australia, without imposing any condition that Japan should make some reciprocal gesture. I admired the pertinacity and skill of the Japanese

Ambassador to Australia in thus securing Australian support for his own country's purposes, but could not compete in Tokyo terms. My reports as to the strong influence in Japan of two foreign exhibitions, one depicting 7,000 years of Iranian art, the other a series of paintings by Van Gogh sent out by the Netherlands Government, had no visible effect in Canberra. Only in later years, well after my departure, did the Australian Government find sufficient virtue in something unrelated to trade to provide funds enabling, for instance, the Australian Ballet Company to tour a number of Asian cities, including Tokyo.

Fortunately, my own activities in Tokyo were substantially under my own control, and I was able to carry out some functions which had no direct relationship to Embassy work. After the departure from Tokyo in 1957 of the British Ambassador, I was asked to succeed him as President of the Tokyo Tennis Club. This contained a wide range of foreign and Japanese members, including the Crown Prince of Japan and his future bride, Miss Michiko Shoda.

There was also a Cambridge and Oxford Society in Tokyo, so-called in that unusual order because it had first been a Cambridge Society. The ex-officio President was always the British Ambassador, chosen, so to speak, as custodian of those two ancient universities. But there was also an Executive Committee, whose Chairman I became. I greatly enjoyed Club Meetings, for which there was one golden rule: traditionally, nothing serious was to be said or done during its monthly lunches or dinners. Here one could escape the stuffiness of diplomatic parties, and indulge as much as one wished in ironical humour, teasing colleagues, even questioning national virtues. When Mr Casey came to Japan the Club had a special celebration in his honour, as a graduate of Cambridge. He too enjoyed the light-hearted occasion, and performed well in accordance with Club tradition.

Finally, towards the end of my term I became President of the Asiatic Society of Japan, whose publications are well known to academic circles. Our Committee meetings were held in the Australian Embassy Dining Room, whose panelled walls listened to more cultural themes and learned discussions than they had ever heard before.

For the rest, my wife and I tried, without much success, to widen our experience of Japan beyond Tokyo and its diplomatic round. At an early stage I had visited Nagoya, Osaka and Kobe to meet business people and inspect some factories and shipyards. A long-planned trip south beyond the main island of Honshu to the islands of Kyushu and Shikoku was only partially successful, as I was recalled to Tokyo on urgent business before we reached Kagoshima or had visited Shikoku. Still, we were able to see the faint relics nears Fukuoka of the successful defence against Mongol invasions in the thirteenth century, and reflect upon the devastating effects of the atomic bomb at Nagasaki.

We had had to decline, with much regret, an invitation to attend the seventy-fifth anniversary of the founding of the University of Hokkaido, but in the summer of 1958 a Trade Fair was being held in the northernmost of Japan's four main islands, and a small squadron of British, including Australian, naval vessels were to visit Hokkaido as part of the general festivities. Two Australian warships, a destroyer and a frigate, had been detailed to visit the fishing-port of Otaru, situated about half-way up the westernmost coast of the island.

The presence of Australian warships in such northerly waters was most unusual, and it seemed to me highly desirable to combine their visit with an official trip by myself to the capital city of Hokkaido, Sapporo, where I could call on the Governor and other officials and give a reception attended, inter alia, by officers from the Australian ships. In the process, we hoped to escape for a week from the humid heat of summer in Tokyo, where Treasury obstinacy from Canberra still denied to the Australian Embassy the air-conditioners approved for a similar climate in Washington D.C.

In due course we set out by train accompanied by Ted Weatherstone, a junior member of the staff who spoke fluent Japanese. The visit proved full of interest, though we ran into a number of minor difficulties and suffered one major disappointment due to the fault of no one but illustrating the unpredictability of developments in the international field.

In Hokkaido we recovered a sense of spaciousness which we had lost in the southern islands of Japan. Here there was *room*—room for man and beast and crops. An experimental sheep-farm; acres and acres of potatoes; horses. The capital city was well laid out in wide, tree-lined streets, with an attractive background of mountains in the distance. It seemed to us surprising that more of the Japanese population did not migrate to Hokkaido, despite the cold winter. Yet, the considerable amount of capital made available by the Japanese Government to develop the island, seemed to have produced disappointing results, judging by the small amount of manufacturing industry, the poor quality of most houses and the seeming poverty of villages. Had some of these funds been diverted in unauthorised directions?

After paying my official calls in Sapporo and visiting the exhibits at the local Fair, my wife and I drove to Otaru along an excellent road through many tunnels. The contrast with all the other roads on which we travelled in Hokkaido—narrow, bumpy, unsealed, dusty—was striking. Otaru proved to be a very run-down fishing port, whose fortunes had obviously not improved since the end of the war. Russian restrictions limited the activities of Japanese fishermen, and if they transgressed against these their boats were seized.

The European-style hotel into which we had been booked proved to be by far the worst I experienced in Japan. Previous occupants of our room had not improved the condition of the furniture; the food was poor; but the distinguishing feature which disturbed us most was the situation of the hotel, on a rising hill at a city intersection, where bells rang every time the lights changed. A loud-speaker also advertised someone's wares during shopping hours, while the noise of traffic, with cars changing gears at the intersection, continued throughout the night and made sleep almost impossible.

However, we had not gone to Otaru for comfort, but for business. My calls on the local Mayor, both on arrival and departure, were scarcely successful, as on each occasion there seemed to be some misunderstanding on his part as to the times of appointment. We toured the local version of the Fair, and Mildred was reluctantly induced to launch a toy ship within the Fair grounds by severing the mooring-rope with the customary Japanese tomahawk.

But the two naval vessels tied up at the nearby wharf were a sight for sore Australian eyes, while local interest in their unusual presence was high. Everything aboard was spick-and-span, and when the ships were decked out with bunting for a late-afternoon cocktail-party, with all members of the crew in formal dress, it was a gay and cheerful occasion for us. There were many Japanese and some foreign guests as well, and it did Australia no harm for these to know that we possessed some warships which our men knew how to handle.

After the cocktail-reception aboard ship, the Officer Commanding insisted on Mildred and myself remaining for an informal meal in his cabin, despite a pressing invitation from the Mayor to watch an unscheduled fireworks display. As we had already spent a considerable time at a party given by the Mayor the same afternoon at a Japanese Inn, I agreed after some hesitation. We greatly enjoyed this relaxed evening, gossiping about Australia and Japan in the security of Australian territory. The Captain was courteous without being deferential, and quickly sprang to the defence of all naval personnel when I told a flippant story of something which had once gone wrong on a warship of another member of the Commonwealth of Nations. We returned to our hotel in a somewhat better mood to face the discomforts of our impending night there.

The reception I was to give in Sapporo on the following day was designed to underline this first, substantial Australian presence in Hokkaido. Those invited included the Governor and other high Japanese officials, foreign consular representatives, the Vice-Chancellor of the University and some of the academic staff. In addition to my wife, Weatherstone and myself, some fifteen Australian naval officers were to attend. Man proposes, God disposes.

After a disturbed night, I received word that the Commander of the Australian warships desired to call on me urgently. When he arrived he told me confidentially that he had received orders to leave Otaru immediately and to sail at high speed for Sasebo on the north-west coast of Kyushu, where he would receive further instructions. Their immediate destination was not to be revealed.

Clearly the instructions were related to the crisis which had broken out in the Middle East, which had led to American troops being landed, by invitation, in the Lebanon. The Captain was apologetic about the inability of his officers to attend my reception in Sapporo, but the orders were peremptory and there was nothing else to be done. He did not need to explain to me that, if the international balloon went up, the ships were in a most exposed position in relation to the Soviet Union. So I made no comment and, at his invitation, accompanied him to his ship while preparations were made for both vessels to back out and disappear without explanation. It would be my responsibility to convey to the Japanese a scarcely credible story to account for their unexpected disappearance.

Once aboard, I was deeply impressed by the change in atmosphere since the cocktail-party of the evening before. Gone was the bunting; an atmosphere of gaiety and ceremonial had given place to one of purposive efficiency. Seated in the Captain's cabin, I waited while officers in working clothes came in to report. Fuel, food, water—everything was ready. Four men still ashore on leave. The Captain asked me to get my staff to ensure they were informed of the sudden departure and to make arrangements for them to fly to Tokyo, where they would be instructed what to do next.

I said good-bye and good-luck, returned to the hotel to collect my wife, and came back to the pier. The ships had already backed out, and were heading for the open sea and a future at which we could only guess.

Weatherstone left messages for the missing sailors in appropriate places, and arranged for their flight to Tokyo, where we looked after them until they moved on to Sasebo. The whole atmosphere of my reception in Sapporo was changed, but it still served a useful purpose. When it was over we left immediately by road for a short, private stay at Lake Toya, where we stayed at a Japanese Inn, sleeping on tatami in a room which opened on to the lake. It was a pleasant place in itself, but a nearby tourist boat with smiling ladies aboard transmitting through loud speakers invitations to take a trip on the lake did not add to its attractiveness. We were soon ready to leave for Chitose airport, passing on the way Showa Shinzan, the new volcanic mountain which rose up suddenly in the early 1940's. We flew back to Tokyo, where we found David Anderson waiting for us at Haneda airport in the Embassy car. Oddly enough, Tokyo did not seem as humid as the heat-wave we had experienced in Hokkaido. But if the road from Haneda to the Embassy was congested, how smooth it seemed.

The Hokkaido trip, though short, refreshed for a while our outlook on life. Before leaving Tokyo I was mentally depressed, and both my wife and I were weary beyond measure. The popular notion of la vie diplomatique as one of ample leisure and opulent facilities has, no doubt, always been a vulgarised image of the facts. It was even more absurd as a picture of the life of an Australian diplomat at that stage of our national development. To omit concrete examples of the kinds of administrative frustrations of Heads of Overseas Missions in those days would be to distort the story of diplomatic life as we experienced it.

This was our third summer in Tokyo and regular requests to Canberra for approval of air-conditioners for bedrooms at least were rejected. As a result, we had insufficient sleep during the three humid summer months. My wife acquired the habit of climbing to the flat roof of the residence well before sunrise, sitting in a deck-chair waiting for daylight to come, hoping that the tip of Mount Fuji would appear on the horizon, but in any event taking comfort in the vista of the garden below and the pot-plants she had persuaded the gardener to take up to the roof.

Eventually I gave up trying to convince Treasury that Tokyo heat in summer was indistinguishable from Washington heat, both of which I had personally experienced. No doubt some clerical researcher in Treasury looked up the weather statistics and found that Washington had one more day of heat or one more degree of humidity than Tokyo. The real difference between the two posts, of course, was that Ambassadors in Washington were ex-Members of Cabinet who were able to exercise political pressures to secure their own comfort and convenience which Treasury was unable to resist; mere officials were different.

Besides, Treasury was introducing order into our overseas representation, under the eagle eye of a senior official brought in for that particular purpose, amongst others. I was Secretary of External Affairs when his appointment was announced. As I had had dealings with him before in another capacity, I saw the Secretary of the Treasury, Dr (later Sir Roland) Wilson, protested against the appointment and warned him of trouble ahead. He replied flippantly and perhaps believed that I was exaggerating.

By the time I reached Tokyo this special custodian of Australian financial resources for overseas posts had produced a volume of 'agreed standards' which was accepted by the Department of External Affairs. An Ambassador was entitled to a room X by Y, with a carpet A by B in size, and a desk of prescribed quality and dimensions. Everything was laid down, in hierarchical order of descent, for every member of the staff, including numbers of bedrooms, cost of curtain material and much else. The only difficulty was that in various foreign cities few or no such prescribed houses existed or were available for purchase or rent only at levels above those permitted. No matter. Every Ambassador must certify personally that the residence of each member of his staff fell within the agreed standards, and accept responsibility for the declaration.

If the standards were to be varied in any particular instance, the Head of Mission had no discretion to make his own decision; a special case must be made out, fully documented, explaining how many houses had been investigated and giving detailed reasons why the book of rules could not be observed. This involved time, energy, diversion from other work, and delay for the officer in question. Meanwhile, having investigated twenty or thirty houses in an effort to find a house within the standards, such an officer could live with his young children in a hotel at high cost to the government and considerable inconvenience and discomfort to the family, until Canberra approval for variation of the standards could be obtained. By the time approval to lease a house outside the standards was obtained, the particular house recommended had often been lost.

This rigid system only encouraged disobedience or evasion. At some posts, including Tokyo, suitable curtain material could not be bought at the limited price prescribed. So a few Heads of Mission made local arrangements for the cost of the tender for the material to be lowered and the cost of making them up increased. From the Treasury point of view that was a different matter; the price for making-up curtains was more flexible.

Eventually we had got rid of the broken-down Humber-Pullman car, for which we received the derisory offer of £30. It was bought for use as a hearse. I imposed, as a condition of sale, a term to the effect that the Australian Coat-of-Arms on the side of the car should be removed before use for its new purposes. The Humber was replaced by an American car, which I had recommended at an early stage because the vast majority of cars in Tokyo were American, and garages had grown accustomed to servicing them. But there was a long-drawn out fight with Treasury regarding the particular make of car to be bought, which had nothing to do with its cost.

I recommended one American car, which I shall call a Splendido, for sound local reasons. Treasury insisted on a Magnifico, made by a different company: I retorted that the Japanese agents were unreliable. After a suitable lapse of time, Canberra advised that Treasury had written to the makers of the Magnifico in America, who replied, oddly enough, that they had very good agents in Tokyo. In desperation I said that I would accept a Magnifico provided Treasury was informed in writing that the Japanese agents of the Magnifico had tried to bribe a member of my staff to stop him sending an adverse report to Head Office in America about the treatment accorded in Tokyo to his own private car. Treasury should also be told that if any repair work were needed for the Magnifico, I would take no responsibility for the cost of work done by the Tokyo agents, as it was notoriously inflated. Whether or not my comments were in fact conveyed to Treasury, I do not know, but the car which eventually arrived was a Magnifico.

No doubt the Magnifico was a great improvement on the Humber-Pullman, but it had its minor disadvantages. It had an enormous flat bonnet, rather like the landing-deck of an aircraft carrier, which did not improve its capacity to pass another car from the opposite direction in the narrow confines of a Japanese village street. For some time it had an unfortunate tendency to refuse to start after I had entered it to leave a diplomatic reception, with ten or fifteen of my diplomatic colleagues standing at the exit of some building anxiously waiting to leave in their own cars. Nothing deterred by the curious audience, my Japanese driver, after unsuccessfully revving the starter for some time, would leap out of the car with a hammer in his hand, open up the bonnet, tap with the hammer on some part of the engine, close the bonnet and start the car, with a smile of triumph on his face. He never quite understood my reactions to this kind of situation.

Finally, after the mudguards on one side were damaged when they were side-swiped by a Japanese car driven by someone who had had too much to drink, the Tokyo agents quoted 75,000 yen or £75 sterling for repairs. As this was the exact price which another Ambassador had predicted I would have to pay, irrespective of the actual damage, I secured a quotation from another firm and managed to reduce the cost of repairs to 47,000 yen.

One other message from Canberra raised my blood-pressure to boiling point. I was suddenly advised that my local allowance in Japan was to be reduced in order to take account of the fact that my wife sometimes used the official car for private purposes. To understand my reaction it is necessary to say something about Canberra and overseas salaries.

After I left Australia, the salaries of first division officers (Heads of Departments) were increased substantially. These increases were not adequately reflected in changes to Heads of Mission salaries. Treasury was determined to hold these at lower levels, arguing that Heads of Mission enjoyed many privileges, such as free residence, servants, an official car etc. These privileges were real, and no one would argue that every Head of

Mission abroad should receive the same salary as the Secretary, Department of External Affairs, particularly where the Missions were small and the posts less important. At the same time, the rate of salary determined one's entitlement to superannuation benefits (and obligations to contribute). I happened to be the only first division officer at an overseas post after the retirement of Colonel Hodgson, and I knew of instances when one or two Heads of other Departments posted overseas after I left Australia had carried their considerable Canberra salaries with them. In all these circumstances I did not regard my salary in Tokyo as adequate or fair.

In Singapore I had bought a small private car for personal purposes, and had taken it with me to Japan. There were quite a number of occasions, in Singapore and Tokyo, when the break-down of the official car had made it necessary to use my private car for official purposes. This fact, of course, had not been taken into account in Canberra. Nor did Canberra seem to be aware that, in substance, the wife of an Ambassador overseas has no private life so far as transport is concerned, particularly in Tokyo where the traffic was such that I would not have allowed my wife to drive a private car. The reduction in allowance which was applied to me seemed therefore unimaginative, petty and pedantic. My reaction was to send my private car back to Australia for the temporary use of one of my sons who happened to need it. Henceforth my wife and I would use only official cars, and if they were not working, one would have to be hired or a taxi used instead.

In 1971, after years of retirement administrative troubles like these seem small and unimportant; yet when they occurred they built up to a point where one became exasperated with the diplomatic life which, despite its many attractions, interests and opportunities, has serious disadvantages in bringing up a family and many strains and stresses in unusual climates and unfamiliar surroundings. I began to feel that, from the point of view of the Australian Treasury, the only crime which a diplomat could commit overseas was financial. If a Mission never overspent, and never underspent (otherwise one would be charged with over-estimating) and never contravened any financial regulation, it would be awarded full marks. The Mission could fail in every major purpose for which it had been established, but that would be irrelevant. In my experience the amount of time and energy I had to spend as Head of Mission on administrative detail seriously interfered with my competence in handling policy matters. In such circumstances it is easy to reach the point where one wants to give the game away.

On 8 November, 1959 my appointment as Australian Ambassador to the Federal Republic of Germany was announced. There was time for a few days rest and quiet in the countryside before the leave-taking began. We drove to Lake Kawaguchi where, for once, the weather favoured us. Brown tints of autumn stood out against a clear, blue lake, with Mount Fuji rising magnificently above us, capped with snow. My wife, who instinctively looks for the top of the mountain when time and opportunity permit, had always wanted to climb Fujiyama before she left Japan. I had made discouraging noises, thinking of the thousands of fellow pilgrims climbing upwards in the summer, and the bitter cold one would experience in winter. But we could drive as far as the fifth station—which we did, over rather bumpy roads and in weather such that the wind tore through our clothing and chilled us to the bone.

I simply could not stand the cold, and decided to stay inside a small shop where a hibachi* gave some measure of inadequate warmth, but Mildred wandered on into forest trees, moving upwards for an agreed period of half-an-hour. She was a little late returning, and I had begun to wonder whether I should not chase after her. I knew full well the strength of her impulse to climb to the top. With magnificent self-control, however, she returned in due course to the shop—and, I suspect, has never forgiven me for preventing her climbing the full 12,000 odd feet, frozen stiff or not.

In Tokyo I paid my final calls. We were entertained at the Palace with two other departing diplomats and a couple of new arrivals; friends arranged farewell dinners for us. One final function we gave at the Embassy brought us much pleasure. It was a regular diplomatic custom in Tokyo to invite a member of the Royal Family, excepting the Emperor, the Empress, the Crown Prince or his recently acquired wife, to a dinner. Often such gatherings were held at Korin Mansion, which belonged to one of the Royal Family, but was made available for diplomatic entertainment. There the arrangements for food and service were faultless; fifty people could be seated at table; both foreigners and Japanese would accept invitations to a dinner in honour of one of the Royal Family.

For the most part dinners, lunches or receptions were given at Korin Mansion by foreign representatives whose own residences were inadequate for purposes of entertainment—and there were many of these. But entertainment at Korin Mansion was impersonal and, so to speak, unrelated to the country of the host. Moreover, so many functions were held there that guests became somewhat blasé—every function was run equally well in precisely the same way, so that any distinctive national flavour was lost.

By attending such functions from time to time, Princess Chichibu, or Princess Takamatsu, or Princess Mikasa showed courtesy, patience and the desire to maintain contact with the foreign diplomatic community. My wife and I, however, felt that too many burdens were being imposed upon these members of the Royal Family by members of the Diplomatic Corps, often, it seemed, primarily for the purpose of lifting the status of the host. So we deliberately refrained from issuing any such invitation, even to a dinner in the privacy of the Australian Embassy where at least we could ensure that no photographers would be present.

But when we were leaving Japan and could no longer be regarded as trying to build up our own position in Tokyo, we decided to invite Princess Chichibu to a farewell dinner at the Embassy. Over a period of nearly four years, we had come to respect greatly the significant social part she played in Japan after the untoward death of her husband. She kindly agreed to come. We invited also only a small group of close friends—Japanese and foreign. It was one of our pleasantest evenings in Japan.

When I called upon the Vice-Minister for Foreign Affairs to inform him a little in advance of the impending announcement of my transfer, I took the opportunity of reminding him that Australian Heads of Mission, following

* a brazier filled with charcoal.

British precedent, were debarred from accepting foreign decorations. In many countries, including Japan, departing Ambassadors are apt to be awarded some local decoration. The British tradition is sound, stemming from the much-quoted statement of the first Queen Elizabeth that 'My dog shall wear no collar but mine own'.

Subsequently, my staff was sounded out by a member of the Imperial Household Board as to whether there was any small memento I should like to take away with me. I responded by saying that a signed photograph of the Emperor and the Empress, and of the Crown Prince and Crown Princess would be appreciated, if such were in accordance with propriety and local custom.

We were booked out to Australia by air on 4 December, 1959. Following upon experience at earlier posts, I made it clear that I would accept no invitation for a function after 30 November. I knew that I would need three full days both to recover from farewell parties and to deal with all the numerous, last-minute details, including packing.

On the afternoon of 2 December I was in my oldest clothes happily hammering down the lid of some box when Shinji San came racing upstairs breathlessly to say that an emissary from the Palace was downstairs asking to see me. I could not guess the reason for such an unusual procedure. As an old diplomatic hand, however, I showed no surprise, instructed Shinji to run into the Chancery and ask my Counsellor, then Keith Brennan, to engage the emissary in conversation and to look after his needs while I changed my clothes. As soon as I could, I made my appearance downstairs.

The visitor proved to be a well-known member of the Imperial Household Board who, after an exchange of courtesies, untied an unusually fine furozhki,* from whose folds he produced four mounted and signed photographs of the Emperor, the Empress, the Crown Prince and the Crown Princess. I expressed appropriate thanks, offered my friend a drink, and he departed.

Convinced that no such event could occur again, during the following afternoon I began to pack some precious books when Shinji San dashed upstairs with the same message as the day before. I gave him the same instructions, hastily changed again and went down-stairs wondering what was about to happen. Again, a fine furozhki was untied, and a fair-sized wooden box lifted out of its folds. I was told it contained a gift from the Emperor to my wife and myself as a token of recognition of our work in Japan. Uncertain whether I was supposed to open it in the presence of the emissary (the Japanese custom is not to open a gift in the presence of the donor), but afraid lest failure to open the box might conceivably be interpreted as a mark of indifference, I asked whether I was permitted to view the gift then and there. Being reassured on this point, I opened the box and found therein two beautiful silver vases, enclosed in white silk covers. The vases were completely plain, except for the Imperial chrysanthemum crest embossed in gold near the top.

During my stay in Japan I had tried never to accept a gift without returning a gift of equal value. But this was different. Only a Head of State,

* a large kerchief, usually of fine silk, used to wrap presents etc.

or of Government could make a return gift to the Emperor. For me to assume the right to do so would merely be an act of discourtesy. So I expressed my deepest thanks for the gift and, as the emissary departed, bowed somewhat lower than I had learned to do during the previous four years.

Before departure on 4 December, my wife and I had a last walk around the garden, and a last walk on the roof together. Yes, this had been a real home for us and we had learned much, whatever the difficulties and frustrations we had experienced. When the servants lined up to bow farewell, the human faults were forgotten and the virtues remembered—with one exception only. We drove to Haneda where we were seen off by our staff, the Chef de Protocol and a few diplomatic friends. The plane door shut tight and soon we were in the air.

The plane took a long turn inland, before heading south. Far away to our right the tip of Mount Fuji, snow-covered, hung like an ethereal scroll in a clear sky. Perhaps, then, we were destined to return someday, if only to justify the Japanese superstition. But I knew that if my wife ever did return, she would do her utmost to climb that mountain. I decided therefore that if she did return I would have to accompany her on the journey.

8

GERMANY

WE arrived in Sydney on 5 December, 1959 and spent three happy months in Australia before leaving for Germany. On arrival there was a family re-union, including one actual and one prospective daughter-in-law. The children took us to dinner at a King's Cross restaurant where, if the surroundings and service were less impressive than they would have been in Japan, the food was more familiar and more in accordance with our habits and tastes.

I retrieved my Zephyr car from John. He was now a research physicist at the Atomic Energy Commission's plant near Sydney, and had found a piece of land at Heathcote on which to build. From there it was an easy run across country to his work at Lucas Heights. The car was a valuable asset during our stay in Canberra.

Fortunately, we had been able to recover our own house in Forrest from Australian tenants who had looked after it well. Though old-fashioned and inadequate in many ways, it was a good summer house, with room enough to put up three children at a time. Mary and Peter stayed with us during their long vacation before returning to their respective colleges at Sydney University. After the humidity of Singapore and of Japan in summer months, the summer season of Canberra was a relief. If it was hot by day, the heat was far drier, while the nights were almost invariably cool enough to sleep without difficulty.

We travelled to Sydney to welcome our eldest son back to Australia after his own considerable Odyssey abroad, marked by independence, pertinacity and success. Years before Alan had left Sydney University without completing his Science course, and for a time led a roving life in different parts of the country, refusing any further assistance from me. In one capacity or another, he managed not only to earn his keep but also to accumulate quickly sufficient capital to justify planning an unorthodox tour overseas.

During my posting in Singapore he had stayed with us for three months, before moving on to India. There he reached the 10,000 foot line of the Himalayas, living on local diets. He then returned to New Delhi whence Peter Heydon, our High Commissioner to India at that time, sent me a message saying that Alan was suffering from malnutrition but would be well looked after until he recovered.

Taking a boat from India to England, Alan was employed for several years on work in the electronics field to keep the wolf from the door while studying to qualify as an electrical engineer. In due course he passed the necessary examinations and was admitted as a member of the British Institution of Electrical Engineers. He then decided to return to Australia, where he began work with an Australian firm in his new field. Soon afterwards he married an English girl whom he had met abroad. All in all, he had made a remarkable recovery from an early period of uncertainty and frustration to which our long absences overseas undoubtedly contributed.

During our three months at home I began to re-discover my own country and to re-occident myself after six years in Asia. My wife and I were well used to the change in style and status from an Embassy Residence overseas to a suburban cottage in Canberra. I recovered my proficiency with an axe, chopping wood for stove and fire-places, while Mildred adapted herself once again to the inconveniences and discomforts of local house-keeping.

I had consultations in the Department of External Affairs and with other Departments about the problems of my new post. To my great satisfaction, it was now accepted policy that Heads of Mission about to proceed overseas should see something of developments in their own country, as far as practicable, before departure. My request for permission to visit New Guinea before leaving for Singapore had been refused by Casey; now I was encouraged to visit the rocket-range at Woomera, see something of research projects at Salisbury, visit the Atomic Energy Reactor at Lucas Heights, inspect the brown coal deposits at Yallourn, and see some of the impressive hydro-electric works in the Snowy Mountains.

There was time also to read much of the biography of Konrad Adenauer, by Paul Weymar, a German edition of which I had bought in Tokyo. This tome of 750 pages had for me the double advantage of teaching me much about pre- and post-war Germany and its most important, current political personality. In addition, it widened my political vocabulary in the German language, and greatly facilitated my reading of German newspapers after arrival in Bonn. I was able to finish the book on the boat, travelling between Sydney and London.

We sailed from Sydney on 5 March, 1960 on the R.M.S. *Oronsay*, on which a comfortable cabin had been booked. The children came to see us off, but as they were now grown up and this was known by them to be our last posting, separation from them was less painful than it had been on frequent other occasions.

On my first sea-voyage to England I had read Tolstoy's *War and Peace* and acted as Sports Secretary. During the voyage I avoided all competitive sports like the plague; for physical exercise, my wife and I preferred long walks around the decks. We did much reading, and after finishing off the Adenauer Biography I read Willy Brandt's *Mein Weg nach Berlin* and *A Companion to German Studies*, edited by Jethro Bithell.

It was pleasant to call at cities around the Australian coast, to visit once more the hills behind Adelaide and to view Perth from King's Park.

At Colombo we lunched with the Australian High Commissioner and soon thereafter the ship was ploughing up the Red Sea. Many of the passengers planned to leave the *Oronsay* at Suez to make a short excursion to Cairo, rejoining the ship at Port Said. I had seen all I ever wanted to see of Cairo, but my wife had never been there. She would be interested, I knew, in the pyramids and the antiquities in the museums, so we decided to join the crowd.

It was rather a ghastly experience, never to be repeated. The interest of the contents of ancient tombs and the visual impression of pyramids and Sphinx was spoiled by crowds of beggars in the streets and the sheer black-mail of the drivers of camels or donkey-carts. We refused to join our fellow-passengers chaffering in cheap bazzars, and eventually joined a weary train to Port Said which seemed nevertheless more likely to arrive on time than broken-down motor cars. On the train we had difficulty in getting anything to eat, while we arrived at Port Said very late and had to fight for transport from the station to the wharf. We joined a launch about midnight, at some risk to life and limb. It was not oversafe and took an inordinate time to reach the ship. Much of the time I wondered whether we were going to be black-mailed (or worse) in mid-stream. There were so many small boats selling cheap merchandise tied up at the ship's landing-barge that we got aboard with some difficulty. Our cabin seemed like home.

We had just passed through the Straits of Gibraltar and turned north-wards when a radio-message from our High Commissioner in London informed us that Her Majesty the Queen would grant us an audience on a specified day. We had not sought this privilege, but I was aware that a practice had grown up in recent years permitting Australian Ambassadors passing through London on their way to new posts to 'kiss hands' on taking up their appointments. As I had not expected this experience to come my way, I had packed my formal clothes in luggage designed to remain un-opened until we reached Germany, but in London Moss Brothers came to the rescue and provided me with the necessary attire for the customary consideration. Fortunately my wife had with her a dress regarded as suit-able for the occasion.

On the prescribed day we drove to Buckingham Palace, and were taken in charge by a senior member of the royal staff, who piloted us through long corridors to a waiting-room. In due course doors to another room were thrown open. Our names were announced and we entered and crossed the room to the point where the Queen stood waiting. No British adviser accompanied us into the room, the doors of which were closed behind us. I had never before realised the constitutional significance of such an audience being given by the Queen of Australia to one of her Australian Ambassadors.

With her vast experience, the Queen quickly put us at our ease, and the conversation revolved around my postings in Japan and in Germany. Such discussions are not for the public record, but I feel I can say that they were not limited to pleasantries and formalities. I left the Palace reflecting upon the extent to which a reigning British monarch can exert personal influence without breach of constitutional proprieties.

Mildred enjoys London in the Spring, and we walked the nearby parks without the need for warnings as to the uncertain future which I had given her before we left London for Moscow in 1947. I took her to Oxford once again and on this occasion we saw much more of the colleges and their surroundings than when the twins had been with us. We stayed at the Mitre Hotel, whose historic charm was not greatly diminished by its scarcely-accessible plumbing. Addison's Walk, edged with daffodils and primroses at that time of the year, uplifted our spirits. Sir David Ross, my senior tutor as an undergraduate, had retired from the Provostship of Oriel, but we had tea with him and found him surprisingly alert in conversation for someone eighty or more.

Having completed shopping in London, we flew to Cologne, where I was met by the German Chief of Protocol and members of the staff of the Australian Embassy, with their wives. Ensconsed in the Ambassadorial car, an ancient Splendido, I noticed with alarm that the speedometer had already clocked 175,000 kilometres. Ralph, my German driver, took us to a house in the pleasant suburb of Marienburg, in which we were to struggle to survive and to operate effectively for the next two years.

The story of this house has to be told if our difficulties in Germany are to be understood. In itself it was quite ample for our needs, though it had a number of disadvantages. Most of the garden was at the rear of the house, which meant that noise from nearby passing trams was distracting both during the day and the night. There was one enormous bathroom, entered through any of four doors, in which the inhabitants of a Japanese village could have abluted collectively; unfortunately, there was no separate bathroom for any guest to use and at the same time leave us our own privacy.

Downstairs there was a pleasant L-shaped sitting room, which led to an adequate dining-room, whose windows looked out on an attractive area of lawn and garden at the rear of the house. Two maid-servants slept in attic rooms, and there were rather gruesome quarters in the basement for a butler, if one could be found. There was no laundry; no washing-machine was provided from official funds (though we had had one in Tokyo); for this reason we had taken over from our predecessors a small and quite inadequate washing-machine which had to be used in the bathroom.

The decision taken by my predecessor to recommend to Canberra that the small house he had in Bonn should be used as a Chancery and that a more ample house available in Cologne should be leased as a residence was, I soon came to believe, a serious misjudgment which haunted me throughout my time in Germany. This is not to say that there were not strong arguments to support the recommendation. Bonn has been, traditionally, a small university city which suddenly found itself the provisional capital of the Republic of Germany after the war, much to the distaste of university staff.

It was impossible to govern Western Germany from West Berlin, isolated within the borders of East Germany by a Communist government sustained by the Soviet Union. To choose another large city, such as Frankfurt, as provisional capital would risk the latter becoming the permanent capital; whereas the political aim was to insist that Berlin must at some time in the future once again become the capital of what, it was hoped, would be an undivided Germany. Konrad Adenauer, the Chancellor, was a Rhinelander, with a home at Rhöndorf, across the Rhine but not far from Bonn. In these circumstances Bonn was chosen as the provisional capital, despite the obvious shortage of housing and other inadequacies.

The immediate results of this decision were inevitable. Bonn was far too small a city for the needs of a federal government, to say nothing of a large Diplomatic Corps. The population increased rapidly, as also did costs, and there was a tremendous demand for houses, few of which were suitable as diplomatic establishments. So the Diplomatic Corps had to spread out along the banks of the Rhine and nearby, from Cologne in the north to Remagen in the south—a distance of some fifty miles. Ambassadors rented or bought houses where they could. Those who could not find adequate accommodation for entertainment gave parties at a large Club in Bad Godesberg, the Redoute, where Beethoven had played. The Redoute was to Bonn what Korin Mansion was to Tokyo.

My predecessor had his children with him, and family needs no doubt played a justifiable part in his decision. In addition, he felt that the small house in Bonn was inadequate for Australian representational purposes. A number of other Missions had residences in Cologne. After a search, he found a more suitable house in Cologne and the Department—no doubt with considerable difficulty—obtained Treasury's assent to a lease, and the provision of some funds for additional furnishing.

This arrangement involved not only him, but also me as his successor, in a daily drive from Cologne to Bonn of twenty miles, fifteen of which were along the first and worst autobahn in Germany. There was scarcely a day when I drove less than 100 miles; on one occasion I had to make the trip three times in the one day and, for special reasons, had to spend four and a half hours in the car. This expenditure of time and energy, which was required of no single member of my considerably younger staff, drove me almost to desperation at times.

Most German autobahns have their attractions, including careful grading, wide curves, the retention of greenery and the prohibition of advertising signs. Nevertheless, at their best they are risky speed-traps. I understand that the experimental autobahn built in the 1930s from Cologne to Bonn has now been re-built and greatly improved; but in my time it was far more dangerous, especially in winter, than any air-travel I have experienced. There was no protected area dividing traffic flowing south from that flowing north. In slush one might pass a truck coming in the opposite direction with a margin of six to twelve inches between the two vehicles which, as they passed, threw dirt and ice onto the respective wind-shields and confused the drivers. Time and again I have passed cars and trucks lying on their sides in the neighbouring fields.

Ralph was an excellent driver, with quick reaction times. But he was German to the core. He would obey the rules of the road, but if he himself was in the right, he was strongly tempted to plough into another car which had broken the rules. Moreover, he had a mania for speed. I learned to read his emotions by the muscles of the back of his neck. Any speed less than 50 m.p.h. distressed him beyond measure. His preference was for a speed of 70 m.p.h. and upwards. He would drive an unnecessary thirty or forty miles in order to get on to an autobahn, which would be sure to skirt attractive towns and villages with restrictive speed-limits. I would travel the same distance in order to drive on the very satisfactory, sealed, side-roads where I could enjoy village and country-side at leisure in peace and quiet.

For the first month or so I became a wretched back-seat driver, telling Ralph what to do and what not to do, and occasionally ticking him off. He would sulk and conform for a couple of days, and then step on the gas again. Eventually I gave up the struggle. On the way from Cologne to Bonn during the early morning, I would comment only in emergency; but on the return journey at the end of the day, when the narrow streets of Bonn had been negotiated and Ralph, sighting the start of the autobahn, rolled up the window and stepped on the accelerator, I taught myself to go to sleep. I only awoke if the car suddenly slowed down, as I knew that some dreadful calamity must be approaching to have induced Ralph to lift his right foot.

In short, the Cologne house might conceivably have been justified if a younger man could have endured the loss of time and expenditure of nervous energy of travelling on the autobahn to Bonn, and if the house had functioned effectively; in my time it never did—indeed, during the first nine months after my arrival it was impossible to entertain in the residence any-one other than close friends.

When we first entered the living room we saw that one of the walls was heavily marked by water stains. The reason, we eventually ascertained, was that the drains on the roof had not been cleared of leaves before the winter, which had been followed by heavy rains. The drains were the landlord's responsibility. As he had changed his mind about leasing the house and was anxious to sell it, any threat by me to abandon the house cheered him tremendously and stimulated his resistance to pressure.

Secondly, the extensive wall-to-wall carpeting which my predecessor had installed in the living-room curved into runnels like the waves of the sea. It was a wool carpet which proved to have been taped down to the floor at intervals as if it had been made of some Ersatz material. Eventually we had to have it pulled up and relaid. Sufficient to add that it took a mere nine months to complete the operation of securing Canberra assent to making our living-room presentable.

If I had my problems on the autobahn, my wife had worse. No doubt we had been spoilt in Tokyo, with a splendid house and grounds, and very competent servants. Germany, we found, was very different. The 'economic miracle' resulted in over-full employment, which had attracted northwards literally hundreds of thousands of workers from Italy, Spain, Portugal and elsewhere. Any German maids or butlers available tended to be the dregs of the local population—unreliable, lazy, quarrelsome or plain insolent.

Two more satisfactory maids had left in the interregnum before our arrival; we had to sack an objectionable and dishonest cook within weeks; another German maid was told in due course that we preferred her room to her company; we engaged a particular individual as a butler solely because no other person was procurable—he proved to be utterly untrained and 'musikalisch'. Eventually, following the advice of more seasoned diplomats in Germany, we decided that we would have to 'go Italian' or 'go Spanish and Portuguese'. At the cost of blood, sweat and tears, digestive upsets and the subsidising of salaries out of private income, we acquired at length a workable household. It consisted, first, of a Portuguese butler who could also drive my wife on occasion in the Mercedes 220 which I bought as a private car. He spoke fluent German and no English. Secondly, we hired a Spanish maid who could understand French, and a Portuguese cook who later married a German. The latter spoke an incredible scramble of French, Portuguese and German which would have made her fortune on the stage. Her conversation was excruciatingly funny, and only my wife could understand it. One awkward aspect of this set-up was that if an Australian telephoned the residence he would in the first instance be answered on the telephone by the Portuguese butler, who spoke no English. Australian visitors thought this a pretty poor show. We admitted the soft impeachment, but invited the critics to try to do better.

Finally, after three months' experience I made a formal recommendation to Canberra. In my judgment the Cologne lease should be surrendered (there would be no difficulty about that); I should lease, for the rest of my time in Germany, the best procurable house in Bonn or Bad Godesberg. This would inevitably be small, but it would be closer to the very satisfactory Chancery we had acquired on the top floor of a new, three-storey building in Godesberg. The Australian Government should purchase land on high ground on the Venusberg near Bonn or on a ridge near Godesberg and, as a longer-term operation, build an ambassadorial residence there.

After consideration in Canberra, my advice was flatly rejected. I can well understand the difficulties which the Department of External Affairs had to face. It would have been necessary to convince the Treasury that the arguments put forward by my predecessor to justify the transfer from Bonn to Cologne were wrong, or at least that subsequent developments had made continued operation from Cologne impracticable.

Yet I have not the slightest doubt that my recommendation was right. Every capital city has its own complications. In some, such as Moscow or Tokyo, the Diplomatic Corps is large and closely-knit, and frequent contacts within the Corps are essential for carrying out one's work. In Germany the situation was different. Because the Corps was scattered up and down the Rhine, close contact was impracticable. In any event, as the wife of the President and the wife of the Head of the German Foreign Office specifically confirmed to my wife, Germans did not relish attending diplomatic dinners where they were outranked, the result being that they were placed alongside juniors whom they found uninteresting. The correct course in Bonn was to operate from a small house with a minimum of servants, to invite mainly Germans to small but frequent dinners or lunches, and to keep in close touch only with those diplomatic missions, Commonwealth or other, whose interests in important respects coincided or overlapped with those of Australia.

When therefore I received the telegram from Canberra rejecting my advice, I set my teeth grimly, continued the long battle to make the house in Cologne usable, and sent a personal letter to the Secretary, Department of

External Affairs, confirming that I would not stay in Germany one day longer than the two-year period for which I had undertaken to serve.

Ironically enough, after my departure from Germany, Treasury approval was obtained for purchase of a small house on the banks of the Rhine in Godesberg, some fifteen minutes quiet driving-time from the Chancery. While this was not the right site, because in winter it was subjected to heavy mist and throughout the year its occupants had to put up with tooting barges on the river, at least my successor was saved the hopeless wear and tear of travelling on the autobahn between Bonn and Cologne.

A second problem was the official car placed at my disposal. In view of its mileage and of my experience of the autobahn to Bonn from Cologne, I strongly supported my predecessor's recommendation, made primarily for local servicing reasons, that it should be replaced by an American Magnifico. Treasury replied that we must have a Splendido of the kind I had recommended in vain in Tokyo. I pointed out that a Splendido would have to be serviced in Frankfurt, approximately 100 miles from Cologne. This would mean the loss of a car and a chauffeur for at least a day every time it was serviced. Treasury insisted that we must have a Splendido.

Eventually I agreed, informing Canberra that I was more interested in physical survival than in a particular make of car or dangerous delay. The Splendido was quite a satisfactory car in itself, but about once a month Ralph streaked to Frankfurt to have it serviced, and on such occasions we had to adapt our programmes to the cars available.

Thirdly, the Australian Treasury forced upon overseas Missions a system of accounting control which caused us endless difficulty. It was not sufficient that our budget for the financial year had been approved by the Minister for External Affairs, Cabinet and Parliament. All important expenditure had to be referred back to Treasury—as in the case of the motor-cars—for approval. From recollection, I think I had discretion to spend a maximum of £250. Further, Treasury issued financial authority to spend, from the annual budget allocation, a specified sum for each three-month period. The sum permitted, at least for the earlier quarters of the financial year, seemed to have been calculated with care somewhat below one-quarter of the approved budget for the year. But even if we had received an exact quarter, the system was ridiculous. International crises do not space themselves conveniently in such budgetary terms. An unexpected crisis—such as that in relation to Berlin—would inevitably call for expense for telegrams exceeding that for which I had authority to spend within a particular, averaged quarter. Obviously, in such a case Treasury regulations had to be ignored and the consequences faced.

If a diplomatic mission cannot function during a crisis without argument with Canberra as to expenditure of funds in a particular period of the year, it would be better to abandon the Mission. Each time my authority to spend within a particular quarter was exceeded, however, I could have been charged with having committed an offence. As someone who had had the responsibility of running the Department of External Affairs as a whole and whose record as an official should have demonstrated that I could be trusted not to abuse power or authority, I found these kinds of controls frustrating and prejudicial to my ability to do the kind of work for which I had presumably been sent abroad.

My official life in Germany began when I presented credentials to President Lübke, reading my short formal speech in German. The President replied in the same language. During the subsequent conversation an interpreter was at hand, but I found I could understand what the President said, although I needed some help in reply at this stage of my re-discovery of the German language.

After the ceremony, I was escorted back to the Chancery by police motor-cyclists. It is customary on such occasions to offer the Chief of Protocol a glass of champagne, and it is not unknown for the escort to receive some polite attention also. I was not amused, however, by the Bonn procedure according to which the Chief of Protocol, during my first visit, informed me of the range of tips which the escort should be given. I deliberately chose *not* to give the highest sum mentioned. Further, I was irritated when I received subsequently a bill for overtime worked by the police on the occasion in question. I had been the fourth and last Ambassador to present credentials that morning, and as a result the return trip to the Chancery had encroached upon the lunch-hour of the escort. To permit such a account to be sent to the Head of a foreign Mission was inconceivable in Japan or the Soviet Union. The incident helped prepare me for a degree of bluntness in dealing with German officials.

It took some time to secure an appointment with the Chancellor, Konrad Adenauer. In the meantime, I called upon thhe Dean of the Corps, who in Bonn is always the Apostolic Delegate, irrespective of the length of his service. The most important and urgent calls were those upon the British, American and French Ambassadors, all of whom, as High Commissioners for their respective countries, had special responsibilities in Berlin under war-time arrangements with the Russians. In the absence of a German Peace Treaty they, and the British, American and French Commandants in Berlin, were my obvious targets for information about any crisis in the divided city.

On the whole, my most fruitful sources were the Americans, although the British, under pressure, were frequently helpful both in Bonn and Berlin. The French Ambassador, splendidly housed in what seemed a minor palace at Remagen, always seemed slightly surprised at my interest in French policy, presumably because Australia was an Anglo-Saxon offspring; still, he appreciated my efforts to understand his country's point of view, and was patient in expounding it.

The Soviet Ambassador, I found, spoke excellent German, was personally approachable, but largely uncommunicative. The Canadian Ambassador had served in Australia and was an old acquaintance. He and his successor made themselves readily available for discussion and advice. The Japanese Ambassador proved to be a capable man whose activities and influence I soon came to respect. Several of the Scandinavian Heads of Mission, as also the Swiss Ambassador, were experienced men and useful sources of information.

My call upon Chancellor Adenauer only confirmed the impressions I had formed of him when reading his biography. As a personality he stood out from all the other political figures. His record during the Nazi period was courageous; indeed, he was lucky to be alive at the end of the war. Starting a federal political career at the age of seventy, he more than any single other German had been responsible for the recovery of Germany's international standing. Although Dr Erhardt might be entitled to claim priority of responsibility for economic recovery, he clearly lacked the political stature and judgment of Adenauer.

The Chancellor was a figure more to be respected than loved, except in his extensive family circle. Authoritarian by temperament, he was determined to get his way, and the means he employed—for instance, in speaking to journalists—showed at times no great loyalty to his colleagues; but these were minor blemishes in a great man. He had an unusual capacity, in speech and action, for simplifying issues and concentrating upon necessary means to reach desired ends. Some of his fellow-countrymen were apt to say that his vocabulary was limited to basic German. If so, he used these few words far more effectively than many others who possessed more extensive vocabularies. In Parliament, official interviews and private contacts, one sensed in him clarity, pertinacity and directness of approach. I soon came to the conclusion that the German people owed him a very great debt for his tireless work on their behalf in the post-war period.

As soon as practicable after presentation of my letters of credence, my wife and I flew to Berlin, where technically I was Head of the Australian Military Mission. There the Australian Government kept a diplomatic officer to maintain daily contact with the Berlin situation. My responsibility was to visit the city from time to time, as appropriate, for discussions with the Governing Mayor and Allied Commandants, to whom I had easier access.

Flying down the air-corridor from Hamburg to Berlin brought back to us memories of Russian days. As we emerged from an allied plane at Tempelhof airport, we were reminded once again of the uncertainty of getting 'out'. Yet after the comparative somnolence of Rhineland Bonn, we always found a visit to Berlin stimulating, even if the prevailing attitude of Berliners were somewhat cynical and harsh. The West Berliners had demonstrated their courage during the blockade of 1948-49; they continued to maintain a rather mordant sense of humour in spite of present difficulties and the uncertain future. Here music was excellent, and drama alive. West Berlin was still the real capital city of the Republic of Germany. The rubble which I had seen in 1948 had now largely been swept away; modern, high-rise flats had been erected; new churches built with impressive modern stained-glass. There were still empty spaces, and war-damaged buildings, but physical re-construction, goods available in the shops and the amount of motor traffic combined to make a striking contrast with conditions in East Berlin at that time.

In 1960 the famous wall dividing the Eastern Sector from the Western Sectors had not yet been built by the Communists. After a drive around the western perimeter, therefore, where half a street was often in one sector and the other half in another, we were able to cross into East Berlin through a check-point, under the guidance of a British military officer. Swinging along the perimeter we had been under frequent observation through field-glasses from attics in East-Berlin houses; once in East Berlin itself, we were literally behind the Iron Curtain again. Apart from the show-piece of the Stalin-Allee, whose bordering buildings exuded a Communist-Russian flavour, the general atmosphere was one of shoddiness and apathy. Buildings were in bad repair, people were in poor clothes, there was a remarkable paucity of vehicular traffic, men and women had resignation written on their faces. At the War Memorial built to perpetuate the 'liberation' of Berlin by Soviet military forces there were some impressive if over-vigorous statues which were being inspected, in separate groups, by Russian soldiers on the one hand and American tourists on the other. Only the theatre, which I managed to visit later, seemed alive—but this, too, had been typical of Moscow in our day.

I was to return to Berlin fairly frequently on official business, particularly during the crisis of the second half of 1961. In May 1960 the 'Summit' Conference in Paris attended by de Gaulle, Eisenhower, Macmillan and Khrushchev had broken down. After his meeting at Vienna in June 1961 with recently-elected President Kennedy, Khrushchev publicly demanded that a settlement of the Berlin and German questions 'must be attained this year'; otherwise the Soviet Union would sign a separate Peace Treaty with East Germany, with whose Government the Western Allies would then have to negotiate questions of access to Berlin. Increasing restrictions upon such access led eventually to Russian pressure on the air-corridors, which constituted the final life-line connecting West Berlin with the outside world. Tension mounted, and it became my responsibility to keep Canberra informed of the worsening situation in Berlin.

Our daughter Mary had joined us in Germany in January 1961 for what proved to be a visit of about nine months. She had taken an Arts degree at Sydney University, one of her main subjects being Music. In Cologne she was able to spend a very useful Semester at the well-known Hochschule für Musik, whose capable Director, Professor Schröter, was kind enough to take her as one of his own limited number of piano pupils. Mary's presence encouraged us to make family arrangements for leave in the United Kingdom during the summer, spending two of three weeks at the Edinburgh Festival, which Mary was keen to attend. I sent Mildred and Mary ahead of me to London, arranging to join them about mid-August.

On 13 August, 1961, Soviet and East German authorities sealed off East Berlin from the Western Sectors, thus cutting off the escape route to the West through which some two or three million Germans had 'voted with their feet' against Herr Ulbricht's regime by fleeing to the West. This action took the Western Allies completely by surprise. There was an immediate crisis. Would the West Berliners take the situation lying down, or would they try to storm across the flimsy barricades? Should British, American and French tanks take the incalculable risks of demolishing the barriers? As the news reached me in Cologne, I saw my carefully-prepared and somewhat costly family plans going up in smoke yet once again.

On this rare occasion, fortune favoured, if not the brave, at least the bold. I waited for two days in Cologne, by which time I judged that the population of West Berlin would be restrained by their own authorities from physical violence across the barriers. In these circumstances it did not seem likely that British or French policy would approve action which, conceivably at least, could lead to an atomic war. As I had earlier cleared with Canberra my departure from my post, I cabled the Prime Minister (who was then holding the portfolio of External Affairs, following the elevation of Mr Casey to a life peerage) expressing my view that the Berlin situation was unlikely now to get out of hand. I added that I was flying to London to join my family as planned, but that I would return to Germany immediately if the Government felt this was necessary. I knew, of course, that prime responsibility for decision would rest on the British, American and French Governments, and that these decisions would be taken, not in Bonn or Berlin, but in London, Washington and Paris. Solely because Menzies was Minister, I incorporated in the telegram a somewhat vain sentence which I would not have sent to anyone else: 'In my judgment there is time to finish my game of bowls'. I had no illusion that Menzies would see in me a modern Sir Francis Drake, but he at least would recognise the reference. In London I joined up with my wife and daughter, and waited for the reply. It came in a telegram giving me generous permission to proceed to Edinburgh, subject to recall if the Berlin situation deteriorated.

So we 'did' our Festival, became saturated with music, and watched two splendid performances by the Old Vic Company of Shakespeare's *King John* and Marlowe's *Dr Faustus*. As a true scion of Scotland I, but not the members of my family, responded duly to a massed-bagpipes performance at night high up on Edinburgh Castle. There was even time for a quick run to Arrochar to see Scottish relatives, Commander and Margaret Bayliss. Then we sped back to Cologne via London, and I hastened to Berlin.

In the isolated city I found the situation quiescent, but extremely sad. Barbed-wire now separated Eastern and Western Sectors; from mounds of earth near the eastern barrier West Berliners waved handkerchiefs to relatives on the farther side, under the watchful eyes of East German soldiers; I heard grim tales of East Germans who had tried to escape to the West despite the wall, and what had happened to those who had not been successful. Except for the unusually bold and imaginative, the 'escape-hatch' was closed. The fifty thousand Grenzgänger who had crossed the border each day to work in the Western Sectors no longer came. Visits from one side to the other, with rare exceptions, were barred. East Germany was now like the Soviet Union—a country whose population was isolated from the world at large and, in a significant sense, a prison. I returned to Cologne and reported to Canberra.

During later visits to Berlin I was greatly assisted in my judgment of the developing situation by two men, namely, General Lucius Clay, whom President Kennedy had appointed his personal representative in Berlin at the end of August, and General Delacombe, British Commandant in Berlin and now Governor of the State of Victoria. General Clay was a man of courage and initiative whose past record in Berlin eminently qualified him to handle a dangerous situation. He was not the sort of person to be intimidated by Soviet pressure or bluff. At one stage he had sent American tanks to the border, where they faced Russian tanks muzzle to muzzle. Later, he ordered his tanks to be withdrawn for half-a-mile. The Russians followed suit, and the world Press hailed this as a diminution of tension. When I questioned Clay about this, he roared with laughter at the Press interpretation. 'When opposing tanks stand muzzle to muzzle', he commented, 'a position from which they have never fought one another, the Press gets excited and talks of the danger of war. When they withdraw half-a-mile, taking up positions from which they really could fight, the Press speaks of a diminution of tension. Don't take too much notice of the Press. Better come to talk to me or my staff.'

Gradually, and largely on the basis of information given me by General Delacombe, I came to realise that the main crisis was not on the ground but in the air. Playing Russian roulette in the air-corridors was not funny, as the Soviet challenge there had to be countered. The Soviet authorities were now applying ground-type salami tactics to the air-corridors, with considerable ingenuity.

Originally, the Soviet Union and the three Western Powers had filed flight-plans with the four-power Air Safety Centre in Berlin, where all four were represented even after serious differences on policy regarding Germany and Berlin had arisen, and the Russians had ceased to file their own flight plans. The practice had grown up of the three Western Powers only filing flight plans, normally for flights at heights from about 8,000 to 10,000 feet. These plans were communicated to the Soviet member of the Centre, who no doubt checked with Soviet authorities. If he raised no objection, the flight plans were regarded as approved. Russian planes might criss-cross the corridors at any time at a height above 10,000 feet, and perhaps well below 8,000 feet. Such flights were not notified in advance to the Centre, but there was no risk of accident, unless Russian planes deliberately 'buzzed' Allied planes flying at approved altitudes. In such latter cases the Russians could be charged with aggressive action.

During the worst of the crisis of 1961, however, the Russians began to adopt a more subtle form of pressure. They filed flight plans once again, for flights within the altitudes which past practice had reserved for Allied planes. At first the plans might be for single, or a small number of flights, at times which would not cut across Allied time-tables. Then they would step up the number of flights to a point where Allied flights would be affected; or claim sole use of a corridor for half-an-hour, an hour, or longer. If these requests were granted, use of the corridors by Allied planes would be diminished until the point could conceivably be reached when the corridors were useless to the Allies. All this would be done under a claim of right, perhaps during a period of alleged manoeuvres.

Despite some hesitation in London and Paris, the Western Commandants —spearheaded by General Clay—felt that this serious challenge to the continuing viability of West Berlin had to be resisted, and there were occasions when Allied military planes were sent through corridors at the same height and time as announced Russian flights, the Soviet authorities having been warned in advance. It must be remembered that during the winter season many flights took place in mist or fog, so that the risk of collision in such cases was high. As there were no such collisions, presumably on these occasions the Western Powers successfully called the Russian bluff; but this was a dangerous operation, the success of which could scarcely be predicted in advance.

Eventually the situation eased as Khrushchev decided not to carry out his threat to sign a Peace Treaty with Eastern Germany before the end of the year, and pressure on the air corridors was relaxed. It was my job, however, not only to explain the Russian tactics to Canberra, but also to point out that similar pressure designed to constrict or strangle the Allied air routes to Berlin could be re-imposed at any time the Soviet Union so decided. If such pressure were maintained irrespective of Allied reactions in Berlin—of which public opinion in Britain, the United States and France was unaware —serious incidents could occur which would be difficult to prevent escalating into war.

Such reporting upon the Berlin problem was the only aspect of my time in Germany in regard to which I felt I was fully earning my keep. It involved, of course, not only visits to Berlin, but regular contact with the Allied Ambassadors in Bonn and with the German Foreign Office, close attention to reports and comments in newspapers (and the quality of the best newspapers in West Germany is very high indeed) and regular attention to television coverage of events in Berlin.

At that date the Australian Treasury still obstinately refused to regard a television set, as distinct from a grand piano, as a diplomatic tool of trade. In Japan I had bought my own set, which enabled me to write one whole despatch on one important occasion, watching the set off and on throughout the day. I did not take my set to Germany, because the voltage was different there; so I bought another set in Cologne which I used almost exclusively for official purposes.

The second major problem in the handling of which I should have hoped to be of some use to Canberra was Britain's first application to join the European Economic Community. Here, however, my hands were tied behind my back—as, I understand, were the hands of other Australian diplomatic representatives in the capital cities of the European Six. I soon drew the inference that this subject was to be regarded as the private property of the Minister for Trade, and of the Secretary of his Department. They alone were to be trusted to deal with it—through public statements, or through personal negotiation at home or overseas—with the sole exception of the Prime Minister of Australia if and when he so chose. Mr Menzies was indeed concerned with the political implications for the Commonwealth of Nations of a successful British application, and made strong and effective statements on the subject. No doubt he was also concerned about the economic implications for Australia, but the handling of this aspect was left, in the main, to Mr McEwen.

In the early stages I was surprised and pleased to receive a telegram from the Department of External Affairs seeking my personal views, and the views of other relevant Australian Ambassadors, on the British application. Such a telegram to an Australian Mission overseas is rare enough to stimulate a quick response, which I readily gave. In the result, the views I expressed had no effect upon Government policy, and I assume they did not please the Department of Trade. I had no complaint at the rejection of my views, but I did object to being expected to report at length on the attitude of the German government towards the British application and Australian reservations, without being provided with sufficient background information on Australian policy or being authorised to do more than ask questions of the Germans.

I regarded this attitude in Canberra as regrettable, because I found the chief economic adviser in the German Foreign Office very ready to discuss Australia's problems if Britain were admitted to the Common Market. But any experienced diplomat knows that if he wants to receive valuable information or comments, he himself must have something to give. On one occasion I received instructions to ascertain German reactions to what had happened at a meeting in London of Commonwealth Finance Ministers, when I had received no confidential information as to what took place at the meeting, let alone any permission to disclose it to the German Foreign Office.

There were no other outstanding problems which occupied my time and energy during my posting in Germany, apart from general reporting, although there was never time to deal adequately with routine matters with the staff available. As to normal trade questions, my Commercial Counsellor was competent, friendly and more than ready to work with me. Our Department of Immigration had a large group of people based in Cologne, and the officer in charge of them was in regular touch with me. Incidentally, as Head of Mission I was supposed to certify that the houses occupied by all his Australian staff were within the agreed standards.

Whenever I could I left Bonn to gain experience of West Germany as a whole. At the Krupp factories in the Ruhr I found the latest owner, Alfried Krupp von Bohlen, completely different in temperament and outlook from the original Krupp, whose armaments had contributed substantially to Germany's victory over France in 1870. After the Second World War Alfried Krupp had decided that the firm would make no more armaments, a fact which was conveniently ignored by those Australians who protested against a visit he had made to Australia. He was a quiet, cultured man, especially interested in colour-photography, and I value the two books of photographs, copies of which he gave me, published privately as mementoes of visits to Australia and to Japan. Inspection of the Krupp factories also made it clear how much attention was given to the welfare of employees.

Visits were also made to the Siemens factories in Berlin, and to various factories in Hamburg and Bremen. These latter ancient, Hanseatic cities were particularly interesting. Their chief citizens seemed far more independent in spirit and more conscious of the world outside Germany than Rhinelanders in Cologne or Bonn. Both cities in the north had been heavily damaged by bombing during the war, but the inhabitants and their governing authorities had girded their loins and set to work to re-build and re-establish shipping and overseas trade without the resentment I had heard expressed by those who had suffered in Aachen and Dresden. Bremen's natural advantages seemed limited to a site on the river Weser not far from the North Sea; yet through magnificent planning of dockyards and loading facilities business had been attracted.

During our first year in Germany my wife and I accepted the annual invitation to members of the Diplomatic Corps to attend sailing and other festivities at Kiel, stopping off at Hanover and Braunschweig on the way north, and pausing at Kassel on the return journey to enable me to give a lecture on Australia. While at Kiel a special train was organised to take visitors to Schleswig, where we inspected relics of ancient Viking long-boats which provided visible evidence of their porterage across the narrow neck of land separating the Baltic from the North Sea.

Whenever practicable, I made contact of one kind or another with German Universities. In West Berlin I saw something of the 'Free Univer-sity' established there after the war; on several occasions we passed through the town of Göttingen, described by Heine as 'famous for its sausages and its university'. Bonn, of course, was close at hand and members of the Diplo-matic Corps attended occasional university functions. In Bonn the most attractive buildings were those parts of the university housed in the old residence of the Elector of Cologne.

The greatest personal pleasure I experienced in Germany was the opportunity to take my wife to places which had meant so much to me as a young man, especially Heidelberg and the Black Forest (Schwarzwald).

Our arrival in Germany in April 1960 was perfect timing for one unusual event—the passion play at Oberammergau. We found it was current practice for the Heads of Diplomatic Missions in Bonn, together with their wives, to receive invitations from the German Government to attend the opening performance of the play. So in mid-May Mildred and I started off by road in the senescent Embassy car.

I had arranged to break the journey in Heidelberg for a day. Inquiries in Bonn elicited the opinion that 'Heidelberg is not what it used to be.' 'It is now an American city'. The last thing I wanted to do was to take my wife to a place which had lost its perennial attraction for me, but I doubted the accuracy of the comments. Moreover, before we left Tokyo our German doctor there, who had a son in Heidelberg, had assured us we would find the hillsides, the old castle and the old bridge untouched; these had not been damaged in the war, and could scarcely be changed by the presence of American tourists or nearby troops.

At long last we approached the Heidelberg hills, and I was on tenterhooks in case a precious memory was about to be destroyed by current reality. As we approached the city there were indeed signs of less pleasant change, but I had arranged for us to be booked into the Schloss Hotel, high on the hill, whence we could look down on castle, church-spires, the old bridge and the swift-flowing Neckar. Our accommodation was supposed to have doors opening upon a small verandah whence we could enjoy this vista. As soon as the porter had placed our bags in the room and departed, I flung open the doors to the verandah and, to my great satisfaction, found the scene almost identical with that I had enjoyed thirty-five years earlier. For me the words of Hölderlin's poem on Heidelberg still rang true.

The afternoon was too short for all I wanted to do. After a hasty lunch we took the cable-car up to Königstuhl, and walked down along paths covered with pine-needles. Unfortunately the weather had clouded over somewhat, and gathering mist blurred the glorious view from the summit over pine-forests towards the river, winding its way across the plain. More could be seen from the terrace within the castle grounds, but we did not delay as daylight would not last long. We descended to river level, crossed the old bridge and climbed to the Philosophenweg on the farther bank, pausing now and then to enjoy the matchless view back across the river over the bridge to the castle. Having completed the walk along the Philosophenweg, we crossed the river by the New Bridge, passed through the old town and climbed slowly to our hotel. Dinner was followed by early retirement and a long night's sleep.

We awoke early, opened the door to the verandah and found the mist cleared and the morning sun bringing up the colour in the pinkish stone which is a dominant feature of Heidelberg's buildings. There was just time to slip downhill to the castle again, where I took colour-photographs and Mildred explored courtyards and grounds. Ralph was waiting when we returned, and soon we were winding our way through the cobbled streets of the old town until we reached newer roads and eventually joined the autobahn once again.

At length we reached Oberammergau, with its charming houses decked with outer-wall paintings. Visitors poured from the railway station. Ralph sought directions to the place where we were staying: it proved to be an inn, of farmhouse style, a little distance from the village. There we found a warm reception and were shown into a simple but spotless room with windows looking on one side up a pleasant valley and on the other side to the distant mountains.

Ralph was despatched to procure a German text of the Passion Play which, oddly enough, had not been procurable in Bonn. After tea on the terrace where the thermometer registered a surprising 78°, we explored the village, noted the wood-carvings for sale in the shops and tried to suppress our vulgar amusement at the thought that the long-haired shop attendant might tomorrow be playing the part of Judas. The village church, with its simple, attractive exterior, horrified us by the profusion of its baroque ornamentation inside.

Next morning we started out early for the performance, which began at 8.15 a.m. Outside the building someone was selling newspapers, and I saw the headline 'Khrushchev's Ultimatum'. However, the crowd was too dense to try to stop to buy a paper. Our seats inside were towards the rear of a large, roofed amphitheatre. The roof covered only the spectators and the stage was open. Beyond the stage the distant mountains could be seen.

We had come to Oberammergau prepared to be disillusioned. We feared that the simple, forceful words of the Biblical story would be overlaid by more complicated, modern verse. The Passion Play was now big business—how could so many people from all over the world be organised without art degenerating into propaganda? We were pleasantly surprised with what we saw and heard. From 8.15 a.m. until 5.30 p.m., with a two-hour break for lunch, we sat and listened. The frequent still tableaux were impressive;

the acting was natural. But most surprising was the quality and quantity of the music. All the singers were from the village, and although they had obviously had training they were not professionals. Yet they performed well, and the music helped to sustain interest. On our way back to the inn, I bought a newspaper and read of the breakdown of the Summit Conference in Paris. Having purchased a few small wood-carving mementoes, we returned to Cologne.

Twice during our stay in Germany we escaped on short leave from the diplomatic round and the frustrations of the house in Cologne, spending ten days in the Schwarzwald and a week in Bamberg. Heads of Australian Missions overseas, irrespective of climate and responsibilities, were entitled to the same three weeks' annual leave granted to a messenger boy in Canberra.

On 13 April, 1961 I celebrated my sixtieth birthday. No birthday in my adult years gave me greater satisfaction. Henceforth I could retire from the Commonwealth Public Service and at least survive on a pension. By that stage the spur of family needs had slackened considerably, and my frustration over administrative red-tape had dampened any ambition for further advancement in the diplomatic service. Indeed, I had lost much confidence in Ministers of the Crown and in my own Department and felt that they had probably come to regard me as a complaining nuisance.

To mark my birthday I suggested to my wife that we should 'play hookey' for a day, leave my jurisdiction without permission and drive to Keukenhof in Holland to see the tulips. She was somewhat surprised at this unaccustomed revolutionary attitude on my part, but readily agreed; so we set out with Mary.

Ralph was delighted at the prospect of pressing down the accelerator of our new Splendido, and at 9 a.m. we shot off like greased lightning. In two hours we had reached the Dutch border, having passed through the industrial haze of the Ruhr valley en route. The autobahns in Holland proved just as crazy as those in Germany so far as speed and risk were concerned, but the houses were smaller and more cheerful, their gardens gay with flowers and alive with children. At Haarlem we paused for lunch in a pleasant restaurant, finding Dutch food somewhat easier to eat and enjoying, for a change, the competent English of the waiter. Outside the window was one of Holland's innumerable canals, in which the spring-green of trees was reflected.

On the farther side of Haarlem we passed miles of open fields brilliant with the colour of massed hyacinths or tulips. The tulips were of every shade. On both sides of the road they provided ample evidence of Dutch initiative and industriousness.

At Keukenhof we left the car and entered the park let by the owner to firms of bulb exporters for public display. Here the flowers were seen to the best advantage. There were also hothouses bursting with brilliant tulips. What a contrast with the iris display in the Meiji Gardens of Tokyo, where the effect is predominantly aesthetic. However, we were not at all critical. It was more than a year since we had seen a blaze of Australian flowers, and the Dutch commercial instinct able to profit from such an improbable field of activity aroused our admiration. By the end of the long trip back to

Cologne we were completely exhausted. My rebellious spirit was curbed, and I began to think about what I could usefully do during the gradual run down-hill of my last year of official service.

My second year in Germany was much happier than my first. I had paid my calls, established my contacts, could return entertainment in the Cologne residence, and had a reasonable chance of survival in a new car on the autobahn between Cologne and Bonn. The American Embassy was consistently helpful and the British Embassy reasonably so. I found high-level officials in the German Foreign Office, with one of whom I played occasional tennis in Bonn when weather permitted, both competent and ready to talk. I should have liked to see more of Adenauer, but only the British, Americans, French and Russians had more or less automatic access to him—for obvious reasons, in view of their special responsibilities stemming from the war. So my news of his attitudes came from some of these foreigners, from statements in Parliament (sessions of which I attended on important occasions when practicable) and from the media.

I found the contrast between the Japanese Diet and the German Parliament interesting. The tradition of both countries had been authoritarian, and democratic forms and practices could scarcely be regarded as well-established in either. Nevertheless, political democracy seemed to me to be much further advanced in Germany than in Japan. In the lower German House (Bundestag) a Minister felt at least bound to argue his case, as distinct from merely stating it. The reasons he advanced for a particular policy would quickly be challenged by the Opposition, forcing the Government to give a considered reply to particular points raised. Of course, Germany as a Western European country had inherited a Greek tradition of argument which the Japanese had not, while I was able to follow the proceedings in Germany without the services of an interpreter.

The constitution of the Upper House (Bundesrat) was also interesting. Although the different states (Länder) of the Federation were represented, the method of representation was quite different from that of the Australian States. Comparable representation in Australia would have resulted in the Premiers of our various States being present personally in our Senate, participating in Federal legislation, and able to take the initiative in introducing Bills. I felt that Australia might have something to learn from such a method, which could well reduce tensions between federal and State governments.

I accepted occasional invitations to address educational and other institutions and usually arranged for a couple of Australian documentary films to be shown at the same time. In Berlin, some 800 people attended such a lecture on Australia under the auspices of the Urania Society. I spoke in German, and the response was immediate when I was able to quote the views of the Australian Prime Minister on the world significance of West Berlin, then subjected to heavy Soviet pressure. Visits to Berlin also enabled me to maintain contact with Willy Brandt, its Governing Mayor, whose political views differed from those of the governing Christian Democratic Party.

There were also a few personal pleasures for my wife and myself, as we came to know our way about and what was going on. Neither of us cared for the atmosphere of Cologne, typified at its worst by Rosenmontag celebrations. Carnival time in Cologne was highly commercialised, and lacked the attractive simplicity of carnivals in smaller German cities and the sophistication of festivals in cities on the French Riviera. Nor was the Opera or drama in Cologne anything like as good as that in Berlin or Hamburg. Yet in Cologne there were musical performances of high quality. There were excellent chamber music concerts. For us, however, the most enjoyable concerts were those organised by the Bachverein. These included performances of the Matthew Passion, the Mass in B. Minor, and the Christmas Oratorio, during which massed choirs and competent orchestras gave splendid renderings of Bach's major choral works, sometimes in Churches rather than concert halls. At the conclusion of the concerts there was no applause, because these were regarded as religious ceremonies.

In September 1961 we accepted an official invitation to the opening of the new Opera House in Berlin. This was to be a significant political occasion, attended by the President of the Federal Republic and members of the Cabinet. It marked not merely the re-building of something which had been destroyed, but also symbolised the determination of the West Berliners to survive and of the West German Government to maintain its claims in Berlin and to encourage the inhabitants. However, as the situation in the air-corridors was tense, we left Mary behind—to her great disappointment.

We flew down the corridor without incident, and my wife and I were soon comfortably ensconced in 'our flat' which formed part of the house occupied by a member of my staff and his wife and family who were based in Berlin. Before the ceremony at the Opera House we had time to inspect parts of the 'wall'. When first erected it had consisted mostly of barbed wire; it was now taller, thicker and stronger, sporting a considerable amount of concrete. Where houses of East Berlin abutted on streets which formed part of the Western Sectors, basements and first-floor windows had been bricked up, while all other windows were kept shut. Much of the Western world had seen photographs of an elderly woman who had tried to jump from an upper window into the arms of friends waiting below. East Berlin soldiers or police had held her by the hands as her body dangled over the pavement. Other East Germans had successfully tunnelled under the wall, or risked swimming across a lake, but many had been shot in the process. The mood of West Berliners standing in groups watching the border was angry and resentful. They glared at armed Vopos on the other side whose nonchalance seemed rather forced. Clearly it would not take much for this resentment to flare into violence.

In the evening we joined the throng of cars crawling to the theatre entrance. The building itself was not particularly impressive outside, but inside it was modern, bright and ample, while the stage had everything which opened and shut. The only disturbing aspect, for me, was a feature of most modern German theatres: the circles above the rear stalls contain a number of toboggan-like structures, holding six or eight people and inclined downhill, looking for all the world as if the toboggan was just about to hurl itself upon the unoffending audience below.

Somewhat to my surprise, Fischer-Dieskau gave a convincing performance as Don Giovanni. The staging was excellent, and the principal singers, with one exception, impressive. The political atmosphere of the occasion and the surrounding tension in Berlin inevitably coloured the reactions of both players and audience, so that it was not possible to judge the production solely from an artistic point of view. Clearly Berliners, both inside and outside the building, were greatly cheered by the fact that the President of the Republic and foreign representatives were present. In short, the performance served its purpose, and we were glad we had been present. After a large reception given by the Oberbürgermeister, Willy Brandt, we got to bed about 1 a.m. As we flew back to Cologne I could not help reflecting upon the fact that, unlike the Sydney Opera House, the new Opera House in Berlin had cost a mere £4 million sterling, and had taken only a couple of years to build.

Early in October 1961 we drove to Frankfurt to put Mary on the plane for Australia. Although she had not taken kindly to the diplomatic life in any country, she had been much happier in Germany than in Japan— partly because much of her time and energy was taken up with piano-study at the Cologne Conservatorium. The house in Cologne seemed empty when we returned, and we missed the sound of the piano, as we had missed the sound of the twins' flutes in Tokyo. There was work for me to do, however, explaining the rapidly-changing political situation to Canberra.

In September the Christian Democratic Party had lost its majority in Parliament and had to bargain in order to form a coalition government, either with the small Free Democratic Party or the larger Social Democratic Party. The bargaining continued for at least a month, and during this period Adenauer maintained an obstinate silence on matters of policy. In the process his prestige began to diminish, and although in due course a bargain was in fact struck with the Free Democrats, I felt that a turning-point was at hand in the local post-war situation.

While the Chancellor's silence continued, I was struck with the part played by the more responsible German Press. Through editorials, special articles and reports from overseas correspondents these newspapers gave a lead to public opinion, exerted influence on the negotiating parties, and at times seemed almost to be the Government.

Before the end of the year we began to plan our departure from Germany in March 1962. After the climate of the Rhineland, we wanted to take my remaining leave in sunshine, preferably in the Mediterranean area, the source of European civilisation. It was impracticable to go as far afield as Persia or Palestine, but we felt that Greece was reasonably close to our homeward route, as we could fly back to Rome and pick up an Orient Line ship at Naples.

I wrote to Canberra about my plans and was astonished to receive a reply expressing broad approval and suggesting that I should make brief official visits to four countries with which we had diplomatic relations without having established diplomatic Missions.

I am afraid that I quickly thought up less worthy motives for the proposal, but I hastily assented before there could be any change of mind.

Mildred and I had every desire to visit Vienna, Belgrade, Athens and Ankara even though, to catch our ship at Naples, we would have to reduce our holidays in Greece by one week.

The first three months of 1962 passed swiftly. I knew that my official career was coming to an end, and that nothing short of a world war or a serious international crisis for Australia would change my decision to retire at the age of sixty-one. Moreover, by now I had not only another ambition, but another opportunity to realise it. For me retirement had never meant concentration on pruning roses. Within the limits imposed upon an ex-official, I wanted to exercise some influence upon public opinion in the field of foreign policy. In particular, I wanted to write a record of Australian foreign policy during the twenty-five years of my public service. The technique of doing this without breach of official confidence had still to be worked out, but the opportunity to try had come. With the help of Sir John Crawford, sometime Secretary, Department of Trade and then Director, Research School of Pacific Studies, Australian National University, I had been invited to become a Visiting Fellow in the Department of International Relations for two or three years, during which my book was to be written.

In my early years of official service, superannuation provisions for Commonwealth Public Servants had been incredibly inadequate. Gradually the benefits (and personal contributions) were raised until, by 1959, the benefits had become respectable, though far from princely. In order to qualify at my age for higher benefits, I had to contribute a large proportion of my salary for several years. This became practicable as my children passed from the university stage and began to earn their own living. I knew that when I returned to Canberra I would be involved in substantial capital expense putting our house in order after occupation by tenants for eight years, but the additional income as a Visiting Fellow would substantially reduce the difficulty of doing this, especially when added to a capital sum I was entitled to claim from the Government in lieu of long-service leave.

In mid-February my wife and I flew to Berlin to make farewell visits there. Conditions in the air-corridors were still somewhat tense. The Russians had been demanding that the corridors should be closed during their own alleged military exercises, and a plane carrying the British Ambassador and Lady Steele to Berlin had been approached rather too closely by a Soviet M.I.G. Our flight was uneventful, except that we seemed to fly rather higher than usual and at one stage we had a couple of American jets as apparent escorts. Soon we were settled in at the house made available to the Australian Military Mission, then occupied by Alf Parsons and his family. Here we were to indulge in somewhat wider entertainment than usual as part of the farewell exercises.

I paid my official call upon Willy Brandt and the three Western Commandants, and my wife and I were entertained at lunch by General Sir Rowan and Lady Delacombe in the beautiful lake-side house they were soon to leave. The General had been far more friendly and helpful to me than his Foreign Office advisers in Berlin, who had mostly served only on the 'inner circle' and found it difficult to understand why Australia should be kept informed on German problems. Our host's job in Berlin had not been an easy one, as he had to carry out a British policy which was less adventurous than the American, while at the same time maintaining friendly relations with the Americans, whose respect he had succeeded in retaining. This was a considerable diplomatic achievement for a soldier by trade.

A large cocktail party enabled us to make some return for past courtesies to a wide range of people. This was followed on a later evening by a dinner to which we invited the Willy Brandts, the Delacombes, some members of the staffs of Allied Military Missions and others. The dinner happened to coincide with the scheduled return to earth of the first American astronaut to orbit the earth. In the Berlin atmosphere we were all tense, as an untoward accident on re-entry or splash-down would affect American prestige. When we sat down at table I kept a transistor-radio by my right foot, ready to be turned up when the crucial moment arrived. Fortunately all went well, and my guests relaxed. The astronaut would have been surprised to know how closely the successful end of his mission had been followed in West Berlin, and how much this had encouraged the local population.

While I was engaged on official visits, my wife was taken over the Documents Centre, where a barrack-like building was enclosed by a high wall topped with barbed-wire and guarded by a sentry. The American in charge, a member of his own country's foreign service, told her that the records contained, *inter alia*, some nine million Nazi Party cards. There were also records evidencing the racial purity of party members, required before marriage, and documents relating to judicial processes during Nazi times.

A final recollection of Berlin is the performance of Lessing's play, *Nathan der Weise*, at the new Schiller theatre. The building itself was modern, functional and pleasing; the acting first-class. This is an eighteenth century play, somewhat stilted in language and faulty in construction. Fundamentally, it is a play of ideas rather than of character, a plea for religious tolerance, put forward eloquently by a Jew. To me the most interesting aspect of the performance was that the play was put on at all in post-war Germany. This showed a degree of courage in facing up to the crimes of Germany's Nazi past, and was in line with the series of some fifteen documentary films of the Nazi period which I had seen on national television. Some of the films were gruesome, and many German viewers must have found them highly unpleasant to watch. Although it would be idle to pretend that there is now no anti-Jewish prejudice in Germany, one must in fairness recognise the efforts of the Adenauer government to diminish it.

During my last days in Bonn it was not difficult to secure from Heads of relevant Diplomatic Missions some understanding of my decision to retire four years before necessary. British Ambassadors retire at the age of 60, and sometimes earlier. I could not, of course, give precise reasons for retirement, but my colleagues knew that I had led a busy life in strenuous posts, and appreciated my desire for greater freedom of decision and activity.

It was more difficult to explain to Germans why I was departing. I was reminded that I had been in Bonn only a short time. Now that I had learned my way about, it was a pity that I was leaving so soon; after all, I was not so old. All these comments had point, and I could only stress my desire to write on foreign policy in the hope that I could have some influence on Australian public opinion. I also took the opportunity, when paying farewell calls on Germans, of trying to stress Australia's predicament as a country of predominantly European descent and cultural tradition, permanently anchored off Southeast Asia, one of the most turbulent areas in the world. This enabled me to add that I hoped in retirement to help my fellow countrymen understand this situation better, calling as it did for more flexibility in policy and tolerance in outlook.

In all cases but one I felt that I had some success in securing understanding of Australia's special problems and of my own point of view. When the Chancellor, Dr Adenauer, expressed mild surprise at my impending departure and asked me what I proposed to do, I tried to explain that I would become a Visiting Fellow at the Australian National University and would have time to do research and to write. Unfortunately the description 'Visiting Fellow' simply does not translate into German, and he concluded that I wanted to become a 'Professor'. Under further questioning by him, I took the risk of being flippant, saying that he must take some responsibility for my decision. At the age of seventy, according to his biography, he had begun a new career: this had encouraged me to do likewise at the age of 61. He took the comment in good part, shook hands, and wished me well.

Both the Foreign Minister, Dr Schröder, and the Head of the Foreign Office, Professor Carstens, listened patiently to my account of Australia's problems and showed some interest in them, but when I tried the same line during my formal call upon the President of the Republic, Heinrich Lübke, I had no success whatever. Australia, he told me, was a land of 'Friede und Sonnenschein' (peace and sunshine). I accepted this as a description of the current situation, but stressed the difficulties of Australian survival over the long-term in anything like its present form. He roundly rejected this approach as well, in such positive terms that I found myself beginning to get annoyed. I had to remind myself that I was still a representative of the Australian Government and that it was not my function to have an argument with the President of the country to whom my successor would have to present credentials. I therefore turned the conversation to matters I had found of special interest in the past two years, and expressed thanks for numerous courtesies received. Though we both relaxed, I left somewhat irritated by the rigidity of his attitude. Back in the Chancery I looked up President Lübke's record and found that, between the years 1933-35 he had been 'deprived of all offices and imprisoned'. With such recollections his references to Australia became more understandable.

On 22 March, 1962 we left Cologne by road for Frankfurt in the official car. I had been asked to speak at the opening of a Qantas office in that city, after which we were to proceed by road to Vienna and Belgrade. Before we left we were given an early morning farewell at the residence by members of my staff and a few friends, including the new Japanese Ambassador and Mrs Narita. Sylvina, the Portuguese maid who had helped save our establishment, was in tears as she gave Mildred a small bunch of red carnations. We too were sorry to leave friends and helpers, but we had no regrets at all at leaving the Ambassadorial Residence in Cologne. Our experience there had been worse than in any other official house in which we had lived overseas, except in Moscow, where conditions were much more excusable and far more difficult to change.

Departure from a post is always an exhausting business, and I was extremely tired during the wintry journey to Frankfurt, which we had to reach by 10.30 a.m. I felt my pockets to make sure that I had with me both my spectacles and the notes for my speech and then dozed most of the way. Ralph brought us to our hotel on time, and my wife retired to bed to try to catch up on some sleep while I went off to perform the opening ceremony. There I carried out my last official duties in Germany. After a stag lunch which followed, I hastened back to the hotel, as we had decided to make a quick departure from Frankfurt to avoid becoming further involved there.

We had planned to spend the night in Stuttgart. Towards evening the car wound down from mountain country into a long valley which led us there. The city seemed to stretch for miles before we reached the Park Hotel, which turned out to be the haven of rest and comfort we needed. Our corner room faced a park, leafless and wintry but blessedly quiet. There were flowers and fruit awaiting us in the room, and the attendant who brought up our luggage smiled in friendly fashion as he asked 'Haben Sie noch ein Wunsch?' (Is there anything more you would like?). At that moment we wanted nothing but baths and sleep, but later we emerged to order a meal which was light, delicious and expensive. Later, glancing through the hotel guest-book, we found the signatures of everyone from Adenauer to Maria Callas, and concluded that the merits of the hotel were well-known.

On the following morning we left for Munich, where we proposed to spend the week-end resting. For one reason or another, I had never found the opportunity to visit the capital of Bavaria before. Munich is not Mildred's favourite city, because she associates it in her mind with Adolf Hitler and a variety of Gemütlichkeit which results from drinking large quantities of beer. However, we enjoyed the simple brick exterior of the Cathedral, with its two tall spires rounded at the top, but not the Nazi-style architecture of the Art Gallery or the pretentious figure of the Bayern Victrix on the shattered Siegestor.

The weather was overcast between Munich and Vienna. The distant haze, however, could not conceal the infinite variety and charm of the villages through which we drove. Near the Austrian border we passed the turn-off to Hitler's eyrie of Berchtesgaden, and later the road to the village where the Führer had been born. These reminded us that this pleasant countryside had been his nursery, as Munich had been the earliest and most receptive scene of his activities.

At the frontier on a hill-top a German officer saluted, the car moved forward, and I was Australian Ambassador to the Federal Republic of Germany no longer: merely an Australian diplomat on temporary special mission on his way home to retirement. Ten yards farther a handsome and dashing Austrian with a fine black moustache and elegant green uniform opened the car door and invited us to alight. In an accent softer than that to which we had become accustomed he asked us to wipe our feet. After an incredulous moment, we learned that there was foot-and-mouth disease amongst cattle on the German side of the border, and visitors were requested to scrape their boots along a stretch of sawdust provided for the purpose. We complied somewhat self-consciously.

The countryside on the Austrian side of the border looked less prosperous, the villages less orderly but more attractive. For a time we enjoyed the absence of an autobahn as our car wound up hill and down dale or passed over cobbled streets. We had decided to turn off the main road to gain a glimpse of Salzburg, where we drew up opposite the simple house in which Mozart had lived. It was off-season in Salzburg, with neither music festival nor winter sports to give a sense of purposeful activity. The fountains were boarded up; nude statues seemed to shiver in a cold wind; there was a general impression of opera from behind stage.

We crossed a pass to the east, reached the Donau basin and followed the river to the capital, picking up again the inevitable autobahn. Soon we were passing the Palais Schaumberg and gaining impressions of the wide streets and impressive buildings of the capital of the Hapsburg Empire. After Bonn, and even after Berlin, Vienna exuded ancient power and style, coupled with a sense of amplitude and a degree of light-heartedness. During the next few days I began to appreciate how bitter the rise of Prussian power must have been for Austrians, and how difficult it must have been for the inhabitants of an erstwhile imperial capital to adjust to the limitations of a truncated, neutralised country.

Our hotel room was elegant. Nothing in it would have been out of place in the eighteenth century. There was so much red carpet in the hotel that I had to wipe the fluff off my heels every time I came into my room. Even the laundry went by the name of Hapsburg. Costs, I might add, corresponded with the degree of antiquity.

There was an Australian Migration Office in Vienna, and the local Australian representative and his wife did all they could to help us. In the absence of Australian diplomatic Missions in the countries I was visiting I had of course made contact with the respective representatives in West Germany of Austria, Turkey and Greece, and with the Swiss Ambassador, if I remember rightly, whose country looked after Yugoslav interests in Germany. Engagements had been arranged through these channels, and Australian Migration Offices in Vienna and in Athens kept informed.

It was bad luck that my visit to Vienna happened to overlap with a formal visit by President Lübke with which the Austrians were naturally preoccupied. This first post-war visit by a German Head of State was a delicate operation, in view of Hitler's forced annexation of Austria. Everyone was preoccupied with the need to avoid untoward incidents, and there were enormous parties and ceremonial events at the Palais Schönbrun and the rebuilt Opera House in which my wife and I were caught up. We would have much preferred exclusion from the German umbrella, whose shadow obscured to some extent the simple purpose of my visit. Yet I did succeed in having useful and friendly talks with Austrian officials, finding the most rewarding subject of discussion—as later in Belgrade, Athens and Ankara— the probable effects upon our respective countries if Britain joined the

Common Market. Clearly the Austrians would like us to open a diplomatic mission in Vienna as soon as possible, but I had no authority to do more than report this wish to Canberra. On the whole they were not unsympathetic to the difficulties I explained in our building up an extensive diplomatic service from scratch.

The experience of the evening reception at the Palais Schönbrunn was one to remember, even if our presence was completely irrelevant and we knew very few of the guests. Everyone was in full evening-dress, wearing— or so it seemed to me—at least one order or decoration. If the current festivities seemed somewhat artificial, the background reflected the splendour of the past. One felt a genuine continuity of history in this entertainment offered to the German Head of State under the coldly-appraising eyes of Metternich, looking down from the wall.

When we left Vienna we were much more conscious of Austria's past power and present weakness than we had been; also, of its significance as a bastion of Western Christianity against the Turk, whose armies had reached the gates of the capital city in 1683. Now we had to adjust ourselves to a very different background, that of Communist Yugoslavia.

Our reception at the Yugoslav frontier could scarcely be described as warm. I was accorded no courtesies, was questioned at some length, and found a woman official rude. Although German was no doubt understood in this area, I had decided to speak only in English or French, in order to avoid awakening resentments stemming from past Austrian and German controls. Eventually we were passed through the barriers, and I began to study the countryside, houses and equipment of the second Communist country we had visited.

Before leaving Germany I had been dubious about taking a German chauffeur to Yugoslavia, and asked my staff to make sure that Ralph had never been there as a member of the German Armed Forces. I had no ambition for him to be arrested as a war criminal. Inquiries were made, and I was assured that Ralph had been in his teens during the war and had not served in the armed forces.

On leaving the frontier post, I instructed Ralph to drive us by the best road, and over the least snow, to Zagreb. He assured us that there was no snow left on any of the roads, and that he was taking the most direct route. As we bumped and rattled over stony by-ways, passed with difficulty a load of hay overturned on a narrow road, climbed hills and wound cir-cuitously into valleys, notices becoming fewer and fewer, I became sus-picious. This was not Ralph's normal speed, and it seemed improbable that there was no better main road to Zagreb. The mystery was solved when, driving into a small town, Ralph turned and said nonchalantly: 'I lived here for a couple of years during the war, and went to school here'. He had taken this route solely for the purpose of re-visiting the scenes of his childhood. Clearly I was no longer the Australian Ambassador to Bonn. He was told to get onto better roads as soon as possible, but did so only when we were fairly close to Zagreb.

The route we had taken off the beaten track had its points of interest, as no care had been taken to conceal normal local conditions. The countryside itself was varied and pleasant, with rolling hills and valleys. In patches of woodland primroses, violets and snowdrops were blossoming. There were fewer cars than we would have expected, less farm machinery and more animals in the fields. Children in villages smiled and waved to us, whether out of friendliness or at the sight of an unusually large, shiny, black car we could not tell.

Zagreb proved to be a busy city, with trams, cars parked down the middle of the roadway, and masses of pedestrians all, it seemed, trying to cross the road just in front of us. We found our way to our hotel with some difficulty, after unsuccessful inquiries in English and better results from questions in German. There a young woman from the Protocol Section of the Foreign Office was awaiting our arrival. She took us in her friendly and competent charge and showed us upstairs into an adequate suite. She preferred to speak French, she said, but battled on bravely in English. Finding that for the moment all we wanted was tea, a bath, dinner and early bed, she left us, promising to come back next morning to take us on a tour of the town.

Next morning we were escorted around the city, having been informed that we were expected in Belgrade at 6 p.m., which would necessitate an early lunch. First we drove to the old town on the hill, with its seventeenth century walls built for defence against the Turks, its cathedral, the smaller church of St Mark with its strange mosaic roof, simple vigorous sculpture and mellow atmosphere. Our guide was happier when we left these relics of the non-Communist past, and drove us to the modern People's University, built of concrete and glass. Here were excellent class-rooms and library facilities, including a wide range of periodicals. The students were adult. There seemed rather too many facilities for too few students, but presumably classes are also held at night when workers could attend. The Director seemed enthusiastic and able.

After my wife had bought a few rough-linen table mats and table-napkins at a craft shop and our Protocol guide had presented us with some books and photographs of Zagreb, we had lunch and then set out again with pleasant memories of the town. This time Ralph stuck to the autobahn. He made good time on the reasonably good highway where there was little traffic, and we sped over the great Hungarian plain, the grain-basket of central Europe, watered by the Sava and the Danube amongst other rivers, any one of which could arouse envy in an Australian. The countryside itself was not particularly interesting. There was a good deal of marsh-land; occasional spires or factory chimneys rose amidst flat pastures.

On the outskirts of Belgrade there was a brilliant sunset, which lit up the river and the old town on the hill as we passed through the more utilitarian, concrete buildings of the New City. A bridge took us over the Danube, here a more impressive stream than in Vienna, and we drove through heavy traffic to a large and impressive hotel. For some time past we had noted that all notices were in Cyrillic script. In Belgrade we found that German was no longer a useful second language.

The welcome we received in the capital of Yugoslavia exceeded all expectations. We had comfortable rooms, were met on arrival by Yugoslav officials and agreed easily upon a programme of official talks, social engagements and tours. In the Soviet Union we had been treated with courtesy; here there was added a personal charm and an infectious enthusiasm to which we responded readily. No one in any country could have done more than one senior member of the Foreign Office, assigned to look after us, together with his wife, and we left feeling that they were friends.

I had formal interviews with Mr Popovic, Minister for Foreign Affairs, and with the Minister for Trade. These were tough members of the Party hierarchy, and the conversations were difficult. Discussions with Foreign Office officials were much easier. I found them capable, vocal in a number of languages and generally sophisticated. They expressed a desire for mutual representation between our respective countries at the diplomatic level, but did not press the issue unduly. As in Vienna, there was interest in the Australian reactions to Britain joining the E.E.C.

Subsequently, we had a pleasant lunch with Mr Leo Mates, Director of the Institute of International Politics and Economics in Belgrade. He had held high posts in his country's diplomatic service, and I had worked with him at United Nations Conferences, especially the Geneva Conference on Freedom of Information and the Press. I had come to respect his intellectual and linguistic capacity and welcomed the opportunity of renewing contact.

For the rest, we were taken to the theatre to a creditable performance of *The Fountain of Bachiserai*, one of my favourite ballets in Moscow days; driven some fifty miles to the old town of Novi Sad, where we inspected a couple of Art Museums and had lunch at the old Petrovardia Fortress; inspected a modern T.B. hospital; managed to survive with some difficulty wine-tasting at an experimental co-operative for wine production; and were shown over the Fresco Museum in Belgrade by the wife of the Foreign Minister. Madame Popovic told us that the Serbs moved north when the Turks came, built monasteries in the hills and decorated them with frescoes. The Turks then destroyed the buildings, or blew off the roofs and covered the frescoes with whitewash. French experts had taught the Yugoslavs to remove the whitewash. The Museum contained copies of those frescoes, and also copies of a number of church door-ways.

On the more practical side, I was taken to inspect a tractor and motor factory, which was less mechanised than in Germany. Working conditions were explained in detail, as also the extent to which workers participated in management. There was a minimum wage, but piece-work could result in a bonus according to profits made. The factory had to operate within the general framework of the national plan, but within these limits there was some freedom of decision, and of competition with other firms. Workers entered the factory at the age of fifteen already partly trained at school; they could study at night and even go on to a university.

Before leaving Belgrade I took the opportunity of calling upon the American Ambassador, Mr George Kennan, some of whose books I had read. Both of us had served in the Soviet Union, while he had mixed diplomacy with academic work. I told him of my future plans at the Australian National University, and was encouraged to find that he believed them sensible, not a mere aberration.

Having re-packed the evening clothes we were sending back to Cologne with Ralph so that we would be free of them while on leave in Greece, I exhorted him sternly to travel by the shortest route to the Yugoslav frontier. Whether he did so I shall never know. Many of the Yugoslavs we had met were at the airport to see us off. As the plane rose I thought of the impressive War Museum in Belgrade which we had inspected, containing models of various battles which had been fought for the possession of the city down the centuries, together with relics of uniforms and arms. Belgrade had been invested—was it fifty times? Was it surprising, I asked myself, if the current outcome of domestic differences and foreign invasions had not resulted in parliamentary democracy on the Westminster model?

Flying south from Belgrade the country seemed poorer, more mountainous and barren. I remembered the comment made by a European diplomat in Belgrade that conditions in Yugoslavia should not be judged by those in the capital city itself, which was something of a show-piece. He had visited Skopje and in its neighbourhood had found poverty worse than any he had seen in the Soviet Union.

Suddenly we found ourselves over Greece, looking at the slopes of Mount Olympus. Beyond the coast the Aegean Sea was incredibly blue. Soon the white, regular houses of Athens were below us, and we caught sight of the Acropolis dominating the city from its height. This was a different and a far more familiar world. Greek myths, the stories of Homer, the persistent questioning of Socrates—these were all part of our own tradition, and we became quite excited at the prospect of our leave in Greece.

The official aspects of my visit to Greece were disappointing. The Australian Migration representative seemed to resent my coming, and the closeness of his relations with Greek authorities did not exactly impress me. I had discussions in the Foreign Office, but they led nowhere in particular. No one in Athens, local or foreign, seemed to do any work between mid-day on Friday and Monday morning—at least in official circles. The British Embassy was helpful, and I gained some insight into Greek economic problems at a lecture given after a lunch organised for others by the Bank of Greece. On the credit side shipping, tourism and remittances from emigrants were the most significant items, but the income from all of these was still below what was needed to pay for necessary imports.

On a Sunday we drove to Cape Sunion through olive groves and around bare, rocky hills, while spring-flowers dotted the nearby fields. There we gazed out at nearby islands, swimming in the bluest of waters, from the vantage point of the ruins of the temple of Poseidon, God of the Sea. At Sunion the clarity of the light was almost painful to the eyes.

Leaving some luggage at the hotel, to which we proposed to return, we took a Lufthansa plane to Ankara, arriving there at night. By this time, what with constant changes in climate and food, strange surroundings, the strain of meeting dozens of people whom we did not know, our physical condition had begun to weaken. In addition, my wife had developed a streaming cold. We were anxious now to complete the official part of the tour as soon as possible.

Australia had no representation of any kind at Ankara, and our arrangements had been left entirely in the hands of the Turkish Foreign Office. As we flew over the capital, we saw a brilliant pattern of lights, as clear as those of Canberra on a winter evening. A member of the Protocol Division of the Foreign Office met us at the airport, and accompanied us to the hotel into which the Foreign Office had booked us, only to be told that no reservation had been made and that no accommodation was available. We felt instinctively that we were in the East again, without sufficient local knowledge to solve the problem. However, the Protocol Officer was in his own country, and after considerable delay and much persistence on his part, we were shown up to a large, odd room which contained a single bed and a divan. After further pressure, bed-clothes were produced for the divan, and our escort retired.

Next morning I signed the President's book and paid my respects at the massive mausoleum built in honour of Kemal Ataturk. Back in the hotel, we found crowds of people, much noise, and considerable difficulty in getting a normal meal. In the evening we were picked up by a pleasant, cultivated Turkish couple who had been at the Turkish Embassy in London and spoke good English. They took us to a ballet, performed by young dancers who had been trained by an English ballerina. The main item on the programme was from *The Rake's Progress*—not precisely what we would have expected to find on the stage at Ankara. The dancers made up in enthusiasm and spontaneity what they lacked as yet in professional skill.

During our few days in Ankara I called upon relevant Turkish Ministers and officials and was entertained by a Turkish host who had invited also the Canadian Ambassador, the British Chargé d'Affaires and the German Chargé d'Affaires. I also sat for a time in Parliament, which was then in session, and made some university contacts. The Turkish authorities seemed to appreciate our visit, and urged politely the desirability of opening diplomatic relations between our two countries.

We had been looking forward to a couple of days in Istanbul on the way back to Athens. Although I had to pay a couple of calls there, the main burden of my official tour would then be over. By the time we reached the ancient capital of Turkey, I had caught the cold from Mildred. Here was our one opportunity to see one of the most interesting cities of the world, without the energy to make the most of it. Nevertheless, we determined not to spend our time in bed. It was very unlikely we would ever come that way again.

We flew from Ankara to Istanbul by day, over country which in some ways reminded us of parts of Australia. Asia Minor was more mountainous, but seemed just as dry and bare. It seemed strange to be flying over country across which the Greek Thousand had fought their way; to be within striking distance of the ancient city of Troy; and to cross a waterway along which Jason and his Argonauts had fared. Here was Istanbul, with its domes and minarets, its bridge of boats joining Asia to Europe, the teeming city of the second Rome which had been an outpost of Christianity for so long before it was overrun by the Turks. Here autocratic Sultans had ruled ruthlessly for some 500 years. As the plane came in to land, historical and literary memories started in my mind lurid images of discarded members of the harem whose skeletons might still be anchored to the sea-bed by heavy stones.

Next day I paid an official call on the chief Turkish representative in Istanbul, and then we set out by car to see some of the city. We went first to the Hagia Sophia. The original exterior had been somewhat spoilt by later building, including brick flying-buttresses to support the crumbling walls. Inside, however, its huge dome, hovering over vast space below, was impressive. The Byzantine mosaics on the walls had been largely obliterated by the Turks with yellow plaster, and the original patterns were being uncovered but slowly. We climbed up into the gallery by a winding ramp, stood where the Empress had sat shielded from view, and then walked round to see the ninth century mosaics which had been restored. Outside the sun shone, but inside there was the cold of the grave. It was a relief to move on to the Blue Mosque, with its uniformity of conception and sense of proportion, and carpets on the floor where the faithful could pray without getting chilled to the bone.

Next day we drove to the Sultan's palace, now a museum. Its site was magnificent; its kitchens had been capable of providing for the 8,000 members of the household, including concubines and slaves; the museum was crammed with priceless objects, a genuine *embarras de richesse*—from a throne inlaid with jewels to, wonder of wonders, what seemed like acres of Chinese celadonware displayed for the most part on walls. Windows and doors opened upon a marble balcony below which the blue waters of the Bosphorus stretched receptively. Such a plethora of wealth was depressing when one reflected upon the ancient and modern poverty which surrounded it.

The British Consul-General in Istanbul was Gordon Whitteridge, whom I had known when he was posted in Bangkok. He and his wife invited us to dinner in the residence which had been occupied by the British Ambassador before the capital was removed to Ankara. It was still used occasionally, but as the Ambassador was out of Turkey on leave the vast reception rooms were shut up. Royal portraits looked down upon a wide marble stairway. Gone were the palmy days of British power when the Ambassador's capacity to influence the Sultan was closely related to the latter's knowledge that British advice or requests might well be reinforced at short notice by the arrival of a British Fleet.

Our hosts promised to take us for a trip up the Bosphorus in the Ambassador's yacht if the weather on the following day were favourable. This we were most anxious to do, despite our colds. Although the weather scarcely qualified, the trip was made, but we stayed mostly behind glass during the voyage. Slowly we churned past Venetian-like palaces and crusader castles until the entrance to the Black Sea was visible in the near distance. Not far from the entrance was a large 'summer' house leased, we were told, by the Soviet authorities. It provided a convenient place from which to view all vessels passing into or out of the Black Sea. Next morning we left Istanbul by air for Athens, our holiday time in Greece reduced now to twelve days.

The story of our private holiday in Greece is scarcely relevant to the life-story of an Australian diplomat who never had the good fortune to be posted there. Suffice it to say that in no other country outside the United Kingdom did we respond so readily to our surroundings. The troubles of modern Greece, I must confess, were less present to our minds than the brilliant achievements of the past.

Less than a fortnight later we left Athens with a wide range of unforgettable memories. The sarcophagus at Eleusis; the Byzantine monastery at Ossias Lukas; three precious days and nights in the mountains at Delphi, sensing the voice of the oracle giving ambiguous advice; the view over a sea of olive trees from a ruined castle at Amphissa; the blue waters of the bay at Naphlion; the narrow passage ways of ancient Tiryns, overhung with great stones; Epidaurus with its magnificent open-air theatre which, in ancient times and now, seats more than 11,000 people; Mycenae; and Athens itself once again. Our experience of Greece was one of the happiest of our lives, making us regret all the more than we had not studied Greek at school. Mentally I reviled the system which had forced me to learn Anglo-Saxon for English Honours at Sydney University, when the time could so much more profitably have been spent on Greek.

In Rome we re-visited some of the places we had seen during our holiday in 1949, and then left for Naples to catch our ship to Australia. Arrangements had been made for Antonio, our Portuguese butler in Cologne, to drive my Mercedes from Cologne to Naples via Rome and to travel back by train at my expense. He was to bring with him portable luggage which we had left behind and ensure that car and luggage were stacked safely aboard at Naples.

After 25 years of diplomatic service, most of it overseas, our luggage was substantial, and the Embassy in Rome decided to send on some of it in an office car to reduce our handling responsibilities on the journey to Naples. In due course Antonio arrived at our hotel, smiling brightly, driving a Mercedes laden down with all he had brought from Cologne, together with most of what we had taken with us on our official visits. He explained that the Embassy car had broken down en route from Rome, so everything had been transferred to the Mercedes. By some miracle the springs survived, but it was a risk which I would never have taken. The incident reminded us of the strange capacity of Australian Embassy cars for breaking down at inconvenient moments.

We left Naples without regret. Our few excursions there in taxis were highly unpleasant, and I came to the conclusion that we were safer aboard ship than seeing the sights. On the voyage home, we followed what was now a familiar route through the Red Sea. At ports around the Australian coast we felt immediately that we 'belonged'. There was no other country in which we wished to retire. The blue haze of distant mountains; the ubiquitous eucalypt; surf pounding on yellow-brown beaches; clear skies at night and familiar stars—we would not wish to exchange these for what we had seen in other countries, however striking or sophisticated.

In Sydney we were welcomed by our children and visited the gradually increasing brood of grand-children. After a few days in the city where we had been born I managed to get the Mercedes through the Customs without payment of duty, under the regulation requiring me to pledge not to sell it for two years, and we drove off to Canberra. When we had passed the built-up area I instinctively stepped on the accelerator. Soon I had to restrain myself severely as I realised that the grades, curves, width and general quality of German autobahns made possible a speed which was dangerous on Australian main roads.

We took over again our somewhat dilapidated house in Canberra, which clearly required considerable expenditure of time, energy and money to make it liveable again. Arriving at the end of May, we experienced a fortnight of winter temperatures below twenty degrees. As we had no central heating, to which we had become accustomed overseas, we froze to the bone. I swung an axe mightily if not efficiently on tough blocks of wood to keep some of the fire-places and a wood-stove burning, while my wife shouldered the customary burdens of a Canberra house-wife, increased substantially by the fact that our numerous tenants had not all treated house and furniture as their own. Both of us soon found that, at our age and with our energy, the physical strains were too great. With some reluctance we gave up our plans to set the old house in order and decided to sell it and move elsewhere. After a few weeks we found a newly-constructed house in the extended area of Red Hill. The house, which we had not designed, had some inconveniences, and no established garden; but our three front rooms looked out northwards over five miles of country towards Mount Ainslie. As we were on a corner block looking down a steep road, the view could not be built out. There was also some oil-heating, which could be supplemented by radiators, and a modern electric stove.

I reported to the Department of External Affairs, and was farewelled by my colleagues. It was a wrench to leave them, but I had no regrets over my decision to retire. I accepted with pleasure the customary presentation which they offered me, but insisted that it should embody working-tools—a desk, a chair and a typewriter. During the past nine years these have been fully used.

After one week at home relaxing, I drove over to the Australian National University. There, in the Department of International Relations, I was made to feel welcome, given a room and stacked my books on shelves. It was a different life, without the staff assistance to which I had become accustomed over the years; but my time was more or less my own and I set myself to learn the art of writing the history of Australian foreign policy from public sources, covering the period 1938-65. Subsequently other opportunities opened out unexpectedly, and during the past nine years I have lived a busy life, writing, lecturing and administering. But that is a separate story unrelated to the experiences of an Australian public servant during the early period of growth of the Department of External Affairs.

EPILOGUE

As suggested in the Preface to these memoirs, the creation of an efficient diplomatic service is a slow, difficult and expensive business. It takes many years to find appropriate staff, to train them at home and abroad, to develop adminstrative techniques for controlling and supporting them, and to induce governments (to say nothing of the Department of the Treasury) to provide necessary funds.

Experience of overseas conditions is built up but slowly; regulations suited to Australian conditions tend to be applied abroad despite the very great difference in circumstances; there is frequently a lack of imagination by permanently home-based staff which has to be overcome gradually; individual members of a Foreign Service and their families are likely to suffer for some time, at least until an adequate system of inspection of overseas posts is developed.

All countries faced with the need to develop a diplomatic service at short notice suffer from growing pains. Officers of my generation in the Australian Department of External Affairs were no exception. It was only gradually that clear distinctions were drawn between, and reasonable provision made for salaries on the one hand and overseas local and entertainment allowances on the other; for child allowances to help meet costs of boarding schools for families of men serving abroad; for children being educated in Australia to visit their parents overseas at sensibly frequent intervals of time; and for retention of control of houses in Canberra during postings out of Australia.

The reader of these pages can scarcely have failed to note that any public servant, like myself, who has held the position of Head of a Department and exercised the responsibility of running it as a whole is likely to feel frustrated when faced with the delays and decisions of other public servants in Canberra whose judgment he feels qualified to question.

Nine years after retirement, I do not complain even though I have felt bound to record. Indeed, I am grateful to the various Australian Governments and Ministers whom I served for the substantial opportunities and responsibilities they afforded me. Of the various men who held the portfolio of External Affairs while I was a Commonwealth Public Servant, only one—Dr H. V. Evatt—caused me seriously to doubt whether I could serve him and at the same time keep my self-respect. Critics will no doubt attribute this to alleged lack of sympathy with some of his policies, but they will be wrong. It was the man and his methods, not his policy, which I found distasteful: I would not have had the least difficulty in serving under Mr Curtin or Mr Chifley.

In all large institutions individuals have their ups and downs. I had my fair share of waiting in hope that what I was losing on the swings I might pick up on the roundabouts. My greatest satisfaction was that, on the whole, I was given interesting posts which stretched my capacity and energy to the full. Although I had not even thought of the possibility of becoming a diplomat before the age of twenty-three, and did not actually do so for a further thirteen years, I believe in retrospect that my early training and native abilities found greater scope in a diplomatic career than they would have done in any of the others of which I have had experience—teaching, academic work, writing and the life of a barrister-at-law.

One of my main aims in writing these memoirs has been to try to convey to the general reader some better understanding of what the life of a diplomat is like. I have met many Australians who still think that it consists primarily in attending cocktail parties dressed in striped pants, and who simply cannot conceive that, so far at least as the senior ranks of the Service are concerned, it involves constant hard work, an unusual measure of adaptability, sound judgment based upon wide experience, a deep sense of public responsibility and exceptional difficulties in bringing up a family. To those who scoff at this catalogue I can only say 'Try it yourself'.

Finally, I hope that the account given in the preceding chapters will help those who form and express speedy and confident judgments on foreign policy issues to gain a better appreciation of the infinite complexity of many such problems, and of the extraordinary obstacles which usually have to be overcome before an effective international consensus can be developed. Amongst those who have a part to play in this process, it is my conviction that the responsible diplomat still stands high in the list —not least in a country like Australia, whose long-term survival in the approximate shape and form we know is far from assured.

APPENDIX I

Publications since the author's retirement in July 1962

Books:
The Evolution of Australian Foreign Policy 1938-65 (Cambridge University Press, London, 1967). Paperback edition in 1968.
Vietnam, An Australian Analysis (F. W. Cheshire, Melbourne, 1968).

Chapters:
'The Australian Diplomatic Service, 1935-65'. Chapter II of *Australia in World Affairs 1961-65*, Gordon Greenwood & Norman Harper (Eds.), (F. W. Cheshire, Melbourne, 1968).
'Southeast Asia in the 1970's'. Chapter III of *Asia and the Pacific in the 1970's*, Bruce Brown (Ed.), (A.N.U. Press, Canberra, 1971).

Articles in Overseas Journals:
Round Table, October 1966 (No. 224)—'Australians at War in Vietnam', pp. 354-362.
Round Table, January 1971 (No. 241)—'Australia's Reaction to Growing Japanese Influence in the Far East', pp. 25-31.
Osterreichische Zeitschrift für Aussenpolitik, 9 Jahrgang, Heft 1, 1969—'Ost und West—Australien und die Probleme Südostasiens', pp. 15-31.
Le Monde Diplomatique, Aout 1969—'L'Australie s'apprête à jouer un rôle nouveau en Asie du Sud-Est', p. 28.
Commonwealth (Journal of the Royal Commonwealth Society, London)—April 1970, vol. xiii, No. 2—'Australia and Commonwealth', pp. 58-66.

Articles in Australian Journals:
Australian Outlook, vol. 17, No. 1 (April 1963)—'Australia and the Munich Agreement', pp. 21-41.
Australian Outlook, vol. 24, No. 1 (April 1970)—'The Anzus Treaty, Past, Present and Future', pp. 17-36.
The Australian Quarterly, vol. 36, No. 4 (December, 1964)—'Australia and the Ambassadorial Issue', pp. 11-18.
The Australian Quarterly, vol. 39, No. 2 (June, 1967)—'The Geneva Agreements 1954 in Relation to Vietnam', pp. 7-23.
Pacific Community, No. 1 (June 1969—Hawthorn Press, Melbourne)—'Australian Defence Policy in Southeast Asia after 1971', pp. 13-23.

World Review (A.I.I.A., Queensland Branch), vol. 3, No. 2 (July, 1964) —'The Australian Commitment to Malaysia', pp. 3-12.

Australia's Neighbours (A.I.I.A., Victorian Branch), (Sept.-Oct., 1965) —'The United Nations in 1965', pp. 1-4.

Australia's Neighbours (A.I.I.A., Victorian Branch), (Nov.-Dec., 1967) —'Elections in South Vietnam, Sept.-Oct., 1967', pp. 1-4.

Arts (Sydney University Arts Association), vol. 2, No. 3, 1963-4— 'Australia in the World of Today—Problems and Responsibilities', pp. 131-134.

Review of the Institute of Public Affairs (Melbourne), vol. 17, No. 3 (July-Sept., 1963)—'Australian Relations with Southeast Asia', pp. 90-96.

Miscellaneous:

Roy Milne Memorial Lecture 1965 (A.I.I.A.)—*The Changing Margins of Australian Foreign Policy.* (published as pamphlet)

Working Paper No. 4, Dept. of International Affairs, Australian National University—*Australian Defence Policy 1951-63; Major International Aspects.* (68 pages of text, 24 pages of documents, published 1964)

Encyclopaedia Britannica Book of the Year 1965 (Australia & New Zealand Supplement, pp. 9-17), 'Australia and New Zealand's Northern Neighbours'.

Articles in Australian Newspapers.

APPENDIX II

Three Political Poems

CANBERRA, 1938-40

I

THE SHEEP MOVE ON (Munich)

In springtime there was grass to eat,
Mist-moistened, green and succulent.
The long blades beckoned at our feet,
We cropped the rich food heaven had sent—
  Then, light at heart, moved on.

But summer came. The fields were swept
By fierce winds, driving from the West.
The grass died first. We few, who crept
By chance to a brackish pool, took rest—
  Then, sick at heart, moved on.

II

WE DO NOT KNOW (Prague)

We do not know whether the dusty road
Will lead us to some sheltered glen of peace
Where each may slip his burden, find abode
And for a brief space watch his flocks increase;
Or whether, stumbling down some mountain track
Shrouded in midnight mist—when every branch
Seems like a weapon lifted in attack—
We may not meet the unheralded avalanche.

We do not know. The impenetrable skies
Contain no certain sign that we may scan
And use to guide us towards the appointed end.
Blindly we move, in fear lest gods devise
Some scheme to quench the flickering spirit of man
And cause primeval darkness to descend.

319

III

TOLL FOR THE BRAVE (Russo-Finnish War)

Toll the bell for Finnish men
Sleeping now beneath the snow
By Wiipuri and Petsamo.

Though the invader stamp again
His ruthless will upon the land
They lie content, a goodly band.

These were men who sallied forth
White-robed, like phantoms, and waylaid
The foe in deadly ambuscade.

Those defied the cannon's wrath
On the scarred Isthmus, till at last
The unending columns trampled past.

Raise no relic where they fell,
But sound their story. Toll the bell.

INDEX

Pearce, Senator George: 21
Pearl Harbour: Japanese attack on, 43
Pearson, Lester: 41, 209
Petain, Marshal: 25-6
Peterson, H. A.: 18, 19, 20, 21
Peterson, Sir Maurice: Brit. Ambassador, Moscow, 104, 118, 128, 155
Peter the Great: 97
Petrov, Vladimir: 267-8
Phelps, Rev. Lancelot: 4-5
Philippines, The: Spender's attitude to possible inclusion in ANZUS, 181, 182-3; and SEATO, 217, 220, 224
Plimsoll, (Sir) James: in Korea, 190; appt. as Ambassador to Washington, 193; Canberra 223; visit to Japan (1957), 258, 259, 260
Plumridge, H.: 85
Pollard, (Lt.-Genl. Sir) Reginald: 197
Popovic, Koca: 308
Popovic, Mme: 308

Quinn, John: 75, 194-5

Radhakrishnan, Dr. Sarvepalli: 155
Raffles, Sir T. S.: 230
Rahman, Tunku Abdul: elections in Malaya (1955), 238; personal simplicity of approach, 230-40
Reading, Lord: 224
Reid, Escott: 41
Rendel, Sir George: 234
Renouf, A. P.: 114
Rhee, Syngman: 186
Ridley, Keith: 248
Roberts, (Sir) Frank: in Moscow, 104, 128, 129
Robertson, Norman: 57
Robinson, W. S.: 46, 48, 56
Rogers, Justice Sir Percival Halse: 11, 13, 47, 168
Roman Catholicism: and Communism in attitudes to 'authority', 153-4
Romulo, Carlos P.: 124
Ronning, Chester: Geneva Confce. (1954), 215-16
Roosevelt, Eleanor: and visit of Lord Gowrie to Washington, 58-9
Roosevelt, Franklin D.: 35, 44, 45, 55, 58, 59, 178, 179; American-British Staff Talks (1941), 39; appointment of Lord Halifax to Washington, 37, 38-9; Casey's decision to leave Washington, 46; Pacific War Council, 50-1, 57; sympathy with Britain before Pearl Harbour, 41; U.S. entry into W. W. II, 43-4
Rosenthal, Commander: 36
Ross, (Sir) David: 5, 8-9, 95, 283

Rowland, J. R.: Charge d'Affaires, Moscow (1947), 114, 116; Indo-China, 196, 244

Schröder, Dr. Gerhard: 303
Scott, Sir Robert: Brit. Commsr.-Genl. for Southeast Asia, 226, 243-4
SEATO: 201, 209, 212, 213, 217, 242, 245; Australian attitude to, 218-19, 221-5; Council meetings, 225; economic aspects, 219; Manila Treaty Confce. (1954), 217-22, 223-4; military planning machinery, 220-1; security guarantees of, 220, 221; U.S. reservation, 221, 224
Sebald, William: 86
Shanahan, Foss: 183, 233
Shann, K. C. O.: 248
Shaw, Patrick: 269
Shedden, Sir Frederick: 190, 191
Shvernik, Nikolai: 101, 102
Sihanouk, Prince Norodom: 244
Singapore: British military facilities on, 237; constitutional developments in, 234-6; Japanese seizure of (1942), 26, 44, 226; Casey's view of importance of Australian representation in, 187; riots (May, 1955), 235-6; appointment to, as Aust. Commr. for Southeast Asia, 203; colonial atmosphere, 229-30; protocol questions, 230-3; re-arrangement of functions of Austn. representative at, 233-4
Sjahrir, Sutan: 80
Slater, W.: 91, 105
Slim, Sir William (Viscount): attitude during visit of Kishi (1957)
Smith, A. S. V.: 46, 48
Sohlman, Rolf: 105
Southeast Asia: Australian interest in, 219, 241-2
Soviet Union, the: methods of representatives at Confces., 67-8; objections to Australian role at Paris Peace Confce. (1946), 82-3; re-opening of relations with Australia after Petrov case, 267-8; use of veto at U.N., 66; appointment and functions as Australian Minister and Ambassador (1947-50), 91-2, 102-3, 130; post-war shortages and living problems, 93-4, 98, 99-101, 107-10, 116-18, 119-20, 141; importance of Diplom. Corps contacts, Moscow, 103-5, 113-14, 127, 128; security in Australian Legation, 105-6; arrangements for Western news in, 106-7; impressions of U.S.S.R., 112-13; New Year in U.S.S.R., 115-16; currency devaluation (1947), 117-19; winter climate, 119-20; theatre, 120-3; Aust. Mission

Watt, (Sir) Alan—*continued*
  cision to retire early, 266-7, 284-8, 301, 302-3; retirement, 313; publications since retirement, App. I; 3 political poems (1938-40), App. II
Watt, George: 1-2
Watt, Dr. James and Dorothy: 4, 72
Watt, Mildred Mary (née Wait): marriage to, 11
Watt, Susan S. R.: 1-2, 11
Wavell, Field-Marshal: 57-8
Weatherstone, 'Ted': 271, 272, 273
Webb, Sidney and Beatrice: views on U.S.S.R., 113
Welles, Sumner: and Evatt, 47, 48, 49, 50

Westerman, (Sir) Alan: 265
Whitlam, E. G.: 24n.
Whitlam, H. F. E.: 24
Whitteridge, Gordon: 311
Wilson, Dr. (Sir) Roland: 62, 63, 170, 274
Wilson, Woodrow: 179
Wylie, (Sir) Francis
Wynes, Dr. Anstey: 77, 93, 158

Yoshida, Shigeru: 188
Yugoslavia: informal mission to (1962), 306-9

Zorin, V. A.: 142, 143